Download Forms on Nolo.com

You can download the forms in this book at:

 www.nolo.com/back-of-book/HFB.html

We'll also post updates whenever there's an important change to the law affecting this book—as well as articles and other related materials.

More Resources
from Nolo.com

Legal Forms, Books, & Software
Hundreds of do-it-yourself products—all written in plain English, approved, and updated by our in-house legal editors.

Legal Articles
Get informed with thousands of free articles on everyday legal topics. Our articles are accurate, up to date, and reader friendly.

Find a Lawyer
Want to talk to a lawyer? Use Nolo to find a lawyer who can help you with your case.

NOLO
LAW for ALL

22nd Edition

How to File for
Chapter 7
Bankruptcy

Attorney Cara O'Neill & Albin Renauer, J.D.

TWENTY-SECOND EDITION	JANUARY 2022
Editor	CARA O'NEILL
Book Design	SUSAN PUTNEY
Proofreading	IRENE BARNARD
Index	ACCESS POINTS INDEXING
Printing	SHERIDAN

ISSN: 2330-3298 (print)
ISSN: 2167-5791 (online)
ISBN: 978-1-4133-2916-2 (pbk)
ISBN: 978-1-4133-2917-9 (ebook)

This book covers only United States law, unless it specifically states otherwise.

Please note

Accurate, plain-English legal information can help you solve many of your own legal problems. But this text is not a substitute for personalized advice from a knowledgeable lawyer. If you want the help of a trained professional—and we'll always point out situations in which we think that's a good idea—consult an attorney licensed to practice in your state.

Acknowledgments

A respectful nod must go out to the original author of this book, the late Stephen Elias, who championed the ability of everyone to advocate on their own behalf. And also, to Trenton, Jacqueline, Christian, and Mia just because you're my favorite people.

—Cara O'Neill

About the Authors

Cara O'Neill is a legal editor and writer at Nolo, focusing on bankruptcy and small claims. She authors, coauthors, and edits several Nolo books, including *How to File for Chapter 7 Bankruptcy, Chapter 13 Bankruptcy, The New Bankruptcy, Everybody's Guide to Small Claims Court, Solve Your Money Troubles, Credit Repair*, and *The Foreclosure Survival Guide*.

Before joining Nolo, Cara practiced for over 20 years as a civil and criminal trial lawyer. During that time, she also served as administrative law judge mediating disputes in the automotive industry and taught undergraduate and graduate law courses and added bankruptcy to her practice after the 2008 economic downturn. Cara earned her law degree in 1994 from the University of the Pacific, McGeorge School of Law, where she served as a law review editor and graduated a member of the Order of the Barristers—an honor society recognizing excellence in courtroom advocacy.

Albin Renauer received his J.D. in 1985 from the University of Michigan Law School, where he served on the *Michigan Law Review*. He worked for various public interest law firms, the California Supreme Court, and Nolo before launching LegalConsumer.com, a website that helps people determine whether or not they're eligible for bankruptcy.

Table of Contents

Your Chapter 7 Bankruptcy Companion

f you're considering filing for bankruptcy, you're not alone. Many Americans turn to the bankruptcy system to get out from under credit card debt, medical bills, car loans, and more, often after being derailed by one of the common life events that can lead to bankruptcy:

- job loss
- health problems (and the resulting medical expenses)
- divorce, or
- a small business failure.

Of course, none of these events would necessarily require bankruptcy if the people who experience them had adequate savings to weather the storm. But most of us lack such savings. In fact, many of us have a difficult time making ends meet and live from paycheck to paycheck. As we all know too well, when a recession hits or when an employer downsizes, many people find themselves turning to bankruptcy for relief.

These are the situations bankruptcy was intended to address. Chapter 7 bankruptcy gives debtors a fresh start by wiping out some or all of their debts. If you decide that Chapter 7 bankruptcy is the right solution for you, this book will guide you through each step of the process.

A straightforward Chapter 7 bankruptcy doesn't require any special courtroom or analytical skills, just that the filer follow these steps:

- Learn the basics of bankruptcy law, including what will happen to your property if you file.
- Get credit counseling from an approved agency before filing for bankruptcy.
- File a packet of official forms and documents.
- Give the trustee certain supporting documents (such as a copy of your most recent tax return).
- Attend a ten-minute meeting with a bankruptcy official called the "trustee."
- Complete a course in budget management.
- Wait a couple of months to receive a debt discharge.

Sounds simple enough, right? But understanding your options, filling out the extensive paperwork, and figuring out the best ways to protect the property you want to keep can get confusing in a hurry. Whether your bankruptcy is routine or you face a complication or two along the way, this book will help you through the process.

First, we explain the alternatives and help you figure out if Chapter 7 bankruptcy is the right choice for you. If you decide you're ready for a fresh financial start, use this book's step-by-step instructions to navigate the bankruptcy process and get back on your feet. It will help you:

- figure out if you can keep your property and which debts (if any) will survive your bankruptcy
- decide how to handle your mortgage, car payment, and other secured debts
- fill out the necessary paperwork
- handle routine bankruptcy procedures, and
- rebuild your credit after bankruptcy.

Don't worry about the size of this book. Most people don't need to read every chapter. For instance, if you know what will happen to your property and debts, you can proceed straight to Ch. 6 and complete the official bankruptcy forms. If you don't own a home or other valuable property, you might be able to skim the chapters that explain how property is handled and what you'll have to do to keep it (Chs. 3 and 4). If none of your debts are "secured" (that is, you haven't pledged collateral or otherwise given the creditor the right to take your property if you don't pay the debt) you can skip Ch. 5.

Use the chart below to figure out where to find the information you need.

Question	Where to Find the Answer
How does Chapter 7 bankruptcy work?	Ch. 1, "An Overview of Chapter 7 Bankruptcy"
Am I eligible to file for Chapter 7?	Ch. 1, "Who Cannot File for Chapter 7" and Ch. 6, "Form 122A"
Is my income low enough to qualify for Chapter 7?	Ch. 1, "Who Cannot File for Chapter 7" and Ch. 6, "Form 122A"
Does it make sense for me to use Chapter 7?	Ch. 1, "Does Chapter 7 Bankruptcy Make Economic Sense?"
Do I have options other than filing for bankruptcy?	Ch. 1, "Alternatives to Chapter 7 Bankruptcy"
Can I avoid being evicted by filing for bankruptcy?	Ch. 2, "Evictions"
Does bankruptcy stop my creditors from trying to collect what I owe them?	Ch. 2
What will happen to my car if I file?	Ch. 3 and Ch. 5
What will happen to my house if I file?	Ch. 4
What personal property might I lose if I file?	Ch. 3
Can I keep property that I've pledged as collateral for a debt?	Ch. 5
Should I sign a reaffirmation agreement promising to repay a debt even after I file for bankruptcy?	Ch. 5
Will I lose my retirement account or pension?	Ch. 3, "Property That Isn't in Your Bankruptcy Estate"
Where can I get the credit counseling required before I file for bankruptcy?	Ch. 1, "An Overview of Chapter 7 Bankruptcy"
Where can I get the budget counseling required after I file for bankruptcy?	Ch. 1, "An Overview of Chapter 7 Bankruptcy"

Question	Where to Find the Answer
Can I get my student loans canceled or reduced in bankruptcy?	Ch. 9, "Debts That Survive Chapter 7 Bankruptcy"
Is there any way I can keep valuable property when I file for Chapter 7?	Ch. 3, "Property You Can Keep"
Which debts will be wiped out after my bankruptcy?	Ch. 9, "Debts That Will Be Discharged in Bankruptcy"
Which debts will I still have to pay after my bankruptcy?	Ch. 9, "Debts That Survive Chapter 7 Bankruptcy"
Can I get my tax debts wiped out in bankruptcy?	Ch. 9, "Debts That Survive Chapter 7 Bankruptcy"
How will my bankruptcy affect someone who cosigned for one of my debts?	Ch. 1, "Does Chapter 7 Bankruptcy Make Economic Sense?"
What will happen if I forget to list a debt on my bankruptcy papers?	Ch. 8, "Newly Discovered Creditors"
Can I give property away to friends or relatives to avoid losing it in bankruptcy?	Ch. 1, "Who Cannot File for Chapter 7"
How will bankruptcy affect my child support obligations?	Ch. 2, "When the Stay Doesn't Apply" and Ch. 9, "Debts That Survive Chapter 7 Bankruptcy"
How do I fill out the bankruptcy forms?	Ch. 6
How do I file my bankruptcy forms?	Ch. 6, "How to File Your Papers"
What happens at the 341 hearing?	Ch. 1, "An Overview of Chapter 7 Bankruptcy" and Ch. 7, "Routine Bankruptcy Procedures"
What documents do I need to bring to the 341 hearing?	Ch. 1, "An Overview of Chapter 7 Bankruptcy" and Ch. 7, "Routine Bankruptcy Procedures"
Can I change my bankruptcy papers once I file them?	Ch. 7, "Amending Your Bankruptcy Papers"

Question	Where to Find the Answer
Will I need an attorney to handle my bankruptcy?	Ch. 10, "Bankruptcy Lawyers"
How can I find a bankruptcy lawyer?	Ch. 10, "Bankruptcy Lawyers"
If I can't afford a lawyer, what other types of help are available to me?	Ch. 10
Can I be fired because I filed for bankruptcy?	Ch. 8, "Postbankruptcy Discrimination"
How can I rebuild my credit after bankruptcy?	Ch. 8, "Rebuilding Credit"

Get Legal Updates and More at Nolo.com

You can find the online companion page to this book at:

www.nolo.com/back-of-book/HFB.html

There you will find important updates to the law; worksheets, charts, and forms; and links to online articles on bankruptcy, debt, credit, and foreclosure.

Should You File for Chapter 7 Bankruptcy?

Your first objective is to figure out whether you can—and should—file for Chapter 7 bankruptcy. This chapter will give you an overview of the bankruptcy process and help you decide whether Chapter 7 bankruptcy is right for you. In the chapters that follow, we explain what will happen to your debts and property and how to complete the required bankruptcy paperwork. And, of course, we also make sure that you know what to expect once your bankruptcy is final.

Bankruptcy in America: The Big Picture

Although you might not care much about the larger bankruptcy picture, understanding it will help you keep your situation in perspective. For many, it's reassuring to know that you're not alone in your financial struggles—and because you're reading this edition, you're likely one of the millions impacted by COVID-19. As you'll see below, a global pandemic isn't a reason in itself for bankruptcy. Instead, it exposes far more people to typical financial insecurities leading to bankruptcy.

Why People File for Bankruptcy

Historically, these are the most common reasons for filing for bankruptcy:
- job loss, followed by an inability to find work that pays nearly as well
- medical expenses that aren't reimbursed by insurance or government programs
- divorce or legal separation, and
- small business failures.

Once a financial catastrophe strikes, many of us wind up taking on significant debt just to weather the storm. If we saved enough, maybe we'd be ready for these unexpected twists and turns. But, for a variety of reasons, many of us aren't prepared. Let's take a closer look at how we become so financially overextended.

Don't Feel Guilty About Filing for Bankruptcy

Perhaps irresponsible spending brought you to this point. It happens. But it's just as likely that isn't the case at all. The cost of living has outstripped salaries for many years now, and if you're like most, you've struggled to make ends meet for some time. If an illness, loss of work, or underemployment struck, you likely depleted any emergency fund quickly, leaving no choice but to turn to credit and fall into debt.

Bankruptcy is in place to provide a financial safety net. It's based on forgiveness rather than retribution and is a truly worthy part of our legal system. It helps keep families together, frees up income and resources for children, reduces suicide rates, and keeps the homeless population from growing even more extensive. In short, bankruptcy provides a chance for a fresh start and a renewed, positive outlook on life.

So if you are grappling with guilt, feel free to let it go. Banks issue credit cards because they are profitable, even though some credit card debts are wiped out in bankruptcies and never repaid. It's a cost of doing business.

What About the Downside?

Despite its many benefits, bankruptcy also has disadvantages—economically, emotionally, and in terms of your future credit rating. The bankruptcy process can get intrusive. As part of your public filing, you must disclose your financial activities during the previous year or two—sometimes more—as well as your income, debts, and current property holdings.

If you have a bankruptcy on your credit report, you might need to explain to those you do business with that you made every effort to meet your financial obligations before resorting to bankruptcy. Whether you are renting or buying a home, purchasing or leasing a car, or seeking financing for a business, your bankruptcy will be counted against you, at least for several years, and will stay on your credit report for up to ten years. You'll likely be able to get credit cards after bankruptcy; however, you will have a high interest rate, at least for a while.

Fortunately, the stigma bankruptcy used to carry has significantly diminished since the 2008 economic downturn. These days, only the older generations seem to prefer struggling under a mountain of debt rather than accepting the label of "bankrupt." But even seniors are coming around. The bottom line is that bankruptcy will give you a financial breather. Plus, you'll learn to live without credit and develop a more manageable relationship with your money.

Changes in Bankruptcy Law

In October 2005, Congress passed a law that changed the way bankruptcy works. One of the purposes of this law, known as the Bankruptcy Abuse Prevention and Consumer Protection Act (BAPCPA), was to cut down on Chapter 7 bankruptcies. It was drafted for the credit card and banking industries under the assumption that many would-be bankruptcy filers could afford to pay back at least some of their debt and should therefore be required to do so.

The hallmark of BAPCPA is what's known as the means test—a questionnaire that helps determine whether filers have sufficient "disposable" income to fund a Chapter 13 bankruptcy plan. In general, those with higher incomes are more likely to fail the test and be forced out of Chapter 7 bankruptcy. Contrary to what the supporters of the BAPCPA thought, the vast majority of those who use Chapter 7 have little or no income to spare. As a result, many people who want to file for Chapter 7 bankruptcy can still do so.

Numerous additional changes make filing for Chapter 7 bankruptcy more complicated and expensive if you use an attorney. But, using our step-by-step instructions, many people can handle their own cases.

This 22nd edition of *How to File for Chapter 7 Bankruptcy* also incorporates the many interpretations of the law handed down by the nation's bankruptcy courts. New court decisions from bankruptcy courts, federal district courts, bankruptcy appellate panels (B.A.P.s), federal Circuit Courts of Appeal, and even the U.S. Supreme Court could come out after this book goes to print. To make sure you have the most up-to-date information and forms, check the companion page at www.nolo.com/back-of-book/HFB.html.

What This Book Doesn't Cover

This book explains the procedures for filing a Chapter 7 bankruptcy if you are an individual, a married couple, or a small business owner with personal liability for your business debts. This book doesn't cover:

- **Chapter 13 bankruptcy.** Chapter 13 allows filers to keep their property and repay some or all of their debt over three to five years. For more information on Chapter 13, see "Pay Over Time With Chapter 13 Bankruptcy," below. You can also get details about Chapter 13 bankruptcy in *Chapter 13 Bankruptcy*, by Cara O'Neill (Nolo).
- **Bankruptcy for business partnerships.** If you're a partner in a business with someone other than your spouse, filing for personal bankruptcy will affect your business; we don't address that situation in this book.
- **Bankruptcy for major stockholders in privately held corporations.** If you're a major owner of a private corporation, filing for bankruptcy could affect the corporation's legal and tax status. This book doesn't cover your situation.
- **Business reorganization.** This book doesn't cover Chapter 11 of the bankruptcy laws, which allows a business to continue operating while paying off all or a portion of its debts under court supervision.
- **Farm reorganization.** A special set of bankruptcy statutes, called Chapter 12, lets family farmers continue farming while paying off their debts over time. Although explained briefly, Chapter 12 isn't addressed in this book.

An Overview of Chapter 7 Bankruptcy

Chapter 7 bankruptcy is sometimes called "liquidation" bankruptcy. It works by canceling most types of debt while allowing you to protect (exempt) property you'll need to work and live. If you're like most, you'll be able to keep all or most of your property. But if you have too much, the bankruptcy trustee will liquidate (sell) it and use the sales proceeds to pay creditors.

Even though bankruptcy falls under federal law, your state decides the type and amount of property you can exempt. Some states are more generous than others, so exemptions vary widely. (See Ch. 3 for exemption information; see www.nolo.com/back-of-book/HFB.html for federal and state exemption lists.)

Here is a brief overview of the Chapter 7 bankruptcy process, from start to finish.

What Bankruptcy Costs

The entire Chapter 7 bankruptcy process takes about three to six months to complete. Usually, it requires one brief meeting with the bankruptcy trustee—the official appointed by the bankruptcy judge to process your bankruptcy. You'll pay $338 in filing fees unless you get a fee waiver. If you use a lawyer, you can expect to pay an additional $1,500 or more in legal fees. Of course, you can save most of this money by representing yourself with the help of this book. (See Ch. 10 for information on finding lawyers.)

Mandatory Credit Counseling

Before you can file for bankruptcy, you must consult a nonprofit credit counseling agency. The purpose of this consultation is to see whether there is a feasible way to handle your debt load outside of bankruptcy without adding to what you owe. You can complete this mandatory credit counseling course online or over the phone.

To qualify for bankruptcy relief, you must show that you received credit counseling from an agency approved by the U.S. Trustee's office within 180 days before you file.

Once you complete the counseling, the agency will give you a certificate showing that you participated. It will also give you a copy of any repayment plan you worked out with the agency.

There are a few exceptions to this counseling requirement. You don't have to participate if you are in the military on active duty, incapacitated, or have a disability that prevents you from participating. Also, suppose you try unsuccessfully to get counseling with an approved agency at least seven days before filing for bankruptcy. In that case, you can ask the court for an additional 30 days to complete your course. You'll have to explain why you weren't able to fulfill the requirement. The court will grant the request if you can show that your honest effort to secure counseling was thwarted due to circumstances beyond your control.

Rules Counseling Agencies Must Follow

In addition to providing services without regard to your ability to pay, counseling agencies must meet several other requirements:

- disclose funding sources, counselor qualifications, the possible impact of the proposed plan on your credit report, and your costs
- provide counseling that includes an analysis of the factors causing your current financial condition and how you can address the problems without adding to your debt
- use trained counselors who aren't paid based on the outcome of the counseling services, and
- maintain adequate financial resources to provide continuing support services over the life of any repayment plan. For example, if they propose a three-year payment plan, they must service your case for three years.

The purpose of credit counseling is to give you an idea of whether you really need to file for bankruptcy or whether an informal repayment plan would get you back on your feet. Counseling is required even if it's evident that a repayment plan isn't feasible (that is, your debts are too high and your income is too low).

The law requires that you participate—not that you go along with whatever the agency proposes. Even if a repayment plan is feasible, you don't have to agree to it. However, you must file any plan with the other required bankruptcy paperwork. (See Ch. 6 for more information on the credit counseling requirement, including how to get the certificate of completion that you'll have to file with your other bankruptcy papers.)

Filing Your Papers

To begin a Chapter 7 bankruptcy case, you must complete a packet of forms and file them with the bankruptcy court in your area. Many filers are shocked to see the long list of documents required in a Chapter 7 case. But don't be alarmed: The forms aren't difficult to complete. But they do take time. Follow the detailed instructions in Ch. 6, and you'll do just fine.

Once you file your paperwork, the court will mail a notice of your bankruptcy filing to you and your creditors. The notice sets a date for the meeting of creditors (see "The Meeting of Creditors (341 Hearing)," below), provides the trustee's name, address, and telephone number, and gives creditors the deadlines for filing objections to your bankruptcy or to the discharge of particular debts.

The Voluntary Petition

You begin a Chapter 7 case by filing a Voluntary Petition. This official court form works like a coversheet and requests a bankruptcy discharge of your debts. You'll provide basic information, including your name, address, and the last four digits of your Social Security number, and information about your creditors, debts, and property. You'll also disclose whether you have lived, maintained a residence or business, or had assets in the district where you are filing for most of the 180 days (91 days or more) before filing. You must meet this condition to have the right to file in that bankruptcy court district. You'll also attest that you completed your prefiling credit counseling (later in your bankruptcy case, you'll prove that you completed budget counseling). You'll find line-by-line instructions for completing the Voluntary Petition in Ch. 6.

Additional Documents

You will have to submit quite a few more documents, either when you file the petition or (with a few exceptions) within 14 days after you file. These additional documents include lists of your creditors, assets, debts, income, and financial transactions; copies of your most recent federal tax return, bank statements, and wage stubs; a list of property you claim is protected by a bankruptcy exemption; and what you plan to do with property serving as collateral for a loan (such as a car or home).

Perhaps the most important forms are the "means test" forms you complete to determine whether you qualify for Chapter 7. You must compute your average gross income during the six months before your bankruptcy filing date and compare that to the median income for your state. If your income is more than the median, another form takes you through a series of questions to determine whether you could pay some unsecured debts in Chapter 13.

(See "Who Cannot File for Chapter 7," below, and Ch. 6 for detailed information about these calculations.)

Emergency Filing

In some situations, speed is essential. If you need to stop creditors quickly, you can do so without filing all of the bankruptcy forms we describe in Ch. 6 (although you'll eventually have to complete the whole set). For example, if you face foreclosure and your house will be sold in a few days, or your car is about to be repossessed, filing an emergency petition will stop the repossession or foreclosure cold.

To temporarily stop the collection efforts, you can simply file the Voluntary Petition form, your credit counseling certificate, a form providing your Social Security number, and a document known as the Creditors' Matrix, which lists the name, address, and zip code of each of your creditors. The automatic stay, which stops collection efforts and lawsuits against you, will then go into effect. (Ch. 2 covers the automatic stay in detail.) You'll have 14 days to file the rest of the forms. (Bankruptcy Rule 1007(c).)

You should file on an emergency basis only if you absolutely must. Many emergency filers fail to meet the 14-day deadline and have their petitions dismissed as a result. Because you are rushing, you are more likely to make mistakes that have to be corrected later, which adds work and potential errors to the process. But if filing an emergency petition is the only way to stop a potentially disastrous creditor action, go for it. Just remember the deadline for filing the rest of the forms.

After you file, you might want to amend some or all of your forms to correct mistakes you discover or to reflect agreements you reach with the trustee. Amending these forms is relatively simple; we explain how to do it in Ch. 7.

The Automatic Stay

Often, people filing for bankruptcy have faced weeks, months, or even years of harassment by creditors demanding payment and threatening lawsuits and collection actions. Bankruptcy puts a stop to all this. Filing your bankruptcy petition creates a federal court order called an "Order for Relief" and informally known as the "automatic stay" that requires your creditors to stop all collection efforts. So, at least temporarily, most creditors cannot call you, write dunning letters, legally take (garnish) your wages, empty your bank account, go after your car, house, or other property, or cut off your utility service or welfare benefits. As explained in Ch. 2, the automatic stay is not absolute. Some creditors are not affected by the automatic stay. Others can get the stay lifted to collect their debts, as long as they get the judge's permission first.

> ⓘ CAUTION
> **Renters beware.** In most cases, the automatic stay's magic will temporarily halt your eviction when you file for bankruptcy. The bankruptcy court will almost always lift the stay and let the eviction proceed upon the landlord's request. Keep in mind that this is what you can expect to occur when eviction moratoriums related to COVID-19 aren't in place. You might have other eviction protections as a result of the coronavirus pandemic. (See Ch. 2 for more information on the automatic stay and eviction proceedings.)

Court Control Over Your Financial Affairs

By filing for bankruptcy, you are technically placing the property you own and the debts you owe in the hands of the bankruptcy trustee (see "The Trustee," below). While your case is open, you can't sell or give away any of the property you own when you file without the trustee's consent. However, you can do what you wish with property acquired and income earned after filing for bankruptcy, with a few exceptions. You are also allowed to borrow money after you file.

The Trustee

The bankruptcy court exercises control over your property and debts by appointing an official called a "trustee" to manage your case. Your trustee's name and contact information will be in the official notice of filing you receive in the mail several days after filing your petition. The trustee (or the trustee's staff) will examine your papers to make sure they are complete and look for property to sell for the benefit of your creditors. The trustee's primary duty is to see that your creditors are paid as much as possible. The trustee will be primarily interested in what you own and claim as exempt and financial transactions made during the previous years. In some cases, past transactions can be unwound, and the recaptured assets can be distributed to your creditors. Also, because the trustee receives a percentage of the recovered assets, the more the trustee finds for creditors, the more the trustee gets paid. So while it is tempting to believe the trustee is there to help you, it isn't the case.

Some courts appoint full-time trustees called "standing" trustees to handle all cases filed in that courthouse. Other courts appoint trustees on a rotating basis from a panel of bankruptcy lawyers called "panel" trustees. Either way, the trustees have the same responsibilities.

How Trustees Get Paid

Trustees receive a flat fee of $60 per Chapter 7 case. In addition, trustees can earn a "commission" if they find property, sell it, and distribute the proceeds to creditors. The percentage of funds received depends on the amount disbursed to creditors: 25% of the first $5,000 paid, 10% of the next $45,000, and so on. Most Chapter 7 cases involve no disbursements (because typically there are no nonexempt assets), so trustees usually have to settle for the $60 fee. But these fee rules give trustees a financial incentive to look closely at bankruptcy filings, especially if debtors appear to have some valuable property.

The U.S. Trustee

The U.S. Trustee Program is a division of the U.S. Department of Justice. Each U.S. Trustee oversees several bankruptcy courts. Individual cases within those courts are assigned to assistant U.S. Trustees, who also employ attorneys, auditors, and investigators. U.S. Trustees work closely with their Department of Justice colleagues from the FBI and other federal agencies to ferret out fraud and abuse in the bankruptcy system. The U.S. Trustees (and the assistant U.S. Trustees) also supervise the work of the panel or standing trustees, who are appointed by the courts.

You will most likely encounter the U.S. Trustee in one of the following cases:
- Your bankruptcy papers suggest that you may be engaging in fraudulent behavior.
- Your case is selected for a random audit.
- Your bankruptcy schedules show that you don't pass the means test (explained later in this chapter).
- You use a bankruptcy petition preparer (BPP) to help you with your paperwork (see Ch. 10 for more on BPPs), and the trustee believes that the BPP has done something illegal—typically, that the BPP has not just helped you complete your papers, but has given you legal advice as well, something that only lawyers are allowed to do. In this situation, your bankruptcy might be affected (particularly if the advice given was incorrect), and the U.S. Trustee may want you to act as a witness against the BPP.

The U.S. Trustee Program also investigates creditor violations, fraud against seniors, mortgage rescue fraud, and more.

The Meeting of Creditors (341 Hearing)

As explained above, you will receive notice of the date of your meeting of creditors (also called the 341 hearing) shortly after you file your bankruptcy papers. This meeting is typically held somewhere in a conference room in the courthouse or federal building (rarely in a courtroom). After checking your identification and swearing you in, the trustee will ask you standard questions all debtors must answer. For instance, you can expect to be asked if everything in your petition is accurate and whether anything has changed. The trustee might ask you additional questions about your particular bankruptcy and the documents you filed, too—for instance, how you arrived at the value for an item of property. This questioning usually takes about five minutes.

Creditors can attend this meeting but rarely do. Creditors who appear can also question you under oath. You might be asked where property serving as loan collateral is located or about the information given to obtain a loan. Some creditors might want to know more about the nature and location of your assets in general.

The good news? While many bankruptcy filers dread the 341 hearing, the concern is unnecessary. Most filers breeze through the process with no problem. And it will likely be the only personal appearance you'll have to make. We discuss the creditors' meeting in more detail in Ch. 7.

When a Disgruntled Ex-Spouse Casts Suspicion on Your Petition

Most of the time, a trustee won't question the accuracy of your personal property schedules unless there is a reason to do so. So what causes a trustee to become suspicious? One source that's hard to ignore is someone close to you. For instance, suppose your disgruntled ex-spouse claims that you didn't list an expensive piece of art or watch. The trustee might look for other undisclosed property by taking an inventory of your home, business, storage facility, or safety deposit box. The easiest way to prevent this type of problem? Be transparent. Your past can indeed come back to haunt you.

What Happens to Your Property

Each state allows debtors to keep certain property types or equity amounts in property. The exemptions available to you depend on where you lived before filing for bankruptcy. In your bankruptcy papers, you'll be asked which items of property you claim as exempt. (For more information, see Ch. 3.)

If you have nonexempt property, you'll have to either surrender it or provide the trustee with its equivalent value in cash after the creditors' meeting. It's unlikely that the trustee will inventory your home (although it can happen) or seize your property. Instead, you'll voluntarily turn over the nonexempt property listed in your schedules or identified through some other means. If you don't turn it over, the bankruptcy judge can order you to surrender the property and hold you in contempt if you don't. Plus, the court can dismiss your bankruptcy petition if you fail to cooperate with the trustee.

If your nonexempt property isn't worth very much or would be hard to sell, the trustee might "abandon" it—which means that you get to keep it, even though it's nonexempt. Unless the debtor has a significant amount of cash, home equity, or luxury goods like a boat or rental property, most of the debtor's property will be essentially worthless to creditors.

Secured Debts

If you've pledged property as collateral for a loan, the loan is a "secured debt." The most common examples of collateral are houses and motor vehicles. If you are behind on your payments, a creditor can ask to have the automatic stay lifted so it can repossess the property or foreclose on the mortgage. However, if you are current on your payments, you can keep the property and continue making payments as before—unless you have built up enough nonexempt equity in the property to make it worthwhile for the trustee to sell it for the benefit of your unsecured creditors. (See Ch. 5 for more information on secured debts.)

If a creditor has recorded a lien against your property without your consent (for example, because the creditor obtained a money judgment against you in court), that debt is also secured. However, in some cases and with certain types of property, you might be able to wipe out the debt and keep the property free of the lien. This is called "lien avoidance," and it is covered in Ch. 5.

Contracts and Leases

If you signed a contract or lease that's still in effect, the trustee might take your place as a party to the contract if it would be beneficial for your creditors. This is known as "assuming" the contract. Alternatively, the trustee can "reject" the contract, in which case you would decide if you wanted the contract to continue in force.

For example, suppose you have a valuable five-year commercial lease at a below-market rate in an up-and-coming part of town. The trustee could hold an auction, assign the lease to the highest bidder, and use the profit to pay unsecured creditors. However, a trustee who doesn't think selling the lease would be worth the trouble will take no action, which is the same as rejecting the lease.

You can keep leases on personal property, such as a car or business equipment, rather than have the trustee assume them. However, you can do this only if you can cure any defaults on the lease, as required by the creditor. (Ch. 6 explains how to list contracts and leases on Schedule G and how to use the Statement of Intention form to notify the trustee and creditors about the leases you'd like to assume.)

Personal Financial Management Counseling

All debtors must attend a course on managing finances to receive a bankruptcy discharge, sometimes referred to as budget counseling, debtor education, or predischarge counseling. You must take this course from an agency approved by the U.S. Trustee Program. You will be charged fees on a sliding scale, but you can't be denied services because of your inability to pay. Once you complete your counseling, you must file a certification form with the court. For a list of approved agencies, go to the U.S. Trustee's website, www.usdoj.gov/ust, and click "Credit Counseling & Debtor Education."

The Bankruptcy Discharge

About 60 days after the 341 hearing—the one hearing all filers must attend— you will receive an Order of Discharge from the court. This notice doesn't list your particular discharged debts. Instead, it provides general information about the types of debts affected by the discharge order. In most cases, all debts are discharged except:

- debts that automatically survive bankruptcy (child support, most tax debts, and student loans are examples), and
- debts that the court has declared nondischargeable due to an action brought by a creditor (such as debts incurred through fraudulent or willful and malicious acts).

Ch. 9 explains which debts are—and are not— discharged at the end of your bankruptcy case. Also, "Who Cannot File for Chapter 7," below, explains the circumstances in which your entire discharge—not just the discharge of a specific debt—might be denied.

What If You Change Your Mind After Filing?

If you don't want to go through with Chapter 7 bankruptcy after filing, you might be out of luck. You can't dismiss it on your own. Instead, you must ask the court to dismiss your case. A court will generally agree, as long as the dismissal won't harm your creditors' interests. But that's often the case because debtors usually want out to prevent property loss. For example, suppose you have substantial nonexempt equity in your house. The court will probably deny your dismissal request so the trustee can sell the house to make some money for your unsecured creditors. (See Ch. 4 for more on what happens to your home in bankruptcy.)

As an alternative to having your Chapter 7 case dismissed, you could exercise your one-time "right to convert" the matter to a Chapter 13 bankruptcy. Chapter 13 offers the benefit of keeping your property out of the trustee's hands. In Chapter 13, you don't surrender the property. However, you do have to pay your unsecured creditors the value of your nonexempt property, as explained in "Pay Over Time With Chapter 13 Bankruptcy," below. If you don't have enough income to pay into a Chapter 13 repayment plan, your case will be dismissed (and unlike Chapter 7, you can dismiss a Chapter 13 case yourself).

After Bankruptcy

Once you receive your bankruptcy discharge, you are free to resume your economic life without reporting your activities to the bankruptcy court. However, a few exceptions exist. Suppose you receive (or become eligible to receive) an inheritance, insurance or lottery proceeds, or proceeds from a divorce settlement within 180 days after your filing date. In that case, you must report the assets to the trustee. If you don't, and they are discovered, the trustee (and the court, if necessary) can order you to turn over the assets and your discharge could be revoked.

After bankruptcy, public or private employers can't discriminate against you solely because of the bankruptcy, although this ban on discrimination has exceptions (discussed in Ch. 8). You can start rebuilding your credit almost immediately, but it might take several years to get decent interest rates on a credit card, mortgage, or car note.

If you fall into debt again, you won't be able to get another Chapter 7 debt discharge until eight years have passed (starting from the last filing date). You won't qualify for a Chapter 13 discharge until four years have passed. Even so, sometimes filing for Chapter 13 is beneficial without a discharge. For instance, filing a Chapter 13 can help stop a wage garnishment or spread out payments on support arrearages.

Who Cannot File for Chapter 7

Filing for Chapter 7 bankruptcy is one way to solve debt problems, but it isn't available to everyone. You might not be able to use Chapter 7 to discharge debt if one of these situations exists.

You Can Afford a Chapter 13 Repayment Plan

Under the bankruptcy rules, filers with higher incomes must pay back some of their debts over time under Chapter 13 rather than discharging their obligations outright in Chapter 7. If the U.S. Trustee decides that your income, debts, and expenses indicate that you can afford a Chapter 13 plan under the rules, it will file a motion to have your case dismissed. The court is likely to grant that motion and throw out your case unless you convert to a Chapter 13 bankruptcy.

To figure out whether you can discharge your debts in Chapter 7, you must first:

- determine your "current monthly income" (your average income during the six months before you file for bankruptcy)
- multiply your current monthly income by 12, and
- compare that figure to the yearly median family income in your state for the same size household.

If your current monthly income (multiplied by twelve) is no more than the state's yearly median income, you'll qualify for a discharge. Your Chapter 7 bankruptcy won't be presumed to be "an abuse" of the bankruptcy process. However, even if you meet this test, if your actual income is significantly higher than your expenses, you might still be forced into Chapter 13 (explained in Ch. 6).

If your income exceeds the state median income, you will have to do some calculations to determine whether you can afford to pay off at least some of your unsecured debts in a Chapter 13 plan. This qualification process is known as the means test. (You can find step-by-step means test instructions in Ch. 6.)

You Have Marijuana Assets

Over the past several years, some states have legalized the personal or medical use of marijuana. Under these laws, an individual or business might possess a relatively small amount of marijuana for personal use or have significant inventory in a dispensary. Either way, filers with marijuana assets might think that they can turn to bankruptcy, believing that the industry is legal in their home state. It's not the case.

Marijuana remains illegal under federal law. The U.S. Trustee Program works to dismiss cases violating the Controlled Substances Act and ensure that marijuana-related assets don't enter the bankruptcy system. For instance, in 2020, an Oregon bankruptcy court dismissed a Chapter 11 case involving two marijuana-growing tenants. Because marijuana possession is a violation of the Controlled Substances Act, a filer could also be subject to criminal penalties. If you're concerned that this problem might arise in your matter, speak with an attorney familiar with the issue.

Some Disabled Veterans Can Skip the Math

If you're a disabled veteran who incurred debt while on active duty or while engaged in homeland defense activities, you don't need to pass the means test. The bankruptcy court must assume your income is less than the state median, so you'll qualify automatically.

The law doesn't clearly indicate what will happen if you incurred some of your debts while you were on active duty. Some courts require you to incur more than 50% of your debts be on active duty; however, other courts might have stricter requirements. If you are unsure about whether you are eligible, talk to a bankruptcy attorney in your area.

Determine Your Current Monthly and Yearly Income

Legally, your income for the means test is your average income over the six months preceding the month in which you filed for bankruptcy. You must include almost all types of income (with a few exceptions such as benefits received under the Social Security Act), taxable or not. The calculations are based on your gross earnings, not the net income you actually take home after taxes and other deductions for the first portion of the test. For filers who lost jobs or other income during the six months before filing, this income figure could be significantly more than what they are actually earning currently.

> **EXAMPLE:** John and Emma are married and have two young children. They fell quickly into debt after John lost his job because of a work-related injury on April 1, 2020. Three months later, on July 1, 2020, John and Emma decide to file for bankruptcy.
>
> To compute their qualifying income, Emma adds up the family's income from January 1, 2020, through June 30, 2020 (the six months before their filing date). This includes John's gross salary for the first three months (he made $8,000 a month as a software engineer), plus $1,800 in workers' compensation benefits for each of the last three months. Emma made $1,000 during each of the first three months and had no income for the previous three months. The total family income for the six-month period is $32,400. Emma will double this amount to arrive at a yearly family income of $64,800.

Use the Current Monthly and Yearly Household Income Worksheet on this book's companion page (www.nolo.com/back-of-book/HFB.html) to calculate your household income. You'll find the figure by:

- adding all income received during the full six months before filing for bankruptcy
- dividing it by six (this is your current monthly household income for the means test), and
- multiplying the current monthly income figure by 12.

You should include all of the following types of income on the form:

- wages, salary, tips, bonuses, overtime, and commissions
- gross income from operating a business, profession, or farm
- interest, dividends, and royalties
- rents and other income from real property
- pension and retirement income
- regular contributions someone else makes to your or your dependents' household expenses, including child or spousal support
- regular contributions of your spouse, if he or she isn't filing for bankruptcy with you
- unemployment compensation (some states will require state unemployment insurance benefits)
- workers' compensation insurance
- state disability insurance
- annuity payments, and
- lump-sum, windfall payments (such as lottery winnings).

Determine Your Household Size

The size of your household is also significant. The more members you have, the less likely it will be that your income will exceed the state median for a family of the same size. You'll qualify for a Chapter 7 discharge without taking the second part of the means test. For example, assume that your yearly household income is $60,000. In your state, the median income for a household of three is $58,000, and the median income for a family of four is $62,000. Being able to count that additional person means you will pass the means test without further calculations.

Unfortunately, neither Congress nor the courts have given clear guidance on how to calculate household size. Many courts adopt the census test for a household. You'd include all of the people, related and unrelated, who occupy a house, apartment, group of rooms, or single room intended for occupancy as separate living quarters. Under this test, you can count your children or stepchildren.

However, some courts allow debtors to count only qualifying dependents. Other courts use the economic unit approach to household size. This formula would include individuals who financially depend on or support the debtor or whose income and expenses are closely intermingled with and connected to the debtor's income.

Roommates are not part of the same household. Typically, they have separate rooms within a house and don't act as a single economic unit by mingling their incomes and jointly paying expenses.

Another issue can arise when children can be counted as part of a household but don't live with the parent exclusively due to a custody and visitation agreement. In general, the answer depends on the rules in your jurisdiction. If you need to count children who also live with another parent to pass the means test, talk to a local bankruptcy attorney and determine how your local court handles this issue. (See Ch. 10 for information on finding a bankruptcy lawyer.)

Compare Your Yearly Income to Your State's Family Median Income

Once you've got your family's yearly income, find out whether it's more or less than the median. You can use the Median Family Income Chart on the companion page (www.nolo.com/back-of-book/HFB.html). The means testing figures change regularly, so be sure to check the current amounts on the U.S. Trustee website at www.usdoj.gov/ust (select "Means Testing Information").

Income You Don't Have to Include

Your income includes income from all sources, *except:*

- income tax refunds
- payments you receive under the Social Security Act (including Social Security retirement benefits, Social Security Disability Insurance, Supplemental Security Income, Temporary Assistance for Needy Families, and possibly state unemployment insurance)
- payments to you as a victim of war crimes or crimes against humanity, and
- payments to you as a victim of international or domestic terrorism.

What to Do Next

If your yearly income is equal to or less than your state's median, then you'll likely qualify for Chapter 7 bankruptcy. As you'll discover, however, the actual monthly income and expenses you report on Schedules I and J could prevent you from receiving a discharge even if you pass the means test. This can happen because the means test averages your income over the six months before you file. As a result, your means test income could be substantially different from your actual monthly earnings. For instance, if you were unemployed for six months but accepted a well-paying position one month before filing for bankruptcy, this problem could crop up.

Here's how this could come up: The trustee appointed to your case will review the monthly income and expenses listed on Schedules I and J. If you earn significantly more than what's needed to pay your monthly expenses, you'll likely have to convert to Chapter 13 or face dismissal.

Let's look at a different problem now. Suppose your yearly income exceeds the state median income. You won't be excluded from Chapter 7 automatically. The second part of the means test will allow you to subtract certain expenses from your income. If you don't have enough left over to make a meaningful payment to creditors, you'll still pass the means test and be eligible for a Chapter 7 discharge.

If you don't qualify after completing the second portion, you'd have to persuade the court that it's appropriate for you to file for Chapter 7 under the circumstances—see "Special Problems" in Ch. 7. You can find the means test forms and step-by-step instructions for completing them in Ch. 6.

If you don't qualify for Chapter 7, consider learning more about Chapter 13 bankruptcy using Nolo's *Chapter 13 Bankruptcy*, by Cara O'Neill. Alternatively, find out about options available outside of the bankruptcy system in "Alternatives to Chapter 7 Bankruptcy," below.

You Previously Received a Bankruptcy Discharge

Because bankruptcy is such a powerful tool, you're limited to how often you can use it. For instance, you can't get another Chapter 7 discharge until eight years have passed. If you previously filed for Chapter 13, your waiting period will be six years.

Note that these eight- and six-year periods run from the date you filed the earlier bankruptcy, not the date you received your discharge.

> **EXAMPLE:** Madison filed a Chapter 7 bankruptcy case on January 31, 2014. She received a discharge on April 20, 2014. Madison files another Chapter 7 bankruptcy on February 1, 2022. The second bankruptcy is allowed because eight years have passed since the filing date of the earlier bankruptcy (even though fewer than eight years have passed since Madison received a discharge in the earlier case).

A Previous Bankruptcy Was Dismissed Within the Last 180 Days

You wouldn't be able to receive a Chapter 7 bankruptcy discharge if you had a Chapter 7 or Chapter 13 case dismissed during the previous 180 days if you:
- violated a court order, or
- requested the dismissal after a creditor asked for relief from the automatic stay. (11 U.S.C. § 109(g).)

You'd have to wait at least 180 days before filing again. This rule is in place to prevent people from gaming the system. For instance, filers have been known to file for Chapter 13 and use the automatic stay to prevent a lender from selling a home at auction with no intention of proposing a feasible plan. If the lender had asked the court to lift the stay to allow the auction to proceed and the filer dismissed the case subsequently, the 180-day rule would apply.

Another rule limits the extent of the automatic stay's protection on subsequent filings within the same year. The automatic stay will only remain in effect for 30 days when filing a second time. It won't go into effect on any filings after that. However, the filer can ask the court to put the automatic stay in place.

You Haven't Met the Credit Counseling Requirements

To file for Chapter 7 bankruptcy, you must satisfy all the requirements for credit counseling. You must receive the counseling within 180 days before you file and file a certificate of completion no later than 14 days after you file. Some exceptions to the counseling requirement exist, but they're challenging to meet. (See Ch. 6 for more on these requirements.)

You Defrauded Your Creditors

Bankruptcy helps honest debtors who get in too deep financially and need a fresh start. A bankruptcy court will not help someone who has played fast and loose with creditors or the court. This type of behavior can lead to a denial of your bankruptcy discharge and even to criminal charges.

The bankruptcy court isn't the place to try to skirt the law. A debtor can only do so many things to try to come out ahead, and filers should assume that anything they could possibly dream up has failed before. Certain activities are red flags to the courts and trustees. If you have done any of these things within the past several years, consult with a bankruptcy lawyer:

- selling assets to friends or relatives for less than what the property is worth
- incurring debts for luxury items when broke and without the intent to pay, and
- any attempt at concealing property or money from creditors.

Converting to Chapter 7 After Filing for Chapter 13

Can you file under Chapter 13 and then convert to Chapter 7 later, without taking the means test? It will depend on the rules in your bankruptcy jurisdiction and the circumstances of your case. However, all courts take steps to prevent debtors from using the conversion process to avoid paying creditors. For instance, in *In re Trotta*, 597 B.R. 269 (Bankr. E.D. Penn. 2019), the court considers the totality of the debtor's financial circumstances, including the means test and the potential of a bad faith motive.

The court in *In re Fox*, 370 B.R. 639 (Bankr. D. N.J. 2007) applies a more lax conversion standard. This court found that the debtor did not have to file the means test form when converting from Chapter 13 to Chapter 7. However, the court emphasized that the debtor must have filed Chapter 13 in good faith and not to avoid taking the means test. This means the debtor must have proposed a feasible (or somewhat plausible) Chapter 13 plan. The test doesn't consider the debtor's current ability to pay and represents a minority approach.

By contrast, in Texas, a debtor must pass the means test when converting from Chapter 13 to Chapter 7 to prevent a debtor living a lavish lifestyle from receiving a Chapter 7 debt discharge. (*In re Croft*, 539 B.R. 122 (Bankr. W.D. Tex. 2015).)

The court in *In re Layton*, 480 B.R. 392 (Bankr. M.D. Fla. 2012) falls somewhere in the middle, finding that the means test isn't necessary if the conversion occurs after a job loss.

Your Filing Constitutes "Abuse"

The court can dismiss your case if it finds that your filing is abusive or your actions demonstrate that you aren't entitled to the remedy offered by Chapter 7. As explained above, if you fail the means test, the court will presume that your bankruptcy filing is abusive and prevent you from using Chapter 7. However, even if you pass the means test, the court might find abuse. For example, if your actual income (listed in Schedule I) exceeds your actual expenses (listed in Schedule J), the court might decide you have too much disposable income for Chapter 7. This can happen even if you pass the means test.

TIP

Here's how much disposable income you can show on Schedules I and J. According to the U.S. Trustee Program's Annual Report, in 2020, a Chapter 7 debtor could have up to $227.50 in disposable income. Cases with disposable income over $227.50 were presumed abusive and subject to dismissal.

Here are some other reasons the court might deny you the benefit of Chapter 7 when you otherwise qualify:

- The court can refuse to grant a Chapter 7 discharge if the debtor fails to keep records that can be used to verify the debtor's financial condition. (*In re Tanglis*, 344 B.R. 563 (Bankr. N.D. Ill. 2006).)
- If the debtor fails to explain what happened to money withdrawn from a business or fails to disclose property, the court can refuse to grant a Chapter 7 discharge. (*In re Beatty*, 583 B.R. 128 (Bankr. N.D. Ohio 2018).)
- Voluntary unemployment can be considered abusive when the debtor could pay back some or all of the debts if employed. (*In re Richie*, 353 B.R. 569 (Bankr. E.D. Wash. 2006).)
- A debtor who can't account for cash advances used during the previous year could be denied a Chapter 7 discharge on the grounds of abuse. (*In re Yanni*, 354 B.R. 708 (Bankr. E.D. Penn. 2006).)

These types of cases are unusual because they're somewhat difficult to prove. For instance, in an omitted asset case, the creditor must first prove that the debtor failed to include an asset. Even if the creditor can do so, the court will accept a reasonably plausible explanation for the omission from the debtor. A creditor would need to be sure of the facts before willingly incurring the cost to try such a case.

You Are Attempting to Defraud the Bankruptcy Court

Misleading the court is a terrible idea. If you lie, cheat, or try to hide assets, your current debt crisis might no longer be your biggest legal problem. You must sign your bankruptcy papers under "penalty of perjury," swearing that everything in them is true. You also have to verify the information you provided under oath at your creditors' meeting. If you get caught deliberately failing to disclose property, omitting material information, using a false Social Security number (to hide your identity as a prior filer), or committing some other inappropriate act, you won't get bankruptcy relief. You may even be prosecuted for perjury or fraud on the court.

The U.S. Trustee Program Actively Investigates Civil and Criminal Fraud

The U.S. Trustee Program, a branch of the U.S. Department of Justice, is charged with uncovering bankruptcy-related fraud. The U.S. Trustee audits "red flag" bankruptcy cases for possible fraud and randomly reviews others. In 2020, the auditing program resulted in nearly 25,000 civil enforcement actions with a "...potential monetary impact of nearly $1 billion in debts not discharged, fines, penalties, and other relief."

The U.S. Trustee Program also made 12,489 bankruptcy-related criminal referrals—a 9.2% increase over the previous year. Potential crimes typically include tax fraud, concealing assets, engaging in bankruptcy fraud schemes, identity theft, and using false Social Security numbers. In 2020, COVID-19 CARES Act violations resulted in 48 criminal referrals. Most involved fraudulent Paycheck Protection Program (P.P.P.) loan applications (bankruptcy debtors are ineligible for P.P.P. loans). Keep in mind that these statistics represent a small percentage of bankruptcy cases filed. As long as you are scrupulously honest in your paperwork and disclosures, there's no need for worry.

Does Chapter 7 Bankruptcy Make Economic Sense?

If you are leaning toward filing for Chapter 7, take a moment to consider whether it makes economic sense. If filing for Chapter 7 won't help with your current debt problems or will force you to give up property you want to keep, then Chapter 7 might not be the best option.

FOR MARRIED COUPLES

If you are married, consider the debts and property of both spouses as you read this section. Married couples usually benefit from filing jointly, but not always. For example, if one spouse brings a lot of debt to the marriage while the other spouse has clean credit, it might make more sense for the debt-ridden spouse to file alone. Filing alone might also be a good idea if one spouse is barred from filing due to a previous bankruptcy. It would also be prudent if filing together would put the nonfiling spouse's separate property at risk or if the couple holds property as tenants by the entirety. You'll find more information on the benefits of filing jointly versus filing alone in Ch. 6.

Are You Judgment Proof?

Most unsecured creditors are required to obtain a court judgment before they can start collection procedures, such as wage garnishment or seizure and sale of personal property. Holders of tax, child support, and student loan debts are exceptions to this general rule. Suppose your debts are mainly of the type that requires a judgment. In that case, the next question is whether you have any income or property that is subject to seizure by your creditors if they obtain a judgment. For instance, if all of your income comes from Social Security (which can't be taken by creditors as long as it isn't commingled with other funds), and all of your property is exempt (see Ch. 3), there is nothing a creditor can do with a judgment. That makes you judgment proof.

While you might still want to file for bankruptcy to get a fresh start, nothing terrible will happen to you if you don't file, no matter how much you owe. (For more on what it means to be judgment proof, see "Alternatives to Chapter 7 Bankruptcy," below.)

Sample Letter Telling Collection Agency to Stop Contacting You

---

Sasnak Collection Service
49 Pirate Place
Topeka, Kansas 69000

November 11, 20xx

Attn: Marc Mist
Re: Lee Anne Ito
Account No. 88-90-92

Dear Mr. Mist:

For the past three months, I have received several phone calls and letters from you concerning an overdue Rich's Department Store account.

This is my formal notice to you under 15 U.S.C. § 1692c(c) to cease all further communications with me at my home or place of employment except for the reasons expressly outlined in the federal law.

This letter is not meant in any way to be an acknowledgment that I owe this money.

Very truly yours,

Lee Anne Ito

Lee Anne Ito

It's not uncommon for a judgment-proof debtor to want to file for bankruptcy to stop harassment by creditors. In most cases, you can stop creditors from making telephone calls to your home or work by simply telling them to stop. Changing your phone number can also help, as well as screening calls. If collection agencies are doing the harassment, you can also send them a letter like the one shown above, which almost always does the trick.

If a collector continues to harass you after you have given written notice, you can sue under the Fair Debt Collection Practices Act. (15 U.S.C. §§ 1692–1692o.) You can ask to be compensated for any damage you suffer (such as medical conditions caused by the harassment) as well as statutory damages. Attorneys' fees are also available, so it should be easier to find an attorney who will represent you without requiring an up-front retainer. Your state may have similar legal protections against harassment by a collection agency or an original creditor—and additional remedies for violations of the law. (For more information on illegal debt collection practices, see *Solve Your Money Troubles*, by Amy Loftsgordon and Cara O'Neill (Nolo).)

Using Bankruptcy to Get New Credit

Even if you are judgment proof, you might want to file for bankruptcy to clear your credit. You will likely be able to rebuild your credit sooner by filing for bankruptcy than by ignoring your debts. In fact, you'll likely receive offers for credit cards and car loans shortly after receiving your discharge. (For more on rebuilding your credit, see Ch. 8.)

Will Bankruptcy Discharge Enough of Your Debts?

Specific categories of debts will survive Chapter 7 bankruptcy, depending on the circumstances. It might not make much sense to file for Chapter 7 bankruptcy if your primary goal is to eliminate these nondischargeable debts.

There are three categories of nondischargeable debts:
- debts that always survive bankruptcy
- debts that survive bankruptcy unless you convince the court that a particular exception applies, and
- debts that survive bankruptcy only if a creditor mounts a successful challenge to them in bankruptcy court.

If most of your debts will survive bankruptcy, hold off on filing Chapter 7 until you have at least read Ch. 9 and learned what is likely to happen to these debts in your case. In particular, you should be concerned about:

- back child support and alimony
- nonsupport debts arising from a marital property settlement agreement or divorce decree
- student loans
- government fines, penalties, or court-ordered restitution
- tax arrearages (including debts incurred to pay a tax—for example, if you used a credit card to pay back taxes), and
- court judgments for injuries or death resulting from your drunk driving convictions.

The following types of debts can survive bankruptcy, but only if the creditor mounts a successful challenge to them in the bankruptcy court:

- obligations incurred on the basis of fraud, such as lying on a credit application or writing a bad check
- luxury items recently bought on credit with no intention of paying for them
- debt resulting from willful and malicious injury to another person or another's property, including assault, battery, false imprisonment, libel, and slander, and
- debt from larceny (theft), breach of trust, or embezzlement.

TIP

Chapter 13 might be a better choice. In some situations, Chapter 13 offers relief that is not available in Chapter 7. For example, if you are facing fore-closure on your home because of mortgage defaults, you have debts that you can discharge in Chapter 13 but not in Chapter 7, or you need an affordable way to pay back your nondischargeable debts, you might want to consider using Chapter 13. (See "Pay Over Time With Chapter 13 Bankruptcy," below, for more information.)

Sorting It All Out

If your debt load consists primarily of debts that will be discharged unless a creditor convinces the court that they shouldn't be, it could make sense to file for bankruptcy and hope that the creditor doesn't challenge the discharge. Many creditors won't—mounting a challenge to the discharge of a debt requires a lawyer, and lawyers don't come cheap. Also, many lawyers advise their clients to write off the debt rather than throw good money after bad in a bankruptcy court challenge.

On the other hand, if your debt load consists primarily of debts that will survive your bankruptcy unless you convince the court otherwise, you must decide whether the debts are large enough to warrant paying an attorney to argue in court that the debts should be discharged. For example, if you owe $50,000 in student loans and have a good argument that they should be discharged, it will be worth your while to file for bankruptcy and pay an attorney $5,000 to push the issue. (You could also do this yourself, although this sort of procedure is challenging to navigate without competent expert help.) If the amount in question is small and your chances of victory slim, however, you might choose to forgo bankruptcy altogether.

Will a Cosigner Be Stuck With Your Debts?

If someone else cosigned a loan or otherwise took on a joint obligation with you, that person can be held wholly responsible for the debt if you don't pay it. If you receive a Chapter 7 bankruptcy discharge, you might no longer be liable for the debt—but your cosigner will still be on the hook. Especially if your cosigner is a friend or relative, you might not want to stick him or her with your debt burden.

If you have a cosigner you'd like to protect, you'll need to use one of the alternatives to Chapter 7 bankruptcy that are outlined below. By arranging to pay the debt over time, you can keep creditors from going after your cosigner for payment. And, if you decide to file for Chapter 13, you can include the debt in your repayment plan to keep creditors off your cosigner's back, at least for the duration of your plan.

Will You Lose Valuable Property?

Chapter 7 bankruptcy essentially offers this deal: If you are willing to give up your nonexempt property (property that isn't protected in bankruptcy) to be sold for the benefit of your creditors, the court will erase your dischargeable debts. If you can keep most of the things you care about, Chapter 7 bankruptcy can be a very effective remedy for your debt problems. But if Chapter 7 bankruptcy would force you to part with treasured property, you may want to look for another solution.

The laws that control what property you can keep in a Chapter 7 bankruptcy are called exemptions. Each state's legislature produces a set of exemptions for use by people who are sued in that state. These same exemptions are available to people who file for bankruptcy in that state and meet the residency requirements described below. In 19 states (and the District of Columbia), debtors who meet the residency requirements can choose between their state's exemptions or another set of exemptions created by Congress known as federal bankruptcy exemptions. States that currently allow debtors this choice are Alaska, Arkansas, Connecticut, Hawaii, Kentucky, Massachusetts, Michigan, Minnesota, New Hampshire, New Jersey, New Mexico, New York, Oregon, Pennsylvania, Rhode Island, Texas, Vermont, Washington, and Wisconsin.

California has adopted a unique system. Rather than using the federal exemptions, California offers two sets of state exemptions for those who meet the residency requirements described below. As in the 19 states that have the federal bankruptcy exemptions, people filing for bankruptcy in California must choose one or the other set of California's state exemptions.

Property that is not exempt can be taken from you and sold by the trustee to pay your unsecured creditors. You can avoid this result by finding some cash to pay the trustee what the property is worth or convincing the trustee to accept some exempt property of roughly equal value as a substitute.

If your nonexempt property isn't worth enough to make selling it worthwhile, the trustee might decide to let you keep it. For instance, few trustees bother to take well-used furniture or secondhand electronic gadgets or appliances. Even if your property is more valuable, the trustee might be willing to let you pay to keep it so the trustee can avoid the trouble and cost of putting it up for sale. For example, if you have a flat-screen television that's worth about $1,500, and only $725 of it is exempt, the trustee might let you keep it if you can pay $400 or so. Even though the trustee could take the television and sell it, that would take time and cost money. While this might seem like buying property you already own, the trustee is entitled to it once you file for Chapter 7 bankruptcy. So yes, in effect, you are paying to get your asset back.

As you've no doubt figured out, the key to getting the most out of the bankruptcy process is to use exemptions to keep as much of your property as possible while erasing as many debts as you can. To make full and proper use of your exemptions, you'll want to:

- learn which exemptions are available to you
- become familiar with the exemptions you can use, and
- use the available exemptions in a way that lets you keep more of your treasured property.

Ch. 3 gives step-by-step instructions for figuring out whether your personal property is exempt under the state laws available for use in your bankruptcy, and Ch. 4 covers exemptions for your home. Here, we provide a brief overview of exemptions.

When Buying Back Nonexempt Property Can Take a Bite Out of Your Tax Debt

While it is no fun to buy back your own property from the bankruptcy trustee, in one situation, it doesn't sting quite so much—when you owe taxes or support arrearages. Here's how it works. It is unlikely that your newish tax debt will be discharged in bankruptcy (see Ch. 9), and your support arrearages most certainly won't go away. You'll be responsible for paying them after your case closes. What's more, taxes and support arrearages are priority debts, which means that if there is money to be distributed, they stand at the head of the line. They get paid before most other debts. As a result, when you rebuy your own property, or when the trustee sells it, the trustee turns around and uses the funds to pay down your tax or support debt—a win-win situation.

Domicile Requirements for Using Exemptions

You can use a state's exemptions if that state has been your "domicile" for at least two years before you file for bankruptcy (called the 730-day rule). Domicile is "the place where a man has his true fixed and permanent home and principal establishment and to which whenever he is absent he has the intention of returning." Your domicile is more than your residence, which generally means wherever you live at any given time.

Your domicile is the place where you are living and intend to live for the indefinite future. Usually, you work, vote, receive your mail, pay taxes, do your banking, own property, participate in public affairs, register your car, apply for your driver's license, and send your children to school there. Your domicile might be different from the state where you are actually living. For example, military members, professional athletes, and corporate officers might spend significant amounts of time working in other states or countries. Still, their domiciles are the states where they make their permanent homes.

If you have not been domiciled in your current state for at least two years before filing, you'll need to do some calculations. You must use the exemptions of the state you lived in for the better part of the 180-day period ending two years before your filing date. So suppose you filed for bankruptcy on January 1, 2021, and you had not lived in your current state for two years. In that case, you would have to use the exemptions available in the state where you lived for most of the period between July 5, 2018, and December 31, 2018. These somewhat odd rules are explained in detail in Ch. 3. A separate law determines whether you can claim your state's homestead exemption—the exemption that protects equity in your home. That rule has a 40-month domicile requirement and is explained in Ch. 4.

The History Behind Convoluted Residency Requirements

Before 2005, if you wanted to keep more of your property, you could move to a state with better exemptions shortly before filing for bankruptcy. That all changed in October of 2005, however, when sweeping bankruptcy law changes went into effect. The new, two-year residency requirement prevents people from maximizing exemptions by strategically moving before filing.

Typically Exempt Property

Certain kinds of property are exempt in almost every state, including:

- equity in your home, up to a certain value (commonly called the homestead exemption)
- equity in a motor vehicle, up to a certain value (usually between $1,000 and $5,000)
- reasonably necessary clothing (no expensive fur coats)
- reasonably necessary household furnishings and goods (the second television might have to go if it has any value)
- household appliances
- jewelry, to a certain value
- personal effects
- life insurance (cash or loan value, or proceeds), to a certain value
- retirement funds necessary for current support
- tools of your trade or profession, to a certain value
- a portion of unpaid but earned wages, and
- public benefits (welfare, Social Security, unemployment compensation) accumulated in a bank account.

Some states also provide a "wildcard" exemption—an exemption for a set dollar amount that you can apply to any property of your choosing. (See Ch. 3 for more on wildcard exemptions.) Also, if you are using the federal exemptions or the California section 703 exemptions and you don't need to protect substantial equity in a home, you can use some or all of the homestead exemption as a wildcard.

How Property Is Valued for Exemption Purposes

Under the old rules, you could value your property at roughly what you could get for it at your own garage sale. The 2005 bankruptcy law uses a different standard: Debtors must value property by determining what it would cost from a retail vendor, taking the property's age and condition into account. For cars, this will be the retail amount listed on www.nada.com or similar price guides. For other property, you will have to use the amount for which similar property is sold on eBay or at used clothing or furniture stores, flea markets, and the like.

Although the bankruptcy code uses the fair market value in valuing property for exemption purposes, how the trustee ultimately decides how to handle the property depends more on the property's auction value (what the trustee would get for it at auction) minus the costs of storage and sale.

Here's an example of how this works. Assume your state provides a $3,000 exemption for car equity. Your car's value is $6,000. If the trustee sells the vehicle at auction, the trustee will incur additional costs associated with picking up, storing, and auctioning the car, probably to the tune of $1,200. So the trustee would net about $4,800 from the vehicle sale after deducting these expenses (sale price of $6,000 less $1,200 in costs). But the trustee would also have to write you a check for the amount of your car equity exemption, which is $3,000, leaving the trustee with about $1,800 to pay to creditors. If the trustee would have recouped less, the trustee would likely "abandon" the property (which means you could keep it).

If Chapter 7 Bankruptcy Won't Let You Keep Treasured Property

If it looks like Chapter 7 bankruptcy will come between you and the property you want to keep, consider filing for Chapter 13 bankruptcy (or an option discussed in "Alternatives to Chapter 7 Bankruptcy," below). Chapter 13 filers retain property regardless of its exempt status. To qualify, you'll show that you have sufficient income to pay monthly bills and any priority debts (such as back child support, alimony, and taxes) in full. But that's not all. In Chapter 13, your proposed plan must also pay your unsecured creditors an amount that equals or exceeds what they would receive in Chapter 7. What does this mean from a practical standpoint? At a minimum, you'll pay unsecured creditors an amount equaling the value of your nonexempt property—the property that would have been sold had you filed for Chapter 7.

Property That Is Typically Nonexempt

In most states, you will have to give up or pay the trustee if you have equity in the following types of property (in legal terms, equity in these items is "nonexempt"):

- expensive musical instruments (unless you're a professional musician)
- cameras, video and computer equipment
- stamp, coin, and other collections
- valuable family heirlooms
- cash, bank accounts, stocks, stock options, bonds, royalties, and other investments
- business assets and inventory
- real estate you're not living in
- boats, planes, and off-road vehicles, and
- a second or vacation home.

> CAUTION
>
> **For those with nonexempt property.** If it appears that you have a lot of nonexempt property, read Ch. 3 before deciding whether to file for bankruptcy. That chapter helps you determine how much of your property is not exempt and suggests ways to:
>
> - buy it from the trustee (if you really want to hold on to it)
> - use exempt property to barter with the trustee, or
> - retain the value of your nonexempt property by selling it and buying exempt property before filing (this can be considered fraudulent—talk to a bankruptcy lawyer first).

> **EXAMPLE 1:** Several years ago, Jack and Chloe inherited their most prized possession, an expensive jade vase worth $100,000. They don't want to give it up, but they owe more than $160,000 and are in desperate financial shape.
>
> If they file for Chapter 7, their debts will be discharged. Still, they will probably lose the vase, assuming it's not exempt in their state and no wildcard exemption will cover its value. In Chapter 13, however, they could keep the vase and pay their debts out of their income over the next three to five years.

However, their unsecured creditors must get at least as much as they would have in Chapter 7. So the monthly Chapter 13 payment would be at least $1,667 for five years ($1,667 x 60 months = approximately $100,000). After several anguished days, Jack and Chloe decide to file for Chapter 7 bankruptcy even though they would lose the vase.

Jack and Chloe might be tempted to hide the vase and hope the trustee doesn't discover it, but that would be a crime for which they could be fined or jailed. It's also an abuse of the bankruptcy process. Hiding property could get their petition dismissed and banned from filing again for six months. Another risky move would be to sell the vase before filing and use the proceeds to buy necessities (always document these purchases) or exempt property. Even though a debtor has the right to sell assets when funds are needed for necessary items, like food, clothing, and shelter, debtors can't pay monthly bills in advance. So it would be hard to justify using all of the vase's sales proceeds for such purposes. The trustee would likely object to this maneuver as an attempt to defraud creditors, so Jack and Chloe would want to consult with a lawyer before considering such action. (See Ch. 3 for information on when you can do this.)

EXAMPLE 2: Over the years, Mari has carefully constructed an expensive computer system that she uses primarily for hobbies and a work tool for her publishing business. The computer system does not qualify for a specific exemption in her state. However, some states might allow her to use the "tools of the trade" exemption. Over a substantial period, Mari has also amassed $100,000 in credit card debts, medical bills, and department store charges.

If Mari files for Chapter 7 bankruptcy, she can discharge all of her debts because they are unsecured and weren't incurred fraudulently. However, unless a wildcard exemption protects the computer system's value, Mari must surrender most of the computer equipment unless it's essential to her publishing business and exempt as a tool of her trade. Otherwise, she might try to convince the trustee to accept exempt property of equivalent value or let her pay for the value of the computer with post-bankruptcy wages or a loan from family or a friend. Mari decides that canceling her debts is far more important than keeping the computer and proceeds to file for Chapter 7 bankruptcy.

Alternatives to Chapter 7 Bankruptcy

In many situations, filing for Chapter 7 bankruptcy is the best remedy for debt problems. In others, however, another course of action makes more sense. This section outlines your main alternatives.

Do Nothing

Surprisingly, the best approach for some is to take no action at all. If you're living simply with little income and property and look forward to a similar life in the future, you might be a judgment-proof debtor. Anyone who sues you and obtains a court judgment won't be able to collect— simply because you don't have anything they can legally take. Except in highly unusual situations (for example, if you're a tax protester or willfully refusing to pay child support), you can't be thrown in jail for failing to pay your debts.

Usually, creditors cannot take your property or income without first suing you and obtaining a court judgment, except for taxing authorities and student loan collectors. Even if the creditor is armed with a court judgment, the law prevents most creditors from taking property protected by your state's exemption laws. Exempt property usually includes food, clothing, personal effects, and furnishings. (See "Will You Lose Valuable Property?" above.) And creditors won't go after your nonexempt property unless it is worth enough to cover the creditor's costs of seizure and sale.

Before taking property, creditors usually try to go after your wages and other income. But generally, a creditor can take only 25% of your net wages to satisfy a court judgment unless it is for taxes, child support, or alimony. Often, you can keep more than 75% of your wages if you can demonstrate that you need the extra amount to support yourself and your family. Income from a pension or another retirement benefit is usually treated like wages. Creditors cannot touch public benefits such as welfare, unemployment insurance, disability insurance, SSI, or Social Security.

To sum up, if you don't have a steady job or another source of income that a creditor can snatch, or you can live on 75% of your wages, and you don't expect your situation to change, you needn't fear a lawsuit. Similarly, if most of your property is exempt, there will be little the creditor can seize to repay the debt. In this situation, most creditors don't bother trying to collect the debt at all.

Now that you have the good news, here's some bad: Judgments usually last for five to ten years. Also, they're typically subject to renewal for similar periods, so you might have to live with your decision to do nothing for a long, long time. And, in many cases, interest on your debt will continue to accrue, which means the $10,000 you owe today could become a $100,000 debt in the future.

Even if you are judgment proof, you might be better off dealing with your debt situation now, either through bankruptcy or through one of the other alternatives discussed below. For example, if you don't file for bankruptcy and later receive a windfall—lottery winnings or an unexpected inheritance—you could lose the windfall to your creditors. On the other hand, windfalls you receive after you file for Chapter 7 bankruptcy are usually yours to keep.

Negotiating With Creditors After the Great Recession

Before the 2008 economic collapse, it was common to negotiate a settlement of 50% or less as soon as six months after you stopped paying a debt with no questions asked—sometimes for even less. However, things have changed. Most creditors now require proof that you're experiencing financial distress just to get the conversation started. This will involve filling out financial questionnaires and turning over documents such as paycheck stubs and bank statements. Of course, it is understandable why creditors do this. Your creditors (and debt collectors) want to get as much information from you as possible. Why? Because they want to get as much money from you as possible. Plus, the information will be helpful if they need to garnish your wages or levy against your bank account later.

Negotiate With Your Creditors

If you have some income or assets you're willing to sell, you might be better off negotiating with your creditors than filing for bankruptcy. Through negotiation, you could develop a new payment plan that would allow you to get back on your feet. Or, you might be able to pay less than you owe in a lump sum payment.

RESOURCE

Negotiating with creditors. How to deal with your creditors is covered in detail in *Solve Your Money Troubles* by Amy Loftsgordon and Cara O'Neill (Nolo).

Get Outside Help to Design a Repayment Plan

Many people have trouble negotiating with creditors. It could be because they don't have negotiating experience to do a good job or because they find the whole process exceedingly unpleasant. Because the ability to negotiate is an art, many people benefit from outside help.

TIP

The best time to negotiate. The end of the month is when you'll have the best chance of getting a reasonable settlement. The reason is simple—collection agency employees (and their managers) are trying hard to meet end-of-the-month collection goals. A good strategy involves calling a few days before the month's end and offering to make a lump sum payment within 24 hours. Cold hard cash will motivate the agent to settle for less; payment plans are not enticing.

If you don't want to negotiate with your creditors, you can turn to a lawyer or a credit counseling agency. These agencies come in two primary varieties: nonprofit and for profit. They all work on the same basic principle: A repayment plan is negotiated with all of your unsecured creditors. You make one monthly payment that the agency distributes to your creditors according to the plan. As long as you make the payments, the creditors will not take any action against you. And, if you succeed in completing the plan, one or more of your creditors might be willing to offer you new credit on reasonable terms.

The nonprofit agencies tend to be funded primarily by reasonable fees paid by the debtor and commissions paid by the major creditors for each repayment plan negotiated. The for-profit agencies are supported by the same sources but tend to charge much higher fees.

Here's the downside to entering into a repayment plan: If you don't make a payment, the creditor could back out of the deal. When that happens, you might find that you would have been better off filing for bankruptcy in the first place.

Tax Consequences of Forgiven Debts

Deciding to ignore your debts could increase your tax burden. The IRS treats certain forgiven debts as taxable income to you. Taxable debts include obligations a creditor has reduced or written off (stopped trying to collect and reported as a loss). (26 U.S.C. § 108.) Any bank, credit union, savings and loan, or other financial institution that forgives or writes off all or part of a debt for $600 or more must send you and the IRS a Form 1099-A or 1099-C at the end of the tax year. When you file your tax return, you must report the write-off as income and pay taxes on it.

There are exceptions to this rule. You don't have to report a debt if you were insolvent when the creditor agreed to waive or write it off. Generally, you are insolvent if your debts, including the debt that was forgiven or written off, exceed the value of your assets.

If you receive a Form 1099-C, you might need to complete IRS Form 982, *Reduction of Tax Attributes Due to Discharge of Indebtedness*, to show that an exception applies. (You can download the form and instructions at www.irs.gov.) Unfortunately, using this form can be complicated, especially if you're claiming the insolvency exception. You might need help from an accountant to complete it correctly.

Pay Over Time With Chapter 13 Bankruptcy

In Chapter 13 bankruptcy, you enter into a court-approved plan to deal with your debts over three to five years. Some debts must be paid in full (back taxes are the most common examples), while others can be paid only in part. The basic idea is that you must devote all of your disposable income to paying your unsecured creditors. So if you experience a significant earnings increase during the plan period, the Chapter 13 bankruptcy judge can increase your plan payments.

With a few exceptions, Chapter 13 doesn't require you to give up any property. However, to ensure that Chapter 13 filers don't receive an advantage over Chapter 7 filers, you'll have to pay for the privilege of keeping nonexempt property. The rule is that unsecured creditors must get at least what they would have received if the property had been sold in Chapter 7.

So while you don't have to give up your property, you have to repurchase the nonexempt portion over three to five years, plus pay 10% (roughly) in trustee fees. In addition to this "buy-back" requirement, the bankruptcy code has guidelines for calculating exactly how much you must pay into your plan, based on your income:

- If your income exceeds your state's median income, you'll pay all of your "disposable income" into your plan for five years. You'll use expense amounts set by the IRS when calculating your disposable income, and they could be significantly less than your actual expenses. If that's the case, you'll be obligated to pay more money into your plan than you actually have leftover each month after paying your bills and living expenses.
- If your current monthly income is less than the state median, you can propose a three-year repayment plan. You can also calculate your disposable income using your actual expenses rather than the IRS standards.

To file for Chapter 13 bankruptcy, you fill out almost the same set of forms used in Chapter 7 bankruptcy and file them with the bankruptcy court along with a filing fee. In addition, you must file your tax returns for the last four years. (You can be delinquent on taxes, but you must have completed the returns.) You'll also need to file and serve a feasible repayment plan on each of your creditors. With the possible exception of current payments on your mortgage and car note, you make plan payments directly to the bankruptcy trustee, who in turn distributes the money to your creditors. When you complete your plan, any remaining unpaid balances on unsecured, dischargeable debts are wiped out.

Chapter 13 requires you to pay down your debts over time. Few filers pay back 100% of what they owe, but it happens—especially if the filer has extensive nonexempt property. Priority debts, like child support and recent back taxes, must be paid in full. (See Ch. 6 for more on which debts qualify as priority debts.) Short-term secured debts (debts that will mature while your plan is in effect) must also be paid in full. However, the obligations that bedevil most people are credit card debts and medical bills, neither of which are priority or secured. These only have to be paid down if you have enough "disposable income" to manage the task after you've met all the other repayment requirements.

For instance, suppose your Chapter 13 paperwork shows that $200 will remain each month after paying your reasonable living expenses. If the funds are needed to pay off an income tax debt or other priority debt, you can propose what's known as a "zero-percent plan." In this type of plan, your unsecured, nonpriority creditors get nothing.

Any money remaining after paying expenses and priority debts will be used to pay your unsecured, nonpriority creditors. (But remember, if you have nonexempt property, your plan must pay your unsecured, nonpriority creditors at least the value of the property, as explained above.) If any unpaid unsecured debt remains when your plan ends (with a few exceptions, like school loans), it will be discharged.

Ultimately, you'll pay an amount equal to your disposable income, your nonexempt property, or any priority debts that must be paid in full, whichever is more.

Another benefit of Chapter 13 is that certain debts are discharged only in Chapter 13. These debts will survive Chapter 7 but be wiped out at the end of your repayment plan if you file under Chapter 13:

- marital property debts (other than for support) created in a divorce or settlement agreement
- debts incurred to pay a nondischargeable tax debt (perhaps you paid your taxes with a credit card)
- court fees
- condominium, cooperative, and homeowners' association fees
- debts for loans from a retirement plan, and
- debts that couldn't be discharged in a previous bankruptcy.

Avoiding Credit Counseling and Debt Repayment Plan Scams

Be careful if you plan to use credit counseling services or enter into a debt repayment plan. According to the Federal Trade Commission, scams involving debt repayment plans are rampant. According to numerous consumer complaints, some of these companies:

- fail to pay creditors on time or at all
- make promises they don't keep, like getting lower interest rates and reduced fees from creditors
- charge unreasonably high fees to consumers
- hide charges or take them out of deposits that are earmarked for creditors, and
- lie about the company's nonprofit status.

Before considering a debt repayment plan, make sure you are dealing with a legitimate nonprofit credit counseling agency. Also, explore all of your other options, get everything in writing, and follow up with your creditors to make sure they are getting paid on time.

Better yet, use an agency that has been approved by the U.S. Trustee for bankruptcy credit counseling. These agencies must be nonprofits and meet specific requirements. They're also overseen by the U.S. Trustee, which gives you some protection against fraudulent practices. You can find a list of approved agencies at the U.S. Trustee's website, at www.usdoj.gov/ust.

You can file for Chapter 13 bankruptcy at any time, even if you received a Chapter 7 bankruptcy discharge the day before. However, you won't be eligible for a discharge if you filed your Chapter 13 case within four years after filing for Chapter 7. Even so, if you can't get a discharge, you can still benefit from being a Chapter 13 debtor. For instance, if you owe taxes or back child support after completing Chapter 7, you can propose a Chapter 13 plan. You'll be able to pay off the arrearages over three to five years while keeping creditors off your back in the meantime.

If you cannot finish a Chapter 13 repayment plan—for example, you lose your job six months into the plan and can't make the payments—you can ask the court to modify your plan. If it's clear you won't be able to complete the plan because of circumstances beyond your control, the court might let you discharge your debts based on hardship. Examples of hardship would be a sudden plant closing in a one-factory town or a debilitating illness.

If the bankruptcy court won't modify your plan or give you a hardship discharge, you still have two options:

- You can convert your case to a Chapter 7 bankruptcy (unless you received a Chapter 7 discharge within the previous eight years).
- You can ask the bankruptcy court to dismiss your Chapter 13 petition and leave you in the same position you were in before filing, except you'll owe less because of the payments made on debts through the repayment plan. However, if your Chapter 13 bankruptcy is dismissed, your creditors could add any interest that was abated during your Chapter 13 case to the total amount you owe.

RESOURCE

Resources for Chapter 13 bankruptcy. For general information on Chapter 13 bankruptcy, get a copy of *The New Bankruptcy* by Cara O'Neill (Nolo). (If you are interested in filing for Chapter 13 bankruptcy, see *Chapter 13 Bankruptcy* by Cara O'Neill (Nolo), which provides comprehensive information about Chapter 13 bankruptcy.)

Do You Qualify for Chapter 13 Bankruptcy?

There are several requirements you must meet in order to qualify for Chapter 13 bankruptcy:

- **You must file as an individual.** Only individuals, not business entities (such as partnerships or corporations), can file for Chapter 13. If you are the sole proprietor of a business, you might be able to keep the business open while including the debt in your repayment plan.
- **Your debt must not be too high.** Your total secured debt (debt for which you have pledged collateral or that otherwise gives the creditor the right to seize property if you don't pay) cannot exceed $1,257,850, and your total unsecured debt may not exceed $419,275 (these amounts will change April 1, 2022).
- **You must be able to propose a legally feasible repayment plan.** If you have sufficient income to pay all of your priority debts (for instance, child support and tax debts), make required monthly payments—and pay back any arrearages—on your secured debts (such as a mortgage or car note), and pay at least some money toward your unsecured debts over the next five years, you can probably propose a Chapter 13 plan that will pass legal muster.

One way to figure out whether you can propose a feasible plan is to take the means test—an eligibility requirement for Chapter 7 that asks higher-income filers to show that they cannot propose a viable Chapter 13 repayment plan. If the means test shows that you will have at least some money left over each month to pay toward your unsecured, nonpriority debts, you should be able to come up with a feasible Chapter 13 plan. The means test is covered in detail in Ch. 6.

Family Farmers Should Consider Chapter 12 Bankruptcy

Chapter 12 bankruptcy, which is similar to Chapter 13 bankruptcy in many respects, is specially designed for family farmers and provides a way to keep the farm while paying off debts over time.

Chapter 13 Might Reduce Interest-Heavy Secured Debts

In some cases, Chapter 13 bankruptcy allows you to break certain secured debts into two parts: the part that is secured by the fair market value of the collateral and any part of the debt that is unsecured because it exceeds the value of the collateral. You must pay the replacement value of the collateral (the secured amount) in your Chapter 13 plan, but you can discharge the unsecured portion along with your other unsecured debts. This procedure is commonly referred to as a cramdown, and it's available on some but not all types of property.

For example, because a car note includes a lot of interest and most cars depreciate in value fairly rapidly, it's common for a vehicle loan balance to be more than the car is worth. In some cases, Chapter 13 allows you to cram down the debt to the car's replacement value (what it would cost to purchase the vehicle from a retail vendor, considering its age and condition) and get rid of the rest of the debt over the life of your plan. You might also be able to cram down debts for other types of property, including real estate that you don't use as your primary residence. However, there are a couple of exceptions to the cramdown rule:

- A car contract cramdown is available only if you bought the car more than 910 days before filing for bankruptcy.
- A cramdown on other types of property is available only if you bought the property more than a year before filing for bankruptcy.
- You can cram down a mortgage on a mobile home if your state law classifies mobile homes as personal property, even though the mobile home is situated on real property. (In re Ennis, 558 F.3d 343 (4th Cir. 2009).)
- You can cram down mortgages owed on second homes, vacation homes, and rental properties.

The tricky part of a cramdown—especially when it comes to rentals and other real property—is that the entire balance must be paid through the Chapter 13 plan.

Only people and entities that meet the following definition of a family farmer qualify for Chapter 12:

- your debts cannot exceed $10,000,000 for farming operations (this amount was more than doubled by the Family Farmer Relief Act of 2019) or $2,044,225 for commercial fishing operations
- 50% or more of your debt (80% for a family fisherman) must have arisen from the farming operation, not including a purchase money mortgage
- 50% or more of your income must have been earned from the farming or fishing operation in the year preceding the filing of the petition, and
- your income must be "sufficiently stable and regular" to enable payments under a Chapter 12 plan.

Like Chapter 13, you must file a schedule of assets and liabilities and a statement of financial affairs. Even though a trustee is appointed to supervise the plan, the farm debtor remains in possession of the farm assets, and actions by creditors are automatically stayed upon filing the petition.

Like Chapter 13, you must file a plan that meets Chapter 12 requirements. A filer who can't pay all unsecured debts in full must use all disposable income to pay down unsecured debt over three years. The period can be extended to five years with court permission. Also, plan payments must pay unsecured creditors at least what they would have received in a Chapter 7 bankruptcy. After completing the plan, all debts are discharged except those that wouldn't be dischargeable in Chapter 7.

Chapter 12 has several advantages over Chapter 13 bankruptcy. The court has unrestricted authority to modify (cram down) secured debts, such as mortgages and car notes, so the debt matches the property's market value. This is different from Chapter 13, where cramdowns cannot be used for mortgages on your primary residence and recent car loans. Another advantage of Chapter 12: Secured debts can be modified to extend beyond the plan. And unlike Chapter 13, priority debts do not have to be paid in full so long as all disposable income over five years is devoted to the plan.

If you are a farmer, consider speaking with a bankruptcy attorney about Chapter 12 before choosing to file a Chapter 7 bankruptcy. (For information on finding a bankruptcy lawyer, see Ch. 10.)

Small and Large Business Entities Might Benefit From Chapter 11 Bankruptcy

The Chapter 11 procedure allows everyone with an economic interest in a struggling business to help create a plan that will enable the company to get on top of its debt and continue operating. (Chapter 11 is also available to individuals whose debt exceeds Chapter 13 limitations.)

A typical Chapter 11 bankruptcy requires lots of meetings and court hearings on various disputed issues. Because everyone must appear through lawyers who are paid out of the bankrupt business's coffers, it's not cheap. And it's not at all unusual for a company to pay more than $50,000 in attorneys' fees, often much more. As a result, until recently, Chapter 11 was only available to large corporations. But as a result of the Small Business Reorganization Act of 2019 (SBRA), that's no longer the case.

SBRA created a new form of bankruptcy—Chapter 11 subchapter V— specifically designed for small companies in need of bankruptcy relief. Any business with debts totaling $2,725,625 or less will qualify. More closely resembling Chapter 13, the process is more cost-effective than a standard Chapter 11 case—two factors that appear well received by business bankruptcy filers. The U.S. Trustee Program reported that approximately 1,100 cases were filed as or amended to subchapter V between its February 19, 2020 inception date and September 30, 2020. (Learn more at www.nolo.com/legal-encyclopedia/chapter-11-bankruptcy-small-business-owners.html.)

The Automatic Stay

One of the most powerful features of bankruptcy is the automatic stay: a court order that goes into effect as soon as you file and protects you from specific actions by your creditors. The automatic stay stops most debt collectors dead in their tracks and keeps them at bay for the rest of your case. Once you file, all collection activity (with a few exceptions, explained below) must go through the bankruptcy court. Most creditors cannot take any further action against you directly while the bankruptcy is pending.

The purpose of the automatic stay is, in the words of Congress, to give debtors a "breathing spell" from their creditors and a break from the financial pressures that drove them to file for bankruptcy. In a Chapter 7 bankruptcy, it serves another purpose as well: to preserve the status quo at the time you file. The automatic stay ensures that the trustee and the court—not your creditors—will be responsible for ultimately deciding which property you will be able to keep, which property you will have to give up, and how the proceeds will be divided if the trustee takes and sells any of your belongings.

This chapter explains how the automatic stay applies to typical debt collection efforts, including a couple of situations in which you might not get the protection of the automatic stay. It also covers how the automatic stay works in eviction proceedings, vital information for any renter who files for bankruptcy.

TIP

You don't need bankruptcy to stop your creditors from harassing you. Many people begin thinking about bankruptcy when their creditors start phoning them at home and on the job. Federal law (and the law of many states) prohibits this activity by debt collectors once you tell the creditor, in writing, that you don't want to be called. And if you orally tell debt collectors that you refuse to pay, they cannot, by law, contact you except to send one last letter making a final demand for payment before filing a lawsuit. While just telling the creditor to stop usually works, you might have to send a written follow-up letter. (You can find a sample letter in Ch. 1.)

Actions Prohibited by the Stay

When you file for any kind of bankruptcy for the first time, the automatic stay goes into effect. It's "automatic" because you don't have to ask the court to issue the stay, and the court doesn't have to take any particular action to make it effective. Once you file, the stay is put in place automatically. The stay prohibits creditors and collection agencies from taking any action to collect your debts unless the law or the bankruptcy court says they can.

In some circumstances, the creditor can file an action in court to have the stay lifted called a Motion to Lift Stay or a Motion for Relief From Stay. In others, the creditor can simply begin collection proceedings without seeking advance permission from the court.

The good news is that the most common type of creditor collection actions are still stopped dead by the stay. These include harassing calls by debt collectors, threatening letters by attorneys, lawsuits to collect payment for credit card and health care bills, and actions to recover property, such as car repossessions, home foreclosures, and wage garnishments. This section explains which collection actions are stopped by the automatic stay.

Credit Card Debts, Medical Debts, and Attorneys' Fees

Anyone trying to collect credit card debts, medical debts, attorneys' fees, debts arising from breach of contract, or legal judgments against you (other than for child support and alimony) must cease all collection activities after you file your bankruptcy case. A creditor or collector cannot:

- file a lawsuit or proceed with a pending lawsuit against you
- record liens against your property
- report the debt to a credit reporting bureau, or
- seize your property or income, such as money in a bank account or your paycheck.

Warning: Stop Your Bank From Draining Your Account

You know it's a bad day when you try to use your debit card only to find out that your credit card company wiped out your bank account. If your rent money is gone, you're probably facing a genuinely catastrophic situation. To put it plainly, it is risky to bank at an institution that also issued you a credit card or loan. If you do, and you fall behind on your payment, the bank can dip into your checking and savings account funds using a nasty collection trick called a "setoff," something you likely gave your bank permission to do when you signed your credit agreement.

Fortunately, you'll only have to worry about this before you file bankruptcy because once filed, the automatic stay prevents your creditors from surprising you with these devastating collection maneuvers. Keep in mind, though, that your bank could still "freeze" funds to cover your debts. (See "Bank Setoffs v. Account Freezing," below.)

In the meantime, there is an easy work-around for this pitfall. To prevent your bank from emptying your account, make sure the bank you get a credit card or loan from is different from the bank where you have a checking or savings account. If they're the same, switch your checking and savings accounts to another bank.

Public Benefits

Government entities seeking to collect overpayments of public benefits, such as SSI, Medicaid, or Temporary Assistance to Needy Families (welfare) benefits, cannot try to get that money back while you're in bankruptcy. If, however, you become ineligible for benefits, including Medicare benefits, bankruptcy doesn't prevent the agency from denying or terminating services on that ground.

Bank Setoffs v. Account Freezing

Setoffs and the freezing of accounts are different banking problems. Setoff can occur *before* you file bankruptcy, but not afterward. Once filed, the automatic stay stops a creditor from taking collection actions against you. (See "Warning: Stop Your Bank From Draining Your Account," above.)

The freezing of your bank account is something that can happen after you file bankruptcy. Some banks—but not all—will freeze your account after receiving notice of your filing as a way of protecting money for creditors. A bank can do this because it isn't taking the money in violation of the automatic stay—only preventing you from removing the money before the trustee decides what should be done with it. If you claimed the money as exempt on Schedule C (you declared you had the right to keep it), the situation should be pretty easy to fix. Call the trustee and explain that you need the money for living expenses. In most cases, the trustee will instruct the bank to release your money. Of course, this can take some time (usually a week or two), so you should do your best to prepare yourself accordingly. An easy way to avoid this problem is to be sure you don't have funds in your bank account when you file.

Debt Associated With Criminal Proceedings

Sometimes people are involved in other court cases when they file for bankruptcy. If the case can be broken down into criminal and debt components, only the criminal portion will be allowed to continue. The debt component will be put on hold while your bankruptcy is pending. For example, if you were convicted of writing a bad check and have been sentenced to community service and ordered to pay a fine, your obligation to do community service will not be stopped by the automatic stay, but your responsibility to pay the fine will. Whether you have to pay the fine after your bankruptcy case ends will depend on whether the penalty was a punishment or reimbursement fine. In Chapter 7, you'll remain responsible for the former but not the latter.

IRS Liens and Levies

Certain tax proceedings are not affected by the automatic stay (see "When the Stay Doesn't Apply," below, for more information). However, the automatic stay will stop the IRS from issuing a lien or seizing (levying against) your property or income.

Foreclosures

Foreclosures are initially stayed by your bankruptcy filing. However, if you filed another bankruptcy case previously and the court lifted the stay related to a specific piece of real property through an "in rem" order, the stay won't apply to the property for two years after the order was entered. In other words, the law doesn't allow you to prevent a foreclosure by filing serial bankruptcies.

Even if this is your first bankruptcy, filing won't stop some periods associated with a state's foreclosure procedures from "running." For example, state law might give a homeowner the right to two or three months' notice before the home is sold. Once a homeowner receives advance notice of foreclosure, the home cannot be sold until the notice period has ended. In these states, filing for bankruptcy won't stop the notice period from elapsing. However, the sale itself can't happen during the bankruptcy unless the foreclosing party gets permission from the bankruptcy judge by filing a motion to lift the stay.

If the lender moves to lift the stay and can show that even with the bankruptcy, the foreclosure will ultimately occur, the court is likely to lift the stay. You might be able to oppose the motion to lift the stay by challenging the lender's right to file the motion. But, even if you are successful in defeating the motion, in Chapter 7 bankruptcy, your victory will only last as long as your bankruptcy—typically only a month or two after the motion is heard.

However, in Chapter 13 cases, you'll stand a better chance of preventing the foreclosure altogether. (See Ch. 7 to learn more about opposing a motion to lift the automatic stay.)

Utilities

Companies providing you with utilities (such as gas, heating oil, electricity, telephone service, and water) can't cut you off because you file for bankruptcy. However, they can shut off your service 20 days after you file if you don't provide them with a deposit or another means to assure future payment. They can also terminate service if you fail to pay for it after you file. (See *In re Jones*, 369 B.R. 745 (B.A.P. 1st Cir. 2007).)

One court has found that cable television isn't a utility, and service can therefore be stopped if the debtor fails to pay the bill before filing for bankruptcy. (*In re Darby*, 470 F.3d 573 (5th Cir. 2006).)

When the Stay Doesn't Apply

The stay doesn't stop every type of collection action or apply in every situation. Congress has determined that certain debts or proceedings are sufficiently important to "trump" the automatic stay. In these situations (described in "Actions Not Stopped by the Stay," below), collection actions can continue as if you had never filed for bankruptcy.

In addition to the specific types of collection actions that can continue despite the stay, there are circumstances in which you can lose the protection of the stay through your own actions. These are described below as well.

Actions Not Stopped by the Stay

The automatic stay does not prohibit the following types of actions from proceeding.

Divorce and Child Support

Almost all proceedings related to divorce or parenting continue unaffected by the automatic stay. These include actions to:

- set and collect current child support and alimony
- collect back child and spousal support from property that is not in the bankruptcy estate (see Ch. 3 for more information on what's in the bankruptcy estate)

- determine child custody and visitation
- establish paternity in a lawsuit
- modify child support and alimony
- protect a spouse or child from domestic violence
- withhold income to collect child support
- report overdue support to credit bureaus
- intercept tax refunds to pay back child support, and
- withhold, suspend, or restrict drivers' and professional licenses as leverage to collect child support.

Tax Proceedings

The IRS can continue certain actions, such as conducting a tax audit, issuing a tax deficiency notice, demanding a tax return, issuing a tax assessment, or demanding payment of an assessment.

Pension Loans

The stay doesn't prevent withholding from a debtor's income to repay a loan from an ERISA-qualified pension (this includes most job-related pensions and individual retirement plans). (See Ch. 3 for more on how pensions are treated in bankruptcy.)

How You Can Lose the Protection of the Stay

Even in circumstances where the stay would otherwise apply, you can lose its protection through your own actions. The stay might not protect you from collection efforts if:

- you had a bankruptcy case pending within the year before filing your current matter, and the court refuses your request to allow the stay to kick in, or
- you don't meet the deadlines set by the bankruptcy code for dealing with property serving as collateral for secured debt.

Prior Cases Pending

The automatic stay will last only 30 days if you had a prior bankruptcy case pending within the year before you file (unless you can get the court to extend it). (11 U.S.C. §§ 362(c)(3) and (4).) And if you had two cases pending in the last year, the automatic stay will not kick in at all (unless the court orders it).

If the automatic stay terminates because of one or two prior pending cases, the property of the bankruptcy estate—in your current bankruptcy filing—is still protected. As explained in more detail in Ch. 3, your bankruptcy estate includes most types of property that you own or are entitled to receive when you file your bankruptcy papers but does not include money earned or most property received after filing. For example, a creditor would not be entitled to seize money that was in your bank account on the date you filed but could levy on wages you earned after filing, which are not part of the bankruptcy estate.

One Dismissal in the Past Year

With a couple of exceptions, if you had a bankruptcy case pending and dismissed during the previous year for any reason, voluntarily or involuntarily, the court will presume that your new filing is in bad faith, and the stay will terminate after 30 days in your new case. You, the trustee, the U.S. Trustee, or the creditor can ask the court to continue the stay beyond the 30-day period, but the court will do this only if you can show that your current case was not filed in bad faith.

The motion to continue the stay must be scheduled for hearing within the 30-day period after you file for bankruptcy and must give creditors adequate notice of why the stay should be extended. This means the motion must:

- be filed within several days after you file for bankruptcy unless you obtain an "Order Shortening Time" from the judge, a procedure in which you ask the judge to shorten the time between service of the motion on your creditors and the hearing on the motion
- be served on all creditors to whom you want the stay to apply, and
- provide specific reasons why your current filing is not in bad faith and the stay should be extended.

When Is a Case Pending?

If you've had a bankruptcy case dismissed within the last couple of years, you might be wondering when that case is no longer "pending" and, therefore, when the one- and two-year time periods for losing the automatic stay start to run. This can be tough to figure out, partly because some cases remain open long after they are dismissed. The general rule is that a dismissed case is no longer pending, even if it continues to be open after that date. In other words, the one- and two-year periods start on the date a case is dismissed.

EXAMPLE: Clayton's Chapter 7 bankruptcy case is dismissed by the court on January 20, 2018, because Clayton missed a deadline for filing required documents. Before the case is closed, Clayton files a motion to set aside the dismissal so he can proceed with his case. The court denies his motion and closes the matter on March 20, 2018. Clayton files for bankruptcy again on January 21, 2020. Because at least one year has passed since Clayton's previous case was dismissed, he is entitled to the protection of the automatic stay.

When deciding whether to extend the stay beyond 30 days, the court will look at the following factors to determine whether your current filing is in good faith:

- More than one prior bankruptcy case was filed by (or against) you in the past year.
- Your prior case was dismissed because you failed to file required documents on time (for instance, you didn't file your credit counseling certificate within 14 days or were unable to amend the petition on a timely basis when required to do so). If you failed to file these documents inadvertently or because of a careless error, that won't help you with the judge—unless you used an attorney in the prior case. Judges are more willing to give debtors the benefit of the doubt if their attorney was responsible for the mistake.
- The last case was dismissed while a creditor's request for relief from the stay was pending.
- Your circumstances haven't changed since your previous case was dismissed.

Two Dismissals in the Past Year

If you had two or more cases pending and dismissed during the previous year, no stay will apply in your current case. You won't even get the initial 30-day stay that would apply if you had only one bankruptcy case pending within the past year. The only way to get the benefit of the stay is to convince the court, within 30 days of your filing, that your current case was not filed in bad faith and that a stay should therefore be granted. The court will look at the factors outlined above to decide whether you have overcome the presumption of bad faith.

Missing Deadlines for Handling Secured Debts

If you have property that secures a debt—that is, property that the creditor has a right to take if you don't pay what you owe—you will have to file a Statement of Intention with the court and serve it on your creditors. The Statement of Intention explains what you want to do with the collateral. You have several choices:

- give the property back to the creditor and get rid of the debt, called "surrendering" the property
- keep the property and pay the creditor what it would cost to replace it, given its age and condition, which is often less than what you still owe on the debt, called "redeeming" the property (redeeming isn't available for all property), or
- keep the property and reaffirm the contract, which means that you will continue to owe some or all of the debt after your bankruptcy (called "reaffirming" the debt).

The bankruptcy rules require you to mail the Statement of Intention to the secured creditor within 30 days after filing your bankruptcy case and to actually carry out your stated intention—by giving back the property, paying its replacement value to the creditor, or signing a reaffirmation agreement—within 30–45 days after your first creditors' meeting. Because the law is contradictory on this time limit, you should take action within 30 days to be on the safe side or simply include it in your initial bankruptcy filing. If you don't meet these deadlines, the stay will no longer apply to that property (although it will continue to protect you otherwise). For example, assume you want to continue paying on your car note, but you don't serve your Statement of Intention on time. The stay will no longer protect your car or prevent the creditor from repossessing it, but your other property will still be protected. The Statement of Intention is discussed in more detail in Ch. 6; you can find lots more information on secured debts, including tips that will help you decide which of these options makes the most sense in your case, in Ch. 5.

Evictions

Temporary eviction moratoriums have offered tenants substantial protection during the COVID-19 pandemic. You can check the status of these protections at www.nolo.com/evictions-ban.

In the past, many people filed for Chapter 7 bankruptcy to stop the sheriff from enforcing a judgment for possession (an eviction order). While landlords could come into court and ask the judge to lift the automatic stay and let the eviction proceed, many landlords didn't know they had this right—and many others didn't have the wherewithal to hire attorneys (or the confidence to handle their own cases). In other words, filing for Chapter 7 bankruptcy often stopped court-ordered evictions from proceeding for the duration of the bankruptcy.

Today, things are a bit different. The 2005 bankruptcy law gives landlords the right to evict a tenant, despite the automatic stay, in either of the following cases:

- The landlord got a judgment for possession before the tenant filed for bankruptcy. If the judgment was for failing to pay rent, there is a possible exception to this rule, discussed below.
- The landlord is evicting the tenant for endangering the property or the illegal use of controlled substances on the property. This isn't automatic, however. The landlord must still follow required bankruptcy procedures.

If the landlord does not already have a judgment when you file, and he or she wants to evict you for reasons other than endangering the property or using controlled substances (for example, the eviction is based on your failure to pay rent or violation of another lease provision), the automatic stay will prevent the landlord from starting or continuing with eviction proceedings. However, the landlord can always ask the judge to lift the stay, and courts tend to grant these requests.

If the Landlord Already Has a Judgment

If your landlord has already obtained a judgment of possession against you when you file for bankruptcy, the automatic stay won't help you with the possible exception described below. The landlord might proceed with the eviction just as if you never filed for bankruptcy.

If the eviction order is based on your failure to pay rent, you might be able to have the automatic stay reinstated. However, this exception applies only if your state's law allows you to stay in your rental unit and "cure" (pay back) the rent delinquency after the landlord has a judgment for possession. Here's what you'll have to do to take advantage of this exception:

Step 1: As part of your bankruptcy petition, you must file a certification (a statement under oath) stating that your state's laws allow you to cure the rent delinquency after the judgment is obtained, and to continue living in your rental unit. Very few states allow this. To find out whether yours is one of them, ask the sheriff or someone at the courthouse if you have legal aid in your area. In addition, when you file your bankruptcy petition, you must deposit with the court clerk the amount of rent that will become due during the 30-day period after you file.

Once you have filed your petition containing the certification and deposited the rent, you are protected from eviction for 30 days unless the landlord successfully objects to your initial certification before the 30-day period ends. If the landlord objects to your certification, the court must hold a hearing on the objection within ten days, so theoretically you could have less than 30 days of protection if the landlord files and serves the objection immediately.

Step 2: To keep the stay in effect longer, you must, before the 30-day period runs out, file and serve a second certification showing that you have fully cured the default in the manner provided by your state's law. However, if the landlord successfully objects to this second certification, the stay will no longer be in effect and the landlord can proceed with the eviction. As in Step 1, the court must hold a hearing within ten days if the landlord objects. The official bankruptcy forms include instructions on this process, as well as the certifications you'll need to file with the court.

> **SEE AN EXPERT**
>
> **If you really want to keep your rental, talk to a lawyer.** As you can see, these rules are somewhat complicated. If you don't interpret your state's law properly, file the necessary paperwork on time, and successfully argue your side if the landlord objects, you could find yourself put out of your home. A good lawyer can tell you whether it's worth fighting an eviction—and, if so, how to go about it.

Endangering the Property or Illegal Use of Controlled Substances

Under the bankruptcy law, an eviction action will not be stayed by your bankruptcy filing if your landlord wants you out because you endangered the property or engaged in the "illegal use of controlled substances" on the property. And your landlord doesn't have to have a judgment in hand when you file for bankruptcy. The landlord can start an eviction action against you or continue with a pending eviction action even after your filing date if the eviction is based on property endangerment or drug use.

To evict you on these grounds after you have filed for bankruptcy, your landlord must file and serve on you a certification showing either of the following:

- The landlord has filed an eviction action against you based on property endangerment or illegal drug use on the property.
- You have endangered the property or engaged in illegal drug use on the property during the 30-day period prior to the landlord's certification.

If your landlord files this certification, he or she can proceed with the eviction 15 days later unless, within that time, you file and serve on the landlord an objection to the truth of the statements in the landlord's certification. If you do that, the court must hold a hearing on your objection within ten days. If you prove that the statements in the certification aren't true or have been remedied, you will be protected from eviction while your bankruptcy is pending. If the court denies your objection, the eviction can proceed immediately.

When the Automatic Stay Protects Against Evictions

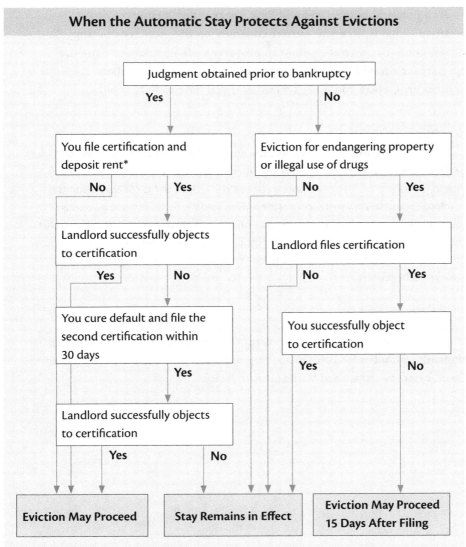

Judgment obtained prior to bankruptcy

Yes — No

You file certification and deposit rent*

No — Yes

Eviction for endangering property or illegal use of drugs

No — Yes

Landlord successfully objects to certification

Yes — No

Landlord files certification

No — Yes

You cure default and file the second certification within 30 days

Yes

You successfully object to certification

Yes — No

Landlord successfully objects to certification

Yes — No

Eviction May Proceed

Stay Remains in Effect

Eviction May Proceed 15 Days After Filing

* This path only applies in the few states that allow a tenant to cure the rent delinquency after the landlord obtains a judgment for possession.

As a practical matter, you will have a very difficult time proving a negative—that is, that you weren't endangering the property or using drugs. Similarly, once allegations of property endangerment or drug use are made, it's hard to see how they would be "remedied." In short, this is another area where you'll need a lawyer if you have to fight it out.

CAUTION
Landlords can always ask the court to lift the automatic stay to begin or continue an eviction on any grounds. Although the automatic stay will kick in unless one of these exceptions applies, the judge can lift the stay upon the landlord's request. And many courts are willing to do it because most evictions will have no effect on the bankruptcy estate—that is, your tenancy isn't something that the trustee can turn into money to pay your creditors. As a general rule, bankruptcy courts are inclined to let landlords exercise their property rights regardless of the tenants' debt problems.

RESOURCE
Need help with your landlord? For more information on dealing with landlords—including landlords that are trying to evict you—see *Every Tenant's Legal Guide*, by Janet Portman and Marcia Stewart (Nolo).

Your Property and Bankruptcy

This chapter explains what happens to your personal property when you file for Chapter 7 bankruptcy. First, we explain what property is subject to the reach of the bankruptcy court. Next, we cover exemptions: state and federal laws that determine what property you can keep when you file for bankruptcy. Happily, most people find that they can keep virtually all or most of their personal property through the bankruptcy process.

If some of your property is not exempt, you might be able to "buy it back" by paying the trustee a discounted price, or sell it and use the proceeds for necessities. Selling nonexempt property and purchasing exempt property is risky, but it can be done in some cases. Below, we offer suggestions—and important cautions—if you want to try this.

> **RELATED TOPIC**
> **More information on homes and collateral.** This chapter covers personal property only, not real estate. If you own your home, Ch. 4 explains how to figure out whether you'll be able to keep it. And, if you own personal property that serves as collateral for a debt, that property is handled a bit differently. The special rules for these debts (called "secured" debts) are explained in Ch. 5.

Property in Your Bankruptcy Estate

When you file for Chapter 7 bankruptcy, almost everything you own when you file becomes subject to the bankruptcy court's authority. The exceptions listed in "Property That Isn't in Your Bankruptcy Estate," below, include pensions, tuition and individual education accounts, and, if you are filing alone, property you own with a spouse as tenants by the entirety.

All property subject to the court's jurisdiction is collectively called your "bankruptcy estate." In addition to the property you own when you file, your estate also includes property you used to own but improperly transferred to someone else. Property you acquire after filing isn't part of your estate, although exceptions apply to a few assets acquired within six months after filing.

The trustee is very interested in your bankruptcy estate because he or she is entitled to a commission on any property that can be taken from your estate and sold to come up with some money for your unsecured creditors. Only property from which the trustee can realize a profit will be sold; you won't lose property worth very little or protected by an exemption.

Using the Information in This Chapter

This chapter will help you:

- **Decide whether bankruptcy is in your best interest.** Knowing what you own and how much you can get for it will help you decide whether to file for Chapter 7 bankruptcy. It might be easier simply to sell off some property and pay creditors directly rather than to go through bankruptcy—especially if you would have to give up the property if you filed for bankruptcy.

- **Determine what property you can keep.** You'll be able to keep some property no matter how much it is worth. However, your right to keep many types of property in bankruptcy often depends on the value of your equity. For instance, many states allow you to keep a car, but only if your equity is less than a certain amount. Vehicle exemptions can range from $1,000 on up depending on the state you live in. If you own considerably more equity than what you can protect with an exemption, you will have to turn the car over to the trustee to be sold or "buy it back" by paying the trustee the equivalent value in cash or other exempt property. If the trustee sells the car, you'll get your exemption amount and your creditors will get the rest.

- **Summarize information about your property before you file.** If you decide to file for bankruptcy, you'll need to fill out forms listing the property you own, how much it's worth, and what you claim as exempt. The work you do in this chapter can be transferred to those forms.

If You Convert From Chapter 13

If you originally filed for Chapter 13 and convert your case to Chapter 7, your Chapter 7 bankruptcy estate consists of everything you owned when you filed Chapter 13 as long as you still own it when you convert to Chapter 7. In one case, a trustee required debtors who converted from Chapter 13 to Chapter 7 to hand over their clothes, $3,660 worth of personal property, and their family dog, all of which were classified as "nonexempt" in their Chapter 13 paperwork. (*In re John*, 352 B.R. 895 (Bankr. N.D. Fla. 2006).) This happened because the debtors did not claim the right to exempt this property when they filed for Chapter 13. If you find yourself in this situation, consult with an attorney. He or she can ask the court to allow you to keep your property because relinquishing it would cause you hardship.

If you convert your case in bad faith, your Chapter 7 bankruptcy estate will include all property of the estate as of the conversion date.

Property You Own and Possess

Property that you own and possess—for example, clothing, books, computers, cameras, TV, iPods, cellphones, furniture, tools, car, real estate, boat, artworks, and stock certificates—is included in your bankruptcy estate.

Property that belongs to someone else is not part of your bankruptcy estate—even if you control the property—because you don't have the right to sell it or give it away. However, you will have to disclose all property you hold on behalf of someone else in your paperwork. Here are some examples.

> EXAMPLE 1: A parent establishes a trust for her child and names you as trustee to manage the money in the trust until the child's 18th birthday. You possess and control the money, but it's solely for the child's benefit under the terms of the trust; you cannot use it for your own purposes. It isn't part of your bankruptcy estate.

> EXAMPLE 2: Your sister has gone to Zimbabwe for an indefinite period and has loaned you her computer while she's gone. Although you might have use of the equipment for years to come, you don't own it. It isn't part of your bankruptcy estate.

EXAMPLE 3: You are making monthly payments on a leased car. You can possess the car as long as you make the monthly payments, but you don't own it. It is not part of your bankruptcy estate (but the lease itself is).

EXAMPLE 4: Your name appears on the title and note to your son's car because he was underage when he bought it. Your son makes all the payments. While the two of you probably consider the car to "belong" to your son, the bankruptcy laws initially consider it to be yours. You can explain that you have "bare legal title" and your son is the equitable owner, which means it shouldn't be considered part of your bankruptcy estate. However, the court could disagree and your son could lose the car unless it fits within an available exemption. Courts have gone both ways on this issue; you should talk to a lawyer if valuable property is at stake.

Property in a Living Trust

A revocable living trust is a popular estate planning tool in which the grantor puts property in trust to be managed by the trustee for the benefit of one or more beneficiaries. The trust is revocable because the grantor can change his or her mind and revoke it at any time.

If you are both the grantor and the trustee of a revocable living trust, property in the trust is considered property of your estate, even though, as a technical matter, the trust "owns" the property. However, if the trust is irrevocable, that is, you can't change your mind and dissolve the trust, property in the trust won't be considered part of your bankruptcy estate, unless the court finds that you created the trust to shelter the property from your creditors or that you improperly transferred the money or assets into the trust.

Property You Own but Don't Possess

Any property you own is part of your bankruptcy estate, even if you don't have physical possession of it. For instance, you might own a share of a vacation cabin in the mountains but never spend time there. Or you might own furniture or a car that someone else is using. Other examples include a deposit held by a stockbroker, stock options, contractual rights to a royalty or commission, or a security deposit held by your landlord or the utility company.

Property You Have Recently Given Away

People contemplating bankruptcy are often tempted to unload their property on friends and relatives or pay favorite creditors before they file. Don't do it. Property given away or paid out in anticipation of filing for bankruptcy is still part of your bankruptcy estate—and in most cases, the trustee has the legal authority to take it back.

Prefiling Transfers of Property

Certain types of actions you take before filing for bankruptcy have such serious consequences that, as a practical matter, they render you ineligible to file for bankruptcy for a period. For example, if you sell or give away property during the two-year period immediately before you file, you will have to disclose those transactions on your bankruptcy papers. The consequences can be very severe—from losing the property to having your whole case thrown out—if the trustee decides that the transfer was fraudulent and the court agrees.

The basic problem here is that some filers are tempted to unload their assets so the trustee won't take them, sell them, and distribute the proceeds to the creditors. These transactions often take the form of selling property to a friend or relative for a nominal amount (such as a dollar), with the understanding that the friend will give back the property once the bankruptcy case is closed. Other common examples include taking one's name off a joint account, deed, or vehicle title, which is really a gift of half of the property to the other joint owner.

Whatever form they take, prefiling gifts and sales of property for substantially less than the property is worth are frequently judged to be fraudulent or improper transfers. This means the property can be taken from its new owner and sold for the benefit of the creditors, and the bankruptcy case could be dismissed. Even if you can convince the trustee that your intentions were good, the trustee can still require the person to whom you gave or sold the property to give it back so it can be sold. In these situations, you usually don't have an opportunity to claim that the property is exempt, so you won't even get any sale proceeds.

The bankruptcy forms require you to list all transfers made during the previous two years, so as long as the transfer didn't fall within that period, you should be fine.

People often wonder how the trustee would find out about a particular transfer. If the transferred property has a title document, as with cars, boats, and real estate, the transfer might show up in the trustee's routine search of state and local databases (for example, at the state DMV). Also, when you attend the creditors' meeting, you must affirm, under oath, that you truthfully answered the questions in your bankruptcy papers, including questions about prefiling transfers. As explained above, trustees stand to profit directly by finding property they can take and sell, so you can expect a trustee to do a bit of research and to pay attention to a tip off by a disgruntled former spouse or business partner. A trustee who senses trouble can follow up by questioning you under oath in a deposition-like proceeding. Most importantly, it's a bad idea to commit perjury.

Often, property that people try to transfer before filing for bankruptcy would have been exempt anyway. In other words, prefiling transfers often occur because the debtor doesn't understand the bankruptcy laws. Had the person just kept the property and claimed it as exempt, he or she could have held on to it and avoided a lot of trouble.

Paying Off a Preferred Creditor

A basic principle of bankruptcy law is that all creditors deserve to be treated fairly. In many cases, money isn't available for creditors and no one gets anything. When money is available, priority unsecured creditors get paid in a particular order, and nonpriority unsecured creditors share equally in the remaining proceeds.

This strict payment order required by law is violated if you pay a creditor off before filing for bankruptcy. Bankruptcy law forbids you from paying more than $600 to any creditor within 90 days before filing for bankruptcy. Also, you must list all payments made to anyone who's an insider—a relative, friend, or business associate, typically—during the year before you file for bankruptcy. So, if you use your tax refund to pay back an emergency loan from your sister, brother, or mother, you have preferred that creditor over your other unsecured creditors. When in bankruptcy, you are required to treat all creditors equally. Your mother and Visa are practically on the same footing, except that payments to your mother will be scrutinized closer.

If the creditor is not an insider (and most of your creditors probably aren't), the court will look at your transactions for only 90 days before you file for bankruptcy. If you are a business debtor—that is, most of your debt arises from your business activities—the court will look only at transactions that exceed $6,825.

At least one court has found that transferring your balance from one credit card to another might be considered a preference. In that case, the debtor used one credit card to pay off her debt on another credit card. Because she made the transfer within three months of filing for bankruptcy, and she could have used the money for any purpose (in other words, she didn't have to use it to pay off her other card), the court ruled that the transfer constituted a preferential transfer. (*In re Dilworth*, 560 F.3d 562 (6th Cir. 2009).)

The consequences of violating the preference rules can be harsh. The trustee is authorized to take back the money and distribute it among your creditors. If you paid back a family member, this could cause some tension. Even if you paid back a creditor that isn't an insider, it could cause some problems. For example, if you paid back a credit card issuer so you could keep your card, that creditor will probably take your card back once it has to return the money.

Even though you can't pay a favorite creditor before you file, nothing prevents you from doing so after you file, as long as you do it with income earned after you file your case or property that isn't in your bankruptcy estate.

Property You Are Entitled to Receive but Don't Yet Possess When You File

Property you are legally entitled to when you file for bankruptcy is included in your bankruptcy estate, even if you haven't actually received it yet. The most common examples are wages or commissions you have earned but have not yet been paid and tax refunds legally owed to you. Here are some other examples:

- Vacation or severance pay earned before you filed for bankruptcy.
- Property you've inherited but not yet received.
- Property you are entitled to receive from a trust. If you receive periodic payments from a trust but aren't entitled to the full amount of the trust yet, the full amount of the trust is considered property of your bankruptcy estate and should be listed in your bankruptcy papers. Although the bankruptcy trustee might not get the money (depending on the type of trust), you don't want to be accused of hiding it.
- Future interest in an irrevocable trust. If you are listed as a beneficiary in an irrevocable trust (that is, the terms of the trust can't be changed) you might have what's called a future interest, which is considered part of your bankruptcy estate. It's hard to assign a value to this type of interest because of potential developments between the time the trust was created and when the time to receive the benefits rolls around. For instance, intervening beneficiaries can often use some of the principal in an irrevocable trust, and there might be little or nothing left by the time it gets to you. Nevertheless, the future interest should be listed in your bankruptcy papers (list the value as "undetermined" if it is unknown).
- Proceeds of an insurance policy, if the death, injury, or other event that triggers payment has occurred. For example, if you were the beneficiary of your father's life insurance policy, and your father has died but you haven't received the money yet, that amount is part of your bankruptcy estate.

- A legal claim to monetary compensation (sometimes called a legal cause of action), even if the claim's value hasn't yet been determined. For example, if you have a claim against someone for injuring you in a car accident, you must include this potential source of money in your bankruptcy papers, even if the amount you will receive has not yet been determined in a lawsuit, settlement agreement, or an insurance claim. As with any other property, you'll have to protect it with an exemption; otherwise, the cause of action will belong to the bankruptcy estate and be pursued by the trustee. If you don't list a legal claim in your bankruptcy petition, you could lose the right to make it in a lawsuit after your bankruptcy. Under a legal principle known as judicial estoppel, failing to raise a legal claim in one judicial proceeding can prevent you from raising it in a later proceeding. (*In re Lopez*, 283 B.R. 22 (B.A.P. 9th Cir. 2002).) If you have a potential lawsuit, you'll want to consult with an attorney. If it is valuable enough, filing for bankruptcy might not be the right course of action.
- Accounts receivable (money you are owed for goods or services you've provided), even if you don't think you'll be paid, is considered part of your bankruptcy estate. It's the trustee's job to go after the money; leaving it off the bankruptcy forms can get you into trouble.
- Money earned but not yet received is property in your bankruptcy estate. This includes, for instance, rent from commercial or residential real estate, royalties from copyrights or patents, and dividends earned on stocks.

Proceeds From Property of the Bankruptcy Estate

If property in your bankruptcy estate earns income or otherwise produces money after you file for bankruptcy, this money is also part of your bankruptcy estate. For example, suppose a contract to receive royalties for a book you have written is part of your bankruptcy estate. Any royalties you earn under this contract after you file for bankruptcy are also property of the estate. The one exception to this rule is money you earn from providing personal services after filing for bankruptcy, which isn't part of your bankruptcy estate. Continuing our example, work on a new edition of the book after you file for bankruptcy would be considered personal services. The royalties you earn for that new work would not be part of your bankruptcy estate.

Another example of money that ends up in your bankruptcy estate (and therefore is not yours to keep unless you can exempt it) are proceeds from what's called a "contingent future interest." This bit of legalese refers to money that you will receive if certain things happen in the future. The mere possibility that you will receive property after filing for bankruptcy is enough to put that property in your bankruptcy estate once you do file. For example, in one case an employee had the right to participate in a profit-sharing plan, but only if he was still employed by the company at the end of the year. He filed for bankruptcy before the end of the year, but remained employed and received a hefty check, which the trustee claimed belonged to the bankruptcy estate, at least in part. The court ruled that the debtor's interest in the profit-sharing plan was a "contingent future interest" (contingent on whether the debtor remained employed) and that the portion of the check that was based on prepetition earnings belonged in the bankruptcy estate even though the debtor didn't receive the actual check until after the filing date. (*In re Edmunds*, 273 B.R. 527 (Bankr. E.D. Mich. 2000).)

Certain Property Acquired Within 180 Days After You File

Most property you acquire—or become entitled to acquire—after filing for bankruptcy isn't included in your bankruptcy estate. But there are exceptions. If you acquire (or become entitled to acquire) certain items within 180 days after you file, you must report them to the bankruptcy court—and the bankruptcy trustee can take them. (11 U.S.C. § 541(a)(5).)

The 180-day rule applies to:

- property you inherit during the 180-day period (some courts have held that property that passes to you as a beneficiary of a revocable living trust is not part of your bankruptcy estate; see, for example, *In re Mattern*, 55 Collier Bankr. Cas. 2d 1677 (Bankr. D. Kan. 2006) and *In re Roth*, 289 B.R. 161 (Bankr. D. Kan. 2003))

- property (not including alimony) from a property settlement agreement or divorce decree that goes into effect during the 180-day period, and
- death benefits or life insurance policy proceeds that become owed to you during the 180-day period.

You must report these items on a supplemental form, even if your bankruptcy case is over. You can find instructions for filing the supplemental form in Ch. 8.

If you convert from Chapter 13 to Chapter 7, the 180-day period runs from the date you originally filed for Chapter 13, not from the date you converted to Chapter 7. (*In re Carter*, 260 B.R. 130 (Bankr. W.D. Tenn. 2001).)

Your Share of Marital Property

How much of your marital property—the property you and your spouse own together—is included in your bankruptcy estate depends on two factors: (1) whether you file jointly or alone, and (2) the laws of your state regarding marital property.

If you file jointly, all marital property that fits into one of the categories listed above belongs to your bankruptcy estate.

However, if you are married and you file for bankruptcy alone, some marital property might not be part of your bankruptcy estate. Whether property is part of the estate depends on whether you live in a community property, tenancy by the entirety, or common law property state.

Community Property State or Territory

These are the community property states: Alaska (if the spouses sign a written agreement to treat the property as community property), Arizona, California, Idaho, Louisiana, Nevada, New Mexico, Texas, Washington, and Wisconsin. Puerto Rico is a community property territory as well.

The general rule is that all property either spouse earns or receives during the marriage is community property and is owned jointly by both spouses. Exceptions are gifts and inheritances received by only one spouse and property owned by one spouse before the marriage or acquired after permanent separation; these are the separate property of the spouse who acquired or received them.

Are Stock Options Part of Your Bankruptcy Estate?

If you own stock options, you have the right to purchase stock at the price assigned when the stock options were granted. Most of the time, you have to wait for a while after you get the options before buying the stock because stock options "vest" when that waiting period is up. Making such a purchase is called "exercising your stock options." Whether stock options are part of your bankruptcy estate depends on when you received them and when they vest.

As a general rule, stock options that you own when you file for bankruptcy are part of your bankruptcy estate. In addition, any stock you purchase by exercising your stock options is also part of the estate, even if you exercise those options after you file for bankruptcy. Courts treat these stock purchases as proceeds earned on property of the estate.

Sometimes, your stock options do not vest; that is, you cannot exercise them until you have been with your company for a certain period of time. In that case, depending on the rules in your jurisdiction, your bankruptcy estate might include only those stock options that have already vested on the date you file for bankruptcy. (*In re Allen*, 226 B.R. 857 (Bankr. N.D. Ill. 1998).)

To calculate the value of your stock options, multiply the number of vested stock options you own by the difference between your option price and the stock's fair market value. (Value of options = [number of vested stock options] × [fair market value – option price].) Even if the value of your options is uncertain, they are still part of your bankruptcy estate and the trustee will take them if they are marketable.

If you are married, live in a community property state, and file for bankruptcy, all the community property you and your spouse own (regardless of whose name is on the title) is considered part of your bankruptcy estate, even if your spouse doesn't file. This is true even if the community property might not be divided 50-50 if you were to divorce.

EXAMPLE: Paul and Emily live in California, a community property state. Emily contributed $20,000 of her separate property toward the purchase of their house. All the rest of the money used to pay for the house is from community funds and the house is considered community property. If Paul and Emily were to divorce and split the house proceeds, Emily would be entitled to $20,000 more than Paul as reimbursement for her down payment. But they aren't divorced, and Paul files for bankruptcy without Emily. Their house is worth $250,000. Paul must list that entire value on his bankruptcy papers—that is, he can't subtract the $20,000 Emily would be entitled to if they divorced.

The separate property of the spouse filing for bankruptcy is also part of the bankruptcy estate. But the separate property of the spouse *not* filing for bankruptcy is not part of the bankruptcy estate.

> EXAMPLE: Paul owns a single-engine Cessna 172 as his separate property (he owned it before he married Emily). Emily came to the marriage owning a grand piano. Because only Paul is filing for bankruptcy, Paul's aircraft will be part of his bankruptcy estate, but Emily's piano won't be.

You might need to do some research into your state's property laws to make sure you understand which of your property is separate and which is community. (See Ch. 10 for tips on legal research.)

Tenancy by the Entirety States

States that recognize some form of tenancy by the entirety for married couples are Alaska, Arkansas, Delaware, the District of Columbia, Florida, Hawaii, Illinois, Indiana, Kentucky, Maryland, Massachusetts, Michigan, Missouri, New York, North Carolina, Ohio, Oklahoma, Oregon, Pennsylvania, Rhode Island (subject to conditions), Tennessee, Vermont, Virginia, and Wyoming.

Real estate (and personal property, in some states) a couple owns as tenants by the entirety belongs to the marriage, rather than to one spouse or the other. If both spouses file for bankruptcy, property held in tenancy by the entirety is property of the bankruptcy estate. If only one spouse files for bankruptcy, this property is not part of the bankruptcy estate and is generally exempt from claims for which only one spouse is liable. Because the property belongs to the marriage, one spouse cannot give it away or burden it with debts on his or her own. The property is not exempt from debts the couple takes on jointly, however. We discuss this, as it applies to real estate, in Ch. 4.

Common Law Property States

If your state is not listed above as a community property or tenancy by the entirety state, it is a "common law" property state. When only one spouse files for bankruptcy in a common law property state, all of that spouse's separate property plus half of the couple's jointly owned property go into the filing spouse's bankruptcy estate.

The general rules of property ownership in common law states are:

- Property that has only one spouse's name on a title certificate (such as a car, a house, or stocks), is that spouse's separate property, even if it was bought with joint funds.
- Property that was purchased or received as a gift or inheritance by both for the use of both spouses is jointly owned, unless title is held in only one spouse's name (which means it belongs to that spouse separately, even if both spouses use it).
- Property that one spouse buys with separate funds or receives as a gift or inheritance for that spouse's separate use is that spouse's separate property (unless, again, a title certificate shows differently).

CAUTION

Check your state's status. The rules regarding tenancy by the entirety can be complicated, so it's best to double-check whether your state is a community property state, tenancy by the entirety state, or common law property state.

Property That Isn't in Your Bankruptcy Estate

Property that is not in your bankruptcy estate is not subject to the bankruptcy court's jurisdiction. The bankruptcy trustee can't take it to pay your creditors under any circumstances.

The most common examples of property that isn't within your bankruptcy estate are:

- property you buy or receive after your filing date (with the few exceptions described in "Certain Property Acquired Within 180 Days After You File," above)

- property pledged as collateral for a loan, if a licensed lender (pawnbroker) retains possession of the collateral
- property in your possession that belongs to someone else (for instance, property you are storing for someone), and
- wages withheld and employer contributions made for employee benefit, and health insurance plans.

TIP

ERISA-qualified retirement accounts are exempt, no matter which exemptions you use. When it passed the new bankruptcy law in 2005, Congress created a broad exemption for all types of tax-exempt retirement accounts, including 401(k)s, 403(b)s, profit-sharing and money purchase plans, IRAs (including Roth, SEP, and SIMPLE IRAs), and defined-benefit plans. These exemptions are unlimited—that is, the entire account is exempt, regardless of how much money is in it—except in the case of traditional and Roth IRAs. For these types of IRAs only, the exemption is limited to a total value of $1,362,800 per person (this figure adjusts every three years for inflation with the next adjustment occurring April 1, 2022). These accounts are exempt regardless of whether you use the federal or a state exemption system.

Funds placed in a qualified tuition program or Coverdell education savings account are also not part of your bankruptcy estate, as long as:

- you deposit the funds into the account at least one year before filing for bankruptcy, and
- the beneficiary of the account is your child, stepchild, grandchild, step-grandchild, or in some cases, foster child.

Funds placed in the account more than two years before you file are excluded from the bankruptcy estate without limit. However, you can exclude only $6,825 of the contributions you make between one and two years before filing. And contributions made within the year before filing are not excluded at all.

For amounts that are not excluded from the bankruptcy estate, you can use a state exemption, if one exists (assuming you are using your state's exemptions and not the federal exemptions).

Property You Can Keep (The Exemption System)

Your property includes everything you own. If you own your own home, land, or buildings of any kind, you are the proud owner of what is called "real property." Everything you own other than real estate is considered personal property.

When filing for Chapter 7 bankruptcy, you might be able to keep your home. (See Ch. 4 for more information.) However, you will probably have to give up any other real estate in which you have equity to be sold for the benefit of your creditors. You will also be able to keep some or all of your personal property. How much you get to keep will depend on whether the property is considered exempt under the state exemption system available to you, or under the federal exemption statute, if the state where you file allows you to choose between the federal and state exemptions.

This section describes how exemptions work and how to figure out which exemptions you can use. Once you know which exemptions are available to you, you can start applying them to your personal property to figure out which items you'll be able to keep. To help you keep track, we've included a Personal Property Checklist, which you can use to take an inventory of your property. Then, using the Property Exemption Worksheet, you'll be able to figure out, item by item, whether you'll be able to hang on to your property. You'll find both the checklist and worksheet on the companion page located at www.nolo.com/back-of-book/HFB.html.

How Exemptions Work

Figuring out exactly what property you're legally entitled to keep if you file for bankruptcy takes some work, but it's crucial. It's your responsibility—and to your benefit—to claim all exemptions to which you're entitled. If you don't claim property as exempt, you could lose it unnecessarily to your creditors.

Exempt property is the property you can keep during and after bankruptcy. Nonexempt property is the property that the bankruptcy trustee is entitled to take and sell to pay your creditors. Therefore, the more you can claim as exempt, the better off you are.

If You Are Named on Someone Else's Bank Account

It's common for older parents to put their son or daughter's name on the parents' bank account. This allows the child to write checks and otherwise manage the account if the parent becomes unable to do so; it also means the account goes straight to the child when the parent dies, outside of probate or other inheritance procedures.

If you are named on someone else's account and file for bankruptcy, however, that account could be considered property of your bankruptcy estate, subject to being taken by the trustee for the benefit of your unsecured creditors. Of course, it's not really your money while your parent is living, but if the trustee thinks you are free to withdraw the money and use it for your own purposes, the trustee might consider at least some of it to be part of your bankruptcy estate.

In these situations it's essential to tell the trustee that it really isn't your money to use as you wish. That would be a breach of your fiduciary duty toward the account holder, and possibly elder abuse. To ensure that the trustee understands why you are named on the account, you should declare the account on your property schedule (Schedule A/B) but explain that it really isn't yours. Also explain that it would be a breach of your duty of trust (fiduciary duty) toward the primary account holder for you to use the money for any purpose other than his or her welfare. You should identify the account and explain why you are named on it on the Statement of Financial Affairs. Finally, you would be well advised to gather documents showing that the sources of the money in the account clearly belong to the principal account owner. (See Ch. 6 for more on these paperwork requirements.)

If you can exempt the account on your bankruptcy Schedule C, you can just list it on Schedule A/B as your own property and avoid any argument over who owns it. For example, suppose your mother has put your name on her savings account, which has a balance of $4,000. If the exemption system you are using in your bankruptcy protects that amount of money, you could list the account on your property schedule (Schedule A/B) and claim the full amount as exempt on your Schedule C. You won't have to argue over who owns the money; either way, the trustee can't take it.

If You Are Named on Someone Else's Bank Account (continued)

To avoid all this trouble, you might be tempted to remove your name from the account before you file bankruptcy. Don't do it. Removing your name makes it look like you are trying to hide the whole issue from the bankruptcy court. The trustee might well convince the court to dismiss your bankruptcy altogether, on the ground that you committed fraud. You're better off leaving your name on the account and explaining the situation to the trustee. If there is significant money in the account, consider consulting with a lawyer about the best way to handle the situation. Incidentally, if you think that the trustee won't find out about the account if you don't list it, don't go there. They have their ways.

Note: If you are listed as a custodian or a trustee of the account funds for a minor under the Uniform Transfers to Minors Act, you don't have to worry about the bankruptcy trustee taking the funds. The law is clear that those funds belong to the minor, not to you in your fiduciary capacity as a custodian or trustee.

Each state's legislature produces a set of exemptions for use by people who are residents of that state. Nineteen states (and the District of Columbia) allow debtors to choose between their state's exemptions or another set of exemptions created by Congress (called the federal bankruptcy exemptions). States that currently allow debtors this choice are Alaska, Arkansas, Connecticut, Hawaii, Kentucky, Massachusetts, Michigan, Minnesota, New Hampshire, New Jersey, New Mexico, New York, Oregon, Pennsylvania, Rhode Island, Texas, Vermont, Washington, and Wisconsin (plus the District of Columbia). You have to choose one system or the other—you can't mix and match some exemptions from both lists. However, if you use one system when you first file your petition and decide that the other system would work better for you, you can amend Schedule C—the form where you list your exemption claims—to change systems.

California has adopted its own unique exemption system. Although California doesn't allow debtors to use the federal exemptions, California offers two sets of state exemptions. With a few important exceptions, the alternative California exemptions are the same as the federal exemptions. People filing for bankruptcy in California must choose one or the other set of state exemptions—they can't mix and match exemptions on both lists.

TIP

You might be able to keep your nonexempt property. If you have the cash to buy it back, the trustee will likely accept less than its value to avoid having to collect, store, and sell the property at an auction (also for less than its full value). If you don't have cash, the trustee might accept exempt property of roughly equal value instead or allow you to pay the value of the nonexempt property through a short payment plan. Finally, the trustee might reject or abandon the item if it would be too costly or cumbersome to sell and let you keep it. So when we say that you have to give up property, it's not always the case.

TIP

Buying nonexempt assets when you owe taxes can be a good idea. If you owe tax debts that you cannot discharge in your bankruptcy and pay the trustee to buy back nonexempt property, the money you give to the trustee will likely be used to repay your taxes (tax debts usually get paid first). A win-win situation. (To learn more about this tactic, see "When Buying Back Nonexempt Property Can Take a Bite Out of Your Tax Debt," in Ch. 1.)

Types of Exemptions

Both state and federal exemptions come in several basic varieties.

Exemptions to a Limited Amount

Some exemptions protect the value of your ownership in a particular item only up to a set dollar limit. For instance, the New Mexico state exemptions allow you to keep $4,000 of equity in a motor vehicle. If you were filing for Chapter 7 bankruptcy in that state and using the state exemption list, you could keep a car you owned outright if it was worth $4,000 or less. You could also keep the car if, after selling it and paying off what you owed, you were left with $4,000 or less. For example, if you own a car worth $20,000 but still owe $16,000 on it, selling it would raise $16,000 for the lender and $4,000 for you. The trustee wouldn't take the car because you would be entitled to the $4,000 exemption amount and there would be nothing left over to pay your other creditors. Instead, you would be allowed to keep it as long as you remained current on your payments. Filing for bankruptcy doesn't change the fact that the auto loan lender can take the car through repossession if you fall behind on your payments.

However, if your equity in the car significantly exceeded the $4,000 exemption, the trustee would sell the vehicle to raise money for your other creditors. For instance, let's say you owe $10,000 on a car worth $20,000. The proceeds from selling the car would pay off the lender in full, pay your $4,000 exemption, and leave $6,000 minus sales costs to be distributed to your other creditors. In this scenario, you are entitled to the full value of your exemption—$4,000—but not to the car itself.

Exemptions Without Regard to Value

Another type of exemption allows you to keep specified property items regardless of value. For instance, the Utah state exemptions allow you to keep a refrigerator, freezer, microwave, stove, sewing machine, and carpets with no limit on their values. For comparison purposes, another Utah state exemption places a $1,000 limit on "sofas, chairs, and related furnishings."

Wildcard Exemptions

Some states (and the federal exemption list) also provide a general-purpose exemption, called a wildcard exemption. This exemption gives you a dollar amount that you can apply to any type of property. For example, suppose you own a $3,000 boat in a state that doesn't exempt boats but does have a wildcard of $5,000. You can take $3,000 of the wildcard and apply it to the boat and the boat will now be considered exempt. If you have other nonexempt property, you can apply the remaining $2,000 from the wildcard to that property.

You can also use a wildcard exemption to increase an existing exemption. For example, if you have $5,000 worth of equity in your car but your state only allows you to exempt $1,500 of its value, you will likely lose the vehicle.

However, if your state has a $5,000 wildcard exemption, you could use the $1,500 motor vehicle exemption and $3,500 of the wildcard exemption to exempt your car entirely. And you'd still have $1,500 of the wildcard exemption to use on other nonexempt property.

Why State Exemptions Vary So Much

Each state's exemptions are unique. The property you can keep, therefore, varies considerably from state to state. Why the differences? State exemptions are used for bankruptcy purposes and to shelter property that otherwise could be taken by creditors who have obtained court judgments. The exemptions reflect the attitudes of state legislators about how much property, and which property, a debtor should be forced to part with when a victorious creditor collects on a judgment. These attitudes are rooted in local values and concerns. But in many cases there is another reason why state exemptions differ. Some state legislatures have raised exemption levels in recent years, while other states last looked at their exemptions many decades ago. In states that don't reconsider their exemptions very often, you can expect to find lower dollar amounts.

Domicile Requirements for Using State Exemptions

Usually filers use the exemptions of the state where they reside when they file for bankruptcy. However, some filers have to use the exemptions of the state where they *used* to live. This is to prevent people from moving to states with generous exemptions just to file for bankruptcy.

Below are the rules that govern which state's exemptions you must use. Keep in mind that your domicile is where you make your permanent home—where you get mail, vote, pay taxes, and so on—even if you are temporarily living elsewhere due to work or military service.

- If you have made your domicile in your current state for at least two years, you can use that state's exemptions.

- If you have had your domicile in your current state for more than 91 days but less than two years, you must use the state's exemptions where you were domiciled for the better part of the 180-day period immediately before the two-year period preceding your filing.
- If you have had your domicile in your current state for less than 91 days, you can either file in the state where you lived immediately before (as long as you lived there for at least 91 days) or wait until you have logged 91 days in your new home and file in your current state. Once you figure out where you can file, you'll need to use whatever exemptions are available to you according to the rules set out above.
- If the state you are filing in offers a choice between the state and federal bankruptcy exemptions, you can use the federal exemption list regardless of how long you've been living in the state.
- If these rules deprive you of the right to use *any* state's exemptions, you can use the federal exemption list, even if it isn't otherwise available in the state where you file. For example, some states allow their exemptions to be used only by current state residents, which might leave former residents who haven't lived in their new home state for at least two years without any available state exemptions. (See, for example, *In re Underwood*, 342 B.R. 358 (Bankr. N.D. Fla. 2006); *In re Crandall*, 346 B.R. 220 (Bankr. M.D. Fla. 2006); and *In re West*, 352 B.R. 905 (Bankr. M.D. Fla. 2006).) If you have recently returned to the United States after being domiciled in another country, and no state exemption system is available to you under these rules, you are also entitled to use the federal exemptions.

A more extended domicile requirement applies to homestead exemptions: If you acquired a home in your current state within the 40 months before you file for bankruptcy, and you didn't purchase it with the proceeds from selling another home in that state, your homestead exemption will be subject to a cap of $170,350 (this figure will adjust on April 1, 2022), even if the state homestead exemption available to you is larger. The principal residence of a family farmer is exempt from this rule. (For detailed information on homestead exemptions, see Ch. 4.)

State "Bankruptcy-Specific" Exemptions Might be Unconstitutional

Most states' exemptions can be used in bankruptcy and in other situations (for example, if a creditor is trying to collect a judgment against you, you can use the state exemption system to exempt some of your property from collection)—we'll refer to these as general state exemptions. However, a few states have particular exemptions or exemption systems that apply only in bankruptcy (often called bankruptcy-specific or bankruptcy-only exemptions.) These states are California (System 2), Colorado, Georgia, Michigan, Montana, New York, Ohio, and West Virginia.

Some trustees have challenged the constitutionality of these bankruptcy-specific exemptions. A few courts have agreed, and ruled that these types of state bankruptcy-specific exemptions are unconstitutional because they aren't authorized by the federal bankruptcy laws. However, the vast majority of courts addressing this issue have upheld the constitutionality of bankruptcy-specific exemptions and allowed bankruptcy filers to use them. (For example, see *Sheehan v. Peveich*, 574 F.3d 248 (4th Cir. 2009) and *In re Applebaum*, 422 B.R. 684 (B.A.P. 9th Cir. 2009).) Most recently, the Sixth Circuit Court of Appeals held that Michigan's bankruptcy-specific exemption statute is constitutional (*In re Schafer*, 689 F.3d 601 (6th Cir. 2012), and in 2013 the U.S. Supreme Court denied certiorari in the case.

For the most part, it's safe to use California's bankruptcy-specific exemptions and bankruptcy-specific exemptions in other states. Just be aware that a trustee or creditor might decide to challenge your right to use the bankruptcy-specific exemptions. If that happens, you might have to amend your paperwork to use the general state exemptions. If that happens, talk to an attorney right away.

EXAMPLE 1: Sammie Jo lives in South Carolina from July 2018 until January 2020, when she gets lucky at a casino, moves to Texas, and buys a car for $15,000. In March 2021, Sammie Jo files for bankruptcy in Texas. Her car is now worth $14,000. Because Sammie Jo has been living in Texas for only 14 months—not two years—she can't use the Texas exemption for cars, which would protect the entire amount. Because Sammie Jo filed in

March 2021, she must use the exemptions of the state where she lived for most of the six-month period (180 days) ending two years before she filed, or March 2019. Sammie Jo lived in South Carolina for the six months before March 2017. As it turns out, the South Carolina exemption for cars is only $6,325, which means that Sammie Jo will probably lose her car if she uses the South Carolina exemptions.

However, Texas gives filers the option of using either its state exemptions or the federal bankruptcy exemptions. Under the law, the rules of the state where a person files determine whether the federal exemptions are available, even if that person has not lived in the state long enough to use its state exemptions. As a result, Sammie Jo can use the federal exemptions instead of the South Carolina state exemptions. Under the federal exemptions, Sammie Jo is entitled to exempt a motor vehicle worth up to $4,000—still not enough to cover her car. But wait: The federal exemptions also provide a wildcard of $1,325, plus $12,575 of unused homestead exemption. Sammie Jo doesn't own her home, so she can add the entire wildcard of $13,900 to her $4,000 vehicle exemption, for a total exemption of $17,900 she can apply to her car.

EXAMPLE 2: Julia lived in North Dakota for many years, until she moved to Florida on January 15, 2019. She files for bankruptcy in Florida on November 30, 2020. Because she has lived in Florida for slightly less than two years when she files, she must use the exemptions from the state where she lived for the better part of the 180-day period that ended two years before she filed—which is North Dakota. As it turns out, Julia's most valuable possession is a prepaid medical savings account with $20,000 in it. While the account would be exempt under Florida law, North Dakota has no exemption for this property type. Nor are the federal exemptions available in Florida. So the trustee will probably seize the medical savings account and use the money in it to pay Julia's creditors. Had Julia waited another month and a half to file, she would have been able to use Florida's exemptions and keep her medical savings account.

If You Are Married and Filing Jointly

If the federal bankruptcy exemptions are available in the state where you file and you decide to use them, you can double all of the exemptions if you are married and filing jointly. (See Ch. 6 for more on whether to file jointly.) You and your spouse can each claim the full amount of each federal exemption.

If you decide to use your state's exemptions, you might be able to double some exemptions but not others. For instance, many states allow you to double all exemptions other than the homestead exemption. For you to double an exemption for a single piece of property, title to the property must be in both of your names. In the exemption charts on the companion page (www.nolo.com/back-of-book/HFB.html), we've noted whether a court or state legislature has expressly allowed or prohibited doubling. If the chart doesn't say one way or the other, it is probably safe to double. However, keep in mind that this area of the law changes rapidly—legislation or court decisions issued after the publication date of this book will not be reflected in the chart. (See Ch. 10 for information on doing your own legal research.)

Applying Exemptions to Your Property

The Personal Property Checklist and Property Exemption Worksheet will help you figure out what personal property you own and whether you will get to keep it if you file for bankruptcy. You also can use this information to complete the official forms that accompany your bankruptcy petition, if you later decide to file. You'll find the checklist and worksheet on the companion page located at www.nolo.com/back-of-book/HFB.html.

Inventory Your Property

If you decide to file for bankruptcy, you will have to list all property that belongs in your bankruptcy estate. Whether or not you can hold on to that property, or at least some of the property's value in dollar terms, depends on what the property is worth and which exemptions are available to you. The best way to start figuring out what you'll be able to keep—and get a jump on your filing paperwork—is to create an inventory of your property.

Use the Personal Property Checklist found on the companion page (www.nolo.com/back-of-book/HFB.html) to create an inventory of your possessions. Place a checkmark in the box next to each item you own. If you are married and filing jointly, list all property owned by you and your spouse.

Using the Property Exemption Worksheet

Now that you have a comprehensive list of your property, you can decide how to use the exemptions available to your best advantage. This will require you to come up with a value for each item, decide which exemption system to use if you have a choice, then figure out how to apply those exemptions to your property.

To do this, use the Property Exemption Worksheet found on the companion page (www.nolo.com/back-of-book/HFB.html). You'll enter the following information into four columns:

- a description of the property
- the property's replacement value
- the exemption (if any) that applies to the property, and
- the number of the statute where that exemption appears.

Complete each of these columns as follows.

Column 1: Using your completed checklist as a guide, describe each item of property and its location.

For personal property, identify the item (for example, 2015 Honda Accord) and its location (for example, residence). For cash on hand and deposits of money, indicate the source of each, such as wages or salary, insurance policy proceeds, or the proceeds from selling an item of property.

Column 2: Enter the replacement value of each item of property in Column 1—what you would pay a retail vendor to buy the property, given its age and condition. It's easy to enter a dollar amount for cash, bank deposits, bonds, and most investment instruments. For items that are tougher to value, such as insurance, annuities, pensions, and business interests, you might need to get an appraisal from someone who has some financial expertise.

For your other property, estimate its replacement value—again, what you could buy it for from a retail vendor, considering its age and condition. As long as you have a reasonable basis for your estimates, the lower the value you place on property, the more of it you will probably be allowed to keep through the bankruptcy process. But be honest when assigning values. Trustees have years of experience and a pretty good sense of what property is worth. It's okay to be wrong as long as you have an arguable basis for the value you list and briefly explain any uncertainties. If you can't come up with a replacement value, leave this column blank. If you file for bankruptcy, you can simply indicate that the value is unknown—although this is risky. A value will be ascertained at some point and it's better to have an idea about what that would be before filing. If the trustee is concerned about the value, you will be asked to provide more detail at your creditors' meeting.

- **Cars.** Unfortunately, the replacement value requirement doesn't exactly square with the way car values are determined by the *Kelley Blue Book*, the most common source for car prices. To be absolutely safe in your estimate, use the average retail price for your car (based on its mileage) listed at the National Automobile Dealers Association website, www.nada.com. If your vehicle is inoperable or in poor condition (with obvious and significant body damage or serious mechanical problems), you can reasonably list whatever you could sell it for on the open market. Because such cars are not sold by car dealers, there's no way to figure out what a retail merchant would charge for such a car.

- **Older goods.** If the items are sold in used goods stores (for example, used furniture stores, Goodwill stores, or hospice outlets), check their prices. If not, you can check the want ads in a local flea market or penny-saver newspaper. eBay is also a good source for values: You can find retail merchants selling a wide variety of used goods at www.ebay.com.

- **Life insurance.** List the current cash surrender value of your policy. You should be able to call your insurance agent to find out what it is. Term life insurance has a cash surrender value of zero. Don't list the amount of benefits the policy will pay, unless you're the beneficiary of an insurance policy and the insured person has died.

- **Stocks and bonds.** Check the listing in a newspaper business section. If you can't find the listing, or the stock isn't traded publicly, call your broker and ask what it's worth. If you have a brokerage account, use the value from your last statement. (For information on how to calculate the value of any stock options you own, see "Are Stock Options Part of Your Bankruptcy Estate?" above.)

- **Jewelry, antiques, and other collectibles.** Any valuable jewelry or collections should be appraised.

Add up the amounts in Column 4 and enter the total in the space provided on the last page.

TIP

Ignore liens against your personal property when computing the property's value. If you owe money to a major consumer lender such as Beneficial Finance, the lender might have a lien on some or all of your personal property. You can often remove this lien in the course of your bankruptcy. Similarly, there might be a lien against your personal property if a creditor has obtained a court judgment against you. These liens, too, can frequently be removed. (See Ch. 5 to find out more about personal property liens and your options for dealing with them.)

Columns 3 and 4: Identify exemptions for your personal property. You can find every state's exemptions on the companion page (www.nolo.com/back-of-book/HFB.html). If the state exemption system you're using allows you to choose the federal exemptions instead of your state's exemptions, you can find these listed directly after Wyoming.

The Trustee Might Abandon Nonexempt Property

Even if you have property that's worth more than the exemption amount, the trustee might not want to deal with it. As in other areas, the bankruptcy laws in this area are somewhat odd. As defined by the bankruptcy code, the replacement value of property will almost always be higher than what the property will likely fetch at an auction held by a trustee. For example, assume you have a piano that would cost you $2,000 from a retail vendor given its age and condition. If the piano is not exempt, the trustee has a $2,000 asset to sell for the benefit of your creditors. However, moving and storing pianos can be expensive, and this particular piano might only fetch $500 at an auction. If the trustee sees that little or no money will be realized from taking the asset, the trustee will abandon it, which means you're free to keep it, even if it isn't technically exempt.

TIP

Focus on the property you really want to keep. If you have a lot of property and are afraid of getting bogged down in exemption jargon and dollar signs, start with the property you wouldn't want to lose. After that, if you are so inclined, you can search for exemptions that would let you keep property that is less important to you.

If You Can Only Use Your State's Exemptions

Unless you are using the exemptions for Alaska, Arkansas, Connecticut, the District of Columbia, Hawaii, Kentucky, Massachusetts, Michigan, Minnesota, New Hampshire, New Jersey, New Mexico, New York, Oregon, Pennsylvania, Rhode Island, Texas, Vermont, Washington, or Wisconsin, you must use your state's exemptions (subject to the domicile rules discussed above).

Step 1: In Column 3, list the amount of the exemption or write "no limit" if the exemption is unlimited. In Column 4, list the number of the statute identified on your state's exemption chart for the exemption that might reasonably be applied to the particular property item. (You'll find the exemption charts on the companion page at www.nolo.com/back-of-book/HFB.html.) If you need more information or an explanation of terms, use the notes at the beginning of the exemption charts and the glossary. In evaluating whether your cash on hand and deposits are exempt, look to the source of the money, such as welfare benefits, insurance proceeds, or wages.

TIP

Err on the side of exemption. If you can think of why a particular property item might be exempt, list it even if you aren't sure that the exemption applies. If you later decide to file for Chapter 7 bankruptcy, you will only be expected to do your best to fit the exemptions to your property. Of course, if you do misapply an exemption and the bankruptcy trustee or a creditor files a formal objection within the required time, you might lose the property that you mistakenly thought was exempt.

Exempting Work-Related Property

"Tools of the trade" is a common exemption category. The term used to mean hand tools, but now it refers more broadly to the things you need to do the job you rely on for support. Here are some examples of property that could be considered tools of the trade in various fields:

- art camera, scanner (artist)
- car, truck, or van that is used for more than just commuting (sales manager, insurance adjuster, physician, firewood salesperson, traveling salesperson, real estate salesperson, mechanic)
- cream separator, dairy cows, animal feed (farmer)
- drills, saws (carpenter)
- electric motor, lathe (mechanic)
- guitar, acoustic amplifier, cornet, violin and bow, organ, speaker cabinet (musician)
- hair dye, shampoo, cash register, furniture, dryer, fan, curler, magazine rack (barber, beauty parlor operator)
- oven, mixer (baker)
- personal computer, printer (insurance salesperson, lawyer, accountant)
- photographic lens (photographer)
- power chain saw (firewood salesperson)
- sewing machine (tailor), and
- truck (logger, tire retreader, truck driver, farmer, electrician).

Review the tools of the trade exemption rules available to you carefully—you might be pleasantly surprised by what you can keep.

Step 2: If a particular exemption has no dollar limit, then apply that exemption to all property items that seem to fall into that category. If there is a limit (for instance, an exemption allows you to keep up to $1,000 worth of electronic products), total the value of all property items you wish to claim under that exemption. Then compare the total with the exemption limit. If the total is less than the limit, then there is no problem. However, if the total is more than the limit, you might have to either give the trustee enough of the property to bring your total back under the limit or apply a wildcard exemption to the extra property, if the state system you are using has one.

Five Steps to Applying Exemptions to Your Personal Property

1. Check the exemptions you are using for specific property items that you want to keep.
2. If the state exemptions don't cover the property you want to keep (either because they don't exempt that property at all or because they exempt substantially less than your property is worth), look for a wildcard exemption in the state exemption list.
3. If the state also lets you use the federal bankruptcy exemptions (or you live in California), see whether a federal exemption (or a System 2 exemption in California) covers your property.
4. If the federal bankruptcy exemptions are available to you but don't seem to cover your property, see whether the federal bankruptcy wildcard exemption will work.
5. If you have the choice of two exemption systems, decide which exemption list you want to use. Don't mix and match. (In California, if you own your home and have considerably more than $29,275 in equity, you'll probably want to use the 704 exemptions. If you don't own a home, the 703 exemptions will often be a better choice.)

   Tip #1: Double your exemptions if you're married and filing jointly, unless the state exemption list on the companion page says that doubling isn't allowed. If you're using the federal bankruptcy exemptions, you can double all exemptions.

   Tip #2: While you're figuring out which of your property is exempt, write down in Column 4 the numbers of the statutes that authorize each exemption. (You can find these on the companion page at www.nolo.com/back-of-book/ HFB.html.) You will need this information when you fill out Schedule C of your bankruptcy papers.

If You Live in California or a State That Allows You to Choose the Federal Exemptions

If the state system you're using allows you to use the federal bankruptcy exemptions or you qualify to use the California exemptions (which give you a choice between two state systems), you'll need to decide which exemption system to use. You can't use some exemptions from one system and some from the other. If you own a home in which you have equity, your choice will often be dictated by which system gives you the most protection for that equity. In California, for example, the homestead exemption in the 704 exemptions protects up to $175,000 in equity, while the 703 exemption list protects only $30,825 (including the $1,550 wildcard).

Unless your choice of exemption lists is dictated by your home equity, you'll be best served by going through the Property Exemption Worksheet twice.

After you apply both exemption lists to your property, compare the results and decide which exemption list will do you the most good. You'll likely find that one set of exemptions is more generous or better protects the property you really want to keep. You might be sorely tempted to pluck some exemptions out of one list and add them to the other list. Again, this can't be done. You'll either have to use one exemption list—you can't mix and match exemptions in two lists.

> **EXAMPLE:** Hannah has lived in Albuquerque, New Mexico, for several years. Other than clothing, household furniture, and personal effects, the only property Hannah owns is a vintage 1967 Chevy Camaro Rally Sport. Hannah often checks out local car magazines and knows that the model she owns typically sells for about $14,000, although this price varies by several thousand dollars based on the car's condition. Hannah wants to know what will happen to her car if she files for Chapter 7 bankruptcy.
>
> Because Hannah has lived in New Mexico for more than two years, she will use that state's exemption rules. Her first step is to locate the exemptions for New Mexico on the companion page. At the bottom of the New Mexico exemption listings for personal property, Hannah finds an entry for motor vehicles and sees that the exemption is $4,000. Hannah begins to worry that she might lose her car, which is worth more than double the exemption limit.
>
> Hannah's next step is to search the New Mexico state exemptions for a wildcard exemption. (See above for an explanation of wildcard exemptions.) Hannah discovers (at the bottom of the list) that she has a $5,500 wildcard exemption to apply to any property, including the Camaro. Add that to the $4,000 regular motor vehicle exemption, and Hannah can now exempt $9,500. This amount still doesn't cover the Camaro's replacement value, which means the trustee would probably sell it, give Hannah her $9,500 exemption, and distribute the rest of the sales proceeds to Hannah's unsecured creditors.

Hannah next checks to see whether New Mexico allows debtors to use the federal bankruptcy exemptions. She looks at the top of the exemption page and sees a note that the federal bankruptcy exemptions are available in her state. Hoping that the federal bankruptcy exemptions will give her a higher exemption limit for her Camaro, she turns to the end of the exemption charts (right after Wyoming) and finds the federal bankruptcy exemption list. Under personal property she sees a listing for motor vehicles in the amount of $4,000—not high enough.

Hannah examines the federal bankruptcy exemptions to see whether they provide a wildcard exemption. She discovers that the federal bankruptcy exemptions let you use up to $12,575 of the homestead exemption as a wildcard. Because Hannah has no home equity to protect, she can apply the wildcard to the Camaro, in addition to the federal exemption for motor vehicles of $4,000. Further, Hannah sees that she can get an additional wildcard exemption of $1,325 under the federal exemption system. Putting these exemptions together, Hannah sees she can exempt $17,900—more than the value of her car.

Because Hannah is most concerned about keeping her car, and because the federal bankruptcy exemptions let her keep her car while the state exemptions don't, Hannah decides to use the federal bankruptcy exemption list.

Using Federal Nonbankruptcy Exemptions

If you are using state exemptions, you are also entitled to use a handful of exemptions called "federal nonbankruptcy exemptions." As the name suggests, these exemptions are generally used in cases other than bankruptcies, but you can also use them in a bankruptcy case. (In California, they apply only if you're using the 704 exemptions.)

Skim the list on this book's companion page at www.nolo.com/back-of-book/HFB.html to see whether any of these exemptions would help you. If they would, you can use them in addition to the state exemptions. If they duplicate each other, though, you cannot add them together for any one category. For example, if both your state and the federal nonbankruptcy exemptions let you exempt 75% of disposable weekly earnings, you cannot combine the exemptions to keep all of your wages—75% is all you get.

Selling Nonexempt Property Before You File

If you want to reduce the amount of nonexempt property you own before you file for bankruptcy, you might consider selling the nonexempt property and using the proceeds to buy exempt property. Or you might want to use the proceeds to pay certain types of debts, such as for necessities of life. But be careful: If the trustee learns that you sold the property and believes that you did so to defraud, hinder, delay, or shortchange a creditor, your efforts to shelter the property could fail. The court might decide to treat any exempt property you purchase as nonexempt property. And, if the court believes you acted fraudulently, your entire bankruptcy discharge could be at risk. In any event, you are allowed to sell property and use the funds for needed living expenses, such as rent and food.

> CAUTION
> **Talk to a lawyer first.** Before you sell nonexempt property, consult a bankruptcy attorney. Your local bankruptcy court might automatically consider these kinds of transfers attempts to defraud a creditor. The only sure way to find out what is and isn't permissible in your area is to ask an attorney familiar with local bankruptcy court practices. A consultation on this sort of issue should not run more than $250 and is well worth the cost if it will help you hold on to valuable property.

You Can Pay Favored Creditors After You File

You might be tempted to leave certain creditors off your bankruptcy papers, perhaps because the creditor is a relative, a local provider of important services (for example, a doctor, lawyer, veterinarian, or department store), or your employer. Unfortunately, bankruptcy requires that all creditors be identified on the appropriate schedules. However, just because you got rid of a debt in bankruptcy doesn't mean you can't pay it. You'll just want to wait until after you file and don't use property of the estate to pay for it. For instance, if you file for bankruptcy on March 12, 2021, you can use income you earn after that date to pay the creditor, because that income is not part of your bankruptcy estate. One last point: While you are free to pay off a discharged debt, the creditor cannot force you to pay it.

Five Guidelines for Prebankruptcy Planning

These five guidelines will help you stay out of trouble when making prebankruptcy transactions.

1. **Don't convert nonexempt property if you have equity in your home.** As noted above, you risk losing some or all of your homestead exemption if you engage in this type of prebankruptcy planning. Our advice is not to do it until you talk to a lawyer.

2. **Accurately report all your prefiling transactions** on the Statement of Financial Affairs. (See Ch. 6 for more on completing the official bankruptcy forms.) Courts see frankness like this as a sign of honorable intentions. If you lie or attempt to conceal property the bankruptcy trustee or court could conclude that you had fraudulent intentions and deny you a bankruptcy discharge (or worse).

3. **Don't make last-minute transfers or purchases.** The longer you can wait to file for bankruptcy after completing a property transfer, the less likely the judge is to disapprove. For example, judges frequently rule that a hasty transaction on the eve of filing shows an intent to cheat creditors. However, the open, deliberate, and advance planning of property sales and purchases is usually considered evidence that you didn't intend to defraud. But even this isn't foolproof. One court ruled that the debtor's deliberate planning more than a year before filing was evidence of an intent to cheat creditors. This conflict reinforces our earlier warning: You must find out your bankruptcy court's approach before selling nonexempt property.

4. **Don't just change the form of property ownership.** Simply changing the way property is held from a nonexempt form to an exempt form is usually considered fraudulent.

   EXAMPLE: Although he's married, Jeff owns a house as his separate property. Also, Jeff incurred virtually all of his debts alone, so he plans to file for bankruptcy alone. In Jeff's state, the homestead exemption is only $7,500. Jeff's equity in his home is nearly $30,000. Jeff's state also exempts property held as tenancy by the entirety, so Jeff transfers ownership of the house to himself and his wife as tenants by the entirety. That would typically exempt the house from all debts Jeff incurred separately. But because Jeff merely changed the form of property ownership, rather than buying exempt property or paying off debts to give himself a fresh start, the bankruptcy court might find the transfer fraudulent and take Jeff's house.

5. **Get the advice of a local bankruptcy attorney before engaging in "bankruptcy planning" of any type.**

CAUTION

Community property warning. As mentioned earlier, if you're married and live in a community property state (Alaska, Arizona, California, Idaho, Louisiana, Nevada, New Mexico, Texas, Washington, or Wisconsin), the trustee can usually take both your share of community property and your spouse's, even if your spouse doesn't file for bankruptcy. But if you're tempted to change all or a portion of the community property into your spouse's separate property, beware: Creditors or the trustee are apt to cry fraud, and the trustee is likely to take the property anyway.

To give you an idea of what judges consider improper behavior shortly before filing for bankruptcy, here are some transactions that courts have found to be fraudulent:

- A debtor bought goods on credit but never paid for them. He then sold those goods and bought property that he tried to exempt.
- A debtor with nonexempt property was forced into involuntary bankruptcy by a creditor. The debtor convinced the creditor to drop the forced bankruptcy. Then the debtor sold the nonexempt property, purchased exempt property, and filed for Chapter 7 bankruptcy.
- A debtor sold nonexempt property worth enough to pay off all her debts (but didn't pay them off).
- A debtor sold nonexempt items for considerably less than they were worth.
- A debtor sold valuable property to a nonfiling spouse for one dollar.
- A debtor transferred nonexempt property the day after a creditor won a lawsuit against him, then filed for bankruptcy.

- A debtor in a state with an "unlimited" homestead exemption sold all her nonexempt property and used the proceeds to pay off a large portion of her mortgage.
- A debtor bought a piano and harpsichord and a whole life insurance policy, all exempt in his state. He didn't play either instrument, and he had no dependents who needed insurance protection.

Taking Out Loans to Pay Nondischargeable Debts

Some people are tempted to borrow money to pay off debts that aren't dischargeable—for instance, a student loan—and then list the new loan as a dischargeable unsecured debt. Be careful if you do this. A court will likely consider your actions fraudulent and dismiss your bankruptcy. If the court doesn't dismiss your case, the creditor could ask the court to declare the debt nondischargeable. If you take out the loan while you're broke and file for bankruptcy soon after, you probably will be penalized. And, if you borrow money or use your credit card to pay off a nondischargeable tax debt, you will not be able to discharge the loan or credit card charge in a Chapter 7 bankruptcy (although you could in a Chapter 13 bankruptcy).

Your House

I f you own a home, Chapter 7 bankruptcy might not be the best strategy to deal with your debts. If you have significant nonexempt equity in your home (that is, equity that isn't protected by a homestead or another exemption), you risk losing your home if you file for Chapter 7 bankruptcy. As long as there will be equity left over after paying off what you owe, paying you the exempt amount, and covering the costs of sale, the trustee can sell your home if you use Chapter 7.

What's more, filing for Chapter 7 bankruptcy won't ultimately prevent a foreclosure on your home, although the automatic stay will put it on hold for a short period while your bankruptcy case is pending. If you want to keep your home, you'll need to make sure your mortgage payments are current before filing and be able to protect all equity with a bankruptcy exemption. See "If You're Behind on Your Mortgage Payments," below.

If you're behind on your payment and want to keep your house, Chapter 13 bankruptcy will likely be the better option. Chapter 13 provides a mechanism for saving a home that isn't available to a Chapter 7 filer. Specifically, you can catch up on the missed payments over three to five years. (For more information, see *The Foreclosure Survival Guide*, by Amy Loftsgordon (Nolo), and *Chapter 13 Bankruptcy*, by Cara O'Neill (Nolo).)

This chapter explains how filing for Chapter 7 bankruptcy—or pursuing alternative strategies—affects your ability to hold on to your home.

How Bankruptcy Affects a Typical Homeowner

As you review this material, keep these basic principles in mind:

- You can keep your home in Chapter 7 bankruptcy unless your home equity exceeds the homestead exemption available and the costs of sale.

- If you are behind on your payments when you file for bankruptcy, your lender can ask the court for permission to lift the automatic stay and proceed with a foreclosure. The court will usually grant this permission, as long as the lender can prove that it is the correct party to be making the request and that the lender's interests will be harmed if the stay isn't lifted.

- Mortgages and deeds of trust have two parts: a promissory note, by which you agree to repay the debt, and a lien on the property, which gives the lender the right to foreclose on the property to get its money back. Unless you reaffirm it (covered in Ch. 5), the promissory note is canceled in the bankruptcy. But the lien will remain, which means you must keep making your payments or face foreclosure.

- You cannot qualify for a mortgage modification after bankruptcy unless you reaffirm the mortgage. Without reaffirmation, there is no promissory note to modify. On the other hand, reaffirming a mortgage can leave you with a huge debt that you'll be responsible for after your bankruptcy—and for that reason it is generally a bad idea. Check with your bank or HUD-approved housing counselor to see how bankruptcy could affect your mortgage modification efforts. The best approach is to hold off filing for bankruptcy until your modification efforts are completed.

- If you don't reaffirm your mortgage, your lender won't report your payments to the credit reporting agencies, which means your payments won't help you rebuild your credit report and score. But it's a bad idea to reaffirm a mortgage solely to rehabilitate your credit, because you'll be on the hook for the mortgage if you can't make your payments later. In fact, certain bankruptcy judges won't approve mortgage reaffirmations at all.

When You Need a Lawyer

We recommend that homeowners talk to a bankruptcy lawyer before filing if they have any concerns about being able to keep their house. The procedures and strategies discussed in this chapter can be complex. A mistake in estimating your equity or applying a homestead exemption could cost you your home. And, your state's law might offer you rights and options that aren't covered here.

You should also consult with a bankruptcy lawyer if:

- You own two homes, or you want to protect equity in a home that isn't your residence.
- You are married, own a home with your spouse, and plan on filing alone. Because the rules for how community property and "tenancy by the entirety" property are treated in bankruptcy can get complicated, it's a good idea to get some legal advice geared to your situation.

Mortgage Payments

You must keep making your mortgage payments if you want to avoid foreclosure. As you probably know all too well, you don't really "own" much of your home—a bank or another lender that has a mortgage or deed of trust on the home probably owns most of it. (Throughout this chapter, we use the term "mortgage" to include deeds of trust.)

Until the mortgage is paid off, the lender has the right to foreclose if you miss mortgage payments. Chapter 7 bankruptcy doesn't change this, although it might put the foreclosure on hold for a while.

Sometimes, a mortgage holder refuses to accept payments from a debtor who is in bankruptcy. If you make your payments but the lender rejects them, create a separate bank account to deposit the payments into each month—and be prepared to make your account current whenever the lender agrees to start accepting payments. Why create a separate bank account? If you leave that money in your regular bank account, you might end up spending it on other necessities, and not have it available at the end of your bankruptcy. For example, if your mortgage payment is $1,500 a month, and your bankruptcy lasts four months, you'll owe $6,000. That's a lot of money that you might be tempted to spend unless you lock it away in its own dedicated account.

Liens on Your House

Chapter 7 bankruptcy won't eliminate liens on your home that were created with your consent or nonconsensual liens, such as tax liens or mechanics' liens. If you've pledged your home as security for loans other than your mortgage—for example, you took out a home equity loan or second mortgage—or a creditor such as the IRS has recorded a lien, those creditors, too, have claims against your home.

If there is a judgment lien on your home—that is, if a creditor sued you, obtained a court judgment, and recorded a lien at the land records office—you might be able to get rid of the lien entirely without paying a cent to the lienholder. And, in some states, if your home is sold in bankruptcy, you will get your homestead amount ahead of secured creditors holding judicial liens.

You can get rid of the lien created by a judgment by filing a Motion to Avoid a Judicial Lien on Real Estate or possibly another action. Lien avoidance is explained in Ch. 5.

Keeping Your House

Even if you keep up with your mortgage payments, you might still lose your house unless a homestead exemption protects your equity. If you were to sell your home today, without filing for bankruptcy, the money raised by the sale would go first to the mortgage lender to pay off the mortgage, then to lienholders to pay off the liens, and finally to pay off the costs of sale and any taxes due. If anything were left over, you'd get it.

How a Homestead Exemption Works: An Example

This chart applies only to those states that use dollar-amount homestead exemptions. If your state bases the homestead exemption on acreage, your lot size will determine whether or not you keep your home.

This example is based on a home worth $100,000, with a $35,000 homestead exemption.

If you have nonexempt equity, the trustee will sell the home. Here, the homeowner's total equity is $60,000 ($100,000 [value of home] − $40,000 [mortgages and liens against home]). The homeowner's nonexempt equity is $25,000 ($60,000 [total equity] − $35,000 [homestead exemption]). Because the home has $25,000 in nonexempt equity, the trustee will sell the house and use the nonexempt equity to pay unsecured creditors.

If you don't have any nonexempt equity, the trustee won't sell your home. Here, the homeowner's total equity is $30,000 ($100,000 [value of home] − $70,000 [mortgages and liens against home]). The trustee would have to give the homeowner $35,000 for the homestead exemption, leaving no nonexempt equity for creditors ($30,000 [total equity] − $35,000 [homestead exemption] = less than zero).

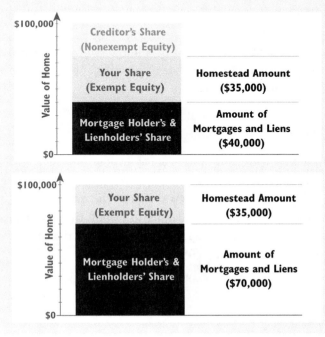

If you file for bankruptcy and the trustee sells your house, the creditors will get paid in pretty much the same order, with one big difference. In a bankruptcy sale, whatever is left after the mortgages, liens, sales costs, and taxes have been paid goes not to you, but to your unsecured creditors—unless a homestead exemption entitles you to some or all of it.

As a practical matter, the trustee won't bother to sell your house if there will be nothing left over for your unsecured creditors. Thus, the amount of your homestead exemption often determines whether or not you'll lose your home in bankruptcy.

If the bankruptcy trustee calculates that there would be excess proceeds from a home sale to give to your unsecured creditors, the trustee will, almost always, take your home and sell it to get that money, unless you can repurchase it—that is, pay the trustee the amount that your unsecured creditors would get from the sale.

We explain how to figure out whether a homestead exemption will prevent the trustee from selling your home in "Will You Lose Your Home?" below.

If You're Behind on Your Mortgage Payments

If you're behind on your mortgage payments but want to keep your house, your first strategy should be to negotiate with the lender and try other nonbankruptcy alternatives discussed in this section.

Chapter 7 bankruptcy's automatic stay won't prevent foreclosure if you fall behind on your mortgage payments. At most, it will postpone foreclosure for a few months. Some lenders will just wait out your bankruptcy (a few months) and then proceed with the foreclosure. Others will file a motion to have the bankruptcy judge lift the automatic stay so that foreclosure can proceed. If successful, doing so will cut short the automatic stay's protection and allow the lender to process the foreclosure.

If you can come up with the money to catch up on your arrearages before the hearing on the motion to lift the stay (this usually means within about 45 days of your bankruptcy filing), you might be able to prevent the foreclosure. But you risk having the trustee question whether you are genuinely bankrupt if you can raise such a large sum of money post-filing. If you can get enough money to bring your mortgage current, then a better course of action is to delay filing for bankruptcy until you pay off the arrearages.

The bottom line: Usually if you want to keep your house, it's best to either wait to file for Chapter 7 until your mortgage payments are current, or file a Chapter 13 bankruptcy and catch up with the payments over time.

RESOURCE

What to do if foreclosure looms. If you're facing foreclosure, you'll want all the help you can get. You can start with *The Foreclosure Survival Guide*, by Amy Loftsgordon (Nolo).). If you're going to try to negotiate a workout with your lender, consider seeking help from a nonprofit, HUD-approved housing counselor. (See "How to Find a HUD-Approved Housing Counselor," below.) You should also consider talking to an attorney to find out whether you have grounds to fight the foreclosure in court, and how filing for bankruptcy might affect your situation. Some lawyers specialize in foreclosure, and most bankruptcy lawyers understand foreclosure defenses. (See Ch. 10 for information on finding an attorney.)

Beware of Scam Artists When Seeking Help With a Foreclosure or Loan Modification

As foreclosures mushroomed in 2008 and beyond, many lawyers and people associated with the real estate business starting offering advice and help on how to fight foreclosures and obtain mortgage modifications from the bank— usually for a steep up-front fee in the neighborhood of $3,000 and up. In many cases, these providers failed to deliver promised results, and instead, kept all or most of the money. While the FTC and laws of some states have made it illegal to take money up front to provide these services, most states (and the FTC) make exceptions for lawyers. Some businesses get around the laws by operating under a lawyer's umbrella.

The fact is, the help you can get from HUD-approved housing counselors is usually as good (or better) as the help you get from for-profit businesses. And the HUD-approved counseling is free. As for foreclosure prevention, you should be able to get a systematic analysis of your case from a real estate or bankruptcy lawyer for less than $1,000—much less in most cases.

Negotiating With the Lender

If you've missed a few mortgage payments, most lenders will be willing to negotiate. What the lender agrees to will depend on your credit history, the reason for your missed payments, and your financial prospects.

> **EXAMPLE:** Doug missed a few house payments because he had a car accident and couldn't work for two months, but he'll be back to work soon. The bank will probably work out a deal with Doug rather than immediately move to foreclose.

Mortgage Modifications

In 2009, the federal government launched an ambitious program designed to get banks to modify the repayment terms of some mortgages so that homeowners would have a better shot at avoiding foreclosure. Known as HAMP (Home Affordable Modification Program), this program encouraged mortgage servicers (banks and companies who manage your mortgage for the mortgage owner) to lower your payments so that your mortgage payment is not more than 31% of your gross income, and add any arrearage on your current mortgage payments to the end of your mortgage term.

HAMP, however, expired at the end of 2016. To replace it, Fannie Mae and Freddie Mac developed the Flex Modification program. This program is similar to HAMP, but allows servicers to also consider how many days delinquent you are and the value of your home. Eligible borrowers can expect to receive around a 20% payment reduction through a Flex Modification.

If you don't qualify for a Flex Modification, you might have other options.

- **Lender/servicer modification procedures.** Almost all of the larger mortgage servicers (and some smaller ones too) have their own modification procedures.
- **State foreclosure prevention mediation.** In response to the foreclosure crisis, some states have implemented mediation programs for those in foreclosure.

- **State hardest hit funds.** The Housing Finance Agency Innovation Fund for the Hardest Hit Housing Markets provided money to individual states to assist homeowners in need. If your state is a recipient, you may be able to get mortgage payment assistance, a principal reduction, or other help. While these programs have been extended through 2020, some have closed early because they ran out of money. If your state has a hardest hit fund program that's still open, it's a good idea to apply for assistance as soon as possible.

For more on these and other options, visit Nolo.com's Foreclosure Center or get *The Foreclosure Survival Guide*, by Amy Loftsgordon (Nolo).

In addition, here are some workout options your lender might agree to:

- Let you pay back missed payments over a few months. For example, if your monthly payment is $1,000 and you missed two payments ($2,000), the lender might let you pay $1,500 for four months.
- Reduce or suspend your regular payments for a specified time, then add a portion of your overdue amount to your regular payments later on.
- Extend the length of your loan and add the missed payments at the end.
- For a period of time, suspend the amount of your monthly payment that goes toward the principal, and require payment of interest, taxes, and insurance only.
- Refinance your loan to reduce future monthly payments.
- Let you sell the property for less than you owe the lender and waive the rest of the loan (called the "deficiency") in a "short sale." Short sales can have negative tax ramifications when the lender waives all or part of the deficiency, so it is important to consult with an accountant or a tax professional before choosing this option.

Before you contact the servicer about a workout, you should prepare information about your situation, including:

- an assessment of your current financial situation and a reasonable budget for the future

- a plan to deal with other essential debts, such as utility bills and car payments
- a hardship letter explaining why you fell behind on your mortgage (for example, you went through a divorce or you had unexpected medical bills)
- information about the property and its value, and
- information about your loan and the amount of the default.

You should also find out whether your mortgage is insured by the Federal Housing Administration (FHA), or guaranteed by the U.S. Department of Veterans Affairs (VA). Borrowers with these types of mortgages have some special rights that those with "conventional" mortgages don't have.

Be advised that modifications are not for everyone—nor will lenders always agree to a modification. Be realistic about your situation before you approach the lender. If it is likely that you will lose your house because of your dire financial situation or because you have other pressing financial problems, it doesn't make sense to keep paying your mortgage even if you are able to get a modification.

How to Find a HUD-Approved Housing Counselor

Here are some ways to find a housing counselor in your area:

- Visit the Making Home Affordable website, www.makinghomeaffordable.gov (the site still offers helpful information).
- The federal Department of Housing and Urban Development (HUD) can help you find a counselor. Call 800-569-4287.
- The Homeownership Preservation Foundation website, www.995hope.org, offers free counseling, among other things. Or you can call 888-995-HOPE and talk with someone.
- The National Foundation for Credit Counseling will get you to a nonprofit counselor (typically HUD certified) through its toll-free hotline, 800-388-2227.

If the Lender Starts to Foreclose

If your debt problems look severe or long-lasting, the lender may take steps toward foreclosure. In most states, before the lender can foreclose, it has to accelerate your loan. This means that the lender declares that you have defaulted and calls for immediate payment of the entire loan, as provided by the terms of the loan agreement.

> **EXAMPLE:** Don and Louise bought a $100,000 home by putting $20,000 down and getting an $80,000 mortgage. Their monthly house payments are $900. After making their payments consistently for several years, they miss four payments in a row. The bank accelerates the loan and demands the entire $76,284 balance left on the loan. Because Don and Louise can't come up with the money, the bank begins foreclosure proceedings.

In most states, this acceleration can be canceled if you are able to make up all the missed payments plus fees and interest; this is called "reinstating" the loan. In many cases, it's the add-ons that prevent homeowners from reinstating their loans. If the add-ons are what's standing between you and reinstatement, consider using a HUD-approved housing counselor to help you negotiate a settlement with the lender. Different states have different time limits for reinstatement. Your counselor should know the time limit for your state; you can also find this information in *The Foreclosure Survival Guide,* by Amy Loftsgordon (Nolo).

Foreclosure can take anywhere from several months to several years, depending on where you live and your individual circumstances. As a result of the federal Dodd–Frank Act, the Consumer Financial Protection Bureau implemented servicing rules, one of which usually prevents a mortgage servicer from moving forward with a foreclosure until a homeowner is delinquent more than 120 days. This waiting period gives the owner time to explore ways to get caught up on missed payments. Your servicer must send you information explaining your right to apply for a workout program. Also, once you submit a completed application, it must be evaluated before the foreclosure can move forward under state law.

You also have several other options:

- Sell your house. If you don't get any offers that will cover what you owe your lender, a short sale might be possible.

- Get another lender to give you a loan that pays off all or part of the first loan and puts you on a new schedule of monthly payments. If the original lender has accelerated the loan, you'll need to refinance the entire balance of the loan to prevent foreclosure. If the lender hasn't accelerated the loan, however, you can prevent foreclosure simply by paying the missed payments, taxes, and insurance, plus interest. But be careful when deciding whether to refinance. In many cases, refinancing hurts more than it helps. Many lenders have figured out clever ways to hide high costs and fees in refinancing deals.

- If you are at least 62 years old and have significant equity in your home, consider getting a reverse mortgage. You can use this type of loan to pay off the lender and receive some money each month, based on your equity. Be aware, though, that reverse mortgages can be risky and aren't a good idea for everybody. These kinds of loans have many downsides, such as taking part or all of your equity, leaving less value for you to pass on to your heirs at your death or less money if you decide to sell the home, as well as high fees.

- File for Chapter 13 bankruptcy if you can't come up with the needed money in a lump sum right away but you can propose a feasible repayment plan. Chapter 13 bankruptcy allows you to "cure the default"—make up missed payments over time and make the regular payments as they come due.

- Use Chapter 13 bankruptcy to get rid of liens. If you have a second or third mortgage that is no longer secured because of the depreciation in your property's value, filing for Chapter 13 bankruptcy allows you to remove them in many, but not all, courts. In some circumstances, it might also allow you to modify a first mortgage down to the property's actual value (for the most part, though, bankruptcy can't be used to modify residential mortgages in this manner).

Defenses to Foreclosure

You may be able to delay or stop the foreclosure if you have defenses to paying the mortgage or if the lender has not properly followed state foreclosure procedures. If you think you might have a defense to foreclosure, contact a lawyer immediately. Some possible defenses are:

- **Interest rate that violates state or federal law.** Some states limit how much interest can be charged on a loan. Federal law prohibits lenders from making deceptive or false representations about the loan and from charging high closing costs and fees. If your interest is very high or your lender didn't tell you the truth about the terms of your loan, consult a lawyer.
- **Violations of the federal Truth in Lending law.** The federal Truth in Lending law, and an amendment known as the Home Ownership and Equity Protection Act (HOEPA), require the lender to give you certain information about your loan before you sign the papers. If the lender failed to provide this information, you might be able to cancel (rescind) the mortgage. But this doesn't apply to loans you used to purchase your home.
- **The servicer made a serious mistake with your account.** You might be able to challenge the foreclosure if, for example, the servicer charged you excessive fees after you fell behind in payments or charged fees that weren't authorized by the loan contract—especially if the servicer then substantially overstated the amount you would have to pay to reinstate your loan. Mistakes about the payment amount to reinstate are particularly serious.
- **Failure to follow foreclosure procedures.** Each state requires servicers and lenders to follow specific procedures when foreclosing on a home. If the servicer or lender doesn't follow these rules (for example, by not giving proper notice of the foreclosure or failing to inform you of certain rights), you might be able to delay the foreclosure.

How to Raise a Foreclosure Defense

About half the states require that foreclosures go through court. The other half allow foreclosure to be brought outside of court under what's known as a "power of sale" clause in the mortgage or deed of trust. If you're facing foreclosure in a state that uses court, you can raise your defense just as you would in any other civil action. If your foreclosure occurs outside of court (called a nonjudicial foreclosure), you have to bring your own action in civil court to stop the foreclosure and then offer your defense.

 RESOURCE
Learn about your options in foreclosure. For detailed information about your options if you are struggling to pay your mortgage or already in foreclosure, get *The Foreclosure Survival Guide*, by Amy Loftsgordon (Nolo). It covers mortgage modification options, foreclosure defenses, short sales, deeds in lieu, and more.

If Foreclosure Is Unavoidable

If you've exhausted the suggestions described above, you have equity in your home, and it looks like foreclosure is inevitable, you should know that losing your home in a bankruptcy sale will often be a better deal than losing it in a foreclosure sale, for two reasons.

First, a forced sale of your home in bankruptcy is supervised by the bankruptcy trustee, who will want to sell the house for as much as possible. In a foreclosure sale, the foreclosing creditor cares only about getting enough to cover its own debt. If you have a homestead exemption on the house, the amount you get increases as the amount your home is sold for goes up.

Second, debtors are rarely entitled to the homestead exemption if the house is sold through foreclosure. In a bankruptcy sale, however, you are entitled to your homestead amount in cash, if there are proceeds left over after the secured creditors have been paid off.

Benefits of Filing Bankruptcy Before the Foreclosure Sale

If you will ultimately lose your home to foreclosure, it often makes sense to file for bankruptcy before the foreclosure sale is final in order to avoid a possible tax hit. Here's why.

If you lose your home to foreclosure, you might end up owing a deficiency. The deficiency is the difference between your mortgage balance and the foreclosure sale price (minus costs and fees related to the sale). For example, if you owed $400,000 on your mortgage, your home sold for $300,000 and the servicer incurred $10,000 to sell the property, you will owe a deficiency in the amount of $90,000 ($400,000 - $300,000 - $10,000).

What happens next depends a lot on the state you live in so it is important to consult your local laws. In some states, your lender can choose whether to come after you for the deficiency or to forgive the debt. In other states, such as California, lenders cannot collect deficiencies for loans used to purchase the property, which are called "recourse" or "purchase money" loans. Because there is no deficiency to collect, so to speak, taxes do not attach. However, this is not true for junior loans used for things other than purchasing the property, such as for remodeling or paying bills. The deficiency rules apply.

Regardless of the state you live in, if, after the foreclosure sale, your lender forgives a deficiency, the government considers the forgiven debt to be taxable income, meaning that you must pay tax on this amount at the end of the year. If the amount of forgiven debt is large, you'll end up with a big tax debt, especially if the extra "income" pushes you into a higher tax bracket.

For many years, most homeowners didn't have to worry about this tax hit because of the Mortgage Forgiveness Debt Relief Act, which absolved people of tax liability for forgiven mortgage debt (assuming the debt was taken out to purchase or improve a principal residence). The protections under the Act however, came to an end.

One of the benefits of filing for Chapter 7 bankruptcy *before* your home forecloses is that it wipes out the debt before any tax obligation attaches. By contrast, once you owe the tax, filing for bankruptcy alone won't get rid of it. There are ways you might still be able to avoid paying it (for example, you meet certain criteria for insolvency), but you'll need the help of an accountant or lawyer to handle the extra steps. Given the uncertainty, it might be better to avoid the tax problem altogether by timing your bankruptcy filing accordingly.

One final note—this stuff gets complicated. If you think you might be on the hook for a tax bill, talk to a lawyer.

In the end, what happens to your home will be up to the bankruptcy trustee. If there is enough equity in your home to produce some money for your unsecured creditors, the trustee will sell it, pay off the mortgage and other lienholders, give you your exemption, and distribute the rest. If there is not enough equity to generate money for your unsecured creditors, the trustee will release his or her authority over the home (called abandonment) and let the mortgage holder pursue any remedies available to it, which will most likely result in foreclosure if you owe an arrearage. In many cases, it's a good idea to give the trustee a chance to sell it and recoup your homestead exemption amount.

Getting Your Equity Out of Your Home

Many people who fall behind on their mortgage payments discover that the longer they can stall the foreclosure, the longer they can live in the home for free. In essence, this is a backdoor way to get a sizable chunk of equity out of your home without selling it or taking it into bankruptcy. For example, if your mortgage payment is $1,500 a month and you manage to live in the house for a year without making your payments, you've pulled the equivalent of $18,000 equity out of your home. And, if you have no equity in your home—even in a home without equity.

The bottom line is that remaining in your home without having to make any payment is a golden opportunity to save some money to help you transition into future housing.

Will You Lose Your Home?

If you file for Chapter 7 bankruptcy, the fact that you've kept up on your house payments might not protect you from losing it. The trustee will still have your house sold if doing so will produce some cash to pay your unsecured creditors (and you aren't able to pay the trustee an equivalent amount). If the sale won't produce cash, the trustee will not take the house.

Whether the sale will produce cash depends on two factors:
- whether you have any equity in your home, and
- if so, whether that equity is exempt.

Use the Homeowners' Worksheet found on the companion page (www.nolo.com/back-of-book/HFB.html) to figure out the answers to these questions. Here are the instructions for filling out the form.

Part I: Do You Have Any Equity in Your Home?

Line 1: Estimated market value of your home

Estimate how much money your home could produce in a quick, as-is sale. The trustee will often use this value in deciding whether to sell the home. However, the trustee might use the full market value of your property. So, if there is a significant difference between the quick sale value and the full value of the home, use the latter to be on the safe side. To get a rough idea of what your home is worth in either type of sale, ask a realtor what comparable homes in your neighborhood have sold for. Or look in newspaper real estate sections. You can also generate rough home valuation estimates from websites such as www.zillow.com, www.realtor.com, www.trulia.com, or www.redfin.com. As stated, these estimates are rough. They won't replace the opinion of a professional appraiser.

Line 2: Costs of sale

Costs of sale vary, but they tend to be about 6%–8% of the sales price. While you aren't supposed to subtract the costs of sale from the fair market value in your bankruptcy paperwork, the trustee likely will when determining whether to take your home. If you want to err on the side of caution, put "0" in this blank.

Line 3: Amount owed on mortgages and other loans

Enter the amount needed to pay off your mortgage and any other loans that are secured by the home as collateral. If you can't come up with a reasonably reliable estimate, contact each lender and ask how much is necessary to cancel the debt.

Line 4: Amount of liens

Enter the amount of all liens recorded against your home other than liens created by mortgages and home equity loans. Liens are claims against your home that have been recorded with the land records office. The three most common types of liens are tax liens, mechanics' liens, and judgment liens. Tax liens can be recorded against your home by the county, state, or federal government for failure to pay property, income, or other taxes. People who do work on your home and claim that you didn't pay them what you owe can record mechanics' or materialmen's liens against your home. And judgment liens can be recorded by anyone who has sued you and won.

If you think there might be liens on your home, visit the county recorder or land records office. Tell the clerk you'd like to check your title for liens. The clerk should direct you to an index that lists all property in the county by the owner's last name. Next to your home should be a list of any liens recorded against it.

Line 5 = Line 2 + Line 3 + Line 4

Add up the total costs that would have to be paid if you were to sell your home.

Line 6 (your equity) = Line 1 − Line 5

If Line 1 is more than Line 5, subtract Line 5 from Line 1, and put the result on Line 6. For bankruptcy purposes, this is your equity in the property—that is, the amount that would be left over after all mortgages, loans, liens, and costs of sale are paid.

If the amount on Line 5 is more than the amount on Line 1, you have no equity; you can stop here. There will be no reason for the trustee to take your home in bankruptcy—once all of the liens and mortgage(s) are paid off, there would be nothing left to distribute to your unsecured creditors.

If you do have equity, go on to Part II to determine how much of it is protected by an applicable exemption.

> TIP
> **Legal research note.** If you do legal research on equity and homestead exemptions, note that the word "equity" has multiple meanings. "Unencumbered" equity is the value of your home, minus the mortgage and the liens you can't get rid of. (That's what we mean when we say equity.) Then there's "encumbered" equity, which is the value of your home minus only the mortgage. Sometimes courts refer to encumbered equity simply as "equity."

The Trustee's Power to Eliminate Liens— And How It May Cost You Your Home

When property has liens on it for more than the property is worth, it is "undersecured." If a trustee sells undersecured property, there won't be enough money to pay off all liens, which means that one or more lienholders will be left with nothing. And there certainly won't be any money to pay unsecured creditors, who get paid only after all lienholders have been paid off.

The trustee's job is to find money to pay unsecured creditors, so the trustee won't bother selling an under-secured home. The picture changes, however, if the trustee can knock out enough lienholders to free up some equity. Once that happens, it might make sense to sell the home.

All states have laws specifying the procedures that must be followed to make a mortgage or another secured agreement or lien valid (called "perfecting" the lien). These typically include a proper acknowledgement signed in front of a notary public and recorded in the local land records office. While real estate practitioners usually have a firm grasp of these rules, mistakes can happen. If a lien hasn't been perfected, the trustee might seek to knock it out, turning an undersecured property into one that, when sold, will yield some cash after the remaining lienholders get their share.

Before you file for bankruptcy, check on the legal status of any liens you are relying on to save your home or other property. In particular, make sure the document creating the lien is recorded and contains a proper acknowledgement. If not, you might have more equity than you think—and the trustee may have a greater incentive to sell your home.

Also, keep in mind that loans between friends and family are the first place that trustee looks when it comes to unperfected liens. The trustee knows that it's easy for laypeople to miss a step when documenting these transactions.

Part II: If You Have Equity, Is It Protected by an Exemption?

We're assuming that, in Part I, you found that you have some amount of home equity. Here in Part II, we'll determine how much of that equity you can claim as exempt—that is, how much of it you're entitled to keep.

Before you can figure out how much of your equity is protected by an exemption, you must determine which set of exemptions to use. The new bankruptcy law imposes strict domicile requirements on filers seeking to use a homestead exemption. Filers who don't meet these requirements may have to use the exemptions of the state where they used to live—and will be subject to a $170,350 limit on the amount of equity they can exempt. (Because many states protect less than $170,350 in home equity, this cap won't affect the majority of filers.) The purpose of these rules is to prevent filers from moving to another state to take advantage of its better homestead protection.

Here are the rules:

- If you bought your home at least 40 months ago, you can use the homestead exemption of the state where your home is.
- If you bought your home at least two years ago, you can use the homestead exemption of the state where your home is. However, if you bought your home within the last 40 months, your homestead exemption is capped at $170,350, unless you bought the home with the proceeds from the sale of another home in the same state.
- If you bought your home within the last two years, then you must use the homestead exemption of the state where you were living for the better part of the 180-day period that ended two years before your filing date. And you are still subject to the $170,350 limit.

EXAMPLE 1: After moving from Vermont to Boston, Julius and his family buy a fine old Boston home for $700,000. A little more than two years later, after borrowing heavily against the home because of financial reversals, Julius files for bankruptcy. At that point, he owns $250,000 in equity. Although the Massachusetts homestead exemption of $500,000 would cover Julius's equity, he can claim only $170,350 of that exemption because he moved to Massachusetts from another state within the last 40 months.

EXAMPLE 2: Eighteen months ago, Fred moved from Florida to Nevada, where he purchased his current home with $400,000 he received from an inheritance. Fred files for bankruptcy in his current home state of Nevada. Because Fred lived in Florida for two years prior to moving to Nevada, he must use Florida's homestead exemption—and because Fred hasn't lived in Nevada for 40 months, his exemption is subject to the $170,350 cap. The cap imposes an extreme penalty on Fred. Florida offers an unlimited homestead exemption, while Nevada's homestead exemption is $550,000. Because of the cap, however, Fred can protect only $170,350 of his equity, which means that the trustee will undoubtedly sell his home, give Fred his $170,350, and use the rest to pay off his unsecured creditors.

EXAMPLE 3: Jessica moves from New Jersey to Vermont, where she buys a home for $250,000, with a $225,000 mortgage. Less than two years after moving, Jessica files for bankruptcy. Because Jessica was living in New Jersey for years before moving to Vermont, she must use either New Jersey's state homestead allowance or the federal homestead allowance (New Jersey gives filers a choice of exemptions). New Jersey provides no homestead exemption at all, but the federal homestead exemption is approximately $25,150. It isn't hard for Jessica to figure out that she should use the federal exemption system if protecting the equity in her home is her top priority. However, if Jessica's personal property is more important to her, and she would be able to keep more of it using the New Jersey state exemptions, she might choose the state exemptions and let the trustee sell her home.

How Appreciation Might Affect the Homestead Cap

As explained above, your homestead exemption will be capped at $170,350 if you acquired your home within the 1,215 days (approximately 40 months) before filing for bankruptcy and you did not purchase it with the proceeds from selling another home in the same state.

But what if you have owned your home for more than 1,215 days, and the *value* of your home has appreciated significantly within the 40 month period prior to the bankruptcy filing? Does the $170,350 cap apply to that appreciated value? Some courts have said "no." (See, for example, *In re Rasmussen*, 349 B.R. 747 (Bankr. M.D. Fla. 2006). Other courts, however, have held that the cap will be applied in this situation. (*In re Nestlen*, 441 B.R. 135 (B.A.P. 10th Cir. 2010)).

If you are filing in a state that allows you to choose between the state and federal exemption lists, you are always entitled to use the federal exemptions, regardless of how long you have lived in the state. The federal homestead exemption allows you to protect about $25,150 in equity, (and you can exempt an additional $1,325 by using the wildcard exemption) and married couples can double that amount.

Homes in Revocable Living Trusts

Revocable living trusts have become a popular way to pass valuable property on when people die. The property owner creates a trust document naming him- or herself as the trustee, another person as successor trustee to take over when the owner dies, and typically one or more beneficiaries to receive the property upon the owner's death. When the original property owner dies, the successor trustee steps in and distributes the property to the beneficiaries. All of this happens without going through court. (It's called a living trust because it takes effect during the property owner's life, not when he or she dies; it's revocable because the property owner can undo it anytime.)

Legally, the trustee owns the property in the trust, although it's common to refer to the trust itself as the legal owner of the property. So, if John Henry creates a revocable living trust and puts his house in it, he will be the initial trustee and own his house as "trustee of the John Henry Revocable Living Trust." If John Henry files for bankruptcy, can he claim a homestead exemption for the house he owns as trustee?

Almost every court to consider this issue has allowed homestead exemptions to be claimed on homes held in typical revocable living trusts. When you create a revocable living trust, you retain actual ownership of the property even though it's titled as a trust rather than outright ownership, so it's only fair to allow you to claim an exemption. Despite this court trend, however, it's probably safest to remove the property from a living trust by executing a new deed (for yourself as trustee(s) to yourself as an individual or a married couple), if your court allows it—talk with a local bankruptcy lawyer. After your bankruptcy, you can execute a new deed placing the property back in the trust.

CAUTION

The cap also applies to filers who commit certain types of misconduct.
No matter how long you have lived in the state where you are filing, your homestead
exemption will be capped at $170,350 if you have been convicted of a felony
demonstrating that your bankruptcy filing is abusive, you owe a debt arising from
a securities act violation, or you have committed a crime or an intentional, willful,
or reckless act that killed or caused serious personal injury to someone in the last
five years. The court might decide to lift the cap if it finds that the homestead
exemption is reasonably necessary for you to support yourself and your dependents.

**Line 7:   Does the available homestead exemption
         protect your kind of dwelling?**

Only two states do not have a homestead exemption. If you are using the
exemptions in one of these two states, enter $0 on Line 11.

States With No Homestead Exemption	
New Jersey	Pennsylvania

For all other states, check the table on the companion page to see if your
type of dwelling is protected. Some types of dwellings may not be covered,
including:

- **Mobile homes.** Most states specifically include mobile homes in their
  homestead exemptions. Other states include any "real or personal
  property used as a residence." This would include a trailer, mobile
  home, or houseboat, as long as you live in it. Some states don't
  detail the types of property that qualify for homestead protection.
  If your mobile home does not qualify for a homestead exemption, it
  would be protected only by the exemption for a "motor vehicle."
- **Co-ops or condominiums.** Some homestead laws specifically cover co-
  ops or use language that says the exemption protects "any property
  used as a dwelling."
- **Apartments.** Most homestead statutes do not protect apartments,
  though a few do.

If your type of dwelling is not covered, enter $0 on Line 11.

If it is unclear whether your type of dwelling is covered by the available homestead exemption, you may need to do some legal research. (See Ch. 10 for help getting started.)

Line 8:   Do you have to file a "declaration of homestead" to claim the exemption?

States That May Require a Declaration of Homestead		
Alabama	Montana	Utah
Idaho	Nevada	Virginia
Massachusetts	Texas	Washington

To claim a homestead exemption in Virginia, you must have a declaration of homestead on file with the land records office for the county where the property is located when you file for bankruptcy. The other states on this list vary in what they require and when. If you are using exemptions for one of these states, the safest approach is to file a declaration of homestead.

Requiring you to record a declaration before you can get the benefit of a homestead exemption might violate the bankruptcy laws. (*In re Leicht*, 222 B.R. 670 (B.A.P. 1st Cir. 1998).) Regardless of the legalities, however, you will be best served by filing your declaration of homestead before you file for bankruptcy.

Other states allow (but do not require) you to file a homestead declaration in certain circumstances. In Texas, for example, you can file a homestead declaration to claim protection for property you own but are not currently living in.

> **EXAMPLE:** John and Molly live in Texas. They have retired and have decided to rent out their spacious country home and move to an apartment closer to town. They can still claim their country home as their homestead by recording a declaration of homestead with the land records office in the county where their country home is.

In some states, a "declared" homestead offers additional protection in situations other than bankruptcy. Also, if you own more than one piece of real estate, some states allow a creditor to require you to file a declaration of homestead to clarify which property you are claiming as your homestead.

Line 9: Is the homestead exemption based on lot size?

Most states place a limit on the value of property you can claim as your homestead exemption, but a few states have no such limits. Find out what kind of homestead exemption system your state uses by looking at the lists below.

Unlimited Homestead Exemption
District of Columbia

If you are lucky enough to be using the District of Columbia exemptions, congratulations: You can skip the rest of this chapter. Your home is not at risk in a Chapter 7 bankruptcy.

Homestead Exemption Based on Lot Size Only		
Arkansas	Kansas	South Dakota
Florida	Oklahoma	Texas
Iowa		

In these states, you can easily determine whether your home is exempt. The homestead exemption is based simply on acreage. Look at the exemption table on the companion page for the acreage limitation for the state. (In Oklahoma, if you use more than 25% of the property as a business, the one-acre urban homestead exemption cannot exceed $5,000.)

If your property is smaller than the maximum allowable acreage, your home is fully protected. You can skip the rest of this chapter.

If your property exceeds the maximum allowable acreage, the trustee will sell the excess acreage if you have any equity in it unless you are able to buy it back from the trustee for a negotiated amount. Enter $0 in Line 11 of the worksheet.

Homestead Exemption Based on Lot Size and Equity		
Alabama	Michigan	Nebraska
Hawaii	Minnesota	Oregon
Louisiana	Mississippi	

These states use the size of your lot and the amount of your equity to determine whether your home is exempt. First look at the exemption table on the companion page for the state acreage limitation and enter it on Line 9.

If your property exceeds the maximum allowable acreage, the trustee will want to sell the excess acreage (or get the equivalent in value from you) if you have enough equity in it.

If your lot size is within the allowed acreage, your exemption is determined by the equity amount limit. Proceed to Line 10.

Homestead Exemption Based on Equity Alone		
Federal exemptions	Maine	Ohio
Alaska	Maryland	Rhode Island
Arizona	Massachusetts	South Carolina
California	Missouri	Tennessee
Colorado	Montana	Utah
Connecticut	Nevada	Vermont
Georgia	New Hampshire	Virginia
Idaho	New Mexico	Washington
Illinois	New York	West Virginia
Indiana	North Carolina	Wisconsin
Kentucky	North Dakota	Wyoming

If the state homestead exemption is based on equity alone, or if you are using the federal exemptions, go to Line 10.

Line 10: Do you own the property with your spouse in "tenancy by the entirety"?

If you are married and live in the right state, you may be able to exclude your home from your bankruptcy estate—which means you can keep it, no matter how much equity you own or how large your state's homestead exemption is—if you own it with your spouse in tenancy by the entirety.

Tenancy by the entirety (TBE) is a form of property ownership available to married couples in about half of the states, some of which have laws that prohibit TBE property from being sold to pay debts that are owed by only one spouse. If this type of law applies, you can keep TBE property, regardless of its value. Some states also protect personal property owned in tenancy by the entirety, such as checking accounts.

States That Recognize TBE

These states recognize TBE home ownership (as does the District of Columbia): Alaska, Arkansas, Delaware, Florida, Hawaii, Illinois, Indiana, Kentucky, Maryland, Massachusetts, Michigan, Missouri, New Jersey, New York, North Carolina, Ohio, Oklahoma, Oregon, Pennsylvania (subject to conditions), Rhode Island, Tennessee, Vermont, Virginia, and Wyoming.

Unlike exemptions, tenancy by the entirety protection generally depends on the law of the state where your property is, not where you live. For example, if you and your spouse live in Minnesota but own a condo in Florida as tenants by the entirety, Florida law protects your condo from being seized to pay debts owed by only one spouse, even though Minnesota law offers no such protection.

To qualify for this type of property protection, all of the following must be true:

- You are married.
- You are filing for bankruptcy alone, without your spouse. If you file jointly, your TBE property is not protected.

- All of the debts you are trying to discharge are yours alone; none are debts that you owe jointly with your spouse.
- You and your spouse own property in one of the states that recognize TBE (see above).
- You and your spouse own the home as tenants by the entirety. In some of these states, the law presumes that married people own their property as tenants by the entirety, unless they specify that they wish to own it in some other way (as joint tenants, for example).

If you meet these five criteria, this protection could be extremely valuable to you. You may want to see a bankruptcy attorney to figure out the best way to take full advantage of it.

Line 11: Is the dollar amount of the homestead exemption limited?

Most states place a dollar limit on the homestead exemption. For example, New York allows you to exempt between $85,400 and $170,825 in equity depending on which county you live in, while Massachusetts allows you to exempt up to $500,000. If the state homestead exemption you're using works this way, write down the amount of equity the exemption protects on Line 11. If your state allows you to use the federal exemptions and you plan to do so, write down the federal exemption instead. (See the exemption tables on the companion page for these figures.)

In some states, if you own your home with your spouse and you file jointly for bankruptcy, you can each claim the full homestead exemption amount (called "doubling"). Other states don't allow doubling. When you look at the exemption table, check to see whether doubling is prohibited. If the chart doesn't mention it, assume that you and your spouse can double.

Line 12: Can you protect more equity with a wildcard exemption?

Some states allow you to add a wildcard exemption to the amount of your homestead exemption. Although these wildcard amounts are usually small, they might be enough to tip the balance in favor of keeping your home.

Check the exemption tables on the companion page to see whether the state where you're filing has a wildcard exemption you can use for real estate; if so, write the amount on Line 12. If your state doesn't have a wildcard exemption that you can use for real estate, leave this line blank.

Line 13: How much of your equity is protected?

Add Lines 11 (the state homestead exemption available to you) and 12 (any wildcard exemption you can add to your homestead exemption). This is the amount of home equity you can protect in bankruptcy. If you aren't subject to the $170,350 cap (explained above), write this amount on Line 13.

Your Homestead Exemption Might Be Reduced If You Converted Nonexempt Property in the Last Ten Years

The court can look back ten years before you filed for bankruptcy to find out whether you have converted nonexempt property to exempt property in order to defraud, hinder, cheat, or delay your creditors. If the court finds that you have converted property for one of these reasons, the value of your homestead exemption will be reduced by the value of the property you converted. (11 U.S.C. § 522(o); *In re Maronde*, 332 B.R. 593 (Bankr. D. Minn. 2005); *In re Lacounte*, 342 B.R. 809 (Bankr. D. Mont. 2005).)

> **EXAMPLE:** In 2010, Peter sold three nonexempt vehicles for a total of $10,000, which he used to pay down the equity on his home, which in turn increased the amount of equity he could claim as exempt. In 2019, Peter files for Chapter 7 bankruptcy. Depending on his reasons for selling the cars and paying down his mortgage, Peter could lose $10,000 worth of homestead protection. If Peter sold his cars so he could keep that money (by putting it into his home) and escape a judgment pending against him, the court might rule that he did so in order to defraud, hinder, cheat, or delay his creditors. If, on the other hand, Peter sold his cars because he legitimately wanted to pay down his mortgage, and he wasn't facing any creditor collection actions at the time, the court would probably find that the conversion was legitimate and would not reduce his homestead exemption.

The takeaway? If you undertook any "asset protection" activities in the last ten years and plan to claim a homestead exemption, talk to a lawyer before you file for bankruptcy.

If you are subject to the $170,350 cap, it might limit the amount of equity you can protect. If the total of Lines 11 and 12 doesn't exceed $170,350, it doesn't matter—the cap won't affect you, and you can write the total amount on Line 13. However, if the total is more than $170,350 and the cap applies, you can protect only $170,350 in equity. Even if your state law would otherwise allow you to take a larger exemption, you'll be limited to $170,350, and this is what you should write on Line 13.

Line 14: Is your home fully protected?

Subtract Line 13 from Line 6, and enter the total on Line 14. If you generate a negative number, all of your home equity should be protected by the applicable exemptions, if your estimates are correct. The trustee probably won't have your home sold, because there would be no proceeds left over (after your mortgage holder was paid off and you received your exempt amount of equity) to pay your unsecured creditors.

If, however, you generate a positive number, your equity exceeds the applicable exemption—in other words, you have unprotected equity in your home. If your estimates are right, the trustee can force the sale of your home to pay off your creditors, unless you can pay the trustee the value of your unprotected equity (perhaps by selling property that would otherwise be exempt). From the proceeds of the sale, your secured creditors will be paid the amounts of their mortgages, liens, and so forth; you will receive the amount of your exemption; and your unsecured creditors will get the rest.

If you have significant unprotected equity, you shouldn't file for Chapter 7 bankruptcy if you want to keep your house. The trustee will almost certainly sell your home, unless you can come up with the cash to keep it. You'll probably fare better—and hold on to your home longer—by using your equity to help pay off your debts, either directly or through a reverse mortgage, or to fund a Chapter 13 reorganization plan.

CAUTION

This worksheet is for estimate purposes only. If this worksheet shows that your equity is equal to or near the maximum amount of your state's homestead exemption, take note: The trustee can challenge the value you claim for your home and may determine that it's worth more than you think. If it looks like property values are rising, the trustee can also leave your case open for a reasonable time and wait to see whether the amount of appreciation will produce some nonexempt property. However at least one court has tacitly disapproved of this practice: It denied the trustee's motion to reopen a case to take advantage of a speculative increase in value in inherited property. (See *In re Saunders*, 2011 WL 671765 (Bankr. M.D. Ga. 2011).)

If these things happen, the trustee may seek to have your home sold. If your estimates show that you might be close to the exemption limit, get some advice from an experienced bankruptcy lawyer. Or, if it looks like the trustee is keeping your case open to capture appreciation in your home's value, ask an attorney to intervene and request a court order that the case be closed.

Secured Debts

This chapter explains how Chapter 7 bankruptcy affects secured debts: debts that give the creditor the right to take back a particular piece of property (the collateral) if you don't pay. We tell you how to recognize a secured debt when you see one and explain your options for dealing with secured debts (and the collateral that secures them) in bankruptcy. This chapter ends with step-by-step instructions on several simple procedures for handling secured debts. (If you opt for one of the more complex procedures, we explain the basics, but you'll probably need the help of a lawyer.)

Here's a brief summary of what's likely to happen to your secured debts and the property that secures them. First, the bad news:

- If you have a mortgage on your home or a home equity loan, bankruptcy will eliminate the debt, but not the underlying lien. The same is true for other secured debts such as car notes and installment payments on business equipment.
- If the government has a lien on your home for unpaid taxes, you can't remove it even if the tax debt itself is discharged in your bankruptcy.

Now, the good news:

- If your property has a lien on it because of a judgment that someone got against you in civil court (a money judgment), you can often get the lien removed. While you can do this yourself (it's called lien avoidance), it's typically more complicated than the bankruptcy itself.
- If you want to get out from under your loan on a car, house, or other property, and return the property without any further liability, you can do it in your bankruptcy case. This is called "surrendering" the collateral.
- If you owe a lot more than the collateral is worth, in some cases you can redeem it—that is, buy the property at its replacement value (what you could buy it for, considering its age and condition). You'll need to come up with a lump-sum payment or arrange for financing; creditors rarely accept installment payments.
- If you aren't in a position to redeem the property but are current on your payments, you might be able to get rid of (discharge) the underlying debt and keep your property by staying current on the payment. This is called the "ride-through" option.

- You can usually keep your car or other personal property by reaffirming the debt and remaining current on your payments. When you reaffirm a debt, you remain personally liable for the debt after the bankruptcy.

That's the big picture for the most common kinds of secured debts. Now it's time to learn the details about:

- which of your debts are secured
- which secured debts you can turn into unsecured ones (via lien avoidance), and
- how to deal with the obligations that remain secured.

RELATED TOPIC

Dealing with leased cars and other property. This chapter addresses secured debts—debts secured by collateral that the borrowers are purchasing or already own. However, many people choose to lease rather than buy their cars (and equipment and commercial space, if they are in business). You must list all leases on Schedule G, then indicate on your Statement of Intention whether you will assume the lease (meaning the lease will continue in effect as if you'd never filed for bankruptcy) or reject the lease (meaning you can walk away from all rights and obligations under the lease). In some bankruptcy courts, you'll also have to get approval from the court in a reaffirmation hearing to assume the lease.

See below for more on reaffirmation hearings. Also, some courts require a written "assumption agreement." You can find more information on leases in bankruptcy, and how to complete these forms, in Ch. 6.

TIP

Chapter 13 might provide better protection for secured property you want to keep. As explained in Ch. 1, debtors who use Chapter 13 can "cram down" many types of secured debts. In a cramdown, the court reduces the principal owed on the debt to the property's replacement value (and often reduces the interest rate, too). Although you can't cram down mortgages on your home or newer car loans, many other types of debts are eligible. If you are significantly upside down on a secured debt and you want to keep the collateral, review the material in Ch. 1 to make sure Chapter 7 is the right bankruptcy choice.

What Are Secured Debts?

A debt is secured if it is linked to a specific item of property, called collateral, that guarantees payment of the debt. Mortgages and car loans are the most common examples of secured debts. If you don't make your payments when they come due, the creditor can repossess the collateral. Often, the collateral is the property you purchased with the debt. For example, a mortgage typically gives the lender the right to foreclose on your home if you don't pay. However, you can also pledge property you already own as collateral for a debt. For example, assume you inherit a new car from a parent, and the car is paid for in full and worth $20,000. You can use the car as collateral for a bank loan—the bank will put a lien on the car as security for repayment of the loan.

An unsecured debt, on the other hand, is not secured by any type of collateral. Credit card and medical debts are typical examples of unsecured debt. Debts owed to lawyers and other professionals are also typically unsecured, as are "deficiency judgments" arising from foreclosures and car repossessions (if the lender sells the property for less than you owe, the remainder of the debt is called a deficiency judgment).

For bankruptcy purposes, there are two types of secured debts:
- those you agree to (called security interests), such as a mortgage or car note, and
- those created without your consent, such as a lien the IRS records against your property because you haven't paid your taxes.

Security Interests

Security interests are secured debts you have taken on voluntarily. If you pledge property as collateral for a loan or line of credit—that is, as a guarantee you will repay the debt—the lien on your property is a security interest. A security interest created to buy the collateral is called a purchase-money security interest. If you use property you already own as collateral (for instance, you refinance a car or pledge business assets as collateral for a loan), the debt is a non-purchase-money security interest. These two types of security interests might be treated somewhat differently in bankruptcy, as discussed later in this chapter.

Usually, you must repay a security interest by making installment payments. If you fail to make your payments on time or to comply with other terms of an agreement (for example, a mortgage lender's requirement that you carry homeowners' insurance), the lender or seller has the right to take back the property.

Lenders Must Perfect Their Security Interests

For bankruptcy purposes, security interest agreements qualify as secured debts only if they have been perfected: recorded with the appropriate local or state records office. For instance, to create a lien on real estate, the mortgage holder (the bank or another lender) must typically record it with the recorder's office for the county where the real estate is located. To perfect security interests in cars or business assets, the holder of the security interest must typically record it with whatever statewide or local agency handles recordings under the Uniform Commercial Code (these are called "UCC recordings," and they are usually filed with the secretary of state or department of state).

Common Examples of Security Interests

Many everyday loans qualify as security interests, including:

- **Mortgages.** Called deeds of trust in some states, mortgages are loans to buy or refinance a house or other real estate. The real estate is collateral for the loan. If you fail to pay, the lender can foreclose.
- **Home equity loans or HELOCs.** You can borrow against the equity in your home to remodel your home, or pay for other things, such as college tuition or a car. No matter how you spend the money, the house is collateral for the loan. If you fail to pay, the lender can foreclose.
- **Loans for cars, boats, tractors, motorcycles, or RVs.** Here, the vehicle is the collateral. If you fail to pay, the lender can repossess it.
- **Loans for business equipment, machines, or inventory.** The lender can repossess the property you pledged as collateral if you don't repay the loan.

- **Store charges with a security agreement.** Almost all purchases on store credit cards are unsecured, as are major credit cards. Some stores, however, print on the credit card slip or other receipt that the store "retains a security interest in all hard goods (durable goods) purchased," meaning that if you don't pay the credit card bill, the store will have the right to take back the purchased items. If you didn't specifically sign a security agreement setting out repayment terms, debts like these are generally considered unsecured debts in bankruptcy. However, if the store makes you sign an actual security agreement setting out the amount financed, the interest rate, and the number of payments (the basics required under the Truth in Lending Act for installment payments) when you use the store's credit card, the debt might be secured. For example, if you buy building supplies on credit, the store could require you to sign a security agreement in which you agree that the items purchased are collateral for your repayment. If you don't pay back the loan, the seller can repossess the property, as long as it perfects its security interest.
- **Title loans, or personal loans from banks, credit unions, or finance companies.** Often, you must pledge valuable personal property you already own, such as a paid-off motor vehicle, as collateral for this type of loan. This is a non-purchase-money secured debt, which will be treated as a secured debt in your bankruptcy as long as it has been perfected by the lender.

Nonconsensual Liens

In some circumstances, a creditor can get a lien on your property without your agreement. These are called nonconsensual liens. In theory, a nonconsensual lien gives the creditor the right to force a sale of the property to get paid. In practice, however, few creditors exercise this right because forcing a sale is expensive and time-consuming. Instead, they typically wait until you sell or refinance the property, at which point the lien has to be paid off with the proceeds, to give the new owner or lender clear title to the property.

For bankruptcy purposes, there are four types of nonconsensual liens:
- judgment liens
- execution liens
- statutory liens, and
- tax liens.

Judgment Liens

A judgment lien can be imposed on your property only after somebody sues you and wins a money judgment against you. In most states, the judgment creditor (the person or company who won) must record the judgment by filing it with the county or state. In a few states, a judgment entered against you by a court automatically creates a lien on the real estate you own in that county—that is, the judgment creditor doesn't have to record the judgment to get the lien.

A judgment lien affects real estate you own in the county where the lien is recorded or the judgment is entered. In many states, a judgment lien also applies to your personal property (property other than real estate) for some time after the judgment, if certain judgment collection techniques are employed. However, judgment liens on personal property are generally ineffective, because most personal property has no title, and the liens are not recorded. This means that the personal property could easily be sold to a third party who has no idea that the lien existed.

A judgment creditor can also file a judgment with your state motor vehicles department to get a judgment lien on any car, truck, motorcycle, or other motor vehicle you own. You might not know about this type of lien unless you check with the motor vehicles department or the creditor files a proof of claim in your bankruptcy case, describing its interest as "secured."

Typically, judgment liens that have been recorded in your county will attach to property that you acquire later. For example, a judgment might be recorded in your county land records office even if you don't own any real estate. If you buy some real estate a few years later, you'll discover that it is now burdened by that pesky old lien that was just sitting there, waiting for you to make a move. Most real estate liens expire after a certain number of years (seven to ten in most states), though they can typically be renewed.

Execution Liens

In some states, a creditor who seeks to collect a judgment under a writ of execution automatically obtains an "execution" lien on your property. Like judicial liens, execution liens can be removed (avoided) as part of your bankruptcy case. (See "How to Avoid Liens on Exempt Property," below, for more on lien avoidance.)

Statutory Liens

Some liens are created by law. For example, in most states, when you hire someone to work on your house, the worker or supplier of materials is entitled to obtain a mechanic's lien (also called a materialman's lien) on the house if you don't pay. In some states, a homeowners' association has the same right if you don't pay your dues or special assessments.

Statutory liens affect only your real estate. They don't attach to your personal property, such as a car or equipment.

Tax Liens

Federal, state, and local governments have the authority to impose liens on your property if you owe delinquent taxes. If you owe money to the IRS or another taxing authority, the debt is secured only if the taxing authority has recorded a lien against your property (and you still own the property) or has issued a notice of tax lien, and the equity in your home or retirement plan is sufficient to cover the debt. For example, in times of upside down or underwater mortgages, an obligation to the IRS might be unsecured even if a lien has been imposed on your home, if you don't have enough equity to secure the debt.

If you don't pay an IRS bill, the IRS can record a Notice of Federal Tax Lien at your county land records office or your secretary of state's office. While the federal tax lien attaches to all of your property, for practical purposes a lien will be effective only if your real estate equity, your retirement account, or your bank account is sufficient to cover the debt. Similarly, your local government can attach a lien to your real estate for unpaid property taxes. And, if your state taxing authority sends you a bill and you don't contest or pay it, the state can record a tax lien against your real estate in that state.

What Happens to Secured Debts When You File for Bankruptcy

Unsecured debts and secured debts are treated differently in Chapter 7 bankruptcy. Creditors with unsecured debts might receive some money in the bankruptcy process if the trustee can take and sell any of your nonexempt property. (The proceeds from a sale of your nonexempt property are divided among all of your unsecured creditors according to priorities established in the bankruptcy code.) Once your case is over, however, unsecured creditors have no rights. Most unsecured debts are wiped out in bankruptcy, whether or not the creditor was paid off, and the creditor has to simply take the loss and move on.

Secured debts are different in two ways: First, if the trustee takes and sells property that secures a debt, the secured creditor is entitled to be paid in full before unsecured creditors get anything. This might effectively allow you to keep the property securing the debt, because the trustee has no incentive to take the property and sell it if the secured creditor would be entitled to all of the nonexempt proceeds.

Second, even though bankruptcy wipes out your personal obligation to repay a secured debt, the creditor's lien on your property survives your bankruptcy case (unless the property is returned to the creditor). A secured debt consists of two parts:

- **Your personal liability for the debt, which obligates you to pay back the creditor.** Bankruptcy wipes out your personal liability for the debt, assuming the debt qualifies for the bankruptcy discharge. (See Ch. 9.) This means the creditor cannot later sue you to collect the debt.

- **The creditor's legal claim (lien or security interest) on the collateral for the debt.** A lien gives the creditor the right to repossess the property or force its sale if you do not pay the debt. If the collateral is unavailable, the lender can sue you for the value of the collateral. A lien sticks with the property even if you give the property to someone else. Bankruptcy, by itself, does not eliminate liens. However, during bankruptcy, you might be able to take additional steps to eliminate, or at least reduce, liens on collateral for security interests.

Unsecured Debt	Secured Debt	Secured Debt After Bankruptcy
IOU $	IOU $ + 🚗 *Lien*	⨯IOU $ + 🚗 *Lien*

EXAMPLE: Madeline buys a couch on credit from a furniture store. She signs a contract agreeing to pay for it over the next year. The contract also states that the creditor (the store) has a security interest in the couch and can repossess it if any payment is more than 15 days late. In this type of secured debt, Madeline's obligation to pay the debt is her personal liability, and the store's right to repossess the couch is the lien. Bankruptcy eliminates her obligation to pay for the couch, but the creditor retains its lien and can repossess the couch if she doesn't pay.

> **CAUTION**
>
> **You could lose property if you have nonexempt equity.** Remember, if your equity in collateral securing a debt is higher than the exemption you can claim in it, the trustee can take the collateral, sell it, pay off the secured creditor, pay you your exemption amount, and distribute the balance to unsecured creditors. Fortunately, most filers are upside down on their secured debts—that is, they owe more than the collateral is worth, primarily because of the interest figured into their payments which is usually front-loaded (meaning, you pay most of the interest off at the beginning of the loan term) and, in the case of personal property, the depreciation of the property's value over time. In these situations, the trustee has no interest in taking the property. The proceeds would all go to the secured creditor and nothing would be left to distribute to unsecured creditors. The filer could then use one of the options discussed in this section.

Eliminating Liens in Bankruptcy

There are several steps you can take during bankruptcy to eliminate or reduce liens. But these procedures are neither automatic nor required: You have to request them.

The most powerful of these procedures lets you eliminate (avoid) some types of liens on certain kinds of exempt property without paying anything to the creditor. (See Ch. 3 for a definition of exempt property.) With the lien eliminated, you get to keep the property free and clear without paying anything more to the creditor.

Other procedures let you eliminate a creditor's lien (and keep the property) by paying the creditor either the amount of the lien or the current replacement value of the property, whichever is less.

Finally, you can rid yourself of a lien simply by surrendering the property to the creditor.

The choice of which procedure to use for each item of secured property is up to you.

If You Don't Eliminate Liens

If you do not take steps to eliminate a lien as a part of your bankruptcy case, the lien will survive your bankruptcy intact, and the creditor will be free to take the property or force its sale if you fall behind on the payments. Fortunately, the courts are very liberal about reopening a case to allow a debtor to file a motion to avoid a lien. So if, after your bankruptcy case is over, you discover a lien that you missed while your bankruptcy case was open, don't worry. Reopening a bankruptcy is a routine procedure.

If the property is valuable and could be easily resold (an automobile, for example), the creditor will surely repossess the item at the first opportunity unless you agree to keep your payments current. (See "Options for Handling Secured Debts in Chapter 7 Bankruptcy," below.) If, however, the property is of little value and not worth the cost of repossessing (such as Mary's couch), the creditor might do nothing.

If the property is of the type with a "title" or ownership document, such as a house or car, and the creditor does nothing, the lien simply remains on the property until you sell it. At that time, the lien must be paid out of the sale proceeds if the buyer wants to have clear title to the property. On the other hand, if the property has no ownership title document, as would be the case with Mary's couch, a computer, or a washer and dryer set, the creditor has no practical way to enforce the lien. In some cases, if the property is declining in value and it is clear that you aren't going to take steps to keep it, the creditor might ask for the bankruptcy court's permission to take the property even before your bankruptcy case is over. For example, if you own a new photocopier subject to a security interest and the copier depreciates in value at a fairly steep rate (say, 30% a year), the creditor would want it back as soon as possible to get the highest resale price.

Options for Handling Secured Debts in Chapter 7 Bankruptcy

As part of your Chapter 7 bankruptcy paperwork, you must list all creditors who hold secured debts. You must also tell the bankruptcy trustee and the secured creditors what you plan to do with the collateral that secures those debts: whether you plan to surrender the property or keep it. You do this in an official form called the "Statement of Intention," which you must file with the court along with your other bankruptcy papers and mail to your creditors. Then, you must carry out your stated intention within the applicable time limits. (You'll find step-by-step instructions on how to complete the forms at the end of this chapter.)

This section explains the basic options for handling secured debts in bankruptcy, including the advantages and disadvantages of each option, any restrictions that might apply, when each option makes sense, and what steps you have to take to use each option. You should review this material carefully and decide how you want to treat the collateral for each secured debt before you file for bankruptcy. If you plan on keeping the collateral, call the lender before filing to see whether you will have to reaffirm the debt (agree to be liable for it after bankruptcy, as explained further below) or whether you can keep the collateral by simply remaining current on your payments even if your liability for the debt is discharged.

Once you've filed for bankruptcy, the automatic stay prevents secured creditors from repossessing property that serves as collateral for a secured debt, unless the court gives permission or you miss the deadline for carrying out your stated intention. It's much easier to hold on to property in the first place than to get it back after the creditor repossesses it. So, if you have some secured property that a creditor is about to take and you haven't filed for bankruptcy yet, you might want to file right away to prevent the seizure.

> ⓘ **CAUTION**
>
> **You may lose your property if you fail to choose.** If you don't make a choice about how you intend to treat collateral, the secured creditor might have the right to repossess the collateral 30 days after you file for bankruptcy, whether or not you have kept up with your payments. Most security agreements contain what's known as an "ipso facto" clause, which says that filing for bankruptcy qualifies as a default allowing the creditor to repossess the property, even if you are current on your payments. If you don't use one of the choices provided by the bankruptcy code, the creditor could use the ipso facto clause to grab your property. However, some states don't honor these ipso facto clauses as long as you remain current on your payments.

Option 1: Surrender the Collateral

If you don't want or need to keep the property, you can surrender it. Surrendering the collateral simply means allowing the creditor to take it back or foreclose on the lien. This is the simplest option for dealing with secured property. It completely frees you from the debt: Giving back the property satisfies the terms of the lien, and the bankruptcy discharges your personal liability for the original debt (and prevents the creditor from seeking a deficiency judgment).

Advantages. A quick and easy way to completely rid yourself of a secured debt.

Disadvantages. You lose the property. Also, if you surrender the property, some bankruptcy courts won't let you use the payments due under the contract as deductions for purposes of the means test. (Ch. 1 explains the means test.) However, other courts let you deduct these payments, reasoning that the means test is backward-looking (that is, it is calculated based on your past expenses) and not concerned with your future intentions.

Restrictions. None. You can surrender any kind of collateral for a secured debt.

When to use it. For property that you don't need or want or that would cost too much to keep.

How it works. On the Statement of Intention form, check the box indicating that you will surrender the property. You must file the form and send a copy to the secured creditor within 30 days after filing for bankruptcy.

It's then up to the creditor to contact you and arrange a time to pick up the property. If the creditor doesn't take the property and the trustee doesn't claim it, it's yours to keep. This might happen if the property isn't worth much. For example, it probably isn't worth the creditor's time to pick up, store, and auction off used household furniture or old computer equipment, no matter how much you still owe on it.

Option 2: Redeem the Collateral

If you want to keep certain types of property, you could "redeem" it by paying the secured creditor the property's current replacement value (what you would have to pay a retail vendor for that type of property, considering its age and condition), usually in a lump sum. Essentially, you are repurchasing the property from the creditor. In return, the creditor delivers the title to you in the same manner as if you had followed your original agreement. You then own the property free and clear.

> **EXAMPLE:** Olivia and Gary owe $500 on some household furniture with a replacement value of $200. They can keep the furniture and eliminate the $500 lien by paying the creditor the $200 replacement value within 45 days after the first creditors' meeting.

Advantages. Redemption is an excellent option if you owe significantly more than the property is worth. The creditor must accept the current replacement value of the item as payment in full. If you and the creditor disagree on the replacement value of the property, the court will decide the issue in a proceeding called a "valuation" hearing. (Ch. 6 explains how to figure out the replacement value of various types of property.)

Disadvantages. Most debtors will have to pay the full replacement value of an item in a lump sum to redeem it. It may be difficult for you to come up with that much cash on short notice. You might be able to get a loan; some companies specialize in lending to people seeking to redeem their collateral in bankruptcy. Or, you can try to get the creditor to agree to accept installment payments, but courts cannot require creditors to make this type of deal.

Restrictions. You have the right to redeem property only if all of the following are true:

- The debt is a consumer debt: one incurred "primarily for a personal, family, or household purpose." This includes just about everything except collateral for loans and credit obtained for business purposes.
- The property is tangible personal property. Tangible property is anything you can touch. A car, furniture, a boat, a computer, and jewelry are all examples of tangible property. Stocks are intangible. The property must also be "personal property," which simply means it can't be real estate.
- The property is either:
  - claimed as exempt (exempt property is explained in Ch. 3), or
  - abandoned by the trustee. A trustee will abandon property that has little or no nonexempt value beyond the amount of the liens. The trustee might notify you of the abandonment or you might have to proactively request it. Once the property is abandoned, you can redeem it by paying the secured creditor its replacement value. If you know you'll want to redeem property if the trustee abandons it, check the "redeem" box on the Statement of Intention. If you haven't done this and the trustee abandons the property, you might have to amend your Statement of Intention (instructions for amending a form are in Ch. 7). Call the trustee to find out.

When to use it. Redemption can be a good idea if you really want to keep personal property, but you don't want your liability for the debt to survive your bankruptcy (this is a consequence of reaffirmation, discussed below). Use redemption only if you owe more than it would cost to purchase the property and you would not be able to get rid of the lien (lien avoidance is covered below in Option 5). It often makes sense to redeem small items of household property that you want to keep because raising money for the lump-sum payment probably would not be that difficult.

Redemption can also be used for cars, which are not eligible for lien avoidance and are likely to be repossessed if a lien remains after bankruptcy and you don't agree to keep making payments. However, if the creditor won't agree to installment payments, raising the cash necessary to redeem a car can be difficult.

How it works. You and the creditor must agree on the value of the property, then draft and sign a redemption agreement. Settling on the replacement value might take a little negotiation. Sometimes, you can get the creditor to accept installment payments if you agree to pay a higher amount. Whatever you decide, put it in the redemption agreement.

Option 3: Retain and Pay (the "Ride-Through" Option)

Before the bankruptcy law changed in 2005, most bankruptcy courts recognized the "ride-through" or "retain and pay" option for dealing with secured debts. Where this option was available, debtors could keep the collateral for secured debts without reaffirming the debts or redeeming the property, as long as they stayed current on their payments. Debtors who took advantage of this option wouldn't owe a deficiency balance if they had to give the property back after receiving their bankruptcy discharge.

The ride-through option is no longer an explicit part of the bankruptcy code, and it isn't recognized in the bankruptcy courts of every state. However, some lenders (and some courts) still allow debtors to keep the collateral without reaffirming secured debts, as long as they remain current on the payments. These lenders would prefer to receive payments from reliable borrowers instead of repossessing and auctioning property only to receive a fraction of what they're owed.

Advantages. The ride-through option allows you to keep property without obligating yourself to a debt that will survive your bankruptcy or having to come up with lump-sum payment. You can keep the property as long as you can keep up with your payments. If you reach a point where you can't afford the payments, you can essentially surrender the property: give it back without owing a deficiency balance.

Disadvantages. Because the ride-through option is no longer part of the bankruptcy code, your lender usually gets to decide whether to allow it or not. And, the ride-through option isn't allowed in every judicial district. Even if you can use this option, you'll have to keep making your payments if you want to keep the property. In contrast, surrendering or redeeming the property allows you to exit your bankruptcy case without ongoing payment obligations (unless your lender will let you redeem on an installment plan).

Restrictions. Generally, your lender gets to decide whether to allow you to use the ride-through option or to require you to redeem or reaffirm the debt. Whether or not your creditor will be so accommodating depends on how close you are to paying off the debt, your history with the creditor, and the creditor's experience with the reaffirmation process.

If your lender doesn't want you to use this option, it might still be available to you if one of the following is true:

- Your state's law forbids lenders from repossessing property as long as you stay current on your payments. In this situation, if you don't redeem or surrender the property, or reaffirm the debt, the debtor can't do anything to enforce its security interest as long as you keep making those payments. (For information on researching your state's law, see Ch. 10.)

- The court rejects your reaffirmation agreement. In this situation, most courts have allowed debtors to keep their property as long as they continue making their payments. These courts have held that, as long as you sign and file a valid reaffirmation agreement promptly and attend the reaffirmation hearing, you will be protected from repossession, even if the court ultimately rejects the agreement (typically, because it looks like you won't be able to make the payments required by the contract). (See *In re Chim*, 381 B.R. 191 (Bankr. Md. 2008) and *In re Moustafi*, 371 B.R. 434 (Bankr. Ariz. 2007).)

In at least one federal judicial circuit—the 11th Circuit covering Alabama, Florida, and Georgia—debtors cannot use the ride-through option. If debtors in these states want to keep property, they must either redeem it or sign a reaffirmation agreement for the debt. (See *In re Linderman*, 435 B.R. 715 (Bankr. M.D. Fla. 2009).)

When to use it. If you think you'll make your payments and your lender will allow it, the ride-through option is often the best choice for property you really want to keep. It allows you to retain the property and avoid any penalty (in the form of a deficiency judgment) if you later have to give it back.

How it works. First, you'll have to contact your lender to see whether it will allow you to "retain and pay for" the collateral rather than reaffirm. If the lender agrees, check the box on the Statement of Intention indicating that you will retain the property. Then, check the "Other" box, and write this in the space provided: "Debtor will retain collateral and continue to make regular payments."

If you default to the ride-through option because the court rejects your reaffirmation agreement, you should complete your Statement of Intention as explained in the instructions for reaffirming a debt, below.

Option 4: Reaffirm the Debt

When you reaffirm a debt, you agree that you will still owe the debt after your bankruptcy case is over. Both the creditor's lien on the collateral and your personal liability for the debt under the original promissory note survive bankruptcy intact—often, just as if you never filed for bankruptcy. For example, if you owe $25,000 on your car before you file for Chapter 7 bankruptcy, you most likely will continue to owe $25,000 on your car after you file for bankruptcy (unless you negotiate a lower amount in your reaffirmation agreement). If you can't keep up your payments and the car is repossessed, you'll owe the difference between the amount you reaffirm for and the amount the lender can sell the car for at auction (considerably less than you owe, in most cases). This is called a "deficiency balance." Nearly all states permit a creditor to sue for a deficiency balance for most types of property. However, about half of the states don't allow deficiency balances on repossessed personal property if the original purchase price was less than a few thousand dollars.

Advantages. Reaffirmation provides a sure way to keep collateral as long as you abide by the terms of the reaffirmation agreement and keep up your payments. Reaffirmation also provides a setting in which you might be able to negotiate new terms to reduce your payments, your interest rate, and/or the total amount you will have to pay over time.

Disadvantages. Because reaffirmation leaves you personally liable for the debt, you can't walk away from the debt after bankruptcy. You'll still be legally bound to pay the deficiency balance even if the property is damaged or destroyed. And because you have to wait eight years before filing another Chapter 7 bankruptcy case, you'll be stuck with that debt for a long time.

For example, if you reaffirm your car note and then default on your payments after bankruptcy, the creditor can (and probably will) repossess the car, auction it off, and bill you for the difference between what you owe and what was received in the auction.

> EXAMPLE: Tasha owns a computer worth $900. She owes $1,500 on it. She reaffirms the debt for the full $1,500. Two months after bankruptcy, she spills a soft drink into the disk drive and the computer is ruined. Although she has lost the computer, because she reaffirmed the debt, she still has to pay the creditor $1,500.

Restrictions. Reaffirmation can be used with any kind of property and any kind of lien, but the creditor must agree to the terms of the reaffirmation if they are different from the current agreement. You or the lender must file the agreement in court as part of your bankruptcy case. Unless an attorney is representing you in the bankruptcy or in the reaffirmation process, the bankruptcy court must review the agreement in a reaffirmation or discharge hearing. At that hearing, the judge will check your bankruptcy paperwork to see how the reaffirmation might affect your post-bankruptcy budget and whether you can afford the payments. The judge can disapprove the agreement if it is not in your best interest or would create an undue hardship for you. The judge is likely to reject the agreement if it looks like you won't make the payments after paying your basic living expenses or if you owe much more on the debt than the property is worth.

When to use it. Because reaffirmation comes with the very serious disadvantage of leaving you in debt after your bankruptcy case is over, you should consider it only if:

- the creditor insists on it
- it's the only way to hang on to collateral that you really need to keep, and
- you have good reason to believe you'll be able to pay off the balance.

Reaffirmation might be the only practical way to keep some property types, such as automobiles or your home. Also, reaffirmation can be a sensible way to keep property that is worth significantly more than what you owe on it.

If you decide to reaffirm, try to get the creditor to accept less than you owe as full payment of the debt. Don't reaffirm a debt for more than what it would cost you to replace the property.

If you need to reaffirm a debt to keep the collateral, make sure you keep up your payments before filing for bankruptcy so you can stay on the creditor's good side. If you fall behind, the creditor has the right to demand that you make your account current before agreeing to a reaffirmation contract, but you will probably have some room to negotiate. In addition, many bankruptcy judges will not approve reaffirmation agreements unless you are current on your payments at the time of the reaffirmation hearing. If the creditor rejects your payments during bankruptcy (which often happens), deposit that money into a separate account so it's available once the creditor decides to accept it. If you can't make these rejected payments when the creditor wants them, you might lose your property.

How it works. Use official bankruptcy Form 2400. You can find this form on the website of the United States Courts. (See in Ch. 6, "Where to Get the Official Forms.") Most large creditors will complete the paperwork, ask you to sign it, and file it with the court. If you're dealing with a smaller creditor, you might have to file it yourself.

The reaffirmation agreement includes several legally required disclosures and warnings. These provisions are intended to put you on notice of how much you'll be paying overall, including the interest rate and your liability to pay the debt in full if something happens to the collateral. In Part D of the agreement, you must explain why you are reaffirming the debt and provide information on your income and expenses, so the court can determine whether the agreement creates an undue hardship for you. Your income and expense information should be in the same ballpark as the information you include in Schedules I and J (see Ch. 6). If these figures indicate that you can't afford the required payments, the court will reject your reaffirmation agreement. If this happens, you will probably be able to keep the property as long as you stay current on your payments under the old loan; see Option 3, above, for more information.

You can cancel a reaffirmation agreement by notifying the creditor before the later of:

- the date of your discharge, or
- 60 days after you filed the reaffirmation agreement with the bankruptcy court.

If your case is already closed, however, you will not be able to switch to the other options listed in this chapter.

If the Court Refuses to Approve Your Reaffirmation Agreement

If the judge disapproves the reaffirmation agreement, does that mean that you will have to surrender your property? Not at all. In fact, disapproval may work to your advantage. A vast majority of the bankruptcy courts that have disapproved reaffirmation agreements have also interpreted the bankruptcy code to protect people from repossession as long as they go along with the program—that is, file the reaffirmation agreement, attend a discharge hearing, and do their best to get it approved. (See *In re Chim*, 381 B.R. 191 (Bankr. Md. 2008); and *In re Moustafi*, 371 B.R. 434 (Bankr. Ariz. 2007).) In other words, by disapproving the agreement the courts are giving the green light to the ride-through option.

If a debtor doesn't cooperate in the reaffirmation process, courts have ruled that the lender is free to exercise whatever rights it has under state law once the judge disapproves of the reaffirmation agreement. In some states, the laws governing commercial transactions forbid repossession as long as the borrower remains current on the debt. Even in states that don't have those laws, experience shows that lenders would rather have money coming in rather than take back the property and resell it at a discounted price—especially if the borrower has faithfully made payments in the past. Simply put, it stands to reason that a lender who has the right to repossess property after a judge disapproves a proposed reaffirmation agreement might not choose to do so.

Option 5: Eliminate (Avoid) Liens

Lien avoidance is a procedure by which you ask the bankruptcy court to eliminate or reduce liens on some types of exempt property. Lien avoidance is neither automatic nor required: You have to request it in a separate legal proceeding in your bankruptcy case.

One common lien avoidance procedure lets you eliminate or reduce liens on certain types of exempt personal property, depending on the value of the property and the amount of the exemption available to you. This procedure is available only for what are called "nonpossessory, non-purchase-money liens": liens on property that you already owned when you pledged it as security for a loan. It can't be used for real estate.

A different lien avoidance procedure allows you to eliminate judgment liens on personal property or real estate that falls within an exemption. By removing the judgment lien, you get to keep the property free and clear without paying anything more to the creditor, assuming the underlying debt can be discharged in bankruptcy (which it usually can).

Nonpossessory, Non-Purchase-Money Liens

If you have pledged some item of personal property (not real estate) that you already owned as security for a loan, and the property is entirely or partially exempt, you might be able to eliminate a lien on the property. (You'll find sample forms for this remedy later in this chapter; you will need to modify them to fit your situation.)

How much of the lien can be eliminated depends on the value and type of property and the exemption amount. If the property (or your equity in it) is entirely exempt, the court will eliminate the entire lien, and you'll get to keep the property without paying anything. If the property (or your equity in it) is worth more than the exemption limit, the lien will be reduced to the difference between the exemption limit and the property's value or the amount of the debt, whichever is less.

EXAMPLE: A creditor has a $500 lien on Hunter's guitar, which is worth $300. In Hunter's state, the guitar is exempt only to $200. He could get the lien reduced to $100. The other $400 of the lien is eliminated (avoided).

$500 lien $300 = value of item

           – $200 = exemption amount

             $100 = amount of lien remaining
                             after lien avoidance

Advantages. This type of lien avoidance costs nothing (if you are representing yourself), involves only a moderate amount of paperwork, and often allows you to keep property without paying anything.

Disadvantages. Some paperwork is involved. Also, by trying to avoid a lien on exempt property, you might reopen the issue of whether the property really is exempt in the first place. This might happen if the property was deemed exempt by default (that is, the property is exempt because the trustee and creditors didn't challenge your claim of exemption within the applicable time limit). Some courts have allowed creditors to argue that the property is not exempt at a hearing on a motion to avoid a lien.

As a practical matter, however, motions to avoid liens are usually not contested.

Restrictions. There are several important limits on this type of lien avoidance. First, as noted above, you can avoid only nonpossessory, non-purchase-money security interests. That sounds complicated, but it makes sense when you break it down:

- Nonpossessory means the creditor does not physically keep the property you've pledged as collateral. It stays in your possession; the creditor only has a lien on it. (In contrast, if you leave your property at a pawnshop to get a loan, that is a possessory security interest—for which this lien avoidance procedure is not available.)
- Non-purchase-money means that you didn't use the money you borrowed to purchase the collateral. Instead, you used property you already owned as collateral for the loan.
- Security interest means the lien was created by voluntary agreement between you and the creditor. In other words, the lien wasn't involuntary, like a tax or judgment lien.

Second, the property you pledged as collateral must be exempt under the exemption system you are using. (Remember that domicile requirements limit the exemptions available to you. See Ch. 3 for more information.) If the property isn't exempt, then the lien doesn't impair your exemption rights, and it can't be eliminated.

Third, only certain types of property are covered. Unfortunately, the property most commonly pledged as collateral for nonpossessory, non-purchase-money security interests doesn't qualify—homes and cars (unless the vehicle qualifies as a tool of the trade, discussed below). You can eliminate a nonpossessory, non-purchase-money security interest lien only if the collateral falls into one of these categories:

- household furnishings, household goods, clothing, appliances, books, and musical instruments or jewelry that are primarily for your personal, family, or household use
- health aids professionally prescribed for you or a dependent
- animals or crops held for your personal, family, or household use, or
- implements, machines, professional books, or tools used in a trade (yours or a dependent's).

What Are Household Goods?

For the purpose of avoiding a consensual lien, household goods are limited to:

- clothing
- furniture
- appliances
- one radio
- one television
- one DVD player
- linens
- china
- crockery
- kitchenware
- educational equipment and materials primarily for the use of your minor dependent children
- medical equipment and supplies
- furniture exclusively for the use of your minor children or your elderly or disabled dependents
- your personal effects (including your wedding rings and the toys and hobby equipment of your minor dependent children) and those of your dependents, and
- one personal computer and related equipment.

Generally, a motor vehicle is considered a tool of the trade only if you use it as an integral part of your business—for example, if you do door-to-door sales or delivery work. It is not considered a tool of the trade if you simply use it to commute, even if you have no other means of getting to work.

Judgment Liens

A nonconsensual judgment lien on property can be avoided if all of the following are true:

- The lien resulted from a money judgment issued by a court.
- You are entitled to claim an exemption in at least some of your equity in the property.
- The lien would result in a loss of some or all of this exempt equity if the property were sold. (That is, the exemption would be impaired.)

If these three conditions are met, you can remove judgment liens from any exempt property, including real estate and cars.

When to use it. Use lien avoidance if it's available, especially if a lien can be completely wiped out. Even if you don't need or want the property, you can avoid the lien, sell the property, and use the money for other things.

To keep things simple, you might want to avoid liens only on property that is completely exempt. The lien will be eliminated entirely and you'll own the property free and clear, without paying anything to the creditor.

Even partial lien avoidance can be beneficial, but sooner or later you'll have to pay the amount remaining on the lien if the property has a title document or is subject to repossession or foreclosure on what's left of the lien. Most often, you'll have to pay off the lien in a lump sum, but some creditors might be willing to accept installments, especially if you compromise on the value of the lien.

How it works. You request lien avoidance by checking the column "Property is claimed as exempt" on the Statement of Intention and by typing and filing a motion. (Complete instructions for preparing and filing a motion to avoid a judgment lien on real estate are at the end of this chapter.) Although it might sound complicated, lien avoidance is often a routine procedure that can be accomplished without a lawyer.

Some bankruptcy filers don't realize they have liens on their property, or don't realize that they could eliminate those liens. Others might not be able to eliminate liens when they file for bankruptcy (typically, because they have no exempt equity in the property), but later they become eligible to do so. Fortunately, bankruptcy courts are very liberal about allowing a debtor to reopen a case to file a motion to avoid a lien. Reopening a bankruptcy case is a routine procedure, described in Ch. 7.

TIP

Lien avoidance on real estate in the current housing market. As home values rise, more and more bankruptcy filers will be able to avoid judgment liens on their homes or other real estate. This is a change from previous years, when the economic downturn meant that many people had no equity in their homes, and therefore usually couldn't avoid judgment liens. If you don't have home equity when you file for bankruptcy, however, and that later changes, you might be able to reopen your bankruptcy case and bring a lien avoidance action.

Lien Elimination Techniques Beyond the Scope of This Book

Deep in the recesses of the bankruptcy code are other procedures for eliminating certain kinds of nonconsensual liens. Section 11 U.S.C. § 522(h) gives a debtor the power to use a wide range of lien avoidance techniques that have been made available to the bankruptcy trustee. The tools are found in Sections 545, 547, 548, 549, 553, and 724(a) of the bankruptcy code. These liens include:

- nonjudgment liens securing the payment of penalties, fines, or punitive damages, and
- nonconsensual liens that were recorded or perfected while you were already insolvent or within the 90 days before filing for bankruptcy.

To use these procedures, you'll need the help of a bankruptcy attorney.

Eliminating Judicial Liens

To determine whether you can eliminate a judicial lien, apply this simple formula. Add the following items:

- all consensual liens on the property (for example, a mortgage and home equity loan)
- all tax liens, and
- your exemption amount.

If the total of all these items is greater than the value of the property, then you can completely eliminate judicial liens on the property. The Judicial Lien Worksheet found on the companion page (www. nolo.com/back-of-book/HFB.html) will help you do the math. Below are a few sample calculations:

One more point to remember: For the purposes of bankruptcy lien avoidance provisions, judicial liens get the lowest priority, behind consensual liens and tax liens, regardless of when the liens were placed on the property and regardless of what state law says. So, in Example C below, it would not matter if the $30,000 judgment lien was created before or after the $40,000 second mortgage: The judicial lien can be eliminated either way.

Example A		Example B		Example C	
Value of property	$ 200,000	Value of property	$ 200,000	Value of property	$ 200,000
Mortgage	$ 100,000	Mortgage	$ 150,000	Mortgage	$ 160,000
Second mortgage	20,000	Second mortgage	20,000	Second mortgage	40,000
Exemption	10,000	Exemption	10,000	Exemption	10,000
Total	$ 130,000	**Total**	$ 180,000	**Total**	$ 210,000
Amount available for judicial liens	$ 70,000	Amount available for judicial liens	$ 20,000	Amount available for judicial liens	$ 0
Amount of judicial lien	$ 30,000	Amount of judicial lien	$ 30,000	Amount of judicial lien	$ 30,000
RESULT: Lien cannot be eliminated.		RESULT: $10,000 of lien can be eliminated; $20,000 of lien cannot be eliminated.		RESULT: Judicial lien can be completely eliminated.	

TIP
You can pay off a lien in a follow-up Chapter 13 bankruptcy.
Another way to handle liens is through what some bankruptcy practitioners call a "Chapter 20" bankruptcy: filing for Chapter 13 bankruptcy after completing a Chapter 7 bankruptcy. Bankruptcy law prohibits you from receiving a Chapter 13 discharge if you file within four years of the date you filed a Chapter 7 case in which you received a discharge. However, even if you can't discharge debts, you can still receive most of the other benefits associated with Chapter 13, including a plan to pay off liens and, in some cases, elimination of the lien altogether. You use the Chapter 13 bankruptcy to deal with or eliminate any liens remaining after your Chapter 7 case has wiped out your personal liability. And, if a lien exceeds the property's value, you can often get the lien fully discharged by simply paying the current replacement value of the item rather than the full amount of the lien.

Be aware that qualifying for a "Chapter 20" can be tricky. Specifically, you'll likely find it somewhat challenging to explain how you qualified for a Chapter 7 discharge previously, yet you now have sufficient income to pay into a Chapter 13 case.

Because this book covers Chapter 7 bankruptcies only, space does not permit us to fully explain how to do a successful follow-up Chapter 13 case. For more information, see *Chapter 13 Bankruptcy*, by Cara O'Neill (Nolo).

Choosing the Best Options

Now it's time to pick the best option for each of your secured debts. If an item has more than one lien on it, you might use a different procedure to deal with each lien. For example, you might eliminate a judicial lien on exempt property through lien avoidance and redeem the property to satisfy a consensual lien.

CAUTION
Don't pay too much. If the option you're considering would require you to pay significantly more than the current market value of the property you want to keep, it's a bad deal. There are frequently ways you or a lawyer can save any item of secured property by paying no more than its current replacement value.

What Property Should You Keep?

Be realistic about how much property you will be able to afford to keep after bankruptcy. Face the fact that you might not be able to keep everything and decide which items you can do without. These questions will help you decide whether an item is worth saving:

- How important is the property to you?
- Will you need the property to help you make a fresh start after bankruptcy?
- How much would it cost to keep the property? (This will depend on the procedure you use.)
- Would it be more expensive to redeem the property or to replace it?
- If you're considering reaffirming the debt, are you sure you'll be able to make the payments after bankruptcy? Or, will you be making a bad investment decision (for instance, agreeing to be liable for $10,000 for a car that is only worth $5,000)?
- If you're considering surrendering your property and buying a replacement item, will you need a loan to purchase it? If so, will you be able to get such a loan after bankruptcy?

EXAMPLE 1: Jasmine bought a sports car two years ago for $16,000. Now Jasmine is unemployed but is about to start a new job. She still owes $13,000 on the vehicle, which is currently worth $10,000. Although she likes the car, she can't come up with the $10,000 in cash to redeem it, and she doesn't want to remain personally liable for the $13,000 debt after her bankruptcy case is over. If Jasmine is willing to lower her standards a little, she can surrender her car and buy a reliable used car to get her to work and back for about $3,000. However, she'll have to come up with the money to buy the car—or make sure she'll be able to borrow it—to make this plan work.

EXAMPLE 2: Jacob owns a ten-year-old Toyota with a replacement value of $5,000. It is security for a debt of $7,500. If Jacob files for bankruptcy, he will probably be able to keep the car by paying the secured creditor only $5,000 (the value of the car). Jacob decides it's worth paying that amount. He knows the vehicle is reliable and will probably last another six years. He also believes it would be a hassle to find a comparable car at that price, and he needs the car to get to work. Jacob offers to redeem the car by making payments, but the creditor demands a lump sum (as it has a legal right to do). Jacob borrows $5,000 from his parents and redeems the car.

Gambling That the Court Won't Approve the Reaffirmation

Since any reaffirmation agreement you sign will have to be approved by the court in a reaffirmation hearing, you might consider gambling that the judge will disapprove the agreement. If that happens, you can still keep the property as long as you continue to be current on your payments, but you won't be liable for the loan after your bankruptcy. A win-win situation for you. (See "If the Court Refuses to Approve Your Reaffirmation Agreement," above.)

What's the chance that the judge won't approve the reaffirmation? Let's take the example of a car note. If your car payment is high compared to your income, you have a very high interest rate, or the car is worth significantly less than the amount you are trying to reaffirm, the judge is less likely to approve the reaffirmation. And the judge definitely will not approve the reaffirmation if your expenses on Schedule J exceed your net income on Schedule I.

What happens if the judge does approve the reaffirmation? You can still bail on the reaffirmation within 60 days of filing the agreement or as long as your case remains open. For instance, if the judge approves the agreement at the hearing, you can say, "Oops, I changed my mind, I no longer want to reaffirm" and the judge should enter that in your case record. So, it's really not much of a gamble after all, although there's a risk that the creditor will repossess the property.

EXAMPLE 3: Now assume that Jacob makes a different decision: Instead of redeeming the debt for $5,000, he decides to discharge the $7,500 debt and continue making payments to the creditor. Jacob figures that the creditor would rather receive the payments than go through the expense and hassle of repossessing a car that would sell for only $5,000. If Jacob is wrong, however, he will have no recourse against the repossession.

Schedule D and the Statement of Intention Form

When you file for Chapter 7 bankruptcy, you must list all creditors who hold secured claims on Schedule D. (See Ch. 6.) You must also tell the bankruptcy trustee and your affected creditors your plans for the property that secures those debts. You do this by filing a form called the Statement of Intention and mailing a copy to each creditor listed on it. (If you have no secured debts, you simply have to sign the Statement of Intention and file it with the court.)

There are line-by-line instructions on how to fill out these forms in Ch. 6. To make the decisions requested on the Statement of Intention, though, you'll need the information from this chapter. Here are some timing tips:

- Try to decide what to do with each item of secured property before you file for bankruptcy.
- The Statement of Intention is due within 45 days after you file for bankruptcy but is often filed at the same time or right after you file your other papers.
- The law requires you to carry out your stated intentions within 30 days after the creditors' meeting. If you miss the deadline, your collateral will no longer be protected by the automatic stay, which leaves the creditor free to take it.

If you change your mind after you file your Statement of Intention, you can amend the form using the amendment instructions in Ch. 7.

Real Estate and Motor Vehicles

Liens on real estate and cars involve special considerations.

Your Home

Filing for bankruptcy when you own your home is discussed in Ch. 4, but here's a reminder: If you own your home and are behind on the payments, Chapter 13 bankruptcy will allow you to keep your house if your proposed repayment plan is feasible. Chapter 7 bankruptcy, on the other hand, does not offer a procedure for catching up on missed mortgage payments ("curing an arrearage"). Unless you can become current on your payments—using property or income you acquire after your filing date—the creditor can ask the court to lift the automatic stay so it can proceed with the foreclosure.

However, if you are current on your mortgage, Chapter 7 bankruptcy might help you eliminate other liens on your house. As explained in "Option 5: Eliminate (Avoid) Liens," above, you can use lien avoidance to get rid of judicial liens if they conflict with your homestead exemption. And you can do this without a lawyer's help.

With the help of a lawyer, you might be able to eliminate other types of liens, including "unrecorded" tax liens and liens for penalties, fines, or punitive damages from a lawsuit.

As for reaffirmation—most bankruptcy courts do not require you to reaffirm a mortgage, even if the bank requests it. And some bankruptcy judges won't approve mortgage reaffirmation agreements at all.

Your Car

Because repossessed motor vehicles can easily be resold, if a lien remains on your car, the creditor will probably act quickly to either repossess it or force its sale (unless you stay current on your payments and the creditor wouldn't gain much by taking and selling the car). Still, if you intend to keep your car, you should deal with liens on it during bankruptcy. If your automobile is exempt, any judicial liens on it can be eliminated through lien avoidance, as explained above.

The purchase-money security interest held by the seller can be dealt with only through redemption or reaffirmation. Raising the lump sum amount necessary for redemption is your best option. If that is not possible, your only realistic option is to reaffirm the debt unless you are willing to gamble that the creditor will let you keep the car as long as you make your payments.

If your automobile falls within the tools of the trade exemption, you can use lien avoidance for any non-purchase-money liens on the vehicle.

Exempt Property

There are four ways to deal with liens on exempt property:

- Give the property back (if there's no property, there's no lien).
- Get rid of the lien in a lien avoidance action.
- Redeem the property.
- Reaffirm the debt.

If you keep the property, you should use lien avoidance whenever possible to eliminate judicial liens and non-purchase-money security interests. Use redemption whenever the lien exceeds the replacement value of the property and you can raise the cash necessary to buy the property back.

If you can't raise the lump sum necessary for redemption, you'll have to either reaffirm the debt or attempt to pay off the lien outside of bankruptcy. The option you choose will depend on how anxious the creditor is to repossess the item. If the property is of little value, you can probably get away with informally paying off the lien. However, if the property is of greater value, you might have to sign an agreement and cooperate in the reaffirmation process. Remember never to agree to pay more than it would cost to replace the property.

Also, remember that even if you can get liens wiped out, you still might not get to keep the property if your equity in the property is worth significantly more than your exemption amount. The trustee might want to sell the property, pay you your exemption amount, and distribute the remaining portion among your unsecured creditors. (See "Nonexempt Property," below, for information on what happens to nonexempt property, including equity that exceeds the available exemption.)

In this situation, the only way to hold on to the property is to buy the equity back from the trustee. How much you will have to pay depends on several factors, but keep in mind this basic rule: The amount you offer to the trustee has to leave your unsecured creditors no worse off than they would have been had the trustee sold the property to somebody else.

> **EXAMPLE:** Mindy has a $1,000 asset on which she can claim a $500 exemption. There is a $200 judicial lien on the asset. Mindy cannot avoid the lien because it does not "impair" her exemption. If the trustee sold the property, Mindy would receive her $500 exemption, the lienholder would get $200, and the remaining $300 would go to Mindy's unsecured creditors. If Mindy wanted to buy the property from the trustee, she'd have to offer $500: $200 for the lienholder and $300 for her unsecured creditors.

As you can see, the amount you have to offer the trustee will vary from case to case, depending on the amount of the liens, the amount of your exemption, and whether you or the trustee can eliminate the liens on the asset. You can consult with the trustee to work out the particulars.

Nonexempt Property

If you want to keep nonexempt property, your options are more limited.

- Redeem the property if the trustee abandons it. (Abandoning property means that the trustee releases it from the bankruptcy estate. A trustee can abandon property that is not valuable enough to justify selling it to raise money for the unsecured creditors.)
- Reaffirm the debt if the trustee abandons the property.

Property Worth More Than the Debt

If your nonexempt property is worth significantly more than the liens on it, you probably won't have a chance to keep it—unless you pay the trustee the net amount the property would realize upon sale, after deducting whatever exemption you are entitled to, the costs of sale and the trustee's commission. Otherwise, the trustee is likely to sell the property, pay off the liens, and distribute the rest of the proceeds to your unsecured creditors.

> **EXAMPLE:** Elena pledges her $4,000 car as security for a $900 loan. The $900 lien is the only lien on her car, and only $1,200 of the $4,000 is exempt. If Elena files for bankruptcy, the trustee will first allow Elena to informally bid on the property. If Elena and the trustee can't reach an agreement, the trustee can take the car, sell it, pay off the $900 lien, give Elena her $1,200 exemption, and distribute the rest of the proceeds to Elena's creditors.

If the trustee does not take the property and you want to keep it, your best bet is to either remain current on your payments or begin the reaffirmation process (if your creditor requires it).

Property Worth Less Than the Debt

If the property is worth less than the liens on it, the trustee will probably abandon it.

> **EXAMPLE:** When Conner bought his $500 sofa on credit from the Reliable Furniture Co., he pledged the sofa as security. Since then, the sofa has declined in value to only $100, but he still owes $250 on it. The trustee will abandon the property, because selling it would yield no proceeds for the unsecured creditors.

The trustee might also abandon property with more than one lien on it if the total of all the liens exceeds the property's value. In this case, the creditors with the lowest-priority liens are called undersecured creditors. (State and federal law determine the priority of the liens. Most of the time, the most recent lien is the lowest-priority lien, but certain types of liens always have priority over others.)

> **EXAMPLE:** Demetrius's car is currently worth $3,000. He pledged his car as collateral for the loan he used to buy it. That loan has a remaining balance of $2,200. He later pledged his vehicle for two personal loans on which he owes $500 each. In addition, there is a judgment lien against his car for $1,000. The total balance of all liens is $4,200.
> In this situation, the original $2,200 purchase-money loan is fully secured, and so is the first personal loan for $500. The other $500 loan is secured only by the remaining $300 in equity, so it is an undersecured claim—nothing is securing the $1,000 judgment lien.

If the trustee abandons the property, you have the right to redeem it at its current replacement value. This is your best option if you can come up with the necessary lump sum payment. Redemption eliminates all liens on the property.

If you are unable to come up with the lump sum required to purchase the property, and the creditor is unwilling to accept installment payments, you'll need to find out whether your lender will require you to reaffirm the debt or whether you can keep the car by remaining current on your payments without reaffirmation.

TIP

Planning reminder. Once you've filed for bankruptcy, a creditor cannot legally take your property unless the court lifts the automatic stay or you miss the deadline for dealing with your secured debts. (One note regarding cars: If you miss the deadline, most creditors will still ask the court to lift the automatic stay before repossessing your vehicle.) It's much easier to hold on to property in the first place than to get it back after the creditor repossesses it. So, if you have some exempt property that a creditor is about to take and you haven't filed for bankruptcy yet, you might want to file right away to prevent the seizure.

Reclaiming Exempt Property Repossessed Just Before Bankruptcy

If a secured creditor took exempt property that would qualify for either lien avoidance or redemption during the 90 days before you filed for bankruptcy, you might be able to get the property back. But you must act quickly before the creditor resells the property. If the creditor has already resold the property, you are probably out of luck. Repossessed cars are usually resold very quickly, but used furniture could sit in a warehouse for months.

If you catch the creditor in time, the creditor must legally give back the property because the repossession is an illegal preference, which means that the property is still part of the bankruptcy estate (as explained in Ch. 3). In practice, however, the creditor won't give the property back unless the court orders it (which usually means you'll need the help of a lawyer) or unless you make a reasonable cash offer for the item.

Assuming you don't want to hire a lawyer, you probably won't be able to get an item back unless you talk the creditor into allowing you to redeem it or reaffirm the debt. The creditor might prefer to have cash in hand rather than used property sitting in a warehouse. If you plan to avoid the lien on the exempt item and not pay anything, however, the creditor probably won't turn over the property unless forced to by court order.

Whether hiring a lawyer is worth the expense to get back an exempt item so you can avoid the lien depends on how badly you need the property and what you'll save through lien avoidance. Compare what it would cost to redeem the property or buy replacement property. If those options are cheaper, or you decide you can get along without the property, don't bother with the court order.

Step-by-Step Instructions

Once you decide what to do with each item of secured property, you must list your intentions on your Statement of Intention, file the form, mail a copy to each secured creditor listed on the form, and then carry out the procedures you commit to within 30 days after the creditors' meeting. (See Ch. 6 for instructions on completing the form.)

How to Surrender Property

If you plan to surrender any secured property, here's how to proceed:

Step 1: When you fill out your Statement of Intention, state that you are surrendering the property that secures the debt.

Step 2: The creditor must make arrangements to pick up the property. It's not your responsibility to deliver. But you can call your creditor, explain the situation, and ask if they want the property back. If they don't, great—you don't have to worry about it anymore. If they do pick it up, get a receipt. (See sample receipt below.)

Receipt for Surrender of Property

1. This receipt certifies that _____ *[name of repossessor (print)]* _____ took the following item(s): *(list items)* _____

   _____

   _____

   _____ .

   on __*[date]*__ , 20__ , because of debt owed to __*[name of creditor (print)]*__ .

2. __*[Name of repossessor (print)]*__ is an authorized agent of __*[name of creditor (print)]*__ .

   Signed: __*[Your signature]*_____   Dated: _____

   Signed: __*[Repossessor's signature]*_____   Dated: _____

How to Avoid Liens on Exempt Property

To avoid a lien on exempt property you'll first need to claim an exemption on the property on Schedule C.

> **SEE AN EXPERT**
>
> **If you miss the deadline, talk to a lawyer.** You might not discover a lien until after the deadline passes for filing a motion. In fact, it's not uncommon to find liens only after a bankruptcy case is closed. If this happens to you, you can file a motion asking the court to let you proceed even though you missed the deadline, or even to reopen the case if necessary. (For sample forms to reopen a bankruptcy case, see Ch. 7.)

What goes in your motion papers depends on the kind of lien you're trying to get eliminated.

Nonpossessory, Non-Purchase-Money Security Interests

You will need to fill out one complete set of forms for each affected creditor —generally, each creditor holding a lien on that property. You'll find sample forms on the companion page (www.nolo.com/back-of-book/HFB.html). Some courts have their own forms; if yours does, use them and adapt these instructions to fit.

> **TIP**
>
> **Do you need to use pleading paper?** Pleading paper is a particular type of paper used in many state and federal courts with numbers running down the left side of the page. The federal bankruptcy rules do not require you to submit motions or other pleadings on pleading paper. However, it's possible that your local court rules do. Check with the applicable court clerk and if numbered paper is required, use the pleading paper found on the companion page (www.nolo.com/back-of-book/HFB.html), or search for "pleading paper" online to find free, downloadable pleading paper.

Step 1: If your court publishes local rules, refer to them for time limits, the format of papers, and other details of a motion proceeding.

Step 2: Type the top half of the pleading form (where you list your name, the court, the case number, and so on) following the motion examples found on the companion page (www.nolo.com/back-of-book/HFB.html). This part of the form is known as the "caption." It is the same for all pleadings.

Checklist of Forms for Motion to Avoid Nonpossessory, Non-Purchase-Money Security Interest

☐ Motion to Avoid Nonpossessory, Non-Purchase-Money Security Interest
☐ Notice of Motion to Avoid Nonpossessory, Non-Purchase-Money Security Interest
☐ Order to Avoid Nonpossessory, Non-Purchase-Money Security Interest
☐ Proof of Service by Mail

Step 3: If you're using a computer to prepare the forms, save the caption portion and reuse it for other pleadings. If you're using a typewriter to prepare the forms, stop when you've typed the caption and photocopy the page you've made so far, so you can reuse it for other pleadings.

Step 4: Using one of the copies that you just made, start typing again just below the caption and prepare a Motion to Avoid Nonpossessory, Non-Purchase-Money Security Interest, as shown in the example located on the companion page.

Step 5: Most courts require you to file the notice and motion with the court and serve the creditor and trustee with both. The notice will explain that the lien will be avoided by default if the creditor doesn't respond and request a hearing on your motion. (These are colorfully called "scream or die" motions—see the sample Notice of Motion and Motion to Avoid Judicial Lien on Real Estate, located on the companion page, for language you can use instead of a formal notice if your district follows this procedure.) Because motions to avoid liens are usually pretty straightforward and are typically granted, many creditors don't bother to respond. If they do, however, either you or the creditor will have to schedule a hearing.

Step 6: If a hearing is required, call the court clerk and give your name and case number. Say you'd like to file a motion to avoid a lien and need to find out when and where the judge will hear arguments on your motion. Some local rules require the clerk to give you a hearing date. Ask for one at least 31 days in the future because you must mail notice of your motion to the creditor at least 30 days before the hearing (unless local rules set a different time limit). Write down the information. If the clerk won't give you the information over the phone, go to the bankruptcy court with a copy of your motion filled out. File that form and schedule the hearing. Write down the information about when and where your motion will be heard by the judge. (Some courts allow you to "self set" your motion by choosing a date online.)

If there will be a hearing, prepare a Notice of Motion that lists the date, time, and location. (See the Sample Notice of Motion to Avoid Nonpossessory, Non-Purchase-Money Security Interest on the companion page.) If you are filing in a district that requires a hearing only if the creditor requests one, use the language in the sample Notice of Motion and Motion to Avoid Judicial Lien on Real Estate on the companion page to give the creditor proper notice of this procedure.

Step 7: Prepare a proposed Order to Avoid Nonpossessory, Non-Purchase-Money Security Interest. This is the document the judge signs to grant your request. In the space indicated in the sample on the companion page, specify what property the creditor has secured. You can get this information from the security agreement you signed. Make two extra copies, and take them with you to the hearing if there is one. The court's local rules might require you to file the proposed order with the rest of your motion papers.

Step 8: Prepare at least two Proofs of Service by Mail, one for each affected creditor and one for the trustee. These forms state that a friend or relative of yours, who is at least 18 years old and not a party to the bankruptcy, mailed your papers to the creditor(s) or the trustee. Fill in the blanks as indicated. Have your friend or relative sign and date the form at the end as shown on the companion page sample. (See "How to Serve the Creditor," below, for more information.)

Step 9: Make at least three extra copies of all forms.

Step 10: Keep the proofs of service. Have your friend mail one copy of the motion, notice of motion, and proposed order to each affected creditor and the trustee.

Step 11: File (in person or by mail) the original (signed) notice of motion, motion (and proposed order, if required in your area), and proof of service with the bankruptcy court.

Step 12: The trustee or creditors affected by your motion might submit a written response. However, most courts will grant your motion if the trustee or creditor doesn't file a response to the motion and you ask the court to enter a default judgment in your favor (see Step 14, below).

Step 13: If there is a hearing, attend it. The hearing usually lasts ten minutes or less. Because you filed the motion, you argue your side first. Explain briefly how your property falls within the acceptable categories of exempt property, that the lien is a nonpossessory non-purchase-money security interest, and that the lien impairs your exemption. (11 U.S.C. § 522(f)(2).) "Impairs your exemption" means that because of the lien, your ownership interest in this item of exempt property has been reduced.

The trustee or creditor (or an attorney) responds. The judge either decides the matter and signs your proposed order or takes it "under advisement" and mails you the order in a few days.

Step 14: If the creditor doesn't show up at the hearing, or if the creditor doesn't file a response to your motion when required to do so (see Step 12, above), file and serve a Request for Entry of Order by Default. (See the sample request with the papers for avoiding a judicial lien on the companion page to get an idea of what this should look like. Of course, you'll have to change the language so it refers to a nonpossessory, non-purchase-money security interest rather than a judicial lien.) This document tells the court that you followed all of the proper procedures and gave the creditor notice of your motion, but the creditor didn't respond as it was required to do. The request asks the court to grant your motion by default. You must prepare another Proof of Service and serve this request on the creditor.

Judicial Lien

To get rid of a judicial lien, follow the steps to eliminate a nonpossessory, non-purchase-money security interest, above, but use the Sample Notice of Motion and Motion to Avoid Judicial Lien on Real Estate and Sample Order to Avoid Judicial Lien on Real Estate forms as examples.

The sample forms are for eliminating a judicial lien on your home. To erase a lien on personal property, you will need to change the language accordingly.

SEE AN EXPERT

Get an attorney, if you need one. If you are having trouble figuring out how to draft the necessary paperwork to avoid a lien, think about asking a lawyer for help—especially if the lien is substantial.

Checklist of Forms for Motion to Avoid Judicial Lien

- ☐ Motion to Avoid Judicial Lien or Motion to Avoid Judicial Lien (on Real Estate)
- ☐ Notice of Motion to Avoid Judicial Lien
- ☐ Order to Avoid Judicial Lien
- ☐ Proof of Service
- ☐ Request for Entry of Order by Default and Proof of Service by Mail (if the creditor doesn't respond)

You will likely have to prove the value of the property in question. Typically, when you file for bankruptcy and assign a value to your property, the only person who will check your figures is the trustee. However, if a creditor opposes your motion to avoid a judicial lien, the creditor can make you prove the property's value because the more the property is worth, the less the lien impairs the exemption. For instance, if you listed property worth $50,000 and the exemption is $45,000, a lien exceeding $5,000 would impair the exemption and entitle you to have the lien removed. But if the evidence you provide at the hearing shows that the property is worth $60,000, a lien of less than $15,000 wouldn't impair the exemption because you would be able to take your $45,000 exemption and still pay the full lien. So be prepared to show how you determined the value of your property.

> **SEE AN EXPERT**
>
> **Use an attorney, if necessary.** If you are having trouble figuring out how to draft the necessary paperwork to avoid a lien, think about asking a lawyer for help—especially if the lien is substantial.

Tax Liens

If your federal tax debt is secured, you might have a basis for challenging the lien. Quite often, the IRS makes mistakes when it records a notice of federal tax lien.

> **SEE AN EXPERT**
>
> **Help from a lawyer.** You will need the help of a tax or bankruptcy attorney—preferably one who has experience in both areas—to challenge a tax lien.

Here are some possible grounds for asking the court to remove the lien:

- The notice of federal tax lien was never recorded, though the IRS claims it was.
- The notice of federal tax lien was recorded after the automatic stay took effect.
- The notice of federal tax lien was recorded in the wrong county: it must be recorded where you own real estate to attach to the real estate in that county.

How to Serve the Creditor

Here are the rules for providing notice to the creditor:
- If the creditor provided you with a contact address and a current account number within the 90 days before you filed for bankruptcy, you must use that address and include the account number and the last four digits of your Social Security or taxpayer identification number with your papers.
- If the creditor was prohibited from communicating with you during these 90 days, you must use the address and account number in the two written communications you received most recently from the creditor.
- If the creditor has filed a preferred contact address with the court, you must use that address.

If your creditor is a business, you must serve a live human being who represents the creditor—you can't just send your motion to "Visa" or "First Bank," for example. Here's how to find that warm body:
- Call the creditor and ask for the name and address of the person who accepts service of process for the business.
- If you don't know how to reach the creditor, contact your state's Secretary of State office and ask for the name and address of the person listed as the registered agent for service of process for the company. Many states make this information available online, too.

Even if the notice of federal tax lien was recorded correctly, you still might have a basis to fight it if either of the following is true:
- The lien expired—liens last only ten years.
- The lien is based on an invalid tax assessment by the IRS.

How to Redeem Property

If you want to redeem exempt or abandoned property, list the property on your Statement of Intention as property to be retained and check the column that says property will be redeemed. (More instructions are in Ch. 6.) You must pay the creditor the current replacement value of the property within 45 days after the creditors' meeting.

TIP

Explore lien avoidance first. If lien avoidance is available, you might be able to get rid of a lien on exempt property without paying anything.

Agreeing on the Value of the Property

Before you can redeem property, you and the creditor must agree on what the property is worth. If you believe the creditor is setting too high a price for the property, tell the creditor why you think the property is worth less—it needs repair, it's falling apart, damaged or stained, or whatever. If you can't reach an agreement, you can ask the bankruptcy court to rule on the matter. But you will probably need an attorney to help you make this request, so it is not worth your while unless the property is worth more than the lawyer will cost, and you and the creditor are very far apart in your estimates of the property's value.

You and the creditor should sign a redemption agreement that sets forth the terms of your arrangement and the amount you will pay if there is a dispute later. (See the sample forms on the companion page.)

If the Creditor Won't Cooperate

The creditor might refuse to let you redeem the property, because the creditor claims that it isn't the type of property you can redeem or because you can't agree on the value. If so, you will need to file a formal complaint in the bankruptcy court to have a judge resolve the issue. You will need an attorney to help you, so think twice about whether you really want to redeem the property. It might be better to let the creditor have it or reaffirm if the creditor insists and you are current on your payments.

Paying in Installments

If you can't raise enough cash to pay the creditor within 45 days after the creditors' meeting, try to get the creditor to let you pay in installments. Some creditors will agree if the installments are substantial and you agree to pay interest on them. But a creditor is not required to accept installments; it can demand the entire amount in cash.

If the creditor refuses to accept installments, you can ask the bankruptcy court to delay your deadline for making the payment for a month or two. But to do so, you will need to file a formal complaint with the bankruptcy court. Again, you will need an attorney to help you, so it might not be worth it.

Paperwork

On the companion page (www.nolo.com/back-of-book/HFB.html) are two sample redemption agreements you can use. Form 1 is for installments and Form 2 is for a lump sum payment. Type the form on pleading paper (the blank paper on the companion page with numbers down the left side) and put your bankruptcy case number on it in case you need to file it later. You should fill out a separate form for every item of property you want to redeem. Have the creditor sign it.

There is no need to file these agreements with the trustee. Keep them with your other bankruptcy papers in case the trustee or the judge wants to see them.

How to Reaffirm a Debt

Bankruptcy courts frown on reaffirmation agreements because they obligate debtors to make payments after bankruptcy, which contradicts the purpose of bankruptcy of providing a fresh start. Nevertheless, if you decide to reaffirm a debt, you must say so on your Statement of Intention. Within 45 days after the 341 hearing, you must be willing to sign a reaffirmation agreement. The law provides that either you or the creditor must file the reaffirmation agreement and, if you aren't represented by an attorney, file a motion asking the court to approve it (the motion is part of the official reaffirmation form). If you are dealing with a major creditor, you can count on the creditor to provide the agreement, get your signature, and file it with the court. After all, these creditors are familiar with reaffirmation agreements, and they want you to be legally obligated to repay the loan after your bankruptcy discharge is granted. You or the creditor can draft an agreement or use the 2400 form series located on the website of the United States Courts (www.uscourts.gov/forms/bankruptcy-forms).

The reaffirmation agreement includes a motion and a request for a reaffirmation hearing. After you file the agreement, you will receive notice of the scheduled hearing in the mail. At the hearing, the judge will make sure that you understand the consequences of signing the agreement. The judge must approve the agreement unless it appears, based on the income and expenses you reported on Schedule I and Schedule J, that you won't be able to make the required payments or that reaffirmation is not in your best interests. In that case, the judge will disapprove the agreement and send you and the creditor back to the drawing board. (See "If the Court Refuses to Approve Your Reaffirmation Agreement," above.)

> **TIP**
>
> **Don't agree to pay too much.** If the creditor requires you to reaffirm the total amount owed on the collateral (an amount that is greater than the current replacement value of the collateral), select another option unless you really want the property and won't be able to get similar property after bankruptcy. In general, you shouldn't reaffirm a debt for more than it would cost you to replace the property.

Your right to cancel a reaffirmation agreement. The bankruptcy code gives you the right to cancel a reaffirmation agreement by notifying the creditor:
- before you receive your discharge, or
- within 60 days after the reaffirmation agreement is filed with the bankruptcy court, whichever is later. (11 U.S.C. § 524(c)(2).)

Notice to the creditor of your cancellation should be by certified mail, return receipt requested. This precludes the creditor from later claiming it didn't receive notification.

Canceling your reaffirmation will leave your debt in the same condition as if you had never filed the reaffirmation agreement. That is, your personal liability for the debt will be discharged (assuming the debt is dischargeable), and the creditor will be able to enforce its lien on your property by either repossessing or foreclosing on it. If your bankruptcy case is still open, you can still try other options discussed in this chapter.

Complete and File Your Bankruptcy Paperwork

This chapter shows you how to take all of the necessary steps to prepare your case for filing under Chapter 7. For the most part, the process is simple, as long as you follow all of the instructions we provide.

> **CAUTION**
>
> **Chapter 7 bankruptcy can be a very straightforward process, but only if you follow the rules.** If you make a mistake—even accidentally—your bankruptcy case might be dismissed. In most cases, you can correct errors with an amendment. But sometimes errors are not correctable and your case will be dismissed with dire consequences: Not only will you continue to owe your debts and face creditor collection actions, but you might also lose the protection of the automatic stay in any future bankruptcy case you file within the next year (see Ch. 2 for more information on the automatic stay).

Gather the Necessary Documents

Along with the official bankruptcy forms, you will also have to provide:

- certification showing that you completed a credit counseling workshop within the last 180 days
- your most recent federal tax return or a transcript of the return (this goes either to the trustee or the court, depending on where you file), and
- your wage stubs for the last 60 days.

Before you can get your bankruptcy discharge, you must also file a certification showing that you completed counseling on personal financial management (Form 423—Certification About a Financial Management Course, covered in Ch. 7) along with a certificate of completion from the counseling agency itself. In addition, the trustee might mail you a request for other documents—or request the documents at your 341 hearing. You should do your best to comply with any reasonable request. Requests related to your financial situation are generally reasonable.

Follow These Rules to Stay Out of Trouble

If you keep these golden rules in mind, you'll save yourself a lot of time and trouble:

- Don't file for Chapter 7 bankruptcy unless you are sure it is the right choice (Ch. 1 explains how to make this decision).
- Don't file until you have assembled all of your documents as directed in this chapter.
- Don't file until you have a certificate showing that you have completed your credit counseling workshop.
- If you can, pay your filing fee in full rather than in installments, so you don't have to worry about your case being dismissed if you miss a payment.
- Be absolutely honest when filling out your paperwork.
- File all of your documents simultaneously (unless you have to file an emergency petition to stop an impending foreclosure, wage garnishment, or repossession).
- Don't file your case until you have your most recent federal tax return (or a transcript) in your hands.
- Serve your tax return (or transcript) on the trustee and any creditors who request it as soon after you file as possible. If you don't serve it at least seven days before the creditors' meeting, theoretically your case could be dismissed, although that is rare. Do the same with your paycheck stubs.
- If you haven't filed a tax return for two or more tax years, send the trustee a written, signed note explaining when you last filed. If relevant, explain why you haven't filed (for instance, your income no longer requires you to file).
- Immediately amend your paperwork if the trustee asks you to.
- Respond to the trustee's request for any supplemental documentation as quickly as possible.
- Don't forget your personal financial management counseling. You won't receive a discharge unless, within 45 days after your creditors' meeting, you file Form 423 certifying that you have completed this course along with the certificate of completion from the counseling agency itself. (Ch. 7 explains how.)

The Credit Counseling Certificate

As explained in Ch. 1, every person who files a consumer bankruptcy must first attend credit counseling within 180 days before filing. The counseling can be done by phone, online, or in person. You'll find a list of approved counselors on the U.S. Trustee's Office website at www.justice.gov/ust (click "Credit Counseling & Debtor Education"). The agencies are listed by state and court district. Select an agency approved by your court.

Once you finish your counseling, the agency should give you a certificate of completion. You'll verify your attempts to obtain counseling on Part 5 of your bankruptcy petition (see the instructions for completing the petition below). The certificate must be filed within 14 days after you file unless you fit within a rare exception. Many agencies will file your certificate for you, but file it with your other paperwork if the agency won't. That way, you won't forget and end up getting your case dismissed.

Repayment Plans

The purpose of credit counseling is to get you to sign up for a debt repayment plan instead of filing for bankruptcy. If the plan makes sense and you believe you can faithfully make the required payments, consider signing up for it. However, keep in mind that even if you make the payments month after month, the creditors can pull out if you fall behind and go after you for the remaining debt. If you decide to file for Chapter 7 afterward, you will have paid back all that money for no good reason. This is why most bankruptcy professionals discourage their clients from signing up for a debt repayment plan.

Even if you have no intention of signing up for a plan, you must cooperate with the debt counseling agency and create a plan if they think one is possible. In many cases, it's clear that a plan won't be feasible. Debtors who have funds to pay creditors will have to file the plan with the court along with the certificate of completion and other bankruptcy papers. If the U.S. Trustee suspects that you might be able to repay creditors in Chapter 13, reviewing the agency's plan will be part of the decision-making process.

Counseling Fees

Most of these credit counseling agencies charge a modest sum ($25–$50 is typical) for the counseling, coming up with a repayment plan (if it gets that far), and the certificate of completion that you'll need to file with your other bankruptcy papers.

Agencies are legally required to offer their services without regard to your ability to pay. (11 U.S.C. § 111(c)(2)(B).) If an agency wants to charge more than you can afford, inform the agency of this legal requirement.

Exceptions to the Counseling Requirement

You don't have to get counseling if the U.S. Trustee certifies no appropriate agency is available in the district where you will be filing. However, counseling can be provided by telephone or online, so it is unlikely that approved debt counseling will ever be unavailable.

However, in one case, a bankruptcy court found that counseling was not "available" to a debtor who spoke Creole because none of the credit counseling agencies in his area could accommodate his language needs. (*In re Petit-Louis*, 344 B.R. 696 (Bankr. S.D. Fla. 2006).) Presumably, this same rule would apply to any debtor who doesn't speak standard English and can't obtain counseling in his or her native language (or through a translator). Since this case was decided, more multilingual credit counseling agencies are available.

You can also avoid the requirement if you ask the court to grant an exception and prove that "exigent circumstances" prevented you from getting counseling. You'll have to show that both of the following are true:

- You had to file for bankruptcy immediately (perhaps to stop a creditor from levying on your paycheck or bank account).
- You were unable to obtain counseling within seven days after requesting it.

> CAUTION
>
> **A foreclosure may not be "exigent" enough.** Several courts have found that a debtor who waits until the last minute to seek credit counseling might not qualify for an exception to the counseling requirement. For example, in *Dixon v. La Barge, Jr.*, 338 B.R. 383 (B.A.P. 8th Cir. 2006), the court found no exigent

circumstances existed when a debtor filed for bankruptcy on the day of a scheduled foreclosure sale. In that case, the debtor claimed to have learned that he could file for Chapter 7 bankruptcy—and that he would have to complete credit counseling—on the night before he filed.

If the court grants an exception, you must complete the counseling within 30 days after you file (you can ask the court to extend this deadline by 15 days).

You can also escape the credit counseling requirement if, after notice and hearing, the bankruptcy court determines that you couldn't participate because of one of the following:

- physical disability that prevents you from attending counseling (this exception probably won't apply if the counseling is available on the Internet or over the phone)
- mental incapacity (you are unable to understand and benefit from the counseling), or
- active duty in a military combat zone.

Consequences of Failing to Get Counseling

Courts have handled a debtor's failure to get counseling in two different ways. Some courts dismiss the debtor's case. Other courts have "stricken" the debtor's case instead. (See *In re Carey*, 341 B.R. 798 (Bankr. M.D. Fla. 2006).) This seemingly technical difference can be very important: If your case is stricken, you can refile without any of the negative consequences of dismissal (including losing the protection of the automatic stay) explained in Ch. 2.

Your Tax Return or Transcript

You must give the trustee and the U.S. Trustee your most recent federal tax return no later than seven days before your creditors' meeting. (11 U.S.C. § 521(e)(2).) You also have to provide the return to any creditor who asks for it. To protect your privacy, you can redact (black out) your birthdate and Social Security number. If you don't provide your tax return on time, your case could be dismissed.

If you can't find a copy of your most recent tax return, you can ask the IRS to give you a transcript containing the basic information in your return—and you can use the transcript as a substitute for your return. Because it can take some time to receive the transcript, you should make your request as soon as you can.

> **CAUTION**
>
> **If you haven't filed tax returns.** As mentioned earlier, if you haven't filed federal tax returns for more than two years, send the trustee a written, signed note explaining the circumstances surrounding your nonfiling. An example of wording might be, "Five years ago I retired from my job and have been living on Social Security. As a result, I've had no need to file taxes."

Wage Stubs

If you are employed, you receive stubs or "advices" with your paycheck. You must produce stubs covering the 60-day period before filing. If you can't access your stubs online and you've already tossed them, you have two options: Wait 60 days before filing (and save your stubs), or go ahead and file, hand over the stubs you have and explain why you don't have 60 days' worth. This second option might not work, however. You'll likely be required to secure some type of proof from your employee since most employers can provide this information in another form, if necessary.

In many courts, you don't file this information. Instead, you send it directly to the trustee. Your bankruptcy court might have a different procedure, however.

If you are not employed, don't worry about this requirement. However, if you receive Social Security or workers' compensation, you should plan on providing proof of those payments. Self-employed individuals will need to turn over monthly and yearly profit and loss statements.

Other Documents

In addition to your tax return and pay stubs, you might have to provide the trustee with other documents before your 341 hearing. Check your local court rules and Chapter 7 trustee standing administration guidelines, or call the trustee's office to ensure you have everything you'll need.

In general, the most commonly requested documents include your:

- bank statements
- retirement account statements
- deed of trust or mortgage payoff information
- car loan statements
- car registrations
- proof of home or car insurance
- marital dissolution agreements, and
- property valuations.

Get Some Information From the Court

Every bankruptcy court has its own requirements for filing bankruptcy papers. If your papers don't meet these local requirements, the court clerk could reject them. So, before you begin preparing your papers, find out your court rules.

In busy courts, you might not get a response to a letter or phone call and will need to visit the court or access information online. Almost every bankruptcy court will keep this information on its website. To find your court's website, visit www.uscourts.gov/federal-court-finder/search.

> **TIP**
>
> **Find out if your court is open.** As of this writing, federal bankruptcy courts are in the process of resuming operations. Because reopening guidelines encourage courts to consider community COVID-19 transmission rates and public health recommendations, the extent of services available will vary, and temporary closures could occur. Check your local court's website for current social distancing information.

Fees

The total filing fee for Chapter 7 bankruptcy is $338. Fees change, however, so verify the amount with the court. This fee is due immediately, unless the court waives the fee or gives you permission to pay in installments. (To make these requests, complete Form 103A or 103B, as explained below.)

Finding the Right Bankruptcy Court

Because bankruptcy is a creature of federal, not state, law, you must file for bankruptcy in a special federal court. There are federal bankruptcy courts all over the country.

The federal court system divides the country into judicial districts. Every state has at least one judicial district; most have more. You can file in any of the following districts:

- where you have been living for the greater part of the 180 days before filing
- where you are domiciled—that is, where you maintain your home, even if you have been living elsewhere temporarily (such as on a military base)
- where your principal place of business is located (if you are a business debtor), or
- where the majority of your business assets are located.

Most readers will use the first option—and many will file in the large city closest to their home. To find a bankruptcy court in your state, use the Federal Court Finder on the U.S. Court's website at www.uscourts.gov/federal-court-finder/search. If you live in a state with more than one district, you can call the court in the closest city and ask whether that district includes your county or zip code.

EXAMPLE: For the past two months, Tom has lived in San Luis Obispo, which is located in California's Central Judicial District. Before that, he lived in Santa Rosa, which is in California's Northern Judicial District. Because Tom spent less of the past six months in the Central District, he should file in the Northern District. If it's too inconvenient, he could wait another month and qualify to file in the Central District.

Local Forms

Along with the official forms every bankruptcy court uses (we list them below), your local bankruptcy court might require you to file a few of its own forms. For example, some courts ask you to include a form with your wage stubs (as explained above). All local forms are available from your local bankruptcy court, or you can download them from your court's website. (Go to www.uscourts.gov/federal-court-finder/search for links to local courts.) Of course, we can't include all local forms in this book or tell you how to fill them out. Most, however, are self-explanatory. If you need help in obtaining or understanding them, see a local bankruptcy lawyer.

Local Court Rules

Most bankruptcy courts publish local rules that govern the court's procedures. These rules mainly govern hearings conducted by the bankruptcy judge and aren't relevant in routine bankruptcy cases. Still, a rule can affect a routine Chapter 7 bankruptcy. You'll find the local rules on the court's website—but be prepared to comb through the table of contents to find the one or two rules that might apply in your case.

Order of Papers and Other Details

Bankruptcy filing offices closed during the COVID-19 pandemic and might (or might not) be open at the time of printing. Because temporary procedures are subject to change and vary by court, the instructions below apply when courts are fully operational.

Check your court's website for filing details. Some courts will want paperwork mailed in. Others have introduced online filing options for non-attorneys (go to www.pacer.uscourts.gov/register-account/non-attorney-filers-cmecf for instructions).

Every court has a preferred order in which it wants to receive forms submitted for filing. Most courts also have rules detailing whether the forms should be stapled or hole-punched, and more. If you make a mistake, most clerks will put your forms in the correct order or punch and staple your papers in the right way. Some, however, will make you do it yourself. This can be a major pain if you are filing by mail. Every court has an exhibit of the standard Chapter 7 filing with the forms arranged correctly. If you want to get it right the first time, carefully examine the court's sample filing, taking notes on the order in which forms fall.

Sample Letter to Bankruptcy Court

Mackenzie Smith
432 Oak Street
Cincinnati, OH 45219
513-555-7890

July 2, 20xx

United States Bankruptcy Court
Atrium Two, Room 800
221 East Fourth Street
Cincinnati, OH 45202

Attn: COURT CLERK

TO THE COURT CLERK:

I am having a difficult time finding bankruptcy filing instructions and would appreciate your assistance. Please send me the following information:

- copies of all local forms required by this court for an individual (not corporation) filing a Chapter 7 bankruptcy and for making amendments
- the number of copies or sets needed for filing
- the order in which forms should be submitted, and
- complete instructions on this court's emergency filing procedures and deadlines.

  I would also appreciate answers to the following questions:

- Do you require a separate creditor mailing list (matrix)? If so, do you have specific requirements for its format?
- Is the filing fee still $338? If not, please advise.
- Should I two-hole punch my papers, or is that done by the court?
- Should I staple the papers, use paper clips, or leave them loose?

  I've enclosed a self-addressed envelope for your reply. Thank you.

  Sincerely,

  Mackenzie Smith
  Mackenzie Smith

Enclosure

You'll likely find the information on the court's website, so look there first. If you can't find what you need, try calling the court (or visiting if it's open). If that doesn't work, you can adapt the sample letter above to your situation and send it to the court along with a large, self-addressed envelope.

If your efforts fail, use paperclips on forms with more than one page and stack them by form number with the voluntary petition on top. Bankruptcy courts scan the documents into a filing system, so avoiding staples is likely the safest approach. Forcing the clerk to remove staples could slow down the process, and hole punching is likely unnecessary.

Number of Copies

Before filing your papers, find out how many copies your court requires. Most ask for an original and one copy. The original will be scanned into the court's database, and your copy will be "conformed" for your records. A conformed copy is either stamped or receives a computer-generated label, with information showing that you filed, the date of your filing, your case number, and the tentative date of your 341 hearing. A few courts still require you to provide an original plus more than one additional copy.

For Married Filers

If you are married, you and your spouse will have to decide whether one of you should file alone or whether you should file jointly. To make this decision, consider how filing together or separately will affect your debts and property.

Are You Married?

If you were married with a valid state license, you are married for purposes of filing a joint petition, and you can skip down to "Should You File Jointly?" below. However, if you were not married with a license and ceremony, read on.

Some states allow couples to establish common law marriages, which the states will recognize as valid marriages even though the couples do not have state marriage licenses or certificates. Contrary to popular belief, a common law marriage is not created when two people simply live together for a certain number of years. In order to have a valid common law marriage, the couple must do all of the following:

- live together for a significant period of time (not defined in any state)
- hold themselves out as a married couple—typically this means using the same last name, referring to the other as "my husband" or "my wife," and filing a joint tax return, and
- intend to be married.

Alabama, Colorado, the District of Columbia, Iowa, Kansas, Montana, New Hampshire (but only for inheritance purposes), Oklahoma, Rhode Island, South Carolina, Texas, and Utah recognize some form of common law marriage. Florida, Georgia, Idaho, Indiana, Ohio, and Pennsylvania previously allowed common law marriage; those states only recognize common law marriages created before a certain date. The rules for what constitutes a marriage differ from state to state.

If you live in one of these states and you meet your state's requirements for a common law marriage, you have the option to file jointly.

Should You File Jointly?

Unfortunately, a simple formula that will determine whether it's better to file alone or with your spouse doesn't exist. In the end, it will depend on which option allows you to discharge more of your debts and keep more of your property. Here are some of the factors you should consider:

- If you are living in a community property state and most of your debts were incurred, and your property acquired, during marriage, you should probably file jointly. Even if only one spouse files, all community property is considered part of the bankruptcy estate. The same is generally true for debts—that is, all community debts are listed and discharged even though only one spouse files. Even if a creditor doesn't agree that all community debts are discharged if only one spouse files, creditors rarely, if ever, go after a nonfiling spouse for a debt unless his or her name is listed as a joint account owner. (See Ch. 3 for more on community property.)

- If you have recently married, you haven't acquired any valuable assets as a married couple, and one of you has all the debts, it might make sense for that spouse to file for bankruptcy alone (especially if the nonfiling spouse has good credit to protect).

- You might want to file alone if you and your spouse own property as tenants by the entirety (see Ch. 3), you owe most of the debts in your own name, and you live in a state that excludes property held as tenancy by the entirety from the bankruptcy estate when one spouse files. This is a particularly important consideration if you own your home as tenants by the entirety: Filing jointly could cause you to lose your home if you have significant nonexempt equity. (See Ch. 4 for more information.)

- If the exemption system you are using allows married spouses to double their exemptions, filing jointly may help you hang on to more of your property. (See Ch. 3 for more information on exemptions, and the companion page at www.nolo/back-of-book/HFB for state-by-state doubling information.)

- If you are still married but separated, you might have to file alone if your spouse won't cooperate. Still, if your debts and property are joint rather than separate, a joint filing would probably be to your best advantage. It's often easier to qualify because you can deduct expenses for two residences.

- If you are married, you and your spouse have shared finances, and your spouse's income is significantly larger than your own, be aware that filing alone won't prevent the court from considering your spouse's income. You must disclose your spouse's earnings on your bankruptcy petition, and the amount left after deducting your spouse's separate debts will be income attributed to you. (This is called the marital adjustment deduction, and is discussed in instructions for Form 122A-2, below.) If you fail to report your spouse's income, or underreport it, the court will likely dismiss your case.

> **SEE AN EXPERT**
>
> **If you are uncertain about how to file, see a lawyer.** The decision to file jointly or alone can have significant consequences. Because the best choice will depend on your unique situation, we advise you to talk to a bankruptcy lawyer if you have any questions about which option makes more sense.

Required Forms and Documents

Bankruptcy uses official forms prescribed by the Federal Office of the Courts. In addition, you must file certain documents, as described above in "Gather the Necessary Documents." Here and on the companion page we provide complete lists of (1) the official forms you will be completing in this chapter, and (2) the documents that you will have to file along with the official forms. We also explain how to get these forms and documents.

> **TIP**
>
> **How the Official Forms are listed.** On the United States Courts' website (www.uscourts.gov), where you find the official bankruptcy forms, you'll see that many of the forms start with the letter "B." We've dispensed with the "B" in this book.

Checklist of Required Official Bankruptcy Forms

These standard forms must be filed in every Chapter 7 bankruptcy:

Form 101—Voluntary Petition for Individuals Filing for Bankruptcy

Form 101A—Initial Statement About an Eviction Judgment Against You (required if your landlord has an eviction judgment)

Form 101B—Statement About Payment of an Eviction Judgment Against You (required if your landlord has an eviction judgment)

Form 103A—Application for Individuals to Pay the Filing Fee in Installments (if you don't want to pay your fee all at once)

Form 103B—Application to Have the Chapter 7 Filing Fee Waived (if you want your fee waived)

Form 106 Declaration—Declaration About an Individual Debtor's Schedules

Form 106 Summary—A Summary of Your Assets and Liabilities and Certain Statistical Information

Form 106A/B—Schedule A/B: Property

Form 106C—Schedule C: The Property You Claim as Exempt

Form 106D—Schedule D: Creditors Who Hold Claims Secured By Property

Form 106E/F—Schedule E/F: Creditors Who Have Unsecured Claims

Form 106G—Schedule G: Executory Contracts and Unexpired Leases

Form 106H—Schedule H: Your Codebtors

Form 106I—Schedule I: Your Income

Form 106J—Schedule J: Your Expenses

Form 106J-2—Schedule J-2: Expenses for Separate Household of Debtor 2 (required if your spouse lives in a separate home)

Form 107—Your Statement of Financial Affairs for Individuals Filing for Bankruptcy

Form 108—Statement of Intention for Individuals Filing Under Chapter 7

Form 121—Your Statement About Your Social Security Numbers

Form 122A-1—Chapter 7 Statement of Your Current Monthly Income

Form 122A-1Supp—Statement of Exemption from Presumption of Abuse Under § 707(b)(2)

Form 122A-2—Chapter 7 Means Test Calculation

Form 423—Certification About a Financial Management Course

Form 2010—Notice Required by 11 U.S.C. § 342(b) for Individuals Filing for Bankruptcy

Creditor mailing list (sometimes called a Creditor Matrix or Mailing Matrix)

Required local forms, if any.

Except for Forms 122A-1 and 122A-2, which might require you to do a fair bit of math, the forms are easy to complete and are designed to be read and understood by the bankruptcy filers themselves. Although you must include every form as part of your filing package (unless indicated otherwise), some won't require much time to complete. For instance, on Schedule A/B, if you don't own real estate, you can simply check "No" in Part 1 and proceed to Part 2.

Fee Waiver
You can ask the court to waive the fees by filing Form 103B. To qualify, you must be unable to pay in installments, and your income must be below 150% of the poverty line. You might have to appear in court so the judge can ask you questions; however, it's unusual.
If the court doesn't grant your request to waive the fee entirely, the court might let you pay in up to four installments. But be careful. If you miss even one installment, the court could dismiss your case without giving you a chance to explain yourself.
The easiest way to pay your fees is online if your court allows it. Check the court website for an "online payment" feature. You'll likely be directed to a www.pay.gov site where you use your bank account, debit card, or PayPal account. If your court is open, paying your fee at the counter will let you get a receipt from the clerk, which you can use to prove payment, if necessary. The final alternative is to send the fees by registered mail, return receipt requested.

Together these forms make up your "bankruptcy petition," although technically, the petition itself is Form 101. (In case you're wondering, Forms 102, 104, and 105 aren't used for voluntary Chapter 7 bankruptcy filings.)

Where to Get the Official Forms

You can find all of the bankruptcy forms on the website of the United States Courts at www.uscourts.gov/forms/bankruptcy-forms. You can complete the forms online and download them at your convenience. You'll notice that the website usually includes the letter "B" before each form number. We dispense with the "B" in this book. So, for example, if we refer to Form 107, that form will be listed as Form B 107 on the court's website.

Tips for Completing the Forms

Here are some tips that will make filling in your forms more manageable and the whole bankruptcy process smoother. You'll find completed sample forms online at www.nolo.com/back-of-book/HFB.html. You can refer to the sample form when reading each form's instructions and filling in your bankruptcy papers. A list of the online resources mentioned in each chapter is at the end of the book.

Use your worksheets and credit counseling plan (if you have one). If you've completed the worksheets in Chs. 1, 3, 4, and 5, you've already done a lot of the work. These worksheets will save you time when you prepare your bankruptcy forms, so keep them handy. If you skipped any of those chapters, refer to the worksheets and accompanying instructions for help in figuring out what to put in your bankruptcy forms.

Make several copies of each form. That way, you can make a draft and change things as you go until the form is complete. Prepare final forms to file with the court only after you've double-checked your drafts.

Prepare your final forms. The easiest, neatest way to complete the forms is by using the fillable forms on the U.S. Courts' website. However, if you wish to print out the forms from the website or get blank forms from your local bankruptcy court, then it's best to type the information into the blanks. You can provide handwritten information, but the trustee handling your case will likely be friendlier if forms are typewritten. If you don't have access to a typewriter, many libraries have typewriters available to the public (for a small rental fee), or you can hire a bankruptcy form preparation service to prepare your forms using the information you provide. (See Ch. 10 for more on these services.)

> CAUTION
> **Interpret the forms literally.** When completing the forms, read each one carefully, including the instructions at the top. Then follow the instructions as closely as possible. You should interpret the instructions literally. If you misinterpret the literal language of the form, and can explain how the misinterpretation arose, you'll be allowed to amend the form without further explanation.

Be ridiculously thorough. Always err on the side of giving too much information rather than too little. If you leave information out, the bankruptcy trustee might become suspicious of your motives. If you leave creditors off the forms, the debts you owe these creditors might not be discharged—hardly the result you would want. In reality, this rarely happens—as long as your case is a "no asset" case, your debt will likely be discharged even if you don't list it. But, if you do have assets that are distributed to your creditors, and a particular creditor doesn't get its share of the distribution because you left it off the form, the debt will likely live on after your bankruptcy. In either event, it's better to list everything.

It gets worse if you intentionally or carelessly fail to list all your property and debts, or fail to accurately describe your recent property transactions. The court, upon a request by the trustee, could find that you acted with fraudulent intent and deny your bankruptcy discharge altogether, causing you to lose some property that you could otherwise have kept.

Respond to every question. Most of the forms have a box to check when your answer is "none." If a question doesn't have such a box and the question doesn't apply to you, type in "N/A" for not applicable. This will let the trustee know that you didn't overlook the question. Occasionally, a question that doesn't apply to you will have several blanks. Put "N/A" in only the first blank if it is evident that this applies to the other blanks as well. If it's not clear, put "N/A" in every blank.

Explain uncertainties. If you can't figure out which category on a form to use for a debt or an item of property, list the debt or item in what you think is the appropriate place and briefly note next to your entry that you're uncertain. The important thing is to disclose the information somewhere. The bankruptcy trustee will sort it out, if necessary.

Be scrupulously honest. As part of your official bankruptcy paperwork, you must complete declarations, under penalty of perjury, swearing that you've been truthful. It's important to realize that you could be prosecuted for perjury if it becomes evident that you deliberately lied.

Use continuation pages if you run out of room. The space for entering information is sometimes skimpy, especially if you're filing jointly. Most of the forms come with preformatted continuation pages that you can use if you need more room. But if there is no continuation sheet, prepare one yourself, using a piece of regular, white 8½" × 11" paper. Write "see continuation page" next to the question you're working on and enter the additional information on the continuation page. Label the continuation pages with your name and the form name and indicate "Continuation page 1," "Continuation page 2," and so on. Be sure to attach all continuation pages to their appropriate forms when you file your bankruptcy papers.

Emergency Filing
Although people usually file all of their bankruptcy forms at once, you don't absolutely have to. If you really need to stop creditors quickly—because of a foreclosure or threatened repossession—you can simply file the Voluntary Petition (including proof of credit counseling), the statement of your Social Security number (Form 121), and a form called a Matrix, which lists the name, address, and zip code of each of your creditors. The automatic stay, which stops most collection efforts against you, will go into effect and you'll have 14 days to file the rest of the forms. (Bankruptcy Rule 1007(c).)
Although it's an option if you're really in a jam, we urge you to not do an emergency filing unless it's absolutely necessary. That 14-day extension goes by fast; many people blow the deadline, then have their cases dismissed. So, if at all possible, file all your paperwork at the same time.

Get help if necessary. If your situation is complicated, you're unsure about how to complete a form, or you run into trouble when you go to file your papers, consult a bankruptcy attorney or do some legal research before proceeding. (See Ch. 10.)

Refer to—but don't copy—the sample forms. Throughout this chapter, we have included links to the completed sample forms of Carrie Anne Edwards, who lives in California. These forms are intended to be used as examples, so you can see what a completed form should look like. However, everyone's bankruptcy situation is different—you will owe different debts, own different property, have different bank accounts and Social Security numbers, and otherwise be utterly dissimilar from this fictional woman. DO NOT COPY THESE EXAMPLES VERBATIM, even if you live in California, because they won't fit your precise situation.

Voluntary Petition for Individuals Filing for Bankruptcy (Form 101)

A completed sample Voluntary Petition is available on the companion page at www.nolo.com/back-of-book/HFB.html. Line-by-line instructions are below.

Fill in the Top of Each Page

In the box at the top of the first page, fill in the name of the judicial district you're filing in and your state, such as the "Central District of California." If your state has only one district, fill in your state's name. Check the "Chapter 7" box. You'll also write your name at the top of each of the eight pages that follow. Don't worry about including a case number. You won't receive it until after you file your paperwork.

Part 1: Identify Yourself

You'll provide identifying information in this first section. Enter your full name as used on your driver's license or other identification card that you will present to the bankruptcy trustee to prove your identity. It's important that you copy your name exactly as it appears on your identification. If there's a discrepancy between your petition and identification, the bankruptcy trustee will likely ask you to correct your petition and your case could be delayed. If you are married and filing jointly, put one of your names as Debtor 1 (on the left) and the other as Debtor 2 on the right. You'll fill out both columns on the form using the instructions below.

All Other Names. The purpose of this box is to make sure that your creditors will know who you are when they receive notice of your bankruptcy filing. If you have used any other name in the last eight years, such as a maiden name, list it here. But don't include minor variations in spelling or form. For instance, if your name is John Lewis Smithsonian, you don't have to put down that you're sometimes known as J.L. But if you've used the pseudonym J.L. Smith, you should list it. If you're uncertain, list any name that you think you might have used with a creditor.

Last Four Digits of Soc. Sec. or Individual Taxpayer I.D. Enter only the last four digits of your Social Security number or taxpayer's ID number. You'll provide your full Social Security number on a different form that won't be a public record.

Business Names and Employer Identification Numbers. If you've operated a business as a sole proprietor during the previous eight years, include your trade name (fictitious or assumed business name) and "dba" names, which stands for "doing business as." Include any employer identification numbers (EIN) you've used in the last eight years. Otherwise, check the "I have not used any business name or EINs" box and move to the next section.

Where You Live. Enter your current street address. Even if you get all of your mail at a post office box, list the address of your personal residence. Next, list the county you live in. If your mailing address is different from your street address (such as a post office box), list it in the last space. If they are the same, put "N/A" in the mailing address section. If your filing spouse does not live with you, insert his or her address to the right. If your spouse doesn't live with you but also isn't filing with you, you don't need to complete the section for Debtor 2.

Your Filing District. Tell the court why you are filing in this particular district. If you've lived in the chosen district longer than any other district over the last 180 days, check the first box. If you have another reason for filing in the district, such as your principal assets are located in the district, check the second box. If you have enough assets to justify filing in a district other than where you live, seek the advice of bankruptcy counsel.

Part 2: Tell the Court About Your Bankruptcy Case

In this section, you'll provide basic information about your case. Start by checking "Chapter 7" in response to the question that asks which chapter you're choosing to file under.

How You Will Pay the Fee. If you will pay the entire fee when you file your case, check the first box. If you plan to ask the court for permission to pay in installments, check the second box. If you wish to apply for a full waiver of the filing fee, check the third box. (For instructions on preparing the forms necessary to pay in installments or apply for a fee waiver, see "How to File Your Papers," below.)

All Prior Bankruptcy Cases Filed Within Last 8 Years. If you haven't filed a bankruptcy case within the previous eight years, check "No." If you have, fill in the district you filed in, the date you filed, and the case number. A previous Chapter 7 discharge bars you from receiving another one until eight years have passed since you filed the last case. A previous Chapter 13 discharge bars you from filing a Chapter 7 case within six years. (See Ch.1 for more details.) And, if you filed a Chapter 7 bankruptcy case that was dismissed for cause within the previous 180 days, you might have to wait to file again, or you might not be able to discharge all your debts. (See Ch. 2 for more information.) If either situation applies to you, see a bankruptcy lawyer before filing.

Pending Bankruptcy Case Filed by a Spouse, Partner, or Affiliate. "Affiliate" refers to a related business under a corporate structure. "Partner" refers to a business partnership. Again, you shouldn't use this book if you're filing as a corporation, partnership, or another type of business entity. A business entity filing bankruptcy must be represented by a lawyer. This is true even if you are the sole member or shareholder of your corporate or LLC entity. If a business or spouse has a bankruptcy case pending anywhere in the country, check "Yes" and enter the requested information. Otherwise, check the "No" box.

Renting Your Residence. If you don't rent your home, check "No," and move to the next section. Otherwise, check "Yes" and tell the court whether your landlord has an eviction judgment against you. If yes, fill out Form 101A, Initial Statement About an Eviction Judgment Against You, and file it with the bankruptcy petition. As explained in Ch. 2, certain evictions can proceed after you file for bankruptcy, despite the automatic stay. The questions in this section (along with the additional forms) help determine whether your landlord obtained a judgment for possession (eviction order) and whether you can postpone the eviction.

Part 3: Report About Any Businesses You Own As a Sole Proprietor

If you don't operate a business, check "No" and go to the next section. For purposes of this form, "business" includes part-time businesses, independent contract projects, and other money-generating ventures. No matter how small or insignificant, report it. For instance, you'll list your Etsy, Tupperware, or dog-walking business, even if you rarely earn anything.

Are You A Sole Proprietor? If you didn't take steps to set up a particular type of business entity, such as a corporation, partnership, or LLC, you run your business as an individual. Check "Yes" and provide the requested information. If your business type falls within one of the described categories, see a bankruptcy lawyer. For instance, if you or your spouse own an assisted living facility (11 U.S.C. § 101 (27A)), you will need a lawyer's services because bankrupting a health care business is complicated.

Filing Under Chapter 11 As a Small Business. Leave this section blank.

Part 4: Report Hazardous Property or Property in Need of Immediate Attention

If you own or have in your possession any property that might cause "imminent and identifiable" harm to public health or safety (for example, real estate polluted with toxic substances because you rented it to a meth manufacturer who hid explosive devices like hand grenades, dynamite, and guns on the property), check "Yes" and provide the requested information. If you are unsure about whether a particular piece of property fits the bill, err on the side of inclusion.

Part 5: Explain Your Efforts to Receive a Briefing About Credit Counseling

Debtors filing for Chapter 7 bankruptcy must participate in debt counseling sessions within 180 days of a bankruptcy filing. Here you tell the court how you have fulfilled the credit counseling requirement. The warning in the left margin explains that you must truthfully check one of four options before filing. If you file without doing so, the court can dismiss your case, you'll lose your filing fee, and your creditors can start collecting against you again.

First Box. Most people will check the first box, which means you obtained a certificate of completion from a credit counseling agency and can attach the certificate (and any debt repayment plan developed through the agency) to your petition.

Second Box. If you have received counseling but haven't received your certificate yet, check the second box. To remain in bankruptcy, you'll need to obtain and file your certificate (and debt repayment plan if any) within 14 days after your bankruptcy filing date.

Third Box. The third box indicates that you have requested credit counseling but were unable to obtain the services within seven days after your request and have not yet received counseling. If you check this box, you'll have to explain why you couldn't complete the credit counseling before your filing date. Read the bold type for additional information regarding your obligations if you wish to remain in bankruptcy.

Fourth Box. Check the fourth box (and one of the additional three boxes describing your exception) if you are not required to take a credit counseling course because you are either incapacitated, disabled, or on active duty. (For more on the exceptions, see Ch. 1.)

Part 6: Answer These Questions for Reporting Purposes

Here you'll provide a summary of type, number, and amount of debt that you have. It's likely that you won't be able to complete this section until after you prepare the other bankruptcy forms.

What Kind Of Debts Do You Have? Check the box for consumer debts if most of your debts are owed personally (typically for household goods and services) and didn't result from attempts to earn money through a business venture. If, however, the bulk of your debts are due to the operation of a business (debt incurred to gain profit), check the business debts box. Filers who owe business debts primarily can skip the means test. If you're not sure which type you have, speak with an attorney.

TIP

Understand the difference between a consumer and business debt. What qualifies as a consumer or business debt isn't always intuitive. For instance, tax debts are usually considered business debts and mortgages consumer debts. To learn more, see the discussion in Part 1 of Form 122A-1Supp ("Identify the Kind of Debts You Have"), below.

Are You Filing Under Chapter 7? Check "Yes." If you think there will be assets available to be sold for the benefit of your unsecured creditors (meaning that after doing all of your schedules, you don't believe you'll get to keep all of your property), check "Yes" again. If you did your homework in Chs. 3 and 4, you will have a good idea about whether all of your assets are exempt, or whether you will have to surrender some to the trustee. If you check "No," your creditors will be told that it is a "no asset" case and that there is no point in filing a Proof of Claim unless they hear differently from the trustee. If you haven't a clue about your property and exemptions, come back to this question after you've completed Schedules A/B and C.

How Many Creditors Do You Owe? Total up your creditors and select the appropriate box. If you aren't sure yet, fill this in after completing Schedules D and E/F.

How Much Are Your Assets Worth? If you have a good estimate of your total assets, check the corresponding box. Otherwise, complete Schedule A/B first.

How Much Are Your Liabilities? Again, if you know the total amount owed to creditors, indicate it by checking the appropriate box. If you're unsure, fill out Schedules D and E/F and return to this question.

Part 7: Sign Below

You (and your spouse, if filing jointly) must sign and date on the available spaces. By signing, you declare that you're aware that you can file under other sections of the bankruptcy code, and that you still choose to file for Chapter 7 bankruptcy. If you think you want to pursue a different option, put your Chapter 7 petition aside and either consult a lawyer or find a book that explains your proposed alternative in more detail. For example, you could check out *Chapter 13 Bankruptcy*, by Cara O'Neill (Nolo).

For Your Attorney. If you represent yourself, type "debtor not represented by attorney" in the space for the attorney's signature. If you are represented by a lawyer, your lawyer will fill in the blanks accordingly, along with the rest of your paperwork.

If You File Without An Attorney. Read this section carefully. It explains that you cannot exclude any debt or any property when you file your bankruptcy papers, even if you plan to repay the debt afterward. You must list everything. It also stresses that a mistake on your part could have serious, long-term financial consequences, and that you are expected to follow all bankruptcy rules and procedures just as if you were an attorney. To file, you must check "Yes" in two boxes, confirming you understand this, and that inaccurately completing forms could constitute fraud leading to a fine or imprisonment. (If a bankruptcy petition preparer typed your forms, enter that person's name and have the preparer complete Form 119 —Bankruptcy Petition Preparer's Notice, Declaration, and Signature.) Sign and date the bottom of the form.

Relating to Eviction Judgments (Forms 101A and 101B)

If your landlord has obtained a judgment for eviction, unlawful detainer, or possession against you, you must complete one or both of the following forms:

- Form 101A—Initial Statement About an Eviction Judgment Against You, and
- Form 101B—Statement About Payment of an Eviction Judgment Against You.

You'll find a copy of the forms on the companion page at www.nolo.com/back-of-book/HFB.html. If you don't have a judgment of eviction against you, you do not complete or file these forms with the court.

Form 106 Schedules

A series of Form 106 schedules provide the trustee and court with a picture of your current financial situation. Most of the information needed for these schedules is included in the Personal Property Checklist, Property Exemption Worksheet, and Homeowners' Worksheet covered in Chs. 3 and 4.

CAUTION

Use the correct address for your creditors. Many of these schedules ask you to provide addresses for the creditors you list. Include the payment address on the last written communication received from the creditor. If the creditor provided more than one address, or if a collection agency is involved, put the alternate address in the "List Others to Be Notified About a Debt That You Already Listed" section of Schedule E/F. The goal is to ensure all creditors receive notice of the bankruptcy, so it is a good idea to err on the side of inclusion. If you no longer have the address of your original creditor, use the address listed on your credit report. If a creditor is a minor child, simply put "minor child" and the appropriate address. Don't list the child's name.

Schedule A/B: Property (Form 106A/B)

Here you list all of the property you own—real and personal—as of the date you'll file the petition. Don't worry about whether a particular asset is exempt; you don't have to claim your exemptions until you get to Schedule C. If you completed the Personal Property Checklist, Property Exemption Worksheet, and Homeowners' Worksheet, and Judicial Lien Worksheet in Chs. 3, 4, and 5, get them out. Much of that information goes on Schedule A/B.

A completed sample of Schedule A/B is on the companion page and line-by-line instructions follow. Even if you don't own any property (which would be unusual), you still must complete the top of this form.

> CAUTION
>
> **List all of your property.** When you complete your paperwork, you must list all real estate and personal property in Schedule A/B. Then, to the extent possible, you claim exemptions for that property in Schedule C. Many people can claim all property as exempt. However, if you don't disclose something, you could lose it, even if it would have been exempt.

Real Property Defined

Real property—land and things permanently attached to land—includes more than just a house. It can also include unimproved land, vacation cabins, condominiums, duplexes, rental property, business property, mobile home park spaces, agricultural land, airplane hangars, and any other buildings permanently attached to the land.

You can own real estate even if you can't walk on it, live on it, or get income from it. This might be true if someone else lives on property that you are entitled to receive in the future under a trust agreement.

There's a separate schedule for leases and time-shares. If you hold a time-share lease in a vacation cabin or property, lease a boat dock, lease underground portions of real estate for mineral or oil exploration, or otherwise lease or rent real estate of any description, don't list it on Schedule A/B. All leases and time-shares should be listed on Schedule G. (See the instructions for that schedule below.)

General Instructions

Schedule A/B consists of separately numbered lines that relate to various categories of property, plus some other lines that ask you to total multiple numbers. For each line, you'll check "No" if you don't own any property in that category. If you do, you'll check "Yes" and provide information about the property. Below are some general instructions and a discussion about questions you'll see throughout the form.

Current value. Most lines in the form ask you to list the "current value" of your property as of the time you file bankruptcy. The court considers the current value to be what's known as "fair market value." In other words, how much it would cost for you to replace the property from a retail vendor given its current age and condition. Because many types of used property can't be purchased from retail vendors (banged-up cars and ripped furniture, for example) it's common to value such property at its market value, or, the value that you—or the trustee—can sell it for. (See Ch. 3 for information on estimating the value of various types of property.)

Community property. Many of the numbered lines on Schedule A/B ask if the item is community property. If you're married and live in a community property state, property acquired during the marriage is community property. Check the "Community Property" box for that particular item. Gifts and inheritances received by one spouse are separate property, as is property a spouse owned before marriage or after separation. Don't check the box if this applies to you, even if you live in a community property state. (To learn more about community property, see Ch. 3.)

Description of property. Some sections ask you to describe the property. If you filled out the Personal Property Checklist and Property Exemption Worksheet in Ch. 3, you already have this information. If not, be sure to go over the Personal Property Checklist, which lists types of property to include in each category. Although the categories in the checklist correspond to categories in Schedule A/B, the checklist describes some of them differently.

Location of property. You'll have to indicate where the property is located. If your personal property is at your residence, just enter "Residence" or your home address beneath the property description. If someone else holds property for you (for example, you loaned your aunt your laptop), insert that person's name and address in this column. The idea is to tell the trustee where all your property can be found.

Who has an interest in the property? You'll need to answer this in the first two sections when listing real property and vehicles. If you are the sole owner, check the first "Debtor 1 only" box. If your filing spouse owns the property exclusively, check the second "Debtor 2 only" box. If you and your spouse own it together, check the third "Debtor 1 and Debtor 2 only" box. If you (or your spouse) own it with someone else, for instance, a family member, then check the last "At least one of the debtors and another" box.

Completing Schedule A/B

A completed sample Schedule A/B is available on the companion page at www.nolo.com/back-of-book/HFB.html. Line-by-line instructions are below.

Fill in the Top of Each Page

Enter the judicial district and state in the box at the top of the first page. For instance, you'd type "Central District of California." If your state has only one district, fill in your state's name only. You'll write your name at the top of each of the ten pages that follow.

Part 1: Describe Each Residence, Building, Land, or Other Real Estate You Own or Have an Interest In

Part 1 deals with your real property (real estate).

Do you own or have an interest in real estate? If no, check the box and proceed to Part 2. If yes, fill in the street address and county where the property is located.

What is the property? Here you'll check the box that best describes the type of property you own. Your choices include single-family home, duplex or multiunit building, condominium or cooperative, manufactured or mobile home, land, investment property, time-share, or something else.

Who has an interest in the property? See "General Instructions," above.

Other Information. Here, you can add additional information about the property, such as a note about a pending foreclosure. You don't have to enter anything here unless you believe it's necessary.

Mobile Home Owners

If you own a mobile home in a park, use the home's value in its current location. Many parks are located in desirable areas, so the park could add to the motor home's value even though you don't have ownership interest in the park itself. A mobile home that might not be worth much on its own could be worth quite a bit if it's sitting in an upscale location.

Current value of the entire property. Enter the current fair market value of the real estate. Don't figure in homestead exemptions, any mortgages, or any other liens on the property. Just put the actual current fair market value as best you can calculate it. You'll likely enter in the price you would offer to sell the home if you listed it with a real estate agent. If you filled in the Homeowners' Worksheet in Ch. 4, use the value you came up with there.

Current value of the portion you own. If you own the property with someone else who isn't joining you in your bankruptcy, list only the amount of your ownership share on this line. For example, if you and your brother own property together (each owns 50%), split the property's current market value in half and list that amount here. If your interest is intangible—for example, you are a beneficiary of real estate held in trust that won't be distributed for many years—enter an estimate provided by a real estate appraiser or put "don't know." You'll later explain to the trustee why you can't be more precise.

Nature of your ownership interest. On this line, you need to provide the legal definition for the interest you (or you and your spouse) have in the real estate. The most common type of interest—outright ownership—is called "fee simple." Even if you still owe money on your mortgage, as long as you have the right to sell the house, leave it to your heirs, and make alterations, your ownership is fee simple. A fee simple interest can be owned by one person or by several people jointly. Normally, when people are listed on a deed as the owners—even if they own the property as joint tenants, tenants in common, or tenants by the entirety—the ownership interest is in fee simple. Other types of real property interests include:

- **Life estate.** This is the right to possess and use property only during your lifetime. You can't sell the property, give it away, or leave it to someone when you die. Instead, the property passes to the person named in the instrument (trust, deed, or will) that created your life estate. This type of ownership is usually created when the sole owner of a piece of real estate wants his surviving spouse to live on the property for the rest of her life, but then have the property pass to his children. In this situation, the surviving spouse has a life estate. Surviving spouses who are beneficiaries of A-B, spousal, or marital bypass trusts have life estates.

- **Future interest.** This is your right to own property sometime in the future. A common future interest is owned by a person who—under the terms of a deed or irrevocable trust—will inherit the property when its current possessor dies. Simply being named in a will or living trust doesn't create a future interest because the person who signed the deed or trust could amend the document to cut you out.

How to List Property That Is Subject to Foreclosure Proceedings

Even if your property is subject to foreclosure proceedings, you still own the property until the foreclosure sale is held and a new deed is recorded either in the lender's name (if the property fails to sell) or in the purchaser's name if the foreclosure auction ends in a successful bid. You should list the property in Schedule A/B and include all of the required information. You should also explain that the house is in foreclosure and provide the foreclosure sale date if it has gotten that far. If not, indicate when you expect the property to be sold.

- **Contingent interest.** This ownership interest doesn't come into existence unless one or more conditions are fulfilled. Wills sometimes leave property to people under certain conditions. If the conditions aren't met, the property passes to someone else. For instance, Emma's will leaves her house to John if he takes care of her until her death. If John doesn't care for Emma, the house passes to Emma's daughter Jane. Both John and Jane have contingent interests in Emma's home.
- **Lienholder.** If you are the holder of a mortgage, deed of trust, judgment lien, or mechanic's lien on real estate, you have an ownership interest in the real estate.

- **Easement holder.** If you are the holder of a right to travel on or otherwise use property owned by someone else, you have an easement.
- **Power of appointment.** If you have a legal right, given to you in a will or transfer of property, to sell a specified piece of someone's property, that's called a power of appointment and should be listed.
- **Beneficial ownership under a real estate contract.** This is the right to own property by virtue of having signed a binding real estate contract. Even though the buyer doesn't yet own the property, the buyer does have a "beneficial interest"—that is, the right to own the property once the formalities are completed. For example, property buyers have a beneficial ownership interest in property while the escrow is pending.

If you have trouble figuring out which of these definitions best fits your type of ownership interest, leave the column blank and let the trustee help you sort it out at your 341 hearing.

Know What Your Property is Worth Before Filing Bankruptcy

In recent years, real property values have been increasing steadily. If you don't know what your property would sell for right now (its market value), you won't know how much equity you have in your home. Filing bankruptcy without knowing what your property is worth can result in an unwelcome surprise, like the loss of your home. For example, if the real estate exemption available to you is $50,000 but you have $100,000 of equity in your home, the trustee will likely sell your home to get the $50,000 worth of nonexempt equity. A word to the wise: Know what your property is worth before you file and consider having your property appraised beforehand.

Totals. Once you've entered all of your real property onto the form, add together the dollar values of the real estate portions you own and write the total in the space provided on Line 2 at the end of Part 1. You'll enter this amount again on Line 55 of this form and on Line 1a on Form 106Sum, Summary of Your Assets and Liabilities and Certain Statistical Information.

> **TIP**
> **Also list time-shares on Schedule G.** Time-shares should be listed on both Schedule A/B and Schedule G. This can be confusing because timeshares sometimes come with deeds and other documents indicating real estate ownership. If you want to keep the timeshare, you'll treat it as an "executory contract" and assert that you want to "assume" the contract on your Statement of Intention. The timeshare company will probably want you to assign an "assumption" agreement, which should then be filed with the court.

Part 2: Describe Your Vehicles

In this section, you list all of your vehicles, including any that someone else is driving. You should also know that "vehicles" pretty much includes anything that has a motor and can transport you from place to place, whether by road, water, or air, so you'll include watercraft, aircraft, motor homes, ATVs, and recreational vehicles. Also list any accessories and trailers used to transport the vehicle.

If you own any cars, vans, trucks, tractors, sport utility vehicles or motorcycles, check "Yes" and describe each vehicle by providing the make, model, mileage, and year of each. Tell the court about any special equipment, the vehicle's condition, and where it's located in the "Other information" section. Check the box that best describes who has an interest in the property (see "General Instructions," above.) List the property's value, without regard to any secured interests (loans or liens on the vehicle) or exemption amount you can claim. For example, suppose you own a car worth $6,000 but you still owe $4,000 on the car note, and your state's motor vehicle exemption is $1,200. You'll put down $6,000 for the current value of the car. Last, list the value of the portion you own.

Move to the next section (Line 4) and provide the same information for boats, personal watercraft, aircraft, motor homes, ATVs, recreational vehicles, and any accessories. You'll add the dollar amount of all vehicle portions you own and enter the total on Line 5. Enter this amount again on Line 56.

> **CAUTION**
>
> **Be honest and thorough.** When listing all of your stuff on a public document like Schedule A/B, you might feel tempted to cheat a little. Don't give in to the temptation to "forget" any of your assets. Bankruptcy law doesn't give you the right to decide that an asset isn't worth mentioning. Even if, for example, you've decided that your CD collection is worthless given the development of newer technology, you still have to list it. Use the form to explain why it has no value. If you omit something and get caught, your case could be dismissed—or your discharge revoked—leaving you with no bankruptcy relief for your current debts. Remember, exemptions will help you keep much of your property; if no exemption is available, you might be able to repurchase the property from the trustee.

Part 3: Describe Your Personal and Household Items

The court wants to know about all of the everyday things you have in your house. Listing all of it might seem daunting since you probably have quite a bit of stuff; however, there are ways to make this simpler. You should separately list all items worth more than the amount allowed for an individual item under the exemption scheme you're using. Combine small items into larger categories whenever reasonable. For example, you don't need to list every pan, spatula, colander, garlic press, and ice cream scoop; instead, group the items into "kitchenware." Other categories might include garden equipment, living room furniture, and linens. If you have many entries for a particular section, you might need to attach a continuation sheet.

You'll put the fair market value of each group of items in the space provided. These figures will reflect the amount you'd be able get if you sold the item. Be fair to yourself when you value the items. For instance, a relatively new sofa would be worth considerably more than an old couch owned by a family with small children and three dogs. Be prepared to justify your valuation if the bankruptcy calls it into question.

After you complete each section, add together the dollar values for your personal and household items and write the total on Line 15. Enter this amount again on Line 57.

Part 4: Describe Your Financial Assets

Here you tell the bankruptcy trustee where all of your money and other financial assets are located. Below you'll find help with the more detailed categories.

Lines 16 and 17. Explain the location of any cash on hand (for example, include the cash that's in your wallet, under your mattress, buried in the yard) or money in financial accounts (list the bank name and branch location). Also, list the source of the funds—for example, from wages, Social Security payments, or child support. This will help you (and the trustee) decide later whether any of this money qualifies as exempt property. Keep in mind that you must list the amount in your account on the day you file for bankruptcy, even if you've written checks that haven't yet cleared. All money in your accounts on the day you file is the property of your bankruptcy estate. The trustee can take the entire balance unless it's exempt, even if you have outstanding checks and it means you bounce a check or two. (*In re Ruiz*, 455 B.R. 745 (B.A.P. 10th Cir. 2011).)

Line 18. Include stock options.

Line 21. Although ERISA-qualified pension plans, 401(k)s, IRAs, and Keoghs will likely be exempt, list them here anyway and describe each plan in detail. (Remember, you must list all of your property. You'll indicate which property is exempt on another form.) Enter the value of the pension, if known. Otherwise, list the value as "undetermined." You'll need to find out the amount at some point because it's likely that you'll have to provide the trustee with a statement showing the account balance (and, to prevent needless delay, it's better to provide it to the trustee with your other financial documents).

Line 24. Although an education IRA and a qualified state tuition plan might technically not be part of the bankruptcy estate, you're required to disclose all assets so list them here.

Line 25. An "equitable or future interest" means that you have a legal right to valuable property currently owned by someone else in the future. For instance, if your parents' trust gives them the right to live in the family home, that's a "life estate." If the trust gives you the home when they die, you have an "equitable interest" in the home while they're alive. "Powers exercisable for the benefit of the debtor" means that a person has been given the power to route property to you, but it hasn't happened by the time you file your bankruptcy petition. In sum, if it looks like property is coming your way eventually, and that property hasn't already been listed in Part 1 of this Schedule, list it here. (Given the complexity of such interests, it would be prudent to consult with a bankruptcy attorney before filing your case.)

Line 26. This question asks about assets commonly known as intellectual property. State what the patent, copyright, trademark, or similar right covers. Give the number assigned by the issuing agency and the length of time the patent, copyright, trademark, or another right will last. Keep in mind that both copyright and trademark rights could exist without going through a government agency. If you claim trademark rights through usage or copyright through the fact that you created the item and reduced it to tangible form, describe them here.

Line 27. List all licenses and franchises, what they cover, the length of time remaining, whom they are with, and whether you can transfer them to someone else.

If You Are Listed on Someone Else's Account

As explained in Ch. 3, if you are named on a parent's bank account (typically, to manage the parent's finances if he or she becomes incapacitated or otherwise needs help), the trustee might believe that account should be part of your bankruptcy estate. To prevent the trustee from getting a false idea about the nature of the account, consider listing it under Part 4 and then describe the true facts, which usually are that the money in the account came from and belongs to the parent, that the bankruptcy filer was only added to the account as a fiduciary (a trusted assistant), and that it would be a breach of the fiduciary duty for the filer to use any of the parent's money for the filer's own purposes.

If the exemptions you are using allow you to exempt bank accounts or cash up to a certain amount, and you have enough of that exemption left over to apply to the money in your parent's account, it makes sense to claim the money in your parent's account as exempt on Schedule C (explained below). The claim of exemption is legally unnecessary, but it will prevent the trustee from trying to prove that the money should be considered part of your bankruptcy estate.

Line 28. If it's early in the year, expect the trustee to be on the lookout for a potential tax return. If you think you'll get one, list it here even though you haven't received it yet. If you don't know how much you'll get, provide an estimate if possible. If your state's exemption system allows you to exempt cash or provides you with a wildcard exemption, you can exempt the tax refund on Schedule C (explained below). If you can't, the trustee will take it and distribute it to your creditors. Therefore, it might be best to wait to file until after you receive your return and use it for necessary living expenses (keep records). Incidentally, some people like to use their tax refund to pay off loans from family members. Don't do it. The trustee will demand the money back from the relative because the payment will qualify as a preference (preferring your relative over your other creditors).

Line 29. List all child support or alimony arrears—that is, money that should have been paid to you but hasn't been. Specify the dates the payments were due and missed, such as "$250 monthly child support payments for June, July, August, and September 20xx." Also list debts owed you from a property settlement incurred in a divorce or dissolution.

Line 30. List all money owed to you that hasn't been paid yet, other than child support, alimony, and property settlements. If you've obtained a judgment against someone, but haven't been paid, list it here. State the defendant's name, the date of the judgment, the court that issued the judgment, the amount of the judgment, and the kind of case (such as "car accident"). Also list things such as unpaid wages, sick and vacation pay, unpaid loans someone owes you, and insurance payments.

Line 33. List all claims that you have against others that might end up in a lawsuit. For instance, if you were recently rear-ended in an automobile accident and are struggling with whiplash, you might have a cause of action against the other driver (and that driver's insurer). You'll need an exemption allowing you to keep the proceeds after you resolve the claim. Otherwise, you'll lose the funds.

Line 34. A contingent and unliquidated claim is an ownership interest that might never arise. If there's a chance that you might come into money, but there's no guarantee of it, list it here.

Line 35. List any financial asset that you possess or are entitled to receive that wasn't listed elsewhere here.

Line 36. Add together the dollar value of your financial assets and write the total on this line. Enter this amount again on Line 58.

Part 5: Describe Any Business-Related Property You Own or Have an Interest In

Here you list the property you use in your business. The title of this section indicates that you're to "List any real estate in Part 1." This is a bit confusing. It does not mean you should list your real estate again in this section. Instead, it is a reminder that you should list all real estate, even if it is business-related, in Part 1 of this form only.

If you are a sole proprietor or an independent contractor, one or more customers or clients likely owe you money. Specify each such debt on Line 38. You'll list office equipment and supplies, machinery, and inventory on Lines 39 and 40, and any customer or mailing lists on Line 43. Add together the dollar value of your business-related property and write the total on Lines 45 and 59.

Part 6: Describe Any Farm- and Commercial Fishing-Related Property You Own or Have an Interest In

Again, the part of the title that says "List farmland in Part 1," means that you should include farmland in Part 1 only; you should not list farmland in Part 6.

You'll use Lines 47 through 51 to list information about the following: livestock, growing or harvested crops, our crops, and all fishing and farm supplies. Include the current value of each property type in the space provided. Add together the dollar value of your farm- and fishing-related property and write the total on Lines 52 and 60.

Part 7: Describe All Property You Own or Have an Interest in That You Did Not List Above

This is where you include property that you didn't list somewhere else, such as a season pass to Disneyland, concert tickets, or anything else of value. Add together the dollar value of all property in Part 7 and write the total on Lines 52 and 61.

Part 8: List the Totals of Each Part of this Form

Enter the totals from each section on the appropriate line (you might have already done so if you used the instructions above). Total all property on Schedule A/B and enter it on Line 63. You'll also transfer the following totals onto Form 106Sum, Summary of Your Assets and Liabilities and Certain Statistical Information: the real estate total from Line 55, the personal property total from Line 62, and the final total from Line 63.

TIP

List exempt property on Schedule C. If you have property that is exempt, list it on Schedule C as well. (If you are unsure about the value of the property, see "How to Exempt Property of Undetermined Value," below.)

Schedule C—The Property You Claim As Exempt (Form 106C)

On this form, you claim all property that you can protect with an exemption from your state (or a federal exemption if you've so elected). An exemption prevents the trustee from selling the property to pay your unsecured creditors. In many individual Chapter 7 bankruptcies, all of the debtor's property is exempt, but this isn't always the case, of course. Even if you must give up some property, if the value of that property is substantially less than the amount of debt that will get wiped out, filing for bankruptcy will likely be a financially sound decision.

A completed sample Schedule C is available on the companion page at www.nolo.com/back-of-book/HFB.html. Line-by-line instructions are below.

CAUTION

If you own a home. Be sure to read Ch. 4 before completing Schedule C.

When you work on this form, you'll need to refer frequently to several other documents. Have in front of you:
- the worksheets from Ch. 3 and Ch. 4
- your draft of Schedule A/B
- the list of state or federal bankruptcy exemptions you'll be using, provided on the companion page, and
- if you're using a state's exemptions, the additional nonbankruptcy federal exemptions, provided on the companion page.

Looking at the sample Schedule C exemptions, you might notice that a particular exemption can apply to more than one category of personal property from Schedule A/B. That's because the exemption laws are written by each state, but the property categories are determined by the federal government employees who created Schedule A/B. As a result, the property and exemption categories don't necessarily match up neatly. For example, the California "tools of the trade" exemption (see the companion page) could apply to a number of the property categories, including Category 39 (Office equipment, furnishings, and supplies), Category 46 (Farming and fishing equipment), and Category 3 (Automobiles, trucks, trailers and other vehicles, and accessories).

Fill in the Top of Each Page

Put the judicial district and state in the box at the top of the first page. For instance, the "Central District of California." If your state has one district, fill in your state's name only. Also, write your name at the top of each page but wait to insert page numbers at the bottom until you know how many pages you need.

Give Yourself the Benefit of the Doubt

When you claim exemptions, give yourself the benefit of the doubt, but don't go too far, and be prepared to lose the property.

The trustee and possibly a creditor or two will examine your exemption claims, although historically, few creditors monitor bankruptcy proceedings. In close cases, bankruptcy laws require the trustee to honor rather than dishonor your exemption claims. In other words, you're entitled to the benefit of the doubt. If the trustee or a creditor successfully objects to an exemption claim, you've lost nothing by trying. (See Ch. 7 for more on objections to claimed exemptions.)

Which set of exemptions are you claiming? If you're using federal exemptions, check the second box. Otherwise, check the first box. (See Ch. 3 for residency requirements you must meet before using a state's exemptions and tips on choosing between the federal and state exemption systems.) As explained in Ch. 3, if you're living in a state that offers the federal exemption system, but you haven't been there long enough to meet the two-year residency requirement, you can choose between the federal system or your previous state's exemptions.

Also, in rare instances, you might not qualify to use any state's exemption system. In that case, you can use federal exemptions, even if the state you're filing in wouldn't usually allow them. (Ch. 3 further explains this situation.)

> **SEE AN EXPERT**
>
> **Property out of state.** You'll generally choose the exemptions of the state you live in when you file as long as you've lived there for at least two years. If you want to protect your equity in a home in a state other than the one you file in, see a lawyer. It will be tricky to file in one place and claim a personal residence in another, and will likely work under only the most unusual of circumstances.

Part 1: Identify the Property You Claim as Exempt. This is where you list the property on Schedule A/B that you claim as exempt. To complete this section, take these steps:

Step 1: Turn to Ch. 3 to determine which exemptions are available to you and which property to claim as exempt. If you have already used the Property Exemption Worksheet to identify your exempt property, skip this step.

Step 2: Decide which of the real estate you listed on Schedule A/B you want to claim as exempt. Remember that state homestead allowances usually apply only to property you live in when you file, but that you can use a wildcard exemption for any type of property.

Step 3: Decide which of the personal property you listed on Schedule A/B (Parts 2–7) you want to claim as exempt.

Step 4: Once you decide what you intend to exempt, use the same description used in Schedule A/B to describe the property again.

Enter the Schedule A/B line number beneath the description. This helps the court clearly identify the right property.

Step 5: Copy the value of the portion you own from Schedule A/B and insert it in the second column.

Step 6: Claim the total exemption amount allowed, up to the value of the item. You'll find the exemption amount allowed on the companion page. Bankruptcy law allows married couples to double exemptions unless the state expressly prohibits it. That means you can each claim the entire exemption amount if you are both filing and have an ownership interest in the property. If your state's chart on the companion page doesn't say your state forbids doubling, go ahead and double. You are entitled to double all federal exemptions if you use them.

Step 7: Specify the law providing for each exemption in the space provided. You'll find citations to the specific exemption laws on the companion page. If you're using part or all of a wildcard exemption in addition to a regular exemption, you'll list both exemption statutes.

Are you claiming a homestead exemption of more than $170,350? Answer the question prompts. If you didn't acquire your home within 1,215 days before filing, and you didn't purchase it using the sales proceeds from a home sold in the same state, your homestead exemption may be capped at $170,350, regardless of the exemption available in the state where your home is located. This amount will increase on April 1, 2022. (See Ch. 4 for detailed information on the homestead exemption cap.)

How to Exempt Property of Undetermined Value

If you have property that is expensive or impossible to value, you can simply put "undetermined" or "unknown" on Schedule A/B and then put the following on Schedule C where you claim the exemption: "Exempt up to its full value under [cite to exemption statute]."

If the exemption available to you for that property is not adequate to cover the property's value, the trustee can file a formal objection and prove his or her case in court. If the trustee doesn't object to your exemption claim within 30 days after your 341 hearing, you may escape with the whole enchilada (but it's not a good idea to count on it).

(!) **CAUTION**
Don't claim more than you need for any particular item. For instance, if you're allowed household furniture up to a total amount of $2,000, don't inflate the value of each item of furniture simply to get to $2,000. Use the values you stated on Schedule A/B.

Schedule D—Creditors Who Have Claims Secured by Property (Form 106D)

In this schedule, you list all creditors who hold claims secured by your property. This includes:
- holders of a mortgage or deed of trust on your real estate
- creditors who have won lawsuits against you and recorded judgment liens against your property
- doctors or lawyers to whom you have granted a security interest in the outcome of a lawsuit, so that the collection of their fees would be postponed (the expected court judgment is the collateral)
- contractors who have filed mechanics' or materialmen's liens on your real estate
- taxing authorities, such as the IRS, that have obtained tax liens against your property
- creditors with either a purchase-money or non-purchase-money security agreement (see "Nature of Lien," below), and
- all parties who are trying to collect secured debts, such as collection agencies and attorneys.

A completed sample of Schedule D is available on the companion page at www.nolo.com/back-of-book/HFB.html. Line-by-line instructions are below.

Fill in the Top of Each Page

Follow the instructions for Schedule C. Line 1 immediately follows below. Check the first box if you don't have creditors holding secured claims and skip to Schedule E/F. Everyone else, check the second box and keep reading.

Part 1: List All Secured Claims

In this section, list all secured creditors, preferably in alphabetical order. If you have more than one secured creditor for a given debt, list the original creditor in Part 1 and the other creditors in Part 2. For instance, if you've been hounded by a collection agency, or sued even, list the information for the collection agency in Part 2. You'll provide additional information in the spaces provided on the form.

List all secured claims. Provide the creditor's name and complete mailing address, including zip code. As mentioned earlier, the mailing address should be the contact address shown on at least two written communications you received from the creditor during the previous 90 days. Call the creditor to get this information if you don't have it. If the creditor is a child, list the child's initials and the name and address of the child's parent or guardian. For example, "A.B., a minor child, by John Doe, Guardian, 111 Alabama Avenue, San Francisco, CA 94732." Don't state the child's name.

Who owes the debt? Tell the court about any other people responsible for paying for this debt (called "codebtors") by checking the appropriate box. Codebtors can be legally forced to pay the debt. Also, list any codebtors in Schedule H as long as the codebtor isn't a spouse filing with you.

Community debt. Similar to the previous discussion about community property, if you're married and live in a community property state, then debt acquired during the marriage is community debt. If this applies, check the box indicating that the claim relates to a community debt. Debts incurred before marriage or after separation are not considered community debt, even if you live in a community property state.

Date debt was incurred. For most claims, the date the claim was incurred is the date you signed the security agreement (contract). If you didn't sign a security agreement with the creditor, the date is most likely the date a contractor or judgment creditor recorded a lien against your property or the date a taxing authority notified you of a tax liability or assessment of taxes due.

Description of property. Describe each item of real estate or personal property that is collateral for the secured debt listed in the first column. For instance, you'll likely list your home as collateral for your mortgage and your vehicle as the security for your car loan. Use the same description you used to describe the property on Schedule A/B. If a creditor's lien covers several items of property, list all items affected by the lien.

Credit Card Debts

Most credit card debts, including cards issued by banks, gasoline companies, or department stores, are unsecured and should be listed on Schedule E/F. However, some department stores claim to retain a security interest in all durable goods, such as furniture, appliances, electronics equipment, and jewelry bought using the store credit card. Also, if you were issued a bank or store credit card as part of a plan to restore your credit, you may have had to post property or cash as collateral for debts incurred on the card. If either of these exceptions apply to you, list the credit card debt on Schedule D. If you are unsure, use Schedule E/F.

The most common codebtors are:

- cosigners
- guarantors (people who guarantee payment of a loan)
- ex-spouses with whom you jointly incurred debts before divorcing
- joint owners of real estate or other property
- coparties in a lawsuit
- nonfiling spouses in a community property state (most debts incurred by a nonfiling spouse during marriage are considered community debts, making that spouse equally liable with the filing spouse for the debts), and
- nonfiling spouses in states other than community property states, for debts incurred by the filing spouse for basic living necessities such as food, shelter, clothing, and utilities.

Contingent, Unliquidated, Disputed. Indicate whether the creditor's secured claim is contingent, unliquidated, or disputed. Check all categories that apply. If you're uncertain of which to choose, check the one that seems closest. If none apply, leave them blank. Briefly, these terms mean:

- **Contingent.** The claim depends on some event that hasn't yet occurred and might never occur. For example, if you cosigned a secured loan, you won't be liable unless the principal debtor defaults. Your liability as cosigner is contingent upon the default.
- **Unliquidated.** This means debt might exist but the exact amount hasn't been determined. For example, say you've sued someone for injuries you suffered in an auto accident, but the case isn't over. Your

lawyer has taken the case under a contingency fee agreement—he'll get a third of the recovery if you win, and nothing if you lose—and has a security interest in the final recovery amount. The debt to the lawyer is unliquidated because you don't know how much, if anything, you'll win.

- **Disputed.** A claim is disputed if you and the creditor disagree about the existence or amount of the debt. For instance, suppose the IRS says you owe $10,000 and has put a lien on your property, and you say you owe $500. List the total amount of the lien, not the amount you think you owe. As long as the debt is listed, it will be discharged. So the actual amount in dispute is not that important.

Nature of Lien. What kind of property interest does your secured creditor have? Here are the possible answers:

- **First mortgage.** You took out a loan to buy your house. (This is a specific kind of purchase-money security interest.)
- **Second mortgage and HELOC (home equity line of credit).** List these loans as well as any other debt that is secured by your home.
- **Purchase-money security interest.** You took out a loan to purchase the property that secures the loan—for example, a car note. The creditor must have perfected the security interest by filing or recording it with the appropriate agency within 20 days. (*Fidelity Financial Services, Inc. v. Fink*, 522 U.S. 211 (1998).) Otherwise, the creditor has no lien and you should list the debt on Schedule E/F (unsecured debt) instead.
- **Nonpossessory, non-purchase-money security interest.** You borrowed money for a purpose other than buying the collateral. This includes refinanced home loans, home equity loans, or loans from finance companies.
- **Possessory, non-purchase-money security interest.** This is what a pawnshop owner has when you pawn your property.
- **Judgment lien.** This means someone sued you, won a court judgment, and recorded a lien against your property.
- **Tax lien.** This means a federal, state, or local government agency recorded a lien against your property for unpaid taxes.

- **Child support lien.** This means that another parent or a government agency has recorded a lien against your property for unpaid child support.
- **Mechanics' or materialmen's lien.** This means someone performed work on your real property or personal property (for example, a car) but didn't get paid and recorded a lien on that property. Such liens can be an unpleasant surprise if you paid for the work, but your contractor didn't pay a subcontractor who got a lien against your property.
- **Unknown.** If you don't know what kind of lien you are dealing with, insert "Don't know nature of lien" after the date. The bankruptcy trustee can help you figure it out later.

How to List Creditors Associated With Foreclosed or Repossessed Property

Until your property is sold in a foreclosure sale and a deed has been recorded showing a transfer of ownership to the lender or new purchaser, you still own the property and any mortgages on the property are considered secured debts. You must list all lenders, mortgage servicers, foreclosing trustees, and attorneys listed on foreclosure papers as secured creditors on Schedule D. List the amounts of the mortgages only once, however. After a deed has been recorded showing that you no longer own the property, your mortgage debt is no longer secured debt. List all these parties on Schedule E/F as unsecured creditors. The same is true with repossessed cars. If you no longer own the vehicle, list the car note on Schedule E/F.

TIP
You're not admitting you owe the debt. You might think you don't really owe a contingent, unliquidated, or disputed debt, or you might not want to "admit" that you owe the debt. However, listing a debt here isn't an admission that you owe the obligation. You're ensuring that if you owe the debt after all, it will be discharged in your bankruptcy (if it is dischargeable; see Ch. 9). To protect yourself from someone claiming that you admitted to owing a debt you don't believe you owe, check the "disputed" box.

Amount of Claim Without Deducting Value of Collateral. For each secured creditor, list the amount it would take to pay off the secured claim, regardless of what the property is worth. The lender can give you this figure. In some cases, the amount of the secured claim may be more than the property's value.

> **EXAMPLE:** Your original loan was for $13,000, plus $7,000 in interest (for $20,000 total). You've made enough payments so that $15,000 will cancel the debt. You would put $15,000 in this column.

If you have more than one creditor for a given secured claim (for example, the lender and a collection agency), list the debt only for the lender and put ditto marks (") for each subsequent creditor.

Value of collateral supporting the claim. Transfer the value of the property listed in Schedule A/B to Column B.

Unsecured Portion, If Any. If the fair market value of the collateral is equal to or greater than the amount of the claim, enter "0," meaning that the creditor's claim is fully secured. If the collateral value is less than the amount of the claim(s) listed, enter the difference here (Column C).

> **EXAMPLE:** If the current value of your car is $5,000 but you still owe $6,000 on your car loan, enter $1,000 in this column ($6,000–$5,000). This is the amount of the loan that is unsecured by the collateral (your car).

If you list an amount in this column for a creditor, do not list this amount again on Schedule E/F (where you will list all other creditors with unsecured claims).

Total. Enter the total of all your Column A entries on the final page of Schedule D. Enter this amount again on Line 2a of Form 106Sum, Summary of Your Assets and Liabilities and Certain Statistical Information.

Part 2: List Others to Be Notified for a Debt That You Already Listed

List all others who need to know about your bankruptcy. The most common example is collection agencies. Entering them here (after you tally your total claims) prevents you from inadvertently listing the claim twice.

> **TIP**
> **Missing creditors.** If, after completing your schedules, you discover that you've missed a few creditors, don't retype your papers to preserve perfect alphabetical order. Simply add the creditor at the end. If your creditors don't all fit on the first page of Schedule D, make as many copies of the preprinted continuation page as needed.

Schedule E/F—Creditors Who Have Unsecured Claims (Form 106E/F)

Schedule E/F identifies unsecured creditors, some of which may be entitled to be paid first—by the trustee—out of your nonexempt assets. Even if you don't have any nonexempt assets to be distributed, you still need to fill this form out if you have any unsecured debts.

A completed sample of Schedule E/F is available on the companion page at www.nolo.com/back-of-book/HFB.html. Line-by-line instructions are below.

Fill in the Top of Each Page

Start by preparing the caption following the instructions for Schedule C.

Part 1: List All of Your Priority Unsecured Claims

Priority claims are claims that must be paid first in your bankruptcy case. The most common examples are unsecured income tax debts and past-due alimony or child support. There are several other categories of priority debts, however. Read further to figure out whether or not you should check this box.

Types of priority claims. These are the categories of priority debts, as listed on Schedule E/F.

☐ **Domestic support obligations.** Check this box for claims for domestic support that you owe to, or that are recoverable by, a spouse, former spouse, or child; the parent, legal guardian, or responsible relative of such a child; or a governmental unit to which such a domestic support claim has been assigned.

☐ **Taxes and certain other debts owed to governmental units.** Check this box if you owe unsecured back taxes or if you owe any other debts to the government, such as fines imposed for driving under the influence of drugs or alcohol. Not all tax debts are unsecured priority claims. For example, if the IRS has recorded a lien against your real property, and the equity in your property fully covers the amount of your tax debt, your debt is a secured debt. It should be on Schedule D, not on this schedule.

☐ **Claims for death or personal injury while debtor was intoxicated.** Check this box if there are claims against you for death or personal injury resulting from your operation of a motor vehicle or vessel while intoxicated from using alcohol, a drug, or another substance. This priority doesn't apply to property damage—only to personal injury or death.

Other priority claims. Here are examples of other priority claims you might want to include in the space provided.

☐ **Wages, salaries, and commissions.** If you own a business and owe a current or former employee wages, vacation pay, or sick leave that was earned within 180 days before you filed your petition or within 180 days of the date you ceased your business, check this box. If you owe money to an independent contractor who did work for you, and the money was earned within 180 days before you filed your petition or within 180 days of the date you ceased your business, check this box only if, in the 12 months before you file for bankruptcy, this independent contractor earned at least 75% of his or her total independent contractor receipts from you. Only the first $13,650 owed per employee or independent contractor is a priority debt.

☐ **Contributions to employee benefit plans.** Check this box if you own a business and you owe contributions to an employee benefit fund for services rendered by an employee within 180 days before you filed your petition, or within 180 days of the date you ceased your business, up to a total of $13,650.

☐ **Certain farmers and fishermen.** Check this box only if you operate or operated a grain storage facility and owe a grain producer, or you operate or operated a fish produce or storage facility and owe a U.S. fisherman for fish or fish products. Only the first $6,725 owed per person is a priority debt.

☐ **Deposits by individuals.** If you took money from people who planned to purchase, lease, or rent goods or services from you that you never delivered, you may owe a priority debt. For the debt to qualify as a priority, the goods or services must have been planned for personal, family, or household use. Only the first $3,025 owed (per person) is a priority debt.

If you didn't check any of the priority debt boxes, go back and check the first box, showing you have no unsecured priority claims to report. Then go on to Part 2.

If you checked any of the priority debt boxes, provide information for each type of priority debt, using the following instructions:

Creditor's Name, Mailing Address Including Zip Code, and Account Number. List the name and complete mailing address (including zip code) of each priority creditor. The address should be the one provided in two written communications you have received from the creditor within the past 90 days, if possible. You might have more than one priority creditor for a given debt. For example, if you've been sued or hounded by a collection agency, list the collection agency and the original creditor.

If the creditor is a child, list the child's initials and the name and address of the child's parent or guardian. For example, "A.B., a minor child, by John Doe, Guardian, 111 Alabama Avenue, San Francisco, CA 94732." Don't state the child's name.

Who incurred the debt? Tell the court about any other people who are also responsible for paying for this debt (called "codebtors") by checking the appropriate box. Follow the instructions for Schedule D.

Community debt. Follow the instructions for Schedule D.

Is the claim subject to offset? If the creditor owes you money, and that amount should be deducted from the amount you owe, you are entitled to an offset. Check "Yes" if this applies to the claim.

Account number. For each priority claim, fill in the last four digits of the account number (not the whole number), if you know it.

When was the debt incurred? State the date you incurred the debt—this might be a specific date or period. Refer to the instructions for Schedule D for more details.

Contingent, Unliquidated, Disputed. Follow the instructions for Schedule D.

Type of priority. Check the box for the category of the priority debt (refer to the explanations provided above).

Total Claim. For each priority debt other than taxes, list the amount it would take to pay off the debt in full, even if it's more than the priority limit. For taxes, list only the unsecured amount (and therefore a priority).

You should list the secured amount on Schedule D. If the amount isn't determined, write "not yet determined" in this column.

Priority Amount. If the priority claim is larger than the maximum indicated on the first page of Schedule E/F (for example, $13,650 of wages owed to each employee), insert the maximum here. If the claim is less than the maximum, include the amount you entered in the Total Claim column here.

Nonpriority Amount. List any portion of the debt that is not entitled to priority here. For example, if you owe an employee $15,000 in wages, only the first $13,650 is entitled to priority. That amount should be listed in the "Priority Amount" column; here, you would list the remaining $1,350.

Part 2: List All Creditors with Nonpriority Unsecured Claims

In the second part of the schedule, list all remaining creditors. You'll follow the instructions provided in Part 1 with one exception: Instead of inserting figures in "Total claim" and "Priority amount," you'll put the amount owed in the space provided for "Amount of claim."

You should include debts that are or may be nondischargeable, such as a student loan. Even if you believe that you don't owe the debt or you owe only a small amount and intend to pay it off, you must include it here. You must list every creditor you owe or possibly owe money. The only way you can legitimately leave off a creditor is if your balance owed is $0.

> **TIP**
>
> **You can pay creditors after you file.** You might be tempted to leave some creditors (like your doctor, favorite electrician, or a relative who loaned you money) off of your bankruptcy schedules to stay in their good graces. That's not a good idea: You must list all of your creditors. However, there is nothing to prevent you from paying a discharged debt after your bankruptcy is complete. The only effect bankruptcy has on the debt is that the creditor can't pursue it through collections or place it on your credit report. If you plan to pay certain creditors after your bankruptcy, let them know before you file. This will lessen the sting of your bankruptcy filing. Although your promise is unenforceable, creditors will gladly accept your money.

Creditors That Are Often Overlooked

One debt could involve several different creditors. Remember to include:

- your ex-spouse, if you are still obligated under a divorce decree or settlement agreement to pay joint debts, turn any property over to your ex, or make payments as part of your property division
- anyone who has cosigned a promissory note or loan application you signed
- any holder of a loan or promissory note that you cosigned for someone else
- the original creditor, anybody the debt was assigned or sold to, any other person (such as a bill collector or an attorney) trying to collect the debt, and
- anyone who might sue you because of a car accident, business dispute, or the like.

Even if you plan to repay a particular creditor, you must list the debt and get it discharged anyway. The creditor will be legally barred from collecting the debt. Still, you can always pay the debt voluntarily out of property or income you receive after you file for bankruptcy.

> **EXAMPLE:** Peter owes his favorite aunt $8,000. Peter files for bankruptcy and lists the debt, which is discharged when Peter's bankruptcy is over. Peter can voluntarily repay the $8,000 out of wages he earns any time after he files, because the wages he earns after filing are not part of his bankruptcy estate. He cannot use property that belongs to the bankruptcy estate, however, until he receives a discharge. The important thing is, repayment is completely voluntary on Peter's part. Peter's aunt can't sue him in court to enforce payment of the debt.

Inadvertent errors or omissions on this schedule can come back to haunt you. If you don't list a debt you owe to a creditor, it might not be discharged in bankruptcy if your estate has assets that are distributed to your other creditors by the trustee, or if the creditor is otherwise prejudiced by being left out (although it is sometimes possible in these circumstances to reopen the bankruptcy and include the creditor). Also, leaving a creditor off the schedule might raise suspicions that you deliberately concealed information, perhaps to give that creditor preferential treatment in violation of bankruptcy rules. (See Ch. 9 for more on what happens to debts not listed on your schedules.)

> **TIP**
>
> **Use your credit reports.** It is often a good idea to order your credit report to determine whether any unknown creditors claim you owe them money. The more complete you are in listing possible creditors (even if you've never heard from them), the more powerful your bankruptcy discharge will be. You can get a free annual credit report from each of the three major credit reporting agencies at AnnualCreditReport.com. Beware of other imposter sites, like www.freecredit report.com, that sound like AnnualCreditReport.com. Most of these sites charge you for your report or require you to sign up for monthly "memberships" to get your report.
>
> It's also a good idea to get a credit report if you are having problems finding a creditor's recent address (however, the bankruptcy court requires that you use the address on the billing statement). (For more information on credit reports and how to obtain them, see Ch. 8.) Don't rely exclusively on credit reports, though. You must disclose every debt on your bankruptcy forms, whether or not it appears in a credit report.

Part 3: List Others to Be Notified About Unsecured Claims

List all others who need to know about your bankruptcy. The most common example is a collection agency. When you fall behind on a debt, it's common to receive bills from multiple debt collectors, all asking to get paid for the same obligation. Entering additional collectors here will ensure that these agencies receive notice of the bankruptcy and stop contacting you. Also, the form provides this space to prevent you from accidentally listing the claim amount more than once. Be sure to put the original creditor's line number in the "line" space so that the court knows which agency is collecting a particular debt.

Part 4: Total Amounts of the Priority and Nonpriority Unsecured Claims

Line 5a. Enter the total for your Part 1 claims.

Line 5b. Enter the total for your Part 2 claims.

Line 5c. Add the line 5a and 5b amounts together and enter the total on Line 5c. Enter this amount again on Line 3b of Form 106Sum, Summary of Your Assets and Liabilities and Certain Statistical Information.

Listing Debts on Foreclosed and Repossessed Property

Secured debts before foreclosure or repossession become unsecured debts after the property title reverts to the lender or vests in a new buyer. Once that occurs, you should list these obligations on Schedule E/F as unsecured debts. List the deficiency amount if you know it. A deficiency is the difference between what you owed and what the lender ultimately got in the foreclosure or repossession sale. If you don't yet know because the foreclosure or repossession was so recent, list the entire debt.

Schedule G: Executory Contracts and Unexpired Leases (Form 106G)

Here you'll list all of your executory contracts and unexpired leases. "Executory" means the contract is still in force—that is, both parties are still obligated to perform important acts under it. Similarly, "unexpired" means that the contract or lease period hasn't run out—it is still in effect. Common examples of executory contracts and unexpired leases are:

- car leases
- residential leases or rental agreements
- business leases or rental agreements
- service contracts
- business contracts
- time-share contracts or leases
- contracts of sale for real estate
- personal property leases, such as equipment used in a beauty salon
- copyright and patent license agreements
- leases of real estate (surface and underground) for the purpose of harvesting timber, minerals, or oil
- future homeowners' association fee requirements
- agreements for boat docking privileges, and
- insurance contracts.

CAUTION

If you're behind in your payments. If you are not current on payments that were due under a lease or an executory contract, the delinquency should also be listed as a debt on Schedule D or E/F. The sole purpose of Schedule G is to identify existing contractual obligations that you still owe or that someone owes you. Later, you will be allowed to state whether you want the lease or contract to continue in effect.

A sample completed Schedule G is available on the companion page at www.nolo.com/back-of-book/HFB.html. Line-by-line instructions are below.

Fill in the Top of Each Page

Start by preparing the caption following the instructions for Schedule C.

Line 1. Check the "No" box if you don't have any executory contracts or unexpired leases and then move on to the next form. Otherwise check "Yes" and keep reading.

Line 2. List each person or company with whom you have a contract or lease. In the first column, provide the name and full address (including zip code) of each party—other than yourself—to each lease or contract. These parties are either people who signed agreements or the companies for whom these people work. If you're unsure who to list, include the person who signed an agreement, any company whose name appears on the agreement, and anybody who might have an interest in having the contract or lease enforced. If you still aren't sure, insert "don't know."

In the second "State what the contract or lease is for" column, for each lease or contract, give:

- a description of the type (for instance, residential lease, commercial lease, car lease, business obligation, or copyright license)
- the date the contract or lease was signed
- the date the contract will expire (if any), and
- the contract number, if the contract is with a government body.

What Happens to Executory Contracts and Unexpired Leases in Bankruptcy

The trustee has 60 days after you file for bankruptcy to decide whether an executory contract or unexpired lease should be assumed (continued in force) as property of the estate or terminated (rejected). If the lease or contract would generate funds for your unsecured creditors, then it will be assumed; otherwise, it will be rejected. As a general matter, most leases and contracts are liabilities and are rejected by the trustee. However, you have the right to assume a lease on personal property (for instance, a car lease) on your own, as long as you give the creditor written notice and the creditor agrees. (11 U.S.C. § 365(p).) You provide this written notice in the Statement of Intention.

As a general rule, people filing Chapter 7 bankruptcies are not parties to leases or contracts that would likely add value to their bankruptcy estates. This isn't an absolute rule, however. If the trustee could sell a lease to someone else for a profit (because you're paying less than market value, for example), the trustee might assume the lease and assign it for a lump sum that could be distributed to your creditors.

It's also possible that you'll want to get out of a contract or lease, such as a residential or an auto lease or a time-share you can't afford. Be sure to state at the bankruptcy meeting or even on your papers that you would like the trustee to terminate the agreement. But remember, it's up to the trustee to decide.

If the lease is assigned or terminated or the contract is terminated, you and the other parties to the agreement are cut loose from any obligations, and any money you owe the creditor will be discharged in your bankruptcy, even if the debt arose after your filing date. For example, say you are leasing a car when you file for bankruptcy. You want out of the lease. The car dealer cannot repossess the car until the trustee terminates the lease, which generally must occur within 60 days of when you file. During those 60 days, you can use the vehicle without paying for it. The payments you don't make during this time will be discharged as if they were incurred before your bankruptcy.

Bankruptcy law has special rules for executory contracts related to intellectual property (copyright, patent, trademark, or trade secret), real estate, and time-share leases. If you are involved in one of these situations, see a lawyer.

Schedule H: Your Codebtors (Form 106H)

In Schedules D and E/F, you identified those debts for which you have codebtors—usually, a cosigner, guarantor, ex-spouse, nonfiling spouse in a community property state, nonfiling spouse for a debt for necessities, nonmarital partner, or joint contractor. You must also list those codebtors here. Also, you must list the name and address of any spouse or former spouse who lived with you in Puerto Rico or in a community property state during the eight years immediately before your bankruptcy filing. If you are married but filing separately, include all names used by your spouse during the eight years.

In Chapter 7 bankruptcy, your codebtors will be wholly responsible for the cosigned debt unless they declare bankruptcy.

A sample completed Schedule H is available on the companion page at www.nolo.com/back-of-book/HFB.html. Line-by-line instructions are below.

Fill in the Top of Each Page

Start by preparing the caption following the instructions for Schedule C.

Line 1. Check the "No" box if you don't have any codebtors; check "Yes" if you do.

Line 2. If you lived in a community property state within the last eight years, check "Yes." Otherwise, check "No" and move on to Line 3. If you checked "Yes," fill in the rest of the requested information in Line 2.

Line 3. In the first column, list the name and complete address (including zip code) of each codebtor. If the codebtor is a nonfiling, current spouse, put all names by which that person was known during the previous eight years. If the creditor is a child, don't state the child's name. Instead, list the child's initials and the name and address of the child's parent or guardian. For instance, "A.B., a minor child, John Doe, Guardian, 111 Alabama Avenue, San Francisco, CA 94732." In the second column, list the creditor to whom you owe the debt. Check the box corresponding to the appropriate schedule and list the line number on which the debt appears.

FOR MARRIED COUPLES

If you are married and filing alone. If you live in a community property state, your spouse may be a codebtor for most of the debts you listed in Schedules D and E/F. In these states, most debts incurred by one spouse are owed by both spouses. In this event, don't relist all the creditors in the second column. Simply write "all creditors listed in Schedules D and E/F, except:" and then list any creditors whom you alone owe.

Schedule I: Your Income (Form 106I)

In this Schedule, you calculate your actual current income (not your average monthly income for the six months before filing used in Form 122A-1, below).

A sample completed Schedule I is available on the companion page at www.nolo.com/back-of-book/HFB.html. Line-by-line instructions are below.

Fill in the Top of Each Page

Start by preparing the caption following the instructions for Schedule C. Ignore the two boxes on the top right-hand side of the form. You won't check these boxes unless you need to change something after filing.

For the rest of the form, if you are married and filing jointly, you must fill in the information in the "Debtor 2 or nonfiling spouse" column. Both you and your spouse are equally responsible for providing accurate information on this form. You also must fill in the "Debtor 2 or nonfiling spouse" column if you are married and not filing jointly, unless you are separated and no longer living under the same roof. If you consider yourself to be separated but still live under the same roof, you don't need to list your spouse's income, but it is better to do so to be on the safe side. Also, if you need additional room to fully answer a question, attach a continuation sheet to your schedule. Be sure to write your name and case number on any additional pages.

Part 1: Describe Employment

Enter your employment status and provide the requested employment information. If you have more than one employer, list each additional employer on a continuation sheet. If you are retired, unemployed, or disabled, enter that in the blank for "occupation."

Part 2: Give Details About Monthly Income

Enter your estimated monthly gross income (this is how much you make before anything is taken out of your check; so don't deduct anything yet—that's coming up) by adding together all of your wages, salary, and commission from "regular employment" (work you usually do regularly). List this figure on Line 2. Put your estimated monthly overtime pay on Line 3. Add Lines 2 and 3 together (your total monthly income) and list this number in two places—on Line 4 of Page 1 and at the top of Page 2 where it says "Copy line 4 here."

Line 5: List all payroll deductions. In the eight blanks, enter the deductions taken from your gross salary. The deductions listed are the most common ones, but you might have others to report, such as state disability taxes, wages withheld or garnished for child support, credit union payments, or perhaps payments on a student loan or a car. List these deductions on Line 5h.

Line 6: Add the payroll deductions. Add all of your payroll deductions together and list the total in this space.

Line 7: Calculate total monthly take-home pay. Subtract your payroll deductions (Line 6) from your income total (Line 4) and enter your total monthly take-home pay on Line 7.

Line 8: List all other income regularly received. In the following eight spaces, you'll list all other types of income you receive.

Line 8a: Net income from rental property, business, profession, or farm. Here, the bankruptcy court wants to know how much money you receive from other income-generating activities. You'll answer this question if you are self-employed, operate a sole proprietorship, are a member of a business partnership, receive money from rental property, or are a farmer.

Attach statements that list the gross receipts, ordinary and necessary business expenses, and net income for each activity. (Subtract the expenses from your gross receipts to get your net income.) Enter your total net income from your rental property, business, profession, or farm on Line 8a.

Line 8b: Interest and dividends. Enter the average estimated monthly interest you receive from bank or security deposits and other investments, such as stock.

Line 8c: Family support payments that you, a non-filing spouse, or a dependent regularly receive. Enter the average monthly amount you, your non-filing spouse, or your dependent receives for support. This includes child support, alimony, spousal support, or maintenance.

Line 8d: Unemployment compensation. Enter the estimated amount you currently receive from unemployment compensation.

Line 8e: Social Security. Enter the total monthly amount you receive in retirement, disability, or survivor benefits from the Social Security Administration.

Line 8f: Other government assistance. Enter the total amount of government assistance you receive each month, such as public assistance, veterans benefits, and workers' compensation. If you receive food stamp assistance or other food programs, specify the source and include the monthly value.

Line 8g: Pension or retirement income. Enter the total monthly amount of all pension, annuity, IRA, Keogh, or other retirement benefits you currently receive.

Line 8h: Other monthly income. Specify any other income (such as royalty payments or payments from a trust) you receive regularly, and enter the monthly amount here. You may have to divide by three, six, or 12 if you receive the payments quarterly, semiannually, or annually.

Line 9: Add all other income. Add together all of your entries from Lines 8a through 8h and enter the amount on Line 9.

Line 10: Calculate monthly income. Add your total monthly take-home pay in Lines 7 to 9. If you are filing jointly, combine your total from Line 10 with your spouse's total and enter your joint monthly income total in the far right space.

Line 11: State all other regular contributions to the expenses that you list in Schedule J. If you receive any help with your expenses regularly, such as from a partner that lives with you (for example, a live-in girlfriend or boyfriend), another member of your household, dependent, roommate, friend or family member, list that amount on Line 11. Include only money that is available to pay expenses and specify the circumstances ("My parents give me $500 each month for rent") on the line provided.

Three Different Income Figures

The bankruptcy law that went into effect in October 2005 produces several strange results. One of these is that you will report three different income figures: the "current monthly income" figure in Form 122A-1, the actual income you report here, and the annual income figures you report in your Statement of Financial Affairs (see below).

Schedule I explicitly states that the income you report will likely be different from your current monthly income on Form 122A-1. That's because the income you report on Form 122A-1 is your average gross income for the six months before filing. Here, the income is the actual net income you expect to receive every month going forward. If, for example, you lost your job a couple of months ago and are now earning much less, your income will be lower than what you reported on Form 122A-1.

Line 12: Add lines 10 and 11 together. Add the total on Line 10 to the number on Line 11. This is your "combined monthly income." Keep this figure handy because you'll use it on two additional forms: the Summary of Schedules and the Statistical Summary of Certain Liabilities and Related Data forms.

Line 13: Expected increase or decrease in income. If you don't expect your income to change in the next year, check the "No" box—you are done with this form. If you expect your income to increase, check "Yes" and explain why you believe so. Be aware that if you indicate that you will soon be enjoying a significantly higher income, you might face a motion from the U.S. Trustee seeking to force you into Chapter 13. But you must be accurate, so you must disclose that fact, regardless of the consequences. Of course, if your income will decrease any time soon, you should use this part of the form to indicate that as well.

Schedule J—Your Expenses (Form 106J)

In this form, you must list your family's total monthly expenditures, even if you're married and filing alone.

Be complete and accurate. Expenditures for items the trustee considers luxuries might not be regarded as reasonable. For instance, the trustee could find payments on expensive cars or investment property questionable.

If this happens and you end up having enough excess income to fund a Chapter 13 plan, Chapter 13 might be your only option if you don't want your case dismissed. Reasonable expenditures for housing, utilities, food, medical care, clothing, education, and transportation will be counted. Be ready to support high amounts with bills, receipts, and canceled checks.

> **EXAMPLE 1:** Joe owes $100,000 (excluding his mortgage and car), earns $4,000 a month, and spends $3,900 a month for the other items listed on Schedule J, including payments on a midpriced car and a moderately priced family home. Joe would probably be allowed to proceed with a Chapter 7 bankruptcy because his monthly disposable income ($100) wouldn't put much of a dent in his $100,000 debt load, even over five years.

> **EXAMPLE 2:** Same facts, except that Joe's Schedule J expenditures total only $2,200 a month. In this case, the court might rule that because Joe has $1,800 a month in disposable income, he could pay off most of his $100,000 debt load over a three- to five-year period, either informally or under a Chapter 13 repayment plan. The court could dismiss Joe's Chapter 7 bankruptcy petition or pressure him to convert it to Chapter 13 bankruptcy.

> **EXAMPLE 3:** Same facts as Example 2, but Joe is incurably ill and will soon have to quit working. The court will more than likely allow him to proceed with a Chapter 7 bankruptcy.

A sample completed Schedule J is available on the companion page at www.nolo.com/back-of-book/HFB.html. Line-by-line instructions are below.

Fill in the Top of Each Page

Start by preparing the caption following the instructions for Schedule C. Just as with Schedule I, ignore the two boxes on the top right-hand side of the form since you haven't filed your petition yet.

CAUTION

Once again, be accurate. Creditors sometimes try to use the information on these forms to prove that you committed fraud when you applied for credit. If a creditor can prove that you lied on a credit application, the debt could survive bankruptcy. (See Ch. 9 for more information.) If being accurate on this form will substantially contradict information you previously gave a creditor, see a bankruptcy attorney for a fraud assessment before filing.

> **TIP**
>
> **Using bankruptcy to eliminate debts before divorce.** If you are getting divorced, one of the best ways to handle marital debt is to discharge qualifying debt in Chapter 7 bankruptcy before the divorce is final. Many people don't realize that if a family law court orders you to pay a debt in the name of both spouses, filing bankruptcy after divorce will not alleviate your responsibility to pay that debt. Even if you discharge the debt, the creditor can collect against your ex-spouse, and your ex-spouse can sue you for violating a court order. Resolving the debt issues through bankruptcy before the divorce allows both parties to truly start fresh without the financial burden from the previous relationship.

Part 1: Describe Your Household

Here, you explain your current living situation. Enter your filing status and tell the court whether you and your spouse live in the same household. If you have dependents, don't list their names. Instead, list them according to their relationship to you, such as "son," "daughter," "granddaughter," "parent." Provide each dependent's age and check the appropriate box indicating where the dependent lives. If you pay expenses for someone other than yourself and your dependents, check "Yes" to question three.

Part 2: Estimate Your Ongoing Monthly Expenses

In this section, you tell the court how much money it takes for you to live each month, otherwise known as your monthly budget. The trustee uses this schedule to decide whether you have enough money left over each month to pay your creditors through a Chapter 13 plan, and if so, how much. In other words, it is important to get it right. Here are some pointers:

- Use the actual cost of your bills on the date you file your bankruptcy.
- If you make some payments biweekly, quarterly, semiannually, or annually, prorate them to show your monthly payment.
- Do not list the payroll deductions you listed on Schedule I.
- Include payments for your dependents' expenses as long as they are reasonable and necessary for the dependents' support.

Most of the line items listed in this form are self-explanatory, but not all. Below you'll find help for the categories that aren't clear, tips to keep you out of trouble with the trustee, and suggestions for expenses you may have forgotten about. As a reminder, make sure to retain receipts for all the expenses you list because receipts are the key to staying in the trustee's good graces.

Line 4b: Home maintenance, repair, and upkeep expenses. If your home is new, you may not have much in the way of upkeep expenses. On the other hand, older homes often need costly loving care. If you anticipate costly repairs shortly, such as painting, plumbing, roofing, or termite repairs, consider getting an estimate and prorating the cost over several months. Here are examples of other common maintenance items (be prepared to explain why you can't perform some of these services yourself):

- yard and pool care
- tree trimming
- pest control
- lightbulb replacement
- heating or air conditioner servicing, and
- smoke detector maintenance.

Line 8: Childcare and children's education costs. If you pay for childcare, it is likely one of your biggest expenses. Listing enrichment activities such as karate and swimming lessons will be difficult to justify.

Line 10: Personal care products and services. Personal care products can add up fast since this category includes toothpaste, soap, razors, shampoo, conditioner, lip balm, talcum powder, lotion, and cotton swabs. Services include haircuts for yourself and your family. Even so, trustees look at this category with a critical eye, so you will certainly want to stay away from budgeting luxurious services like manicures and pedicures unless, of course, you can demonstrate such services are necessary for your profession or that you need them for health reasons.

Line 14: Charitable contributions and religious donations. There is no limit to how much you can claim for charitable contributions or religious donations. As a rule of thumb, however, it is wise to consider limiting your charitable contribution budget to an amount that reflects prior contributions. Also, your tithing budget should be no more than ten percent of your income. In both cases, be prepared to show receipts of past contributions so the trustee can see that you have an established history of donating at that level.

When Expenses on Schedule J Trigger an Audit

One thing that will trigger a bankruptcy audit is listing higher than expected expenses on Schedule J. So what is considered to be higher than expected? A good rule of thumb is that anything over and above the IRS National and Local Standards used in the means test calculation could be considered suspect. Of course, this doesn't mean that you shouldn't list the actual amount of your expenses. To the contrary, you are required by law to be accurate on your schedules (and you should be fair to yourself, as well). Just realize that the trustee might not be the only one questioning you about expenses that are higher than the "standards." If your figures trigger an audit, the U.S. Trustee's Office will contact you. In both instances, be prepared to show documentation in the way of receipts.

Line 17: Installment or lease payments. Since your budget reflects the expenses you anticipate paying, you should only include your car payment if you plan to keep the car. Don't include payments for credit cards and other debts you won't be responsible for once you receive your discharge.

Line 22. Your monthly expenses. To complete Schedule J, add all of your expenses on Lines 4 through 21 and enter the total amount on Line 22.

Line 23. Calculate your monthly net income. Enter your combined monthly income figure from Schedule I onto 23a. Enter your total monthly expenses (the amount you listed on Line 22) on Line 23b. To determine your monthly net income (how much you have left over each month after paying your bills), subtract your monthly expenses (Line 23b) from your monthly income (Line 23a) and enter the result on Line 23c.

While it is okay to have a small negative number, be cautious. Expenses that greatly exceed your income could cause the trustee to question the accuracy of the information provided. In most cases, your income and expenses should be reasonably close.

Do you expect an increase or decrease in expenses? To finish the form, indicate whether you anticipate an increase or decrease in expenses within the following year. If so, check "Yes," and explain why in the box immediately to the right. If not, check "No." You are done with Schedule J.

Dismissal for Abuse

As explained in Ch. 1, bankruptcy law has an eligibility requirement called the "means test" to determine who qualifies for Chapter 7 bankruptcy. Debtors whose "current monthly income"—their average income over the six months before they filed for bankruptcy—exceeds their state's median income must take the means test. In the means test, debtors calculate their disposable income by subtracting certain allowable expenses (in amounts set by the IRS) and deductions from their current monthly income. If they have enough disposable income to fund a Chapter 13 repayment plan, their Chapter 7 case will be a "presumed abuse" of the bankruptcy laws and will be dismissed or converted to Chapter 13.

If you either pass the means test or don't have to take it, your case won't be presumed abusive. However, the court can still find that allowing you to use Chapter 7 would be an abuse of the bankruptcy process if circumstances show that you could afford a repayment plan. Some courts have dismissed Chapter 7 cases or converted them to Chapter 13 under this theory if the debtor's Schedule I and Schedule J show that the debtor has significantly more income than expenses.

Because the law on abuse is unsettled, we suggest that you be very cautious claiming expenses for luxury items. If your income exceeds your expenses on these schedules by more than a small amount, you may want to talk to a lawyer before filing. Either of these situations might result in the U.S. Trustee challenging your right to use Chapter 7.

CAUTION

Don't underestimate your expenses. As indicated above, a significant net income might lead the trustee to challenge your Chapter 7 filing. Sometimes people give low estimates of their expenses because they don't want to appear to be living beyond their means. Or sometimes people's expenses are low because they have been unemployed, but have increased or will increase soon because they have recently started working again. If this describes your situation, go back over your expenses and make sure they are accurate in light of your actual situation.

Summary of Your Assets and Liabilities and Certain Statistical Information (Form 106Sum)

A sample completed Summary is available on the companion page at www.nolo.com/back-of-book/HFB.html. Line-by-line instructions are below.

Fill in the Top of Each Page

Start by preparing the caption following the instructions for Schedule C.

Part 1: Summarize Your Assets

Turn to the last page of Schedule A/B. Copy the total on Line 55—the value of your real estate—onto line 1a of the Summary. Copy the total on Line 62—the value of your personal property—onto Line 1b. Finally, copy the total on Line 63—the total value of all of your property—onto Line 1c of the Summary. Move on to Part 2.

Part 2: Summarize Your Liabilities

Here you'll need both Schedule D and Schedule E/F. Again, turn to the last page of each schedule and transfer the necessary totals.

Part 3: Summarize Your Income and Expenses

Copy the totals from Schedule I and Schedule J and enter them where indicated.

Part 4: Answer These Questions for Administrative and Statistical Records

This part of the form asks you to transfer information from other bankruptcy schedules. Check the boxes and fill in the blanks using your completed forms. You'll check "Yes" in response to the first question since you are filing Chapter 7. You'll likely check that your debts are primarily consumer debts, meaning that they are not business-related. (To learn more, see the discussion of consumer and nonconsumer debts in Form 122A-1Supp, below.)

You'll need to return to this form to fill in Line 8 because you won't have your current monthly income until after completing Forms 122A-1, 122B, or 122C (instructions for these forms are below). Finally, you'll use Schedule E/F to complete Line 9 and its subparts.

Declaration About an Individual Debtor's Schedules (Form 106Dec)

In this form, you are required to swear that everything you have entered on your schedules is true and correct. Deliberate lying could cost you your bankruptcy discharge, a fine of up to $250,000, and up to 20 years in prison.

A sample completed Declaration is available on the companion page at www.nolo.com/back-of-book/HFB.html. Line-by-line instructions are below.

Fill in the Top of Each Page

Start by preparing the caption following the instructions for Schedule C.

Sign below. If you hired someone other than an attorney to complete your petition, check the "Yes" box, enter the person's name on the line, and attach Form 119. Otherwise, check "No." Read the statement above the signature line. By signing the form, you declare under penalty of perjury that the information in the summary and schedules is true and correct. Enter the date and sign the form. Be sure that your spouse signs and dates the form if you are filing jointly.

Statement of Financial Affairs for Individuals Filing for Bankruptcy (Form 107)

This form gives information about your recent financial transactions, such as payments to creditors, sales, or other property transfers and gifts. Under certain circumstances, the trustee may be entitled to take back property that you transferred to others before filing for bankruptcy, and sell it to benefit your unsecured creditors.

The questions on the form are, for the most part, self-explanatory. Spouses filing jointly combine their answers and complete only one form, but they're equally responsible for supplying correct information.

If you have no information for a particular item, check the "None" box. If you fail to answer a question and don't check "None," you will have to amend your papers—that is, file a corrected form—after you file. Add continuation sheets if necessary.

CAUTION

Be honest and complete. Don't give in to the temptation to leave out a transfer or two, assuming that the trustee won't find out or go after the property. You must sign this form under penalty of perjury. And, if it appears to the trustee that you left information out intentionally, your bankruptcy could be dismissed—you could even be criminally prosecuted, although this is extremely rare.

On the other hand, you are entitled to take the form and its instructions quite literally. Carefully read the form's general instructions and the instructions for each separate item, and then answer according to the literal meaning of the form's words. If you do this, you won't be held to account for wrong answers. Of course, you might have to amend your paperwork if your interpretation is not the same as that of the trustee. Still, at least you won't be suspected of lying or playing fast and loose with the bankruptcy forms.

A sample completed Statement of Financial Affairs is found on the companion page. Line-by-line instructions appear below.

Fill in the Top of Each Page

Start by preparing the caption following the instructions for Schedule C.

Part 1: Give Details About Your Marital Status and Where You Lived Before

The first question asks for your marital status. Check the appropriate box. On Line 2, if you've lived somewhere other than at your current address within the last three years, check "Yes" and provide your prior addresses and the dates you lived at each. List any other places where your filing spouse has lived. If none, check the "Same as Debtor 1" box and enter the dates.

If you've lived with a spouse in a community property state within the last eight years, check "Yes" on Line 3. While you do not list the name of your nonfiling spouse or former spouse here, the form reminds you to include them on Schedule H: Your Codebtors.

Part 2: Explain the Sources of Your Income

Enter your gross income from your employment or business for this year (the amount you've made year-to-date) and for the previous two years. Gross income is the amount you receive before subtracting taxes and other payroll deductions or business expenses. Make sure you provide amounts consistent with the income disclosed on the tax returns provided to the trustee. For instance, if you claim $25,000 gross income for the previous year on this form, your tax return for that year should list the same or a similar figure.

You'll include information about income from all other sources on Line 5. Such income includes interest, dividends, royalties, workers' compensation, other government benefits, alimony, child support, rental income, money from lawsuits, royalties, gambling winnings, and all other money you have received from sources other than your job or business during the last two years. Provide the source of each amount and the gross amount you received before any deductions.

CAUTION

Be prepared to explain inconsistencies in reported income. You list income three separate times in your bankruptcy papers. On Schedule I, you report your current income. On Form 122A-1, you report your income for the previous six months. On the Statement of Financial Affairs, you report your annual gross income for the previous two to three years. None of these numbers will be the same, but if the income you report on your Statement of Financial Affairs is substantially higher than your income reported on the other forms, the trustee may want to know why. For example, if on the Statement of Financial Affairs you report your annual gross income for the previous year as $100,000 but on Form 122A-1 report your current monthly income as $4,000 a month (annualized to $48,000), the trustee might want you to explain the discrepancy.

CAUTION

Don't use your tax refund to repay a debt. Many people use their tax refunds to repay loans from relatives. If you repay more than $600, however, it counts as a preference that the trustee can take back. The better strategy is to hang on to the money, declare it on Schedule A/B, and claim it as exempt on Schedule C assuming that the exemptions you are using provide for it. Then, after your bankruptcy, it will be yours to do with what you want. If you've already repaid the loan, perhaps the relative can return the money and you can exempt it as described above. If the money is gone, your relative can reject the trustee's demand and say, in effect, "sue me." For amounts less than $1,000 or so, it's unlikely that the trustee will sue; the expense will likely outweigh whatever the trustee could recover. But you never know. If you have no way to exempt your tax refund, you can spend it on living expenses and necessities before filing bankruptcy, but make sure to document your expenditures.

Part 3: List Certain Payments You Made Before You Filed for Bankruptcy

The purpose of these questions is to find out whether you have favored or preferred any creditor over another.

Line 6. Check "Yes" if your debts are primarily consumer debts. (See Form 122A-1Supp, on the companion page, for more on consumer and nonconsumer debts.) List payments made to a regular creditor that total more than $600 for everything other than child support or alimony, or payments to an attorney for your bankruptcy case. Include the creditor's name and address, dates of payment, the total amount paid, and the amount you still owe. Then check the box that best describes the type of debt payment.

If your debts are primarily business debts, list all payments or other transfers made to a creditor within 90 days of filing that total $6,825 or more.

Lines 7 and 8. An insider—defined in this section—is essentially a relative or close business associate. All other creditors are regular creditors, even friends. List all payments or other property transfers made within one year before you filed your petition if you made the payment directly to an insider creditor or if the payment or property transfer benefited an insider, meaning it paid off the debt of a family member or business associate (Line 8).

Part 4: Identify Legal Actions, Repossessions, and Foreclosures

Line 9. Include all court actions you're currently involved in or were involved in during the year before filing. Court actions are either civil or criminal in nature. You'll include the following information:

- **Case title.** The case title consists of those involved in the suit (such as *Carrie Edwards v. Ginny Jones*).

- **Case number.** The court clerk assigns a case number that will appear on the first page of any court-filed paper.
- **Nature of the case.** A short phrase, or even a one-word description, is sufficient. Here are a few examples: civil, criminal, personal injury, class action, divorce, foreclosure, collection, or contract.
- **Court or agency.** This information is on any summons (or just about any other court document) you receive or prepare for filing.
- **Status of the case.** State whether the matter is awaiting trial, pending a decision, on appeal, or concluded (finished).

Line 10. If, at any time during the year before you file for bankruptcy, a creditor took any of your money or property from you, enter it here. Enter all of the requested information and check the box that describes what happened. Here is an explanation of relevant terms:

- **Property was repossessed.** If you failed to make your payments as agreed on personal property—such as a car or a boat—and the creditor took back the property (the collateral), then check this box. For instance, if your vehicle, boat, or electronic equipment was repossessed because you failed to pay (defaulted on your payments), describe it here. If you voluntarily returned property to a creditor because you couldn't keep up the payments, you'd enter that information here, too.
- **Property was foreclosed.** Check this box if your creditor took back your house or other real estate (such as rental property or land) because you weren't able to make your payments.
- **Property was garnished.** Check this box if your employer took money out of your paycheck (often called a "wage garnishment") to pay a judgment creditor or outstanding tax debt.
- **Property was attached, seized, or levied.** If you lost other money or property in a different manner, check this box. A typical example is a judgment creditor or taxing agency deducting money from your bank account.

Line 11. A setoff occurs when a creditor, often a bank, uses money in a customer's account to pay a debt owed to that creditor. For example, many credit unions tie loans to the borrower's savings and checking accounts, so that any default on the loan can be deducted from those accounts. Here, list any setoffs that your creditors have made during the previous 90 days.

The trustee might require the bank (or anyone else) to turn over the money obtained through setoff and use it to repay your creditors. (To learn how to prevent setoff from happening to you, see "Warning: Stop Your Bank From Draining Your Account," in Ch. 2.)

Line 12. Check "Yes" if any of the following things happened during the one year before you file for bankruptcy (although you don't have to list the property, expect the bankruptcy trustee to ask for more details).

- **Assigned property.** You assigned (legally transferred) your right to receive benefits or assets to a creditor to pay a debt. Examples include assigning a percentage of your wages to a creditor for several months or assigning a portion of a personal injury award to an attorney. The assignee is the person to whom you made the assignment, such as the creditor or attorney.
- **Court-appointed receiver or custodian seized property.** The court allowed someone to take control of your property (often to prevent it from being mishandled during a pending lawsuit).

Part 5: List Certain Gifts and Contributions

Line 13. Provide the requested information about gifts you've made in the past year. The bankruptcy court and trustee want this information to make sure you haven't improperly given property away—due to either financial mismanagement or a desire to cheat creditors—before filing for bankruptcy.

You don't have to list gifts to family members that are "ordinary and usual." Still, there is no easy way to identify such gifts without more guidance—which is why the court requires you to list all gifts over $600 per person. Any gift over that amount is considered extraordinary. Forgiving a loan is also a gift, as is charging interest substantially below the market rate. Other gifts include giving a car or prepaid trip to a business associate.

Line 14. List all charitable donations of more than $600 given within the two years before you filed for bankruptcy, including both money—such as church tithing or monthly payroll deductions to a charitable organization—and property donations of used clothing, toys during the holiday season, and the like.

Part 6: List Certain Losses

Line 15. Provide information about losses suffered during the year before filing for bankruptcy. Include events such as fire, theft, natural (and other) disasters, and gambling losses. Also, provide information about any insurance covering the loss. If the loss was for an exempt item, most states let you keep the insurance proceeds up to the exemption limit. (See the exemption charts on the companion page at www.nolo.com/back-of-book/HFB.html.) However, you'll need to claim the exemption on Schedule C. If the item was nonexempt, the trustee is entitled to the proceeds. In either case, list any proceeds you've received or expect to receive.

Part 7: List Certain Payments or Transfers

Line 16. If you paid an improperly high fee to an attorney, bankruptcy petition preparer, debt consultant, or debt consolidator, the trustee might try to get some of it back to distribute to your creditors. Be sure to list all payments someone else made on your behalf (including bankruptcy costs that friends or family members helped you with), as well as payments you paid directly. Be sure to include amounts for bankruptcy counseling courses, too.

Line 17. Before filing bankruptcy, it is common for people to look for other answers to debt problems by exploring options like credit consolidation services. List any paid services you used within the year before filing bankruptcy to help you with debt issues.

Line 18. List all property (real estate and all other types of property) that you sold or gave to someone else (including a spouse) during the two years before you file for bankruptcy. Some examples are selling or abandoning (junking) a car, pledging your house as security (collateral) for a loan, granting an easement on real estate, or trading property. Also, describe any transfer within the past two years to your ex-spouse as part of a marital settlement agreement.

Don't include any gifts you listed in Part 5. Also, don't list property you've parted with as a regular part of your business or financial affairs. For example, if you operate a mail order book business, don't list the books you sold during the past year. Similarly, don't put down payments for regular goods and services, such as your phone bill, utilities, or rent. The idea is to disclose transfers of property that might legally belong to your bankruptcy estate.

Be accurate about the value of the transferred property. If you sell the property for roughly the same amount that it's worth, there shouldn't be a problem. Assets transferred for less than the fair market value will likely raise the inference that it was unloaded to avoid paying creditors.

> **EXAMPLE 1:** Three years before filing for bankruptcy, Jack sold some personal electronic equipment to a friend for a modest sum. Because the sale wasn't made within the previous two years, Jack needn't list it here.

> **EXAMPLE 2:** Santiago has accumulated a collection of junked classic cars to resell to restoration hobbyists. Within the past year, Santiago has sold three of the vehicles for a total of $20,000. Because this is part of Santiago's regular business, he needn't report the sales here.

> **EXAMPLE 3:** Within the year before filing for bankruptcy, Bailey, a nurse, sold a vintage Jaguar E-type for $17,000. Because this isn't part of her business, Bailey should list this sale here.

Line 19. List all property transfers you've made in the previous ten years to an irrevocable trust that lists you as a beneficiary. These types of trusts—referred to as self-settled trusts—are commonly used by wealthy people to shield their assets from creditors and by disabled people to preserve their right to receive government benefits. In bankruptcy, however, assets placed in a self-settled trust are considered nonexempt. There is an exception that applies to assets placed in certain special needs trusts. (*In re Schultz*, 368 B.R. 832 (D. Minn. 2007).) If you are the beneficiary of a self-settled trust, you should talk to a bankruptcy attorney before filing.

Part 8: List of Certain Financial Accounts, Instruments, Safe Deposit Boxes, and Storage Units

Line 20. Provide information for each account in your name (or opened for your benefit) that was closed or transferred to someone else during the past year.

Line 21. Provide information for each safe deposit box you've had within the previous year. Explain who had access to it, as well as the contents.

Line 22. List information about any storage facility you've had within the past year. Again, list those with access to it and the contents.

If You Are Listed on Someone Else's Account

In the instructions for completing Schedule A/B, we explained that you should list any bank accounts you have been added to for money management purposes. Here, you should describe the account and explain, as you did on Schedule A/B, that you are on the account only to manage it for your relative, and that the money in the account belongs to the relative, not to you.

Part 9: Identify Property You Hold or Control for Someone Else

Line 23. Describe all the property you are currently borrowing from, storing, or holding in trust for someone else. Examples include arrangements as simple as storing your neighbor's tractor on your property to more complicated things such as funds in an irrevocable trust held for someone else as beneficiary but controlled by you as trustee, and assets you're holding as executor or administrator of an estate. This type of property isn't part of your bankruptcy estate. However, you must disclose it so the trustee is aware of it and can ask for more details.

A trustee interested in assets described here can invoke several court procedures designed to get more information. However, it is unlikely that the trustee will invade your house to seize the property (although if you have valuable property, a trustee might inventory your residence). If you can establish that the property actually belongs to someone else—by producing the trust document, for example—you needn't worry about losing it in your bankruptcy case.

> **EXAMPLE:** You are renting an unfurnished apartment owned by a friend. The friend has left a valuable keyboard and mixing equipment in your care. If and when you decide to move, you have agreed to place the equipment in storage for your friend. Because you don't own the items but instead take care of them for your friend, you would describe it here.

Part 10: Give Details About Environmental Information

Few individuals will have much to say here. It's intended primarily for businesses that do business on polluted premises. Still, read the questions carefully and provide the requested information, if applicable. You'll also want to read the definitions provided on the form for "environmental law," "site," and "hazardous material" before answering this section.

Part 11: Give Details About Your Business or Connections to Any Business

The questions in this section ask about the nature, location, and name of any business you're associated with. Provide all of the information requested if you are in business or have been in business for the previous four years. Check "No" if you don't have any business ties and move on to Part 12.

Line 27. Check the appropriate box if you've been involved with a business within the last four years. The definition of "business" is broad. You might need to check the "Sole proprietor or self-employed in a trade, profession, or other activity full-time or part-time" checkbox if you engage in a money-generating activity. Such activities can include anything from a full-time, self-employed plumbing business, to a part-time endeavor, such as personalized crafting, tutoring, or home cosmetic sales. You must answer this question completely so that the trustee will understand how you've earned your money over the past four years and what you did with your business interests (if you are no longer in business).

The remaining boxes are intended for a filer who has an interest in a business entity, such as a partnership, corporation, or limited liability company. Our book is designed for individuals only, so you probably won't check one of these items. If you have business entity interests, consult with a bankruptcy lawyer before filing.

If you report a business, then complete the sections below the checkboxes.

- **Nature of the business.** Describe the product your company sells or the service provided.
- **Name of accountant or bookkeeper.** Identify every person other than yourself—usually a bookkeeper or an accountant—who was involved in the accounting of your business during the previous four years. If you were the only person involved in your business's accounting, write "None."

- **Employer Identification Number and dates business existed.** Provide the requested information.

Line 28. You might have prepared a financial statement if you applied to a bank for a loan or line of credit for your business or in your own name. If you're self-employed and applied for a personal loan to purchase a car or house, you probably submitted a financial statement as evidence of your ability to repay. Such statements include:

- balance sheets (these compare assets with liabilities)
- profit and loss statements (these compare income with expenses), and
- financial statements (these provide an overall financial description of a business).

Part 12: Sign Below

Sign and date this section. You're declaring under penalty of perjury that the answers in the statement are true and correct. If you're filing jointly, be sure your spouse dates and signs it as well. If you attach additional pages to this form, check "Yes." If you paid or promised to pay someone to help you fill out your forms, check "Yes," write in that person's name. Attach Form 119, Bankruptcy Petition Preparer's Notice, Declaration and Signature (the preparer should fill it out). If either or both of these last questions don't apply to you, check "No." You're done with this form.

Statement of Intention for Individuals Filing Under Chapter 7 (Form 108)

This form is critical if you owe any secured debts (Schedule D) or are a party to an executory contract (such as a time-share) or unexpired lease (Schedule G). This is where you inform the trustee and your secured creditors about the contract or lease and what you want to happen to the collateral for each of your secured debts. Briefly, you may:

- reaffirm the debt under a reaffirmation agreement that will continue your liability for all or part of the debt despite your bankruptcy
- redeem the debt by buying the collateral at its replacement value, or
- voluntarily surrender the collateral.

These options were discussed in detail in Ch. 5; you should return to that chapter now if you want more guidance on your options here.

If you are a party to a lease (for instance, a car lease or an executory contract), you may indicate on this form that you want to assume the lease or contract.

If you want to walk away from the lease or contract, you can indicate that you are rejecting it. The bankruptcy trustee can assume the lease, but this is rarely done in personal Chapter 7 cases. The trustee might do so if you had a long-term lease as part of your business and the trustee believes it can be sold to a third party for the benefit of your creditors.

Under 11 U.S.C. Section 365p, you must provide the lessor with written notice that you intend to assume the lease or contract. You do this by sending the lessor or party to the executory contract a copy of the Statement of Intention. The statute gives the lessor or contract party the option to agree to the assumption and notify you of any conditions you must meet (for example, catching up on your payments, if you're behind). The lessor or contract party is very likely to let you assume the lease or contract; the alternative would be for you to walk away without any penalty.

CAUTION

Check your mileage on a leased car. Before you decide to assume your car lease, check your mileage first. If your mileage substantially exceeds the limit in your lease and you plan on turning your car in when the lease is up, think again about whether it makes sense to keep the vehicle. You might be better off letting it go and getting out from under the excess mileage charges.

A sample completed Statement of Intention is available on the companion page at www.nolo.com/back-of-book/HFB.html. Line-by-line instructions are below.

Fill in the Top of Each Page

Start by preparing the caption following the instructions for Schedule C.

Part 1. List Your Creditors Who Have Secured Claims

Here you list each of your secured debts and indicate what you plan to do with the property securing the debt (the collateral). You'll start by identifying the creditor and asset. For each debt, list the creditor's name and describe the property that serves as collateral for the debt, as you did on Schedule D. The form provides space for four items; attach extra sheets if you have more.

Next, you'll need to explain what you intend to do with the property. You're given four choices. Check the appropriate box depending on what you plan to do. (You'll find detailed coverage of these options in Ch.5.)

- **Surrender.** Check this if you intend to give the property back to the lender.
- **Retain and redeem.** Check this box if you can redeem the property by paying the lesser of what you owe or the replacement value of the property. Very few debtors can afford this option.
- **Retain and reaffirm.** Check this box if you plan to enter into a reaffirmation agreement with the lender.
- **Retain the property and explain.** If you are retaining the property for another reason, check this box and explain. For example, in some cases your lender will not require you to reaffirm if you remain current on payments. If this is your situation, write "Debtor will retain collateral and continue to make regular payments." Or, if there is equity in your property and you qualify to avoid the lien because it impairs an exemption, write "avoid the lien."

Finally, if you claimed the property as exempt on Schedule C, check "Yes." Otherwise, check "No."

> **CAUTION**
>
> **Think long and hard before reaffirming a mortgage.** Although you can reaffirm a mortgage like any other secured debt, bankruptcy professionals often advise against it because it will leave you with a large debt after your bankruptcy case is over. If you don't reaffirm, there are some consequences. Your lender won't report your continued payments on the mortgage to the credit reporting agencies, so your payments won't help you rehabilitate your credit. Also, you might not be able to modify your mortgage unless you reaffirm it because many mortgage servicers take the position that once your bankruptcy filing wipes out the promissory note, there's nothing left to modify. Despite these benefits, reaffirming a mortgage is usually a bad idea. The better approach is to modify your mortgage before filing for bankruptcy and find another way to rebuild your credit.

Do You Have to Reaffirm Your Mortgage to Keep Your Home?

Some mortgage lenders are under the impression that you can be forced to reaffirm your mortgage debt as a condition of retaining your home. The majority of courts considering this issue disagree—ruling that the reaffirmation rule only applies to personal property. (See *In re Pope,* 2011 WL 671972 (Bankr. E.D. Va. 2011).) However, one Florida bankruptcy court held that your mortgage lender can require you to reaffirm your mortgage, subject to the court's ultimate approval. (*In re Steinberg,* 447 B.R. 355 (Bankr. S.D. Fla. 2011).)

CAUTION

Save up those monthly payments. Often, secured creditors will not accept payments while your bankruptcy case is open but will expect you to get current after the bankruptcy discharge when the automatic stay is no longer in place. If a creditor refuses your payments during bankruptcy, be sure to save the money so you'll be able to catch up on payments for the property you intend to keep.

The Ride-Through Option and the Statement of Intention

If yours is a jurisdiction that allows the ride-through option, and your lender agrees to its use, then check the "Other" box and write in "retain and pay." If the ride-through option is not available in your jurisdiction, or your lender does not favor this option, you may be able to get a similar result by doing the following: Check the "Reaffirm" box on the Statement of Intention, make sure the reaffirmation agreement is filed with the court, and then see what the judge does at the reaffirmation hearing. If the judge does not approve the reaffirmation, case law indicates that you will be entitled to use the ride-through option, as long as you remain current on your payments. (See Ch. 5 for more on the ride-through option.)

Part 2: List Your Unexpired Personal Property Leases

For each unexpired lease, list the creditor's name (lessor) on the first line and then describe the leased property underneath. Use the same description used in Schedule G. Check "Yes" if you want the lease to continue after bankruptcy and "No" if you want to walk away from the lease.

Part 3: Sign Below

Sign and date the form. Even if you have no secured debts or leases to include, you must file the form with your signature and the date.

Your Statement About Your Social Security Numbers (Form 121)

This form requires you to list your Social Security number. It will be available to your creditors and the trustee but, to protect your privacy, will not be part of your public bankruptcy case file.

The Means Test Forms

Two forms—Forms 122A-1 and 122A-2—make up what's known as the means test. This important test helps the U.S. Trustee decide whether your income and expenses allow you to file for Chapter 7 bankruptcy or whether you will have to repay your creditors in Chapter 13. If you don't have to take the means test, you'll fill out a third form, Form 122A-1Supp. Here's what each form does:

Form 122A-1. The first form determines whether your income is below the median income for your state. If it is, you qualify for Chapter 7 bankruptcy and do not need to fill out the second form.

Form 122A-1Supp. If you don't have to take the means test, you fill out the supplement to Form 122A-1. (The circumstances that allow you to skip the means test are discussed below.)

Form 122A-2. If your income is above the state median, you fill out the second form and complete the actual means test calculation.

What Is Income?

While it is pretty clear that the money you receive from your job is income, you might not realize that almost all other money you receive is considered income, too. In fact, the list of the funds not considered income is somewhat shorter than that of reportable income.

Here's what you *won't* include:
- Social Security benefits
- tax refunds and loan proceeds
- COVID-19 "stimulus" payments made under the National Emergencies Act (50 U.S.C. 1601 et seq.)
- payments received as a victim of a war crime, a crime against humanity, or international or domestic terrorism, and
- compensation, pension, pay, annuity, or allowance paid by the U.S. government related to a disability, combat-related injury or disability, or death of a uniformed service member.

Here's what you *will* include:
- gross wages, salary, tips, bonuses, overtime, and commissions
- income received from operating a business
- real property income, such as rents
- pension and retirement income, including from the government
- income payments received from your 401(k) and IRA
- interest and dividends from investments
- royalties from things such as oil, music, or book rights
- spousal support and child support received for your dependent
- money received for household expenses from a family member or roommate
- unemployment compensation and private disability income
- gambling and litigation proceeds
- trust income, and
- cash gifts.

> **SKIP AHEAD**
>
> **Debtors with primarily business debts, or qualifying military service, can skip ahead.** Forms 122A-1 and 122A-2 are only for debtors whose debts are primarily consumer debts. If more than 50% of your debt is attributable to the operation of a business, you are a business debtor and do not need to complete the entire form. Instead, check Box 1, "There is no presumption of abuse," in the top right corner of Form 122A-1 and then complete Form 122A-1Supp, the Statement of Exemption from Presumption of Abuse form. The same is true if you have qualifying military service. Check Box 3, "The Means Test does not apply now because of qualified military service but it could apply later," and complete the Statement of Exemption from Presumption of Abuse form. You'll find a sample Statement of Exemption from Presumption of Abuse form, along with instructions for completing it, later in this chapter.

If You Fail the Means Test

If the information you provide on this form shows that your income exceeds the state median and you can pay more than $13,650 or at least 25% of the debts you listed in Schedule E/F over a five-year period, your Chapter 7 filing will be presumed to be abusive, and the U.S. Trustee will ask the court to either dismiss your Chapter 7 filing or, with your consent, convert your case to Chapter 13. If this happens, we highly recommend that you obtain the services of an attorney to help you stay in Chapter 7 unless you are willing to sign up for a five-year Chapter 13 repayment plan. If you convert, you can use most of the bankruptcy papers filed in your Chapter 7 case in your Chapter 13 case. However, you'll need help coming up with a repayment plan.

Chapter 7 Statement of Your Current Monthly Income (Form 122A-1)

You'll find a copy of Form 122A-1 on the companion page. Instructions for filling it out are below. To get started, follow the instructions for Schedule C to complete the top left box. For now, leave the top right box as it is. You'll complete this box after you finish filling out the forms.

Part 1: Calculate Your Current Monthly Income

Line 1 asks you to provide your filing and marital status. The boxes you check will determine whether you provide information for yourself only or if you need to provide your spouse's information, as well. If you are not married, married and legally separated, or married and living separately, complete Column A only. If you're married and filing jointly, or married but your spouse is not filing with you, complete Columns A and B.

> CAUTION
>
> **Use the right figures.** The figures you provide should be the *average* monthly income that you received during the six *full* months before you file your bankruptcy. For example, if you file on January 15, 2021, provide information from July 1, 2020 through December 31, 2020 (the six full months before January 15th). Be sure to state each amount as a monthly figure, regardless of how often you receive that income. Also, if your income varied during that time, add it all together and divide it by six. Don't include income you and your spouse received jointly, such as rental income, more than once. If you don't have income to report for a particular question, simply write $0.

Line 2. Gross wages, salary, tips, bonuses, overtime, and commissions. Enter your average monthly earnings over the last six months from gross wages, salary, tips, bonuses, overtime, and commissions. ("Gross" means before any taxes, Social Security, or any other amounts are withheld.)

Line 3. Alimony and maintenance payments. Enter any alimony, spousal support, and maintenance payments you receive from someone other than your current spouse.

Line 4. All amounts from any source are regularly paid for household expenses of you or your dependents, including child support. Enter the monthly average of any amounts regularly contributed by someone else to your household income. This includes regular contributions from an unmarried partner, members of your household, your dependents, parents and roommates. If you are filing separately but your spouse's income is included in Column B, don't include any contributions that your spouse makes to your household; his or her income is already being taken into account.

What If You Receive Income During the Six-Month Period That You Earned Before That Period?

Some courts insist that you include all income actually received during the reporting period, even if you earned it or became entitled to receive it before the six-month period began. (*In re Miller*, 519 B.R. 819 (B.A.P. 10th Cir. 2014).) Another court found that income earned but not received during the reporting period is omitted. (See *In re Arnoux*, 442 B.R. 769 (Bankr. E.D. Wash. 2010).)

As with everything involving bankruptcy, unless you are familiar with the requirements and practices in your particular court, it is better to err on the side of being conservative. That would mean reporting all income received during the six-month period. Check with a local attorney if this would make the difference between passing or not passing the means test.

Line 5. Net income from operating a business, profession, or farm. In the first blank, list your monthly gross receipts before deductions (add everything for the six months and then divide by six). Compute your average ordinary and necessary monthly expenses for the business for the six months and insert the figure in the second blank. Subtract your monthly expenses from your gross receipts to obtain the net monthly income. Transfer the net monthly income to Column A if it is your business or a joint business with your spouse. Transfer the number to Column B if the company belongs to your spouse only.

Line 6. Net income from rental and other real property. Follow the instructions for Line 5 to find the net monthly income for your rental or other real property. Transfer the net monthly income to either your income column or your spouse's income column, but not both.

Line 7. Interest, dividends, and royalties. Enter your average monthly income from interest, dividends, and royalties over the last six months.

Line 8. Unemployment compensation. Your average monthly unemployment compensation goes here. If the amount received was a Social Security benefit, do not list it in Column A or B. Instead, list it in the specific spaces provided for you or your spouse.

Line 9. Pension or retirement income. This is where you include your average monthly pension and retirement income. Don't include Social Security retirement benefits or compensation, pension, pay, annuity, or allowance paid by the U.S. government related to a disability, combat-related injury or disability, or death of a uniformed service member.

Line 10. Income from all other sources not listed above. If you received any income that you didn't already list, you identify it here using continuation pages if necessary. Don't include money received under the Social Security Act, COVID-19 "stimulus" payments made under the National Emergencies Act (50 U.S.C. 1601 et seq.).

Line 11. Calculate your total current monthly income. Add together all of the entries in Column A and all of the entries in Column B (enter a zero in Column B if there is no codebtor). Add the two income totals together and enter the result in the far right space. This is your total current monthly income.

Part 2: Determine Whether the Means Test Applies to You

This is where the rubber meets the road. In this part, you compare the current monthly income figure you calculated in Part 1 of this form to the median family income for your state. If your income is more than the median, you'll have to fill out another form, Form 122A-2; depending on that form's figures and calculations, you might be barred from using Chapter 7. If your income is equal to or less than the median, you can skip Form 122A-2 and file your Chapter 7 papers. Keep reading to find out where you stand.

Line 12. Calculate your current monthly income for the year. First, copy your total current monthly income from Line 11 to Line 12a. Then, convert your monthly figure to an annual one by multiplying it by 12. This is your current annual income and it goes on Line 12b.

Line 13. Calculate the median family income that applies to you. Fill in your state and family size. (If you're not sure which household members to count, see "Determine Your Household Size," in Ch. 1.) The most recent state median income figures as of the publishing date of this book are on the companion page (www.nolo.com/back-of-book/HFB.html). You can find the current amounts on the U.S. Trustee's website at www. justice.gov/ust. Click "Means Testing Information" and then scroll down to the link "State Median Family Income."

Line 14. How do the lines compare? Do the math. If your income (Line 12a) is less than your state's median income (Line 13), you pass the means test without further calculations. Check Box 14a and the first box on the top of page 1 of this form, "There is no presumption of abuse." Because your income is low enough, you don't need to complete another means test form.

If your income (Line 12b) is more than your state's median income (Line 13), you must do more calculations to see if you qualify for Chapter 7. Check Box 14b and the second box on the top of page 1 of this form, "The calculation to determine if a presumption of abuse applies will be made under Chapter 7 Means Test Calculation (Form 122A-2)." Now you must complete Form 122A-2.

Part 3: Sign Below

By signing Form 122A-1, you declare under penalty of perjury that all information you provided is true and correct. The instructions at the bottom of the page tell you whether you must file Form 122A-2.

> **TIP**
>
> **Consider postponing your filing.** If you conclude that you'll have to take the means test, think about whether your income will decrease in the current or future several months. If you recently lost a high-paying job or had a sudden decrease in commissions or royalties, your average income over the past six months might look pretty substantial. But in a few months, when you average in your lower earnings, it will come down quite a bit—perhaps even to less than the state median. If so, you might want to delay your bankruptcy filing if you can.

Chapter 7 Means Test Calculation (Form 122A-2)

If you're still reading, you probably make more than your state's median household income, and, as a result, you must complete the means test calculation. The purpose of the means test calculation is to find out whether you have enough income to pay some of your whether you have enough income to pay some of your unsecured, nonpriority debts over five years. (Your unsecured, nonpriority debts are those you listed in Schedule E/F, above.)

A blank Form 122A-2 is available on the companion page. Step-by-step instructions for filling it out are below. Getting started is simple enough—fill out the box in the top left by following the instructions for Schedule C. As with Form 122A-1, don't fill out the box in the top right just yet. You'll do that after you finish the form.

Part 1: Determine Your Adjusted Income

The first part of the means test calculation allows you to subtract the portion of your spouse's income that isn't used to pay for monthly household expenses. (If you and your spouse are filing together, then you don't get to adjust your income here.)

Line 1. Start by copying Line 11 from Form 122A-1 onto Line 1. This is your current monthly income.

Line 2. Next, select the box that most accurately describes your filing status.

Line 3. If you're married but filing individually (without your spouse), you can deduct the portion of your spouse's income used to pay for things other than household debts. Be aware that the U.S. Trustee takes the position that you can deduct only the following debts:

- your spouse's student loans
- your spouse's tax debt, including tax withholdings from earnings
- repayment of a loan that benefits only the other spouse, such as the repayment of a 401(k) loan, or
- funds used to support another person, such as a child from another marriage or spousal support for an ex-spouse.

For example, if your nonfiling spouse has a monthly income of $2,000, but your spouse contributes only $400 a month to your household, you can enter $1,600 here as long as the excluded income goes to pay a debt meeting the criteria above. (Also, don't include a deduction for credit cards used for household expense.) This is commonly referred to as the marital adjustment deduction.

Line 4. Adjust your current monthly income by subtracting the amount in Line 3 from the amount on Line 1. This is your adjusted current monthly income.

Part 2. Calculate Your Deductions From Your Income

In this part, you will figure out what expenses you can deduct from your current monthly income. After you subtract all allowed expenses, you will be left with your monthly disposable income—the amount you would have remaining, in theory, to pay into a Chapter 13 plan.

While you're allowed to deduct living expenses from your income, there's a catch. Since the bankruptcy court does not allow for lavish living, you can't deduct the actual costs for all of your expenses, only allowed expenses. Instead, you must calculate certain expenses according to the standards set by the IRS. (The IRS uses these standards to decide how much a delinquent taxpayer should have to give the agency each month to repay back taxes on an installment plan.)

> **RESOURCE**
>
> **Where to find the IRS standards.** To find the IRS standards, go to the U.S. Trustee's website at www.justice.gov/ust. Choose "Means Testing Information" from the left column. Choose the correct filing date from the drop-down menu and click "Go." As you scroll down, you'll see links for the National Standards and Local Standards (you will have to select either your state or your region for the Local Standards, depending on the type of expense). You can also get these figures from your court clerk.

Here are some tips for filling out Lines 6 through 15.
- Deduct the expense amounts set forth by the IRS regardless of your actual expenses.
- Do not "double dip" by deducting amounts that you already subtracted from your spouse's income in Line 3 or business operating expenses you already subtracted in Lines 5 and 6 on Form 122A-1.
- If your actual expense is higher than the standard deduction, you'll get a chance to include the actual amount later.
- "You" refers to both you and your spouse if you were required to fill in Column B on Form 122A-1.

Line 5. Number of people used in determining your deductions from income.
List the number of people you support. Typically, you'll count the people living in your household that you support. This is informally known as the "heads on beds" rule. If you're supporting someone who doesn't live in your household, call your local trustee's office and ask whether that individual would count as a dependent.

Items Using the National Standards

Use the IRS National Standards for Lines 6 and 7. (See "Where to find the IRS standards," above.)

Line 6: Food, clothing, and other items. Enter the total IRS National Standards for Food, Clothing, and Other Items for your family size and income level. This is the amount the IRS believes you should get to spend for food, clothing, household supplies, personal care, and miscellaneous other items.

Line 7: Out of pocket health care allowance. Enter the amount you are allowed to claim for health expenses from the IRS National Standards for Out-of-Pocket Health Care. You can claim more for household members who are at least 65 years old. The total amount you can claim is relatively small; if you spend more than you're allowed to claim here, you can list the rest on Line 22. Lines 7a through 7f ask you to split the expenses into two groups—expenses for those over 65 and those under 65. Enter your total deduction amount on Line 7g.

Local IRS Standards

Use the IRS Local Standards for Lines 8 through 15. (See "Where to find the IRS standards," above.)

Line 8. Housing and utilities—insurance and operating expenses. Enter the amount of the IRS Housing and Utilities Standards listed for your county, using the figure under the "Non-Mortgage" column.

Line 9. Housing and utilities—mortgage or rent expenses. Calculate your mortgage or rent expenses using Lines 9a through 9c.

Line 9a. Enter the amount of the IRS Housing and Utilities Standards for your county for mortgage or rent expenses according to your family size. Use the figure under the "Mortgage/Rent" column, and enter it on Line 9a.

Line 9b: Here you calculate your total average monthly payment for all mortgages and debts secured by your home. On the lines provided, list each of your secured creditors and the average monthly payment to each. To get the average monthly payment, add up all payments due in the next 60 months, and then divide by 60. Total the payments for all creditors, and list that number in the "Total average monthly payment" box. Copy that number in two other places: The line immediately to the right (there is an arrow pointing to it) and on Line 33a.

Line 9c. Subtract the amount listed on Line 9b from the amount listed on Line 9a. Enter that number twice on Line 9c in the two blanks right next to each other. If you get a negative number, enter "0." This is your net mortgage or rent expense. (You will use this information later on in the section on Deductions for Debt Payments. The extra steps in this section ensure that you don't end up double-counting the mortgage deduction.)

Line 10. If you think the IRS Local Standards are incorrect, explain why and list your additional expenses here. If you believe your housing expenses are higher than the IRS Local Standards because the standards are wrong, and the incorrect standards affect your monthly expense calculation, explain why on the lines provided and list any additional amount you claim on Line 10.

CAUTION

Stay away from Line 10. Seriously. After combing through the opinions of the brightest bankruptcy minds in the land, it appears no one really knows the purpose of Line 10. In fact, even the U.S. Trustee's official position fails to shed much light on this dilemma, and instead, chooses only to warn debtors—rather mysteriously at that—that claiming additional housing expenses leads to unwanted objections by trustees. Since no one can figure out what else could be listed on Line 10, and taking into account that the bankruptcy court's favorite phrase is "Pigs get fat, hogs get slaughtered," unless you think up (and list) a great justification for your adjustment, the prudent course of action is to take what you get on Lines 8 and 9 and skip Line 10 altogether.

Line 11. Local transportation expenses. Indicate the number of cars you pay operating expenses for. If you don't have a car, check "0" and go to Line 14 (you'll get to deduct public transportation expenses on that line). If you have one car, select the second box and proceed to Line 12. If you have two or more cars, check the third box and go to Line 12.

Line 12. Vehicle operation expense. These are your expenses for operating a car (maintenance, gas, etc.). On Line 12, enter the IRS Local Transportation Standards amount for your area and the number of cars you claim expenses for (the amount differs depending upon where you live).

Line 13: Vehicle ownership or lease expense. These are your expenses for owning or leasing a car. Start by listing the year, make, model and mileage of Vehicle 1 on the lines following the instruction "Describe Vehicle 1." You'll do the same for Vehicle 2 immediately following Line 13c. You figure out your vehicle expense by completing Lines 13a through 13f.

CAUTION

You must have car payments to make this deduction. Keep in mind that you can only claim an ownership/lease expense on Line 13 for a car that you actually make loan or lease payments on. If you own your car free and clear, you are not entitled to the ownership/lease expense deduction. (*Ranson v. FIA Card Services, N.A.*, 562 U.S. 61 (2011).)

Line 13a: On Line 13a, enter the IRS Local Transportation Standards for ownership of a first car. The amount is actually a national figure; at the time of printing, it was $533 for one car and $1,066 for two cars. (See "Where to find the IRS standards," above. Scroll down to the Local Transportation Expense Standards drop-down menu and choose your region. The ownership figure is near the bottom of the page.)

Line 13b: On Line 13b, enter your average monthly payment (over the next five years) for all debts secured by your first car. For example, assume you have three years left to pay on the car and the monthly payment is $350. The total amount you will owe in the next five years is $12,600 (36 months times $350). If you spread that amount over the next five years—by dividing the total by 60, the number of months in five years—you'll see that you have an average monthly payment of $210. You'll enter this number three times:

Under the heading "Average monthly payment"; in the "Copy 13b here," blank; and on Line 33b.

Line 13c: Subtract Line 13b from Line 13a and enter the amount on Line 13c. Also copy the same number on the blank immediately to the right. This is your net vehicle ownership or lease expense for Vehicle 1.

Lines 13d through 13f. If you have another car, go through the same calculations for Vehicle 2 as you did for Vehicle 1.

Line 14. Public transportation expense. If you don't have a car and use public transportation, enter the amount listed under "Public Transportation" from the IRS Local Transportation Expense Standards. This is a national figure and was set at $217 at the time of printing. (To get the most up-to-date figure, see "Where to find the IRS standards," above. Scroll to the Local Transportation Expense Standards drop-down menu and choose your region. The public transportation cost is toward the middle of the page.)

Converting Taxes to a Monthly Figure

If you are paid weekly, biweekly, or twice a month, you will have to convert the tax amounts on your pay stubs to a monthly amount. And, if you pay quarterly taxes (estimated income taxes, for example), you'll need to convert that figure as well. Here's how to do it:

- Weekly taxes: Multiply by 4.3 to get a monthly amount.
- Biweekly taxes: Divide by 2 to get a weekly amount, then multiply by 4.3.
- Bimonthly taxes: Divide by 2.
- Quarterly taxes: Divide by 3.

Line 15. Additional public transportation expense. If you have a car and use public transportation, you can claim a public transportation expense. Find the correct amount by following the instructions for Line 14 above.

Other Necessary Expenses

While the below expenses are based on IRS expense categories, you list your actual expenditures (there isn't a standard IRS figure).

Line 16. Taxes. Enter the total average monthly expense that you actually incur for all taxes *other than real estate or sales taxes*. Examples of taxes that you enter here are income taxes, self-employment taxes, Social Security taxes, and Medicare taxes. In some cases, these taxes will show up on your wage stub. You'll need to convert the period covered by your wage stub to a monthly figure. (Use the conversion rules above to arrive at monthly figures.) Once you have figured out how much you pay each month for each type of tax, add them together and enter the total in the column on the right.

Line 17. Involuntary deductions. Enter all of your mandatory payroll deductions here. Use the conversion rules above to arrive at monthly figures. Make sure you deduct only mandatory deductions (such as mandatory retirement contributions, union dues, and uniform costs). Don't include contributions to a 401(k) because they are voluntary.

Line 18. Life insurance. Enter any monthly payments you make for term life insurance. Do not enter payments for any other type of insurance, such as credit insurance, car insurance, renter's insurance, insurance on your own life, and whole life insurance policies. (Whole life insurance is the type that allows you to borrow against the policy.)

Line 19. Court-ordered payments. Enter the amount of any payments you make pursuant to a court order. Child support and alimony are the most common examples, but you may also make payments to satisfy a court money judgment or a criminal fine. Do not include court-ordered payments toward a child support or alimony arrearage; only the payments you need to stay current should be entered here.

Line 20. Education. Enter the total monthly amount that you pay for education required by your employer to keep your job, and the total monthly amount you pay for the education of a physically or mentally challenged dependent child if there is no public education available that provides similar services. Included in this amount would be the actual costs of after-school enrichment educational services for a physically or mentally challenged child, and the actual education expenses you are paying in support of an individual educational plan.

Line 21. Childcare. Enter the average monthly expense of childcare, including babysitting, preschool, nursery school, and regular childcare. If your employment is seasonal—and therefore your need for regular childcare is seasonal—add your childcare costs up for the year and divide the total by 12. Remember that childcare and education are not the same. For instance, childcare for a child who is of public education school age should only cover the hours before and after school.

Line 22. Additional health care expenses. Enter the average monthly amount you pay for out-of-pocket health care expenses, but only to the extent it exceeds the amount you were allowed to claim on Line 7. Do not include payments for health insurance or health savings accounts; those go on Line 25.

Line 23. Optional telephones and telephone services. Enter the average monthly expenses you pay for any communication devices (other than basic home telephone and cellphone services) that are necessary for the health and welfare of you or your dependents. Examples provided by the form are pagers, call waiting, caller identification, special long distance services, or business cellphone service. Arguably virtually all of these devices are necessary for the health and welfare of your family; however, some expenses might not be allowed—for example, a cellphone you use for your business or Internet service. When in doubt, list the expense.

Line 24. Add all of the expenses allowed under the IRS expense allowances. Add together all amounts listed on Lines 6 through 23 and enter the total amount on Line 24.

Additional Expense Deductions

The means test allows you to deduct certain types of expenses not included in the IRS categories. These go on Lines 25 through 32. However, you can't list an expense twice. If you already claimed an expense elsewhere, don't list it again here.

Line 25. Health insurance, disability insurance, and health savings account expenses. Here, list your reasonably necessary monthly expenses for health insurance, disability insurance, and health savings accounts (HSAs) on the lines provided. The form allows you to list a "reasonable" expense whether you actually pay that amount each month or not. If, however, you pay less than the reasonable amount you list, you must indicate how much you actually spend each month on the additional line provided. If the U.S. Trustee or one of your creditors later wants to challenge your expense claims—for example, to argue that you really have more disposable income than the form indicates—they can use this information.

Line 26. Continued contributions to the care of household or family members. Anything you spend to care for a member of your household or immediate family because of the member's age, illness, or disability can be deducted here. If your contributions are episodic—a wheelchair here, a vacation with a companion there—estimate your average monthly expense and enter it here.

> CAUTION
>
> **Your response here could affect eligibility for government benefits.** Expenses you list here could render the person you are assisting ineligible for Social Security or other government benefits. For example, if you state that you are spending $500 a month for the care of a relative, and that relative is receiving SSI, your relative might receive a lower benefit amount each month, to reflect your contribution. On the other hand, if you are making such expenditures, you are required to disclose them here. If you find yourself in this predicament, talk to a lawyer.

Line 27. Protection against family violence. The average monthly expense for security systems and any other method of protecting your family should be entered here.

Line 28. Additional home energy costs. If your actual home energy costs exceed the figure you entered on Line 8, enter the extra amount you spend here. As the form indicates, you may need to prove this extra expense to the trustee. Whether you need to provide proof will depend on the results of this means test. If the amount you enter here is the deciding factor in determining that you don't have enough disposable income to fund a Chapter 13 plan, proof will definitely be required.

Line 29. Education expenses for dependent children. This item is for money you spend on your children's education. If your average monthly expense is $170.83 or more, you can claim $170.83 per child in this blank; that's the maximum you can deduct (this figure will adjust on April 1, 2022). If your average monthly expense per child is less than $170.83, enter the actual expense amount. Remember not to list an amount twice; if you already listed an expense on Line 20 or 21, for example, don't repeat it here.

Line 30. Additional food and clothing expense. Here, you can list the amount by which your actual expenses for food and clothing exceed the IRS allowance for these items as entered in Line 19. However, you cannot list more than 5% over the IRS allowance.

Line 31. Continuing charitable contributions. If you have been making charitable contributions to an organization before your bankruptcy filing date, you can enter them here as long as the group is organized and operated exclusively for religious, charitable, scientific, literary, or educational purposes; to foster national or international amateur sports competition (but only if no part of its activities involve the provision of athletic facilities or equipment); or for the prevention of cruelty to children or animals. The organization also can't be disqualified from tax exemption status because of its political activities.

Line 32. Add all of the additional expense deductions. Enter the total of Lines 25 through 31 in the column on the right.

Deductions for Debt Payment

Here, you deduct average monthly payments you will have to make over the next five years. Once you complete this section, you can put all the numbers together to figure out whether you pass the means test.

Line 33. Secured debts. This is where you add your monthly house and car payments (which you've already calculated) together with monthly payments on other secured debts. To get the monthly figure for each secured creditor, add up the total amount that will come due within the next 60 months, and then divide the total by 60.

Line 33a. Copy the amount you listed on Line 9b (you may have already done so). This is your average monthly mortgage payment.

Line 33b. Copy the amount you listed on Line 13b. This is your average monthly payment for Vehicle 1.

Line 33c. Copy the amount you listed on Line 13e. This is your average monthly payment for Vehicle 2.

Line 33d. For each additional secured creditor, list the creditor's name, the property securing the debt, and the average monthly payment on the debt. Also, check the box that indicates whether the payment includes taxes or insurance.

Line 33e. Add Lines 33a through 33d and enter the amount in both blank spaces on this line. This is your total average monthly payment on secured debts.

Line 34. Arrearages on property you need to support yourself. Here you'll list amounts you'd need to pay in order to catch up on past-due payments for property that you need to support yourself or your family. Property necessary for support typically includes a car, your home, and anything you need for your employment (like work tools). If you listed any property on Lines 33a through 33d that you need to support yourself and your dependents, check "Yes." Next, you list any past due amounts you owe those creditors. In the spaces provided, list the creditor, the property involved, and the total past due amount (the past due amount goes in the "Total cure amount" column). For each entry, divide the cure amount figure by 60 and enter the result in the "Monthly cure amount" column. Add up the monthly cure amounts and enter that figure on the two lines next to "Total."

Line 35. Past-due priority debts. List the average monthly amount you will have to pay for priority claims over the next five years (list past-due amounts only; don't list ongoing payments you make to stay current). Your priority claims are the ones you listed in Schedule E/F. They include certain tax debts, child support, and alimony. Divide by 60 to arrive at the monthly average.

Line 36. Are you eligible to file a case under Chapter 13? Here you determine whether you are eligible to file for Chapter 13 bankruptcy. You can skip this section for now. If you pass the means test (meaning that your income calculated on Line 39d is less than $8,175 as of March 31, 2022—the figure will adjust on April 1, 2022), you won't need to fill it out anyway. If your income is $8,175 or more after you finish the form, come back to this section and follow these steps:

1. Add Lines 33, 34, and 35.
2. Divide Line 41b by .25 (this provides the average monthly payment you would have to make to pay down 25% of your unsecured debt over five years).
3. Add this number to the total of Lines 33, 34, and 35. Put the resulting number on the space in Line 36 labeled, "Projected monthly plan payment if you were filing under Chapter 13." This is the average

amount you would have to pay into a Chapter 13 plan to cover your secured debts, arrearages on those debts, priority debts, and 25% of your unsecured debts.

4. On the "Current multiplier for your district…" line, enter the multiplier percentage from the U.S. Trustee's website for your state and district or the Administrative Office of the United States Courts for districts in Alabama and North Carolina. (See "Where to find the IRS standards," above. Scroll to the bottom of the page to the section called "Administrative Expenses Multipliers," and click "Schedules," then scroll down to your district to get the percentage.)

5. Multiply the two amounts. This is your average monthly administrative expense if you were filing under Chapter 13.

Line 37. Add all of the deductions for debt payment. Add Lines 33e through 36 and enter the total on Line 37.

Total Deductions From Income

Here you total up everything you can deduct from your income.

Line 38. Add all of the deductions. Copy Line 24 (your IRS expense allowances) onto the first line. Copy Line 32 (your additional expense deductions) onto the second line. Copy Line 37 (your deductions for debt payment) onto the third line. Total the three lines and enter the result twice as directed.

Part 3: Determine Whether There Is a Presumption of Abuse

This is where you find out whether you pass the means test. If you have enough income left over after your allowable deductions to fund a Chapter 13 plan, the presumption of abuse arises and you probably cannot file for Chapter 7 bankruptcy. This is one of the rare moments in life that you hope you have less money after you pay all your bills rather than more, because if you don't have enough discretionary income left over to fund a Chapter 13 plan, you're good to go.

Line 39. Calculate monthly disposable income for 60 months. Follow the prompts in Lines 39a through 39d to determine your monthly disposable income.

Line 39a. Copy Line 4, your adjusted current monthly income, here.

Line 39b. Copy Line 38, your total deductions, here.

Line 39c. Subtract Line 39b from Line 39a. Enter your monthly disposable income in the two spaces provided on Line 39c.

Line 39d. Multiply Line 39c by 60 and enter the amount in the two spaces provided on Line 39d.

Line 40. Find out whether there is a presumption of abuse. Here you must check one of three boxes.

- If the amount on Line 39d is less than $8,175, check the top box. This means that you don't have enough money left over to make a Chapter 13 plan feasible so you can file for Chapter 7. If you checked the top box, go back to the first page and check the box at the top, right-hand side of the page ("There is no presumption of abuse."). Then move on to Part 5 where you sign the form.

- If the amount on Line 39d is more than $13,650, you have enough income to make a Chapter 13 plan feasible, and you probably won't be allowed to stay in Chapter 7. Go back to the first page and check the second box at the top, right-hand side of the page ("There is a presumption of abuse."). Then move on to Part 5 where you sign the form.

- If the amount on Line 39d is at least $8,175, but not more than $13,650, you will have to do a few more calculations to see where you fall. To do so, complete Lines 41(a) and (b). (These figures will adjust on April 1, 2022.)

Line 41a. Enter the amount listed on Line 3b of A Summary of Your Assets and Liabilities and Certain Statistical Information Schedules. (This is the total amount of your unsecured nonpriority debt.)

Line 41b. Multiply Line 41a by 0.25. Enter the amount in the two spaces provided.

Line 42. Determine whether your leftover income will pay at least 25% of your unsecured, nonpriority debt. Here, you determine whether the income you have left after your allowed deductions (listed on Line 39d) is sufficient to pay 25% of your total nonpriority, unsecured debt (listed on Line 41b).

If the amount on Line 39d is less than the amount on Line 41b, congratulations! You have passed the means test. Go back to the first page, check the box on the top right-hand side of the page ("There is no presumption of abuse") and move to Part 5 where you will sign the form.

If the amount on Line 39b is greater than the amount on Line 41b, then unfortunately, you did not pass the means test. The form instructs you to go back to the first page, check the bottom box at the top right-hand side of the page ("There is a presumption of abuse"), and move to Part 5 where you will sign the form.

Part 4: Give Details About Special Circumstances

If you don't pass the means test, you might still be allowed to file for Chapter 7 if you have expenses stemming from an unusual or catastrophic situation that the trustee finds compelling. These types of expenses are listed on Part 4 of Form 122A-2 so that the trustee can evaluate your particular situation and determine whether the expenses are reasonably necessary to support you and your family.

You can list two types of expenses in Part 4—additional expenses not listed elsewhere and expenses already listed elsewhere that need explanation as to why they are reasonable and necessary.

Higher-than-expected expenses can also be listed here too. Say a tornado hits your town, destroys your house, and paralyzes a family member. In Part 4, you would list the increased costs involved in temporarily relocating elsewhere, buying replacement clothes and basic supplies, rebuilding the house, and healing the hurt family member.

Part 4 provides the trustee with a snapshot of your financial picture so he or she can determine whether a valid justification exists to waive the presumption of abuse.

What Happens If You Fail the Means Test?

If, after completing Form 122A-2, you check "The presumption arises" box on the top of Page 1, the court clerk will issue a notice to that effect shortly after you file your bankruptcy, and the United States Trustee will decide, upon further examination of your paperwork and within 30 days after your 341 hearing, whether to seek to have your case dismissed or converted to Chapter 13. While it's not automatic, a dismissal or conversion will most likely be sought in cases where the presumption arises.

TIP

Double-check your expenses. Before signing the form in Part 5, review the form and carefully examine the expense items that aren't mandated by the IRS. Often, people underestimate their actual expenses. If you find that you underestimated one or more expenses, or left out an expense that is provided for in the form, make the adjustments and see whether you can get a passing grade. Because this form is so complex, we recommend that you go through it at least twice before arriving at your final figures.

SEE AN EXPERT

See a lawyer if the presumption arises and you want to stay in Chapter 7. If you have to check the box stating that the presumption (of abuse) arises, your Chapter 7 filing could be in trouble. Unless you are willing to proceed under Chapter 13, or have your bankruptcy dismissed, we strongly suggest that you find a bankruptcy lawyer to help you from this point on.

Part 5: Sign Below

Sign and date the form. You are done.

Statement of Exemption from Presumption of Abuse (Form 122A-1Supp)

Some people automatically qualify for Chapter 7 bankruptcy even if their income is too high or they can't pass the means test. Those include:

- people whose debts are primarily business debts
- disabled veterans who incurred most of their debts while on active duty or performing a homeland defense activity, and
- certain Reservists and members of the National Guard.

You fill out this form to find out if you qualify for one of these exemptions. A copy of 122A-1Supp is available on the companion page. Step-by-step instructions are below.

To get started, follow the instructions for Schedule C to complete the top left box. Since you haven't filed anything yet, you don't need to worry about the top right-hand side box. Leave it unchecked. If you are filing jointly, and you think your spouse qualifies for an exemption, your spouse should fill out a separate Form 122A-1Supp. You will both also fill out separate 122A-1 forms—you'll see why below.

Part 1: Identify the Kind of Debts You Have

This part asks whether your debts are primarily consumer debts. If they are not, then they are business debts and you qualify for the exemption.

What Are Consumer Debts?

Consumer debts are those that are "incurred by an individual primarily for a personal, family, or household purpose." This includes things such as food, clothing, shelter, childcare, and entertainment; in other words, everyday living expenses and personal extravagances. For example, using your credit cards to buy clothes for yourself and your family, to purchase a television, and go the movies would be typical ways people incur consumer debts.

What Are Nonconsumer Debts?

Nonconsumer debts are any debts that don't fall into the consumer debt category. That is, to declare that your debts are primarily nonconsumer debts (and avoid the means test), over 50% of your debt must be for something other than personal, family, or household purposes. The purpose of your debt is determined at the time you incurred it.

Below are some of the most common types of nonconsumer debts.

Business debts. Expenses you incur to run a business are nonconsumer debts. These include expenses such as:

- rent or mortgage on your office space or storefront
- vehicles used in your business
- building and fixture expenses
- products used in or sold by your business
- utilities, such as heating and air, at your place of business
- your business phone
- personal guarantees for business debt
- business-related legal fees, and
- liabilities arising from accidents related to your business.

It is common for businesses to keep track of expenses by using a credit card to purchase supplies and needed services. If you've used a credit card exclusively in your business, it will be considered a business debt. For instance, if you ran a plumbing business and used credit to buy necessary supplies such as pipes, toilet fixtures, trucks, and plumbing tools, those debts would be considered "business debt." If those debts constituted more than 50% of your total debt, then you would qualify for the exemption.

Tax debts. Many types of tax debts are considered to be nonconsumer, even income tax debts. The reasoning is that no one intentionally incurs tax debt for personal, family, or household expenses. Check with a lawyer if you are unsure.

Other debts. It's not always obvious which debts are consumer and which are not. For example, sometimes student loans are considered nonconsumer debts, especially if they were incurred to attend a professional school and the money went toward tuition (not housing or food). (See *In re De Cunae*, 2013 WL 6389205 (Bankr. S.D. Tex. 2013).)

> ☼ **TIP**
>
> **If your debts might be nonconsumer, check with a lawyer.** If you are unsure whether a certain category of debt is consumer or nonconsumer, and if it were non-consumer, you'd be able to skip the means test, consider talking to a lawyer. Of course, if you would pass the means test anyway, don't bother.

Line 1. If more than 50% of your debts fall into the consumer category, check "Yes," and proceed to Part 2 of this form. (When we say 50%, we mean 50% of the total amount of your debt load; not the number of debts you have in each category. So for example, if you have one mortgage in the amount of $200,000 and three separate business debts that total $50,000, your debts would be primarily consumer because more than half of your total debt load ($250,000) is made up of your mortgage.)

If more than 50% of your debts are nonconsumer in nature, check "No," go to the top of Form 122A-1 and check Box 1, "There is no presumption of abuse," and then skip the rest of Form 122A-1 (other than signing it in Part 5). Attach Form 122A-1Supp to Form 122A-1.

Part 2: Determine Whether Military Service Provisions Apply to You

This part assesses whether you are a part of a small group of military personnel who qualify for this exemption. You qualify for a military service exemption if you fall into one of the following categories:

- you are a disabled veteran and incurred most of your debts while on active duty or while performing a homeland defense activity
- you have been on active duty for at least 90 days (with your duty beginning sometime after September 11, 2001)
- you were released from active duty less than 540 days before filing bankruptcy (with your duty lasting at least 90 days and beginning sometime after September 11, 2001)
- you are performing a homeland defense activity that will last for at least 90 days, or
- you performed a homeland defense activity fewer than 540 days before filing bankruptcy and the activity lasted for at least 90 days.

If you meet one of these conditions, read and check the appropriate boxes on Form 122A-1Supp. Next, check Box 3 at the top of Form 122A-1 and skip the rest of Form 122A-1 (other than signing it in Part 5). Attach Form 122A-1Supp to Form 122A-1.

Notice Required by 11 U.S.C. § 342(b) for Individuals Filing for Bankruptcy (Form 2010)

This form gives you information about credit counseling and the various chapters of bankruptcy available. It also warns you of the consequences of lying on your bankruptcy papers, concealing assets, and failing to file the required forms on time.

Like all of the official forms, you can find these on www.uscourts.gov/forms/bankruptcy-forms.

Creditor Mailing List

As part of your bankruptcy filing, you are required to submit a list of all of your creditors so the court can give them official notice of your bankruptcy. Depending on the jurisdiction, this might be called the mailing matrix, master address list, creditor mailing matrix, or something else. This list must be prepared in a specific format prescribed by your local bankruptcy court. Your court might also require you to submit a declaration, or "verification," stating that your list is correct (as always, be sure to check your court's local rules). The mailing list will be uploaded online with your other paperwork. If you need to provide notice of a motion or another event, you can use the list to print out mailing labels, which is handy when you have a lot of creditors to notify.

Here's what you'll want to do:

Step 1: Make a list of all of your creditors, in alphabetical order. You can copy them from Schedules D, E/F, and H. Be sure to include cosigners and joint debtors. If, however, you and your spouse jointly incurred a debt and are filing jointly, don't include your spouse. Also include collection agencies, sheriffs, and attorneys who either have sued you or are trying to collect the debt. And, if you're seeking to discharge marital debts you assumed during a divorce, include both your ex-spouse and the creditors. Finally, if you have two or more debts owed to the same creditor at the same address, you'll list the creditor once.

Step 2: Compile the information gathered in Step 1 in the format required by your local court.

CAUTION

It is very important to be complete when preparing the creditor mailing list. If you leave a creditor off the list and the creditor does not find out about your bankruptcy by some other means, that debt might survive your bankruptcy if there is a priority distribution in your case. (See Ch. 9 for more information about the discharge of debts not included in your bankruptcy papers.)

How to File Your Papers

The instructions below apply when courts are fully operational. New filing procedures introduced during the COVID-19 pandemic might still apply. Check your court's website to determine whether you can file in person or by mail, or if you should upload your documents using an online non-attorney filing system (go to www.pacer.uscourts.gov/register-account/non-attorney-filers-cmecf for instructions).

Gather your completed forms and the documents you set aside at the beginning of this chapter. Ensure you have everything on the Bankruptcy Forms Checklist and Bankruptcy Documents Checklist (you can find these checklists on the companion page).

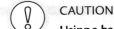 CAUTION

Using a bankruptcy petition preparer increases the paperwork. If you use a petition preparer, there will be several additional forms to file.

Basic Filing Procedures

Once you've got all of your papers together, follow these filing instructions.

Step 1: Put all your bankruptcy forms in the proper order.

Step 2: Check that you, and your spouse if you're filing a joint petition, have signed and dated each form where required.

Step 3: Make the required number of copies, plus one additional copy for you to keep just in case your papers are lost in the mail (if you file by mail). In addition, make:

- one extra copy of the Statement of Intention for each person listed on that form, and
- one extra copy of the Statement of Intention for the trustee.

Step 4: If your court requires you to hole-punch your papers when you file them, use a standard two-hole punch (copy centers have them) to punch the top center of your original set of bankruptcy papers. Don't staple any forms together.

Serving the Statement of Intention

The bankruptcy rules require you to serve (by mail) the Statement of Intention on each creditor listed on the statement (although in some jurisdictions, filing it with your other paperwork is sufficient—check with your court). You have between 30 and 45 days to do this. We recommend you do it immediately so you don't forget. If you don't serve your Statement of Intention on time, the creditor can repossess the collateral. The trustee must also be served. The trustee's contact information will be provided either on the copy of your papers that the clerk returns to you or on the notice of filing you receive several days after you file.

Have a friend or relative (other than your spouse, if you are filing jointly) over the age of 18 mail, by first class, a copy of your Statement of Intention to the bankruptcy trustee and to all the creditors listed on that form. Be sure to keep the original.

On a Proof of Service by Mail (a copy is on the companion page), enter the name and complete address of the trustee and all creditors to whom your friend or relative sent your Statement of Intention. Have that person sign and date the Proof of Service.

Step 5: If you plan to mail your documents to the court, address a 9" × 12" envelope to yourself and affix adequate postage to handle one copy of all the paperwork. Although many people prefer to file by mail, we recommend that you personally take your papers to the bankruptcy court clerk if at all possible. Going to the court will give you a chance to correct minor mistakes on the spot.

Step 6: If you can pay the filing fee, clip or staple a money order to the petition, payable to the U.S. Trustee (courts won't accept a check and sending cash in the mail is unwise). If you want to pay in installments, attach a completed Application for Individuals to Pay Filing Fee in Installments (Form 103A), plus any additional papers required by your court's local rules (see "Paying in Installments," below). If you don't think you can afford installment payments, you may be able to obtain a fee waiver by filing the Application to Have the Chapter 7 Filing

Fee Waived (Form 103B) (see "Waiver of Filing Fee," below). For both installment payments and fee waivers, you might have to appear before the bankruptcy judge to justify your request.

Step 7: Take or mail the original and copies of all forms to the correct bankruptcy court.

Paying in Installments

You can pay in up to four installments over 120 days. You can ask the judge to give you extra time for a particular installment, but all installments ultimately must be paid within 180 days after you file. You'll file the request along with your bankruptcy petition. If the judge refuses your request, you will be given some time to come up with the fees (probably ten days, perhaps longer).

If you are applying to pay in installments, you must file a completed Application for Individuals to Pay Filing Fee in Installments (Form 103A) when you file your petition. You can find this form along with all the other bankruptcy forms at www.uscourts.gov/forms/bankruptcy-forms.

The application is easy to fill out. At the top, fill in the name of the court and your name (and your spouse's name if you're filing jointly). Leave the Case No. space blank. Then enter:

- the chapter you are filing (Item 1)
- the amount you propose to pay when you file the petition (Item 2, first blank)
- the number of additional installments you need (the total maximum is four), and
- the amount and date you propose for each installment payment.

You (and your spouse, if you're filing jointly) must sign and date the application. Leave the rest blank.

> CAUTION
> **Make installment payments on time.** If you pay the fee in install-ments, make sure you make each payment on time. If you don't, the court could dismiss your bankruptcy and you'll then have to pay the entire fee to reopen your case.

Waiver of Filing Fee

You also can apply to have your fees waived altogether by filing the Application to Have the Chapter 7 Filing Fee Waived (Form 103B). This form is relatively complex and asks for a lot of the information you've provided in the schedules completed earlier in this chapter. You can find this form on the official U.S. Courts website at www.uscourts.gov/forms/bankruptcy-forms. In most cases, the court will tell you whether the judge granted the request by mail and you won't need to appear before the judge. If you receive a waiver and it later turns out that you could pay the fee, the court can revoke your waiver. (*In re Kauffman*, 354 B.R. 682 (Bankr. D. Vt. 2006).)

If the court denies your application, you'll have to pay the full filing fee within a week to ten days, although the judge might set up a fee payment schedule if it appears warranted.

Emergency Filing

If you want to file for bankruptcy in a hurry because you need to get an automatic stay in place, you can file what's known as an emergency or "skeleton" filing. You'll file Form 101—Voluntary Petition, the Mailing Matrix, Your Statement About Your Social Security Numbers (Form 121), a credit counseling certificate, and the filing fee. Some courts also require you to file a cover sheet and an Order Dismissing Chapter 7 Case, which will be processed if you don't file the rest of your papers within 14 days. (Bankruptcy Rule 1007(c).) If the bankruptcy court for your district requires this form, you can get it from the court (possibly on its website), a local bankruptcy attorney, or a bankruptcy petition preparer.

If you don't follow up by filing the additional documents within 14 days, your bankruptcy case will be dismissed. You can file again, if necessary. You'll have to ask the court to keep the automatic stay in effect once 30 days have passed after you file. (See Ch. 2.)

For an emergency filing, follow these steps:

Step 1: Check with the court to determine exactly what forms must be submitted for an emergency filing.

Step 2: Fill in Form 101—Voluntary Petition.

Step 3: On a Mailing Matrix (or whatever other form is required by your court), list all your creditors, as well as collection agencies, sheriffs, attorneys, and others who are seeking to collect debts from you.

Step 4: Fill in the Statement of Social Security Number and any other papers the court requires.

Step 5: File the originals and the required number of copies, accompanied by your fee (or an application for payment of fee in installments), counseling certificate, and a self-addressed envelope with the bankruptcy court. Keep copies of everything for your records.

Step 6: File all other required forms within 14 days. If you don't, your case will be dismissed.

After You File

Filing a bankruptcy petition has a dramatic effect on your creditors and your property.

The Automatic Stay

The instant you file for Chapter 7 bankruptcy, your creditors are subject to the automatic stay, as described in detail in Ch. 2. If you haven't read that chapter, now is the time to do it.

The Trustee Takes Ownership of Your Property

When you file your bankruptcy papers, the trustee becomes the owner of all the property in your bankruptcy estate as of that date. (See Ch. 3 for an explanation of what's in your bankruptcy estate.) However, the trustee won't actually take physical control of the property. Most, if not all, of your property will be exempt, which means the trustee will return it to your legal possession after your bankruptcy is closed. If you have any questions about dealing with property after you file, ask the trustee or the trustee's staff.

While your bankruptcy is pending, do not throw out, give away, sell, or otherwise dispose of the property you owned as of your filing date—unless and until the bankruptcy trustee says otherwise. Even if all of your property is exempt, you are expected to hold on to it, in case the trustee or a creditor challenges your exemption claims.

If some of your property is nonexempt, the trustee might ask you to turn it over. Or, the trustee could decide that the property is worth too little to bother with and abandon it. (Typically, the trustee doesn't let you know that property is abandoned, but once you receive your discharge, the property is deemed abandoned.)

What Happens to Business Property

If you are operating a sole proprietorship or a solely owned corporation or limited liability company (LLC), you might have to shut down the business—at least temporarily—until the trustee can assess the nature and value of your inventory and assets, as well as any exemptions you can claim in the property. This shut-down period could last for a couple of months and perhaps even longer. If your business is service-oriented and lacks machines or inventory, you can probably continue in business without interruption. The trustee might require proof of liability insurance, however.

Business entities aren't part of a personal bankruptcy. Even so, if you (or you and your spouse) are the sole owner of an entity like a corporation or an LLC, the trustee can step into your shoes, vote your shares to dissolve the business, and sell off whatever inventory and assets you can't personally exempt. Because it takes some time to assess the business assets and go through the necessary corporate procedures, you might have to shut down your business at least while that process is going on. And if you aren't able to exempt your business assets, you'll have to shut down for good.

TIP

If you are worried about losing property or your business, contact the trustee sooner rather than later. If you have any property that you might have to surrender, the best course of action is to contact the trustee as soon as possible. This accomplishes two things: It establishes your forthrightness (which is important in bankruptcy) and provides insight into what the trustee might do. Ask the trustee what you can expect and answer the trustee's questions. The trustee might give you particular instructions, such as to forward rental or trust fund payments, or might arrange to set up a time to view the property. It also isn't unheard of for a trustee to quickly decide that your accounting or Etsy business is of no value to the bankruptcy estate. This type of advance information could give you time to figure out how to buy your property back at a discounted price, afford you the relief of knowing your property is not at risk, or simply give you time to acclimate to it being sold.

In a Chapter 7 case, with a few exceptions, the trustee has no claim to property you acquire or income you earn after you file. You are free to spend it as you please. The exceptions are property from an insurance settlement, a marital settlement agreement, or an inheritance that you become entitled to receive within 180 days after your filing date. (See Ch. 3.)

Handling Your Case in Court

For most people, the Chapter 7 bankruptcy process is fairly straightforward. In fact, it proceeds pretty much on automatic pilot. The bankruptcy trustee decides whether your papers are in order and, if not, what amendments you need to file. Ordinarily, you have few decisions to make.

This chapter tells you how to handle the routine procedures that move your bankruptcy case along, and how to deal with complications that may arise if any of the following occur:

- You or the trustee discovers an error in your papers.
- A creditor asks the court to lift the automatic stay.
- You decide to object to a creditor's claim.
- A creditor objects to the discharge of a particular debt.
- A creditor or the trustee objects to your claim that an item of property is exempt.
- You decide to dismiss your case or convert it to another type of bankruptcy, such as a Chapter 13 bankruptcy.
- You need to reopen your case for some reason after it has been closed.
- Your case is dismissed, and you want to refile it and keep the protection of the automatic stay.

Some of these problems—fixing a simple error in your papers, for example—you can handle yourself. For more complicated problems, such as fighting a creditor in court about the discharge of a large debt, you'll probably need a lawyer's help.

RESOURCE

If you're going to court. If you face any of the special problems covered in this chapter, your first step should be to take a look at *Represent Yourself in Court*, by Paul Bergman and Sara Berman (Nolo). In addition to valuable information about handling federal court proceedings, this book has a special chapter on bankruptcy court.

Routine Bankruptcy Procedures

A routine Chapter 7 bankruptcy case takes three to six months from beginning to end and follows a series of predictable steps.

The Court Sends a Notice of Bankruptcy Filing

Shortly after you file for bankruptcy, the court sends an official notice to you and all of the creditors listed in your mailing matrix. This notice contains several crucial pieces of information.

Your Filing Date and Case Number

This information puts the creditors on notice that you have filed for bankruptcy and gives them a reference number (your case number) to use when seeking information about your case.

Whether the Case Is an Asset Case or a No-Asset Case

When you filled in the bankruptcy petition, you had to check one of the following two boxes:

☐ Debtor estimates that funds will be available for distribution to unsecured creditors.

☐ Debtor estimates that, after any exempt property is excluded and administrative expenses paid, there will be no funds available for distribution to unsecured creditors.

The box you check determines the type of notice the court sends to your creditors. If you checked the first box, your case is known as an "asset case" and your creditors will be advised to file a claim describing what you owe them. If you checked the second box, your case will be known as a "no-asset" case and your creditors will be told to not file a claim. However, they will also be informed that they will have an opportunity to file a claim later if it turns out that there are assets available after all.

How a Routine Chapter 7 Bankruptcy Proceeds

Step	Description	When It Happens
You begin your case by filing bankruptcy papers.	You file the petition and supporting schedules with the bankruptcy clerk, who scans them into the court records.	When you decide to do so. Once you file, most creditors are barred from taking collection actions.
The court notifies creditors that you have filed for bankruptcy.	A notice of your filing is mailed to you and your creditors, stating the date of the 341 hearing and contact information for the trustee.	A few days after you file.
The court assigns a trustee to the case.	The trustee's job is to review your paperwork and take possession of any nonexempt property.	The trustee is appointed at the same time the notice to creditors is mailed.
You provide your most recent tax return to the trustee.	You must give the trustee your most recent tax return but can black out sensitive information, such as your Social Security number and date of birth.	Seven days before the 341 hearing.
The 341 hearing is held.	The 341 hearing is the only personal appearance most filers make. The judge is not there and creditors seldom attend. The trustee questions you about your paperwork. Most meetings last a few minutes.	Between 20 and 40 days after the date you file.
The means test is applied in appropriate cases.	The U.S. Trustee starts a process leading to dismissal or conversion of your case to Chapter 13 if your papers show that you have adequate income to fund a Chapter 13 debt repayment plan.	The U.S. Trustee must file a statement within ten days after the 341 hearing if it appears from the paperwork or information gleaned in the 341 hearing that your income is over the state median and you can't pass the means test.

How a Routine Chapter 7 Bankruptcy Proceeds (continued)

Step	Description	When It Happens
Objections to exemption claims are filed.	If the trustee or a creditor disagrees with an exemption you have claimed, a formal written objection must be filed with the court.	Within 30 days after the 341 hearing.
Secured property is dealt with.	If you owe money on property, you must either redeem or reaffirm the debt if you want to keep the property.	Within 30 days after the 341 hearing.
You attend budget counseling.	You must undergo personal financial management counseling before you can get your discharge.	Within 60 days after the 341 hearing, you must file proof that you completed counseling.
The court holds a reaffirmation hearing.	If you reaffirm a debt and aren't represented by a lawyer, you must attend a court hearing where the judge reviews your reaffirmation agreement.	Roughly 60 days after your 341 hearing.
The court grants your discharge.	The court mails a notice of discharge that wipes out all debts that can legally be discharged, unless the court has ruled otherwise in your bankruptcy case (very rare). The automatic stay is lifted at this time.	Roughly 90 days after you file, and no less than 60 days after your 341 hearing.
Your case is closed.	The trustee distributes any property collected from you to your unsecured creditors.	A few days or weeks after your discharge in a no-asset case; longer in an asset case.

The 341 Hearing Date

As of this writing, all trustees are holding 341 meetings by phone or video conference. While bankruptcy courts are in the process of reopening, dates will vary depending on COVID-19 transmission rates in the local community. Check your court's website for current appearance information.

The notice also sets a date for the meeting of creditors (also called the "341 hearing"), usually several weeks later. Mark this date carefully—it is very important for several reasons:

- You must attend the 341 hearing; if you don't, your case can be dismissed.
- Your creditors must file their claims (if it is an asset case) within 60 days after this meeting.
- Your creditors must file any objections they have to the discharge of their debts within 60 days after this meeting.
- The trustee and your creditors must file any objections they have to your exemption claims.

Contact Information for the Trustee

The notice of filing will also provide the name, address, and telephone number of the trustee assigned to your case. You will probably be able to find the trustee's email address on the notice since most trustees agree to allow the court to contact them by email, which is called "electronic service." If you can't find it, call the trustee's office, get the trustee's email address, and communicate in that way if possible.

Your Creditors Must Cease Most Collection Actions

When the court mails your creditors official notice of your filing, the creditors will learn that the automatic stay is in effect. The automatic stay prohibits most creditors from taking any action to collect the debts you owe them until the court says otherwise.

There are some notable exceptions to the automatic stay, however. Ch. 2 provides detailed information on the automatic stay, including which actions it does—and does not—prohibit.

In addition, the bankruptcy court can lift the automatic stay for a particular creditor—that is, allow the creditor to continue collection efforts. (Lifting the automatic stay is covered in "Special Problems," below.)

Creditors won't know that they have to stop their collection efforts until they receive notice of your bankruptcy filing. The notice sent by the court could take a week or more to reach your creditors. If you need quicker results, send your own notice to creditors (including any bill collectors, landlords, or sheriffs about to enforce an eviction order). A sample letter notifying your creditors is shown below. You can also call your creditors. Be prepared to give your bankruptcy case number, the date you filed, and the name of the court in which you filed.

Notice to Creditor of Filing for Bankruptcy

Lynn Adams
18 Orchard Park Blvd.
East Lansing, MI 48823

June 15, 20xx

Cottons Clothing Store
745 Main Street
Lansing, MI 48915

Dear Cottons Clothing:

On June 14, 20xx, I filed for Chapter 7 bankruptcy, Case No.: 20xx-67361 *in pro per*. Under 11 U.S.C. § 362(a), you cannot do the following:

- take any action against me or my property to collect any debt
- enforce any lien on my real or personal property
- repossess any property in my possession
- discontinue any service or benefit currently being provided to me, or
- take any action to evict me from where I live.

A violation of these prohibitions may be considered contempt of court and punished accordingly.

Very truly yours,

Lynn Adams

Lynn Adams

If a creditor tries to collect a debt in violation of the automatic stay, you can ask the bankruptcy court to hold the creditor in contempt of court and to award you money damages. The procedures for making this request are beyond the scope of this book.

Attend the 341 Hearing (Meeting of Creditors)

At the 341 hearing, the trustee will ask all debtors questions about the accuracy of the petition and whether any information changed. The trustee will also ask specific questions to individual debtors to resolve any issues in your paperwork. Some trustees question a debtor more closely about items in the bankruptcy papers than others. The trustee might want to see documentation of some of your figures, such as the value of a house or car. If you don't have this paperwork with you, the trustee will postpone the meeting to another date to give you time to find the necessary documents. Typically, you won't have to appear at another meeting if you submit these documents by mail or email beforehand (the trustee will give you instructions).

For most people, the 341 hearing is brief. Very few, if any, creditors show up, but *you* must show up. If you don't appear and haven't notified the trustee in advance, your case will likely be scheduled for dismissal. Some trustees will automatically give you a second chance without seeking dismissal. Either way, if you have a good excuse for not attending, the trustee is likely to reschedule. But it's best to inform the trustee that you can't participate well before the meeting date.

> **FOR MARRIED COUPLES**
>
> **If you're married and filing jointly.** Both you and your spouse must attend the first scheduled 341 hearing. If the meeting is continued to another date for a technical reason—to provide identification, for example (sometimes people need additional time to get a Social Security card)—only one spouse may have to attend. Ask the trustee whether both of you have to come back, or whether one will do.

If You Can't Appear

Sometimes, a person who has filed for bankruptcy cannot attend the 341 hearing for a legitimate reason, such as a serious illness or a weather-related issue, like a flood or hurricane. If that is true in your case, contact the trustee for information on how to proceed. Here is what the U.S. Trustee's office tells the regular trustees about how to handle people who are unable to appear:

"The trustee should consult with the United States Trustee regarding the general procedures for approving a debtor's alternative appearance when extenuating circumstances prevent the debtor from appearing in person. Extenuating circumstances may include military service, serious medical condition, or incarceration. In such instances, a debtor's appearance at a § 341(a) meeting may be secured by alternative means, such as telephonically. When the debtor(s) cannot personally appear before the trustee, arrangements should be made for an independent third party authorized to administer oaths to be present at the alternate location to administer the oath and to verify the debtor's identity and state the Social Security number on the record.... On the rare occasion when other arrangements need to be made to address a particular situation, the trustee should consult with the United States Trustee about the appropriate safeguards to follow. The trustee also may allow such debtors to provide proof of identity and Social Security numbers at the trustee's office at their convenience any time before the next scheduled meeting.

"When a trustee becomes aware of a debtor's disability, including hearing impairment, the trustee must notify the United States Trustee immediately so that reasonable accommodation can be made. The United States Trustee has procedures in place to address the special needs of debtors."

Preparing for the 341 Hearing

Before the hearing, call the regular trustee whose name and phone number appear on the notice of bankruptcy filing from the court. Explain that you're proceeding without a lawyer ("*in pro se*") and ask what records you're required to send to the trustee before the hearing.

You should expect to send:

- evidence of your current income
- statements from financial institutions for all of your deposit and investment accounts through the date you filed bankruptcy
- your most recent tax return, and
- if you had to take the means test, proof of your monthly expenses (if the trustee questions an expense, you'll be asked to provide proof).

You have a right to redact (black out) all but the last four digits of your Social Security number on any papers you submit. You can also redact the names of your minor children, full dates of birth, and full Social Security numbers. The trustee will expect to receive these documents no later than seven days before the hearing.

Some people become anxious at the prospect of answering a trustee's questions and consider having an attorney accompany them. But if you were completely honest in preparing your bankruptcy papers, it's unlikely that you'll need an attorney with you at the 341 hearing. If the trustee does have tough questions, it is you, not the attorney, who will have to answer them. That said, there's nothing wrong with retaining counsel if it would make you feel more comfortable.

If you think you've been dishonest on the forms or with a creditor, or have attempted to unload some of your property before filing, you'll want to see a lawyer before you go to the hearing.

You can visit the hearing room where your district holds 341 hearings (typically, the nearest federal building) and watch other 341 hearings if you think that might help alleviate some anxiety. Just check with the U.S. Trustee's office in your district to find out when these hearings are held.

A day or so before the 341 hearing, thoroughly review the papers you filed with the bankruptcy court. If you discover mistakes, make careful note of them. You'll probably have to correct your papers after the hearing, but that's an easy process. Instructions are in "Amending Your Bankruptcy Papers," below.

After reviewing your papers, go over the list of questions the trustee will likely ask. You'll find examples in "What Will the Trustee Ask You?" below. It's a good idea to answer them all, if they relate to your situation.

At the beginning of the hearing, the trustee will ask you whether you have read the Notice Required by 11 U.S.C. § 342(b) for Individuals Filing for Bankruptcy (Form 2010). You filed it with your petition. Reviewing it before the meeting will mean you have one less thing to worry about at the hearing. If you forget, there will likely be copies of the form available at the 341 hearing.

> ⚠ CAUTION
>
> **Don't forget your ID.** You'll need identification at the 341 hearing. Bring both a photo ID (such as a driver's license, a passport, or an identification card) and proof of your Social Security number. Many trustees require a Social Security card, so if you can't find yours, it's a good idea to order one as soon as possible. Otherwise, call the trustee's office and ask about acceptable substitutions.

The Routine 341 Hearing

Most 341 hearings are quick and simple. You appear in the designated meeting place at the date and time stated on the bankruptcy notice. Several other people who have filed for bankruptcy will be there, too, for their own 341 hearings. When your name is called, you'll be asked to sit or stand near the front of the hearing room. The trustee will swear you in and ask you for your identification. At that point, you'll be asked whether everything in your papers is 100% true and correct. To prepare, it's important that you:

- review your papers before filing them
- file amendments before the 341 hearing if you discover any errors after you file (refer to "Amending Your Bankruptcy Papers," below)
- review your papers again shortly before the 341 hearing, and
- volunteer any additional changes at the hearing.

Then you can confidently answer "yes" to the trustee's first question. The trustee will probably be most interested in:

- how you came up with a value for a big ticket item, such as your home or car
- anticipated tax refunds
- any possible right that you have to sue someone because of a recent accident or business loss
- reasons for inconsistencies in your paperwork or omitted information (such as answering "none" to the questions about clothing or bank accounts when it's obvious that you have either or both)

- recent large payments to creditors or relatives, and
- possible inheritances or insurance proceeds coming your way.

In other words, the trustee will want to know if you expect to receive any money from any source that could be used to pay something to your creditors.

If your answer to a trustee's question differs from the information in your bankruptcy papers, the trustee will have reason to suspect your entire case—and your bankruptcy might change from a routine procedure to an uphill battle. If you know that you have made mistakes, you should call them to the trustee's attention before the trustee raises the issue. If you are caught in a contradiction, immediately explain how it happened. Even if someone else prepared your papers for you, you can't use that as an excuse. You are responsible for the information in your papers, which is why you should thoroughly review them before signing and filing them.

When the trustee is finished questioning you, any creditors who have appeared will have an opportunity to ask you questions. Most often, no creditors show up. If any do appear, they are likely gathering evidence to see whether it is worthwhile to object to your discharge. In most cases, it will be a creditor you've been in a dispute with, and you likely won't be surprised that they're there. For instance, a creditor might ask for an explanation if the information in your bankruptcy papers differs from what was on your credit application. When the creditors are through asking questions, the hearing will end.

Except in highly unusual situations, the trustee and creditors should be finished questioning you in five minutes or less. When the trustee and creditors complete the questioning, the hearing might or might not be concluded depending on whether the trustee needs anything further. If the trustee needs more information or documents, the meeting will be continued to another date. Many trustees won't make you appear on the continued date if the outstanding issue is resolved beforehand.

If you don't have secured debts or nonexempt property, and no one will be asking the court to rule on the dischargeability of a debt or the continuing effect of a lien, your case will effectively be over, other than you'll need to file your debtor education certificate if you didn't do so. You won't need to worry about someone coming to your house to inventory your property or calling your employer to confirm the information on your papers. You'll simply wait until the court sends you your notice of discharge and case closure. That should happen 60 to 75 days after your 341 hearing.

Some trustees have their own questionnaires and requests for documents to complete. They will either mail these to you so you can complete them before the 341 hearing, or ask you to complete them while you are waiting for your turn to be questioned. Also, you might be asked to complete a brief form asking who assisted you in filling in your paperwork and who explained some of the choices you made (such as why you chose to file a Chapter 7 bankruptcy). The purpose of this form is to smoke out nonlawyer bankruptcy petition preparers who are providing legal advice as part of their service. (See Ch. 10 for more on bankruptcy petition preparers.)

Finally, if you pay a domestic support obligation, expect to provide information about the amount and to whom you pay on one of the trustee's forms. The trustee must provide notice of the bankruptcy case.

Angry Creditors

Creditors with an ax to grind with the debtor—such as wronged business partners and bitter ex-spouses—tend to show up frequently. Don't worry about being taken by surprise, though. It's unlikely. Most people are well aware of the people who are unhappy with them and might choose to make their dissatisfaction known publicly.

Potential Problems at the 341 Hearing

If you or your papers give any indication that you own valuable nonexempt property, the trustee might question you about how you decided what it's worth. For instance if you have valued your real estate at $150,000, and the trustee thinks it's worth a lot more, you will be asked where you got your figures. Or, a creditor who's owed a lot of money might question you about the circumstances of the debt, hoping to show that you incurred the debt without intending to pay it, or by lying on a credit application, and that therefore it should survive bankruptcy. (See Ch. 8.)

What Will the Trustee Ask You?

Here are questions you can expect the trustee to ask, many of which are required, but not all:

- State your name and current address for the record.
- Have you read the Bankruptcy Information Sheet provided by the U.S. Trustee?
- Did you sign the petition, schedules, statements, and related documents you filed with the court? Did you read the petition, schedules, statements, and related documents before you signed them, and is the signature your own?
- Please provide your picture ID and Social Security card for review.
- Are you personally familiar with the information contained in the petition, schedules, statements, and related documents?
- To the best of your knowledge, is the information contained in the petition, schedules, statements, and related documents true and correct?
- Are there any errors or omissions to bring to my or the court's attention at this time?
- Are all of your assets identified on the schedules?
- Have you listed all of your creditors on the schedules?
- Have you previously filed for bankruptcy? (If so, the trustee must obtain the case number and the discharge information to determine your discharge eligibility.)

The trustee might also ask additional questions, such as these:

- Do you own or have any interest in any real estate?
  - Property that you own: When did you purchase the property? How much did the property cost? What are the mortgages encumbering it? What do you estimate the present value of the property to be? Is that the total value or your share? How did you arrive at that value?
  - Property that you're renting: Have you ever owned the property in which you live? Is its owner in any way related to you?
- Have you made any property transfers or given any property away within the last year (or a more extended period if applicable under state law)? If so, what did you transfer? To whom was it transferred? What did you receive in exchange? What did you do with the funds?
- Does anyone hold property belonging to you? If so, who holds the property, and what is it? What is its value?
- Do you have a claim against anyone or any business? If there are significant medical debts, are the medical bills from injury? Are you the plaintiff in any lawsuit? What is the status of each case, and who is representing you?

What Will the Trustee Ask You? (continued)

- Are you entitled to life insurance proceeds or an inheritance as a result of someone's death? If so, please explain the details. (If you become a beneficiary of anyone's estate within six months of the date your bankruptcy petition was filed, the trustee must be advised within ten days through your counsel of the nature and extent of the property you will receive.)
- Does anyone owe you money? If so, is the money collectible? Why haven't you collected it? Who owes the money, and where is that person?
- Have you made any payments over $600 to anyone in the past year?
- Did you file federal income tax returns on a timely basis? When was the last return filed? Do you have copies of the federal income tax returns? At the time of the filing of your petition, were you entitled to a tax refund from the federal or state government?
- Do you have a bank account, either checking or savings? If so, in what banks and what were the balances as of the date you filed your petition?
- When you filed your petition, did you have:
  - any cash on hand
  - any U.S. Savings Bonds
  - any other stocks or bonds
  - any certificates of deposit, or
  - a safe deposit box in your name or in anyone else's name?
- Do you own an automobile? If so, what is the year, make, and value? Do you owe any money on it? Is it insured?
- Are you the owner of any cash value life insurance policies? If so, state the name of the company, face amount of the policy, cash surrender value (if any), and beneficiaries.
- Do you have any winning lottery tickets?
- Do you anticipate that you might acquire any property, cash or otherwise, as a result of a divorce or separation proceeding?
- Regarding any consumer debts secured by your property, have you filed the required Statement of Intention concerning the exemption, retention, or surrender of that secured property? Please provide a copy of the statement to the trustee. Have you performed that intention?
- Have you been engaged in any business during the last six years? If so, where and when? What happened to the assets of the company?

You might also be questioned about why you claimed that particular property is exempt. If this happens to you, simply describe the process you went through in selecting your exemptions from the charts on the companion page. If you consulted an attorney about exemptions or other issues, mention this also. This questioning won't affect your case unless the trustee disagrees with your exemption claims.

Make Sure the 341 Hearing Is Closed

The 30-day period in which the trustee and creditors can file objections to exemptions starts running when the 341 hearing is concluded or "closed." The hearing is officially closed—and the clock starts to run on objections—only when the trustee so notes in the court's docket. The trustee's oral statement alone at the 341 hearing isn't enough to officially close the hearing. Check the court file to ensure that the trustee closed (adjourned or concluded) the 341 hearing, and follow up with the trustee if you don't see an entry like that. Otherwise, the 30-day period to file objections won't start to run, and the trustee and creditors will have unlimited time to file objections.

CAUTION

You're responsible for your paperwork, even if you used a bankruptcy petition preparer. You must provide the property valuation and other information in your bankruptcy papers. You cannot shift responsibility for the accuracy and thoroughness of your petition to the preparer, whose job is just to enter the information you supply. If you use a preparer, check all of your paperwork carefully before signing it and filing it with the court.

Deal With Nonexempt Property

After the 341 hearing, the trustee is supposed to collect all of your nonexempt property and have it sold to pay off your creditors. Typically, but not always, the trustee accepts the exemptions you claim on Schedule C and goes after property you haven't claimed as exempt. If, however, the trustee or a creditor disagrees with an exemption, the trustee will likely try to resolve the issue informally. If you can't agree and the trustee files a written objection with the bankruptcy court within 30 days of the 341 hearing, the court will schedule a hearing. After listening to both sides, the judge will decide the issue. (See "Special Problems," below.)

If you really want to keep a nonexempt item and can borrow money from friends or relatives, or you've come into some cash since you filed for bankruptcy, you might be able to trade cash for the item. The trustee, whose sole responsibility at this stage is to maximize the amount paid creditors, is interested simply in how much money your property can produce, not in taking a particular item. So the trustee will probably be happy to accept cash instead of the nonexempt property you want to keep. In fact, many will discount the property value by approximately 20% to take into account sales costs.

> **EXAMPLE:** Maura files for Chapter 7 bankruptcy and claims her parlor grand piano as exempt. The trustee disagrees, and the judge rules that the piano is not exempt. To replace the piano on the open market might cost Maura $7,000. The trustee determines that the piano would probably sell for $4,500 at an auction, and is willing to let Maura keep the piano if she can come up with $3,600, to avoid the cost of moving the piano, storing it, and selling it at auction.

The trustee might also be willing to let you keep nonexempt property if you volunteer to trade exempt property of equal value. For instance, the trustee might agree to let Maura keep her nonexempt piano if she gives up her car, even though Maura could claim the car as exempt. Again, the trustee is interested in squeezing as many dollars as possible from the estate and usually won't care whether the money comes from exempt or nonexempt assets.

Deal With Secured Property

When you filed and served your Statement of Intention, you told the trustee and your creditors whether you wanted to keep property that is security for a debt or give it to the creditor in return for cancellation of the debt.

The law contradicts itself on the time limits for carrying out your intentions. Depending on which provision you believe, you have either 30 or 45 days after the date set for your first 341 hearing to deal with your secured property. If you miss the deadline, the creditor can repossess the collateral— the automatic stay no longer applies (see Ch. 2). Because of these serious consequences, we strongly recommend that you file your Statement of Intention with the rest of your paperwork, or, at least handle your secured property within 30 days of the hearing, just in case the court follows this earlier deadline. (Ch. 5 explains how to decide what to do with your secured property and how to carry out your intentions.)

Complete an Approved Debtor Education Course

After you file for bankruptcy but before receiving your discharge, you must take a two-hour course in personal financial management. Known as "debtor education," this course is typically offered by the same agencies that provide the credit counseling you must complete before you file. (You can find counseling agencies at www.justice.gov/ust; click "Credit Counseling & Debtor Education.") As with credit counseling, you can expect to pay about $35 for this course, and you can ask for a fee waiver if you can't afford the fee.

Once you complete the counseling (and no later than 60 days after the first date set for your 341 hearing), you must file Form 423 with the court to certify that you've met the requirement and the certificate you get from the counseling agency (although some providers will file the certificate for you—consider asking). If you don't file these documents on time, the court will close your case without granting you a discharge of your debts, which means your bankruptcy case was pointless. While it's possible to reopen your case to file the required form, it will cost you. You'll have to repay the $338 filing fee and prepare the request. It's obviously much easier to get the counseling and file the form as soon as possible. Although you have 60 days from your 341 hearing to get this done, you're better off not delaying it.

You might be able to obtain a disability waiver of this counseling requirement—which means you wouldn't have to take it if the following apply:

- You have a severe physical impairment.
- You make a reasonable effort, despite the impairment, to participate in the counseling.
- You are unable, because of your impairment, to meaningfully participate in the course.

(See *In re Hall*, 347 B.R. 532 (Bankr. N.D. W.Va. 2006).)

Attend the Reaffirmation Hearing

If you have signed and filed a reaffirmation agreement, the court will hold a hearing. At the hearing, the judge will determine whether making payments under the reaffirmation agreement would impose an undue hardship on you and your family, and whether it would be in your best interest to reaffirm the debt. You can find a complete explanation of the reaffirmation process—including what happens if the judge won't approve the agreement—in Ch. 5.

Understand Your Discharge Order

About 60 to 75 days after the 341 hearing, the court will send you a copy of your discharge order. On the form, it says that all debts you owed as of your filing date are discharged—unless they aren't. It then lists the types of debt that are not discharged. (A sample discharge order is available on the companion page at www.nolo.com/back-of-book/HFB.html.) You will notice that the order does not state which of your specific debts are or aren't discharged. To get a handle on this crucial information, carefully read Ch. 9.

Make several photocopies of the discharge order and keep them in a safe place. Send them to creditors who attempt to collect their debt after your case is over, or credit reporting agencies that still list you as owing a discharged debt. Refer to Ch. 8 regarding postbankruptcy collection efforts.

Amending Your Bankruptcy Papers

One of the helpful aspects of bankruptcy procedure is that you can amend any of your papers at any time before your final discharge. If you make a mistake, you can correct it quickly.

Despite this liberal amendment policy (as stated in Bankruptcy Rule 1009), some judges will not let you amend your exemption schedule after the deadline for creditors to object to the exemptions has passed. If you run into one of these judges, you'll need to talk to a bankruptcy attorney. (Although in light of a recent U.S. Supreme Court case, this may no longer be allowed. See *Law v. Siegel*, 134 S. Ct. 1188 (2014).)

In most courts, you will have to pay to amend your bankruptcy papers if you are amending Schedules D, or E/F to add a new creditor or change an address, because these changes require the court to make an additional mailing. The fee for adding a new creditor is currently $32. You won't be charged to change the address of a creditor or attorney already included in your paperwork.

If you become aware of debts or property you should have included in your papers, amending your petition will avoid any suspicion that you're trying to conceal things from the trustee. If you don't amend your papers after discovering this kind of information, your bankruptcy petition might be dismissed or one or more of your debts might not be discharged if that new information comes to light.

Even if your bankruptcy case is already closed, some courts will allow you to reopen it and amend your papers to add an omitted creditor who tries to collect the debt. (See Ch. 8.)

CAUTION

Try to get it right the first time. Too many changes can make you look dishonest, which can get your case dismissed and investigated. Of course, if the facts have changed since you filed your petition, or you notice mistakes, you should amend. But the more accurate your papers are at the outset, the less likely your case will run into trouble.

Common Amendments

Even a simple change in one form can require changes to several other forms. Here are some of the more common reasons for amendments and the forms you might need to amend. Exactly which forms you'll have to change depends on your court's rules. (Instructions for making the amendments are below.)

Add or Delete Exempt Property on Schedule C

If you want to add or delete property from your list of exemptions, you must file a new Schedule C. Depending on the omission you might need to change:

- Schedule A/B, if the property is real estate or personal property and you failed to list it

- Schedule D and Form 108—Statement of Intention for Individuals Filing Under Chapter 7, if you need to add collateral property securing a debt
- Form 107—Your Statement of Financial Affairs for Individuals Filing for Bankruptcy, if you forgot to include a transaction, or
- the Mailing Matrix, if the exempt item is tied to a particular creditor.

Add or Delete Property on Schedule A/B

You might have forgotten to list some of your property on your schedules. Or, you may have received property after filing for bankruptcy. The following property must be reported to the bankruptcy trustee if it's received or you become entitled to receive it within 180 days after filing for bankruptcy:

- property you inherit or become entitled to inherit
- property from a marital settlement agreement or divorce decree, and
- death benefits or life insurance policy proceeds. (See Ch. 3.)

If you have new property to report for any of these reasons, you may need to file amendments to:

- Schedule A/B, if the property is real estate
- Schedule A/B, if the property is personal property
- Schedule C, if the property was claimed as exempt and it's not, or you want to claim it as exempt
- Schedule D and Form 108—Statement of Intention for Individuals Filing Under Chapter 7, if the property is collateral for a secured debt
- Form 107—Your Statement of Financial Affairs for Individuals Filing for Bankruptcy, if any transactions regarding the property haven't been described on that form, or
- the Mailing Matrix, if the item is tied to a particular creditor.

If your bankruptcy case is already closed, see Ch. 8.

Change Your Plans for Secured Property

If you've changed your plans for dealing with an item of secured property, you must file an amended Form 108—Statement of Intention for Individuals Filing Under Chapter 7.

Correct Your List of Creditors

To correct your list of creditors, you may need to amend:

- Schedule C, if the debt is secured and you plan to claim the collateral as exempt
- Schedule D, if the debt is a secured debt
- Schedule E/F, if the debt is a priority debt (as defined in Ch. 6)
- Schedule E/F, if the debt is unsecured
- Form 107—Your Statement of Financial Affairs for Individuals Filing for Bankruptcy, if any transactions regarding the property haven't been described on that form, or
- the Mailing Matrix, which contains the names and addresses of all your creditors.

If your bankruptcy case is already closed, see Ch. 8.

Add an Omitted Payment to a Creditor

If you didn't report a payment to a creditor made within the year before you filed for bankruptcy, you must amend your Form 107—Your Statement of Financial Affairs for Individuals Filing for Bankruptcy.

How to File an Amendment

To make an amendment, take these steps:

Step 1: Fill out the Amendment Cover Sheet on the companion page, if no local form is required. Otherwise, use the local form. If you use our form, here's how to fill it in:

- Put the appropriate information in the top blanks (for instance, "Western District of Tennessee").
- Enter your name, the name of your spouse if you're married and filing jointly, and all other names you have used in the last eight years.
- Enter your address, the last four digits of your Social Security number, and a taxpayer ID number (if you have one because you own a business).
- Enter your case number.

- Check the boxes of the forms you are amending. If you add new creditors or change an address, check the box that you have enclosed the appropriate fee (currently $32).
- Sign the form.
- Continue to the declaration about the truth of the amendment.
- Enter your name (and the name of your spouse if you're filing jointly) after "I (we)."
- Enter the number of pages that will be accompanying the cover sheet.
- Enter the date you are signing the document.
- Sign (both you and your spouse, if you're filing jointly) at the bottom to swear under penalty of perjury that your amendment is accurate.

Step 2: Make copies of the forms affected by your amendment.

Step 3: Check your local court rules or ask the court clerk whether you must retype the whole form to make the correction, or if you can just type the new information on another blank form. If you can't find the answer, ask a local bankruptcy lawyer or nonattorney bankruptcy petition preparer. If it's acceptable to just type the new information, precede the information you're typing with "ADD," "CHANGE," or "DELETE" as appropriate. At the bottom of the form, type "AMENDED" in capital letters.

Step 4: Call or visit the court to learn what order the papers must be in and how many copies are required.

Step 5: Make the required number of copies, plus one copy for yourself, one for the trustee, and one for any creditor affected by your amendment.

Step 6: Have a friend or relative mail a copy of your amended papers to the bankruptcy trustee and to any creditor affected by your amendment.

Step 7: Enter the name and complete address of every new creditor affected by your amendment on the Proof of Service by Mail (a copy is on the companion page). Also enter the name and address of the bankruptcy trustee. Then have the person who mailed the amendment to the trustee and new creditors sign and date the proof of service.

Step 8: Mail or take the original amendment and proof of service and copies to the bankruptcy court. Enclose a money order for the filing fee, if required. If you use the mail, enclose a prepaid self-addressed envelope so the clerk can return a file-stamped set of papers to you.

If the 341 hearing occurred before you file your amendment, the court will likely schedule another one.

Filing a Change of Address

If you move while your bankruptcy case is still open, you must give your new address to the court, the trustee, and your creditors. Here's how to do it:

Step 1: Make one or two photocopies of the blank Notice of Change of Address and Proof of Service forms on the companion page.

Step 2: Fill in the Change of Address form with your old address, new address, and date you moved.

Step 3: Make one photocopy for the trustee, one for your records, and one for each creditor listed in Schedules D, E/F or the Mailing Matrix.

Step 4: Have a friend or relative mail a copy of the Notice of Change of Address to the trustee and to each creditor.

Step 5: Have the friend or relative complete and sign the Proof of Service by Mail form, listing the bankruptcy trustee and the names and addresses of all creditors to whom the notice was mailed.

Step 6: File the original notice and original Proof of Service with the bankruptcy court.

Special Problems

Sometimes, complications arise in bankruptcy. For instance, a creditor might file a motion or object to the discharge of a debt or the entire bankruptcy. If a creditor does this, you'll receive a Notice of Motion or Notice of Objection. At that point, you might need to go to court yourself or get an attorney to help you. Here are some of the more common complications that could crop up.

You Failed the Means Test

If you didn't pass the means test (described in Ch. 6) but decided to file for Chapter 7 anyway, you might face a motion to dismiss or convert your case to a Chapter 13 bankruptcy.

Presumed Abuse

If you don't pass the means test, your Chapter 7 bankruptcy will be presumed to be abusive. This means that you won't be allowed to proceed unless you can establish that the presumption of abuse should be set aside because of special circumstances.

However, none of this is automatic. To stop your Chapter 7 bankruptcy on the grounds of abuse, someone—a creditor, the trustee, or, most likely, the U.S. Trustee—must request a court hearing to dismiss or convert your case. The U.S. Trustee must file a statement, within ten days after your 341 hearing, indicating whether your case should be presumed abusive. (This statement is required if your income is more than the state median; see Ch. 1 for more information.) Five days after the U.S. Trustee's statement is filed, the court must send it to all of your creditors to inform them of the U.S. Trustee's decision and give them an opportunity to file a motion to dismiss or convert your case.

Within 30 days after filing this statement, the U.S. Trustee must either:

- file its own motion to dismiss or convert your case on grounds of abuse, or
- explain why a motion to convert or dismiss isn't appropriate (for example, because you passed the means test).

These duties and time limits apply only to the U.S. Trustee. If your income is more than the state median, your creditors can file a motion to dismiss or convert any time after you file, but no later than 60 days after the first date set for your 341 hearing.

Defending a Motion to Dismiss or Convert

If the U.S. Trustee (or a trustee or a creditor, in some cases) files a motion to dismiss or convert your case based on presumed abuse, you are entitled to notice of the hearing at least 20 days in advance. You will receive papers in the mail explaining the grounds for the motion and what you need to do to respond. Because abuse is presumed, you will bear the burden of proving that your filing really isn't abusive, and that you should be allowed to proceed.

There are two basic defenses to this type of motion:

1. **You didn't fail the means test.** To defend on this basis, you must be able to show that you actually passed the means test and the party bringing the motion to dismiss or convert misinterpreted the information you provided in Form 122A-1 and Form 122A-2 or misinterpreted the applicable law (for example, by including Social Security benefits in your current monthly income when the law says they should be excluded).

2. **Special circumstances exist that allow you to pass the means test.** Bankruptcy law gives a serious medical condition or a call to active duty in the armed forces as examples of special circumstances, but this isn't an exhaustive list. However, it isn't enough just to show that special circumstances exist: You must also show that they justify additional expenses or adjustments to your current monthly income "for which there is no reasonable alternative."

To prove special circumstances, you must itemize each additional expense or adjustment of your income, and provide:

- documentation for the expense or adjustment, and
- a detailed explanation of the special circumstances that make the expense or adjustment necessary and reasonable.

You will win only if the additional expenses or adjustments to your income enable you to pass the means test. (Ch. 6 explains how to make this calculation.)

> **EXAMPLE:** Madison and Ryan have a child with autism. Sophia is making remarkable progress in her private school, for which Madison and Ryan pay $1,000 a month. No equivalent school has lower tuition. Under the means test guidelines, Madison and Ryan are entitled to deduct only $170.83 a month from the income for private school expenses. If Madison and Ryan were allowed to deduct the full $1000 monthly tuition, they would easily pass the means test. By documenting Sophia's condition, the necessity for the extra educational expense, and the fact that moving her to a less expensive school would greatly undermine her progress, Madison and Ryan might have a chance of convincing the court to allow the $1,000 expense, which would, in turn, rebut the presumption of abuse.

Bankruptcy courts have issued written decisions on a variety of special circumstance claims. If you need to prove special circumstances to pass the means test, you will definitely want to check with a local attorney or do your own research to find out how bankruptcy courts in your state have treated the special circumstances you're claiming. (See Ch. 10.)

A frequently addressed issue is whether payments on nondischargeable student loans can be considered a special circumstance. While a few courts have held that they can be, more courts have gone the other way and ruled that student loan payments do not constitute special circumstances.

Here are some cases in which the court has allowed special circumstances claims. But remember that courts in your area might see the issue differently:

- unusually high transportation expenses (*In re Batzkiel*, 349 B.R. 581 (Bankr. N.D. Iowa 2006))
- reduction in income (*In re Tamez*, No. 07-60047 (Bankr. W.D. Tex. 2007) (reduction in income due to voluntary job changes))
- joint debtors who have two separate households (*In re Graham*, 363 B.R. 844 (Bankr. S.D. Ohio 2007); *In re Armstrong*, No. 06-31414 (Bankr. N.D. Ohio 2007))
- slightly higher rent expenses (*In re Scarafiotti*, 375 B.R. 618 (Bankr. D. Colo. 2007)), and
- court-ordered child support payments arising after filing petition (*In re Littman*, 370 B.R. 820 (Bankr. D. Idaho 2007)).

A Creditor Asks the Court to Lift the Automatic Stay

Your automatic stay lasts from the date you file your papers until the date you receive your bankruptcy discharge, the date your bankruptcy case is closed, or when the judge orders it lifted, whichever happens first. For example, assume you receive a discharge but the trustee keeps your case open because the trustee is waiting to collect your tax refund or inheritance you are due to receive in the future. In this situation, the automatic stay would not be in effect after your discharge, even though your case would still be open.

As long as the stay is in effect, most creditors must get permission from a judge to take any action against you or your property that might affect your bankruptcy estate. (See Ch. 2 for information on which creditors are affected by the stay and which are free to proceed with collection efforts despite the stay.) To get this permission, the creditor must file a request in writing called a Motion to Lift Stay. The court will schedule a hearing on this motion and send you written notice. You will have a certain period of time to file a written response. Even if you decide not to file a response, you may still be able to appear in court to argue that the stay shouldn't be lifted. Check your local rules on this point.

If you don't show up for the hearing—even if you filed a written response —the stay will probably be lifted as requested by the creditor, unless you show that the requesting creditor won't be harmed by the stay, or unless lifting the stay would potentially harm other creditors. For instance, if the creditor is seeking permission to repossess your car, and your equity in the car is sufficient to repay the requesting creditor and would produce some income for your unsecured creditors if sold by the trustee, the court might refuse to lift the stay whether or not you show up.

After hearing the motion, the judge will either rule "from the bench" (announce a decision right then and there), or "take it under submission" and mail a decision in a few days. A creditor can file the motion asking a judge to lift the stay within a week or two after you file, but a delay of several weeks to several months is more common.

Grounds for Lifting the Stay

The bankruptcy court might lift the automatic stay for several reasons:

- The activity being stayed is not a legitimate concern of the bankruptcy court. For instance, the court will let a child custody hearing proceed, because its outcome won't affect your economic situation.

- The activity being stayed is going to happen no matter what the bankruptcy court does. For instance, if a lender shows the court that a mortgage foreclosure will ultimately occur, the court will usually lift the stay and let the foreclosure proceed. (If you want to keep your house, you may be better off filing for Chapter 13 bankruptcy. See Ch. 4.)

- The stay is harming the creditor's interest in property you own or possess. For instance, if you've stopped making payments on a car and it's losing value, the court may lift the stay. That would allow the creditor to repossess the car now, unless you're willing and able to periodically pay the creditor an amount equal to the ongoing depreciation until your case is closed.

- You have no ownership interest in the property sought by the creditor (ownership interests are explained just above). If you don't own some interest in property that a creditor wants, the court isn't interested in protecting the property—and won't hesitate to lift the stay. The most common example is when a month-to-month tenant is behind on rent and files for bankruptcy to forestall an eviction. Because the tenancy has no monetary value, it is not considered property of the estate, and the stay will almost always be lifted.

Do You Have an Ownership Interest in the Property?

There are many kinds of ownership interests. You can own property outright. You can own the right to possess it sometime in the future. You can co-own it jointly with any number of other owners. You can own the right to possess it, while someone else actually has legal title.

For most kinds of property, there's an easy way to tell if you have an ownership interest: If you would be entitled to receive any cash if the property were sold, you have an ownership interest.

For intangible property, however—property you can't see or touch—it might be harder to show your ownership interest. This most often arises in cases involving contracts concerning residential real estate.

For instance, if you have a lease (a type of contract) on your home when you file, most bankruptcy courts would consider it an ownership interest and would not lift the stay to let a landlord go ahead with eviction without more. But if the lease expired by its own terms before you filed—which converted your interest from a "leasehold" to a month-to-month tenancy—most courts would rule that you have no ownership interest in the property and would lift the stay, allowing the eviction to go forward.

Another ownership interest is the contractual right to continued coverage that an insured person has under an insurance policy. The automatic stay prevents insurance companies from canceling insurance policies.

Opposing a Request to Lift the Stay

Generally, a court won't lift the stay if you can show that it's necessary to preserve your property for yourself (if it's exempt) or for the benefit of your creditors (if it's not), or to maintain your general economic condition. You might also need to convince the court that the creditor's investment in the property will be protected while the bankruptcy is pending.

Here are situations and some possible responses you can make if creditors try to get the stay lifted:

- **Repossession of cars or other personal property.** If the stay is preventing a creditor from repossessing personal property pledged as collateral, such as your car, furniture, or jewelry, the creditor will probably argue that the stay should be lifted because you might damage the collateral or because the property is depreciating (declining in value) while your bankruptcy case is pending. Your response should depend on the facts. If the property is still in good shape, be prepared to prove it to the judge.

   If the property is worth more than you owe on it, you can argue that depreciation won't hurt the creditor, because the property could be repossessed later and sold for the amount of the debt or more. But if you're like most debtors and have little or no equity in the property, you'll need to propose a way to protect the creditor's interest while you keep the property—assuming you want it. One way to do this is to pay the creditor a cash security deposit to offset the expected depreciation.

   If you intend to keep secured property (see Ch. 5), you can argue that lifting the stay would deprive you of your rights under the bankruptcy laws. For example, if you intend to redeem a car by paying its replacement value, the court should deny the motion to lift the stay until you have an opportunity to do so.

- **Utility disconnections.** For 20 days after you file your bankruptcy petition, a public utility—electric, gas, telephone, or water company—cannot alter, refuse, or discontinue service to you, or discriminate against you in any other way, solely based on an unpaid debt or your bankruptcy filing. (11 U.S.C. § 366(a).) If your service was disconnected before you filed, the utility company must restore it within 20 days after you file for bankruptcy—without requiring a deposit—if you request it.

Twenty days after the order to continue service, the utility is entitled to discontinue service unless you provide adequate assurance that your future bills will be paid. (11 U.S.C. § 366(b).) Usually, that means you'll have to come up with a security deposit.

If you and the utility can't agree on the size of the deposit, the utility can cut off service, and you'll likely need a lawyer to ask the bankruptcy court to have it reinstated. If the utility files a motion to lift the stay, argue at the hearing that your deposit is adequate.

- **Evictions.** Filing for bankruptcy has been a favorite tactic for some eviction defense clinics, which file a bare-bones bankruptcy petition to stop evictions even if the tenant's debts don't justify bankruptcy. However, the automatic stay doesn't apply if your landlord obtained a judgment for eviction before you filed for bankruptcy, or if the eviction is based on your endangerment of the property or use of illegal controlled substances on the premises. These exceptions to the general rules (which have their own exceptions) are explained in Ch. 2.

- **Foreclosures.** If the lender cannot show proof that it owns the mortgage, you might be able to oppose a lender's motion to lift the stay by arguing the lender had no right to file the motion in the first place.

    If the lender proves that it owns the mortgage, you might be able to oppose the motion if you can show that you can resume regular payments and catch up on your arrears. In that case, the judge might allow you additional time to cure your default under the protection of the automatic stay instead of granting the lender's motion.

The Trustee or a Creditor Disputes a Claimed Exemption

After the 341 hearing, the trustee and creditors have 30 days to object to your claimed exemptions. If the deadline passes and the trustee or a creditor wants to challenge an exemption, it's usually too late, even if the exemption statutes don't support the claimed exemption. (*Taylor v. Freeland and Kronz,* 503 U.S. 638 (1992).) The objections must be in writing and filed with the bankruptcy court. Copies must be served on the trustee, you, and your lawyer, if you have one.

In some cases, the trustee can object to an exemption after the 30 days passes. For instance, in one case, the debtor stated that the value of certain stock options was unknown and used a $4,000 or so wildcard exemption to cover the value, whatever it was. Eight months after the bankruptcy case was closed, the trustee asked the debtor what happened to the stock options. As it happened, they had been cashed out for nearly $100,000. The trustee sought to have the case reopened to recover the excess value. The debtor argued that the 30-day period prevented a reexamination of the exemption claim.

Reasons for Objecting

The most common grounds for objecting are:

- You aren't eligible to use the state exemptions you claimed. You can use a state's exemptions only if you have made that state your domicile (your true home) for at least two years before filing. If you haven't been domiciled in your current state for at least two years, you must use the exemptions for the state where you were living for the better part of the 180-day period ending two years before you filed for bankruptcy. (See Ch. 3 for more on these rules, and Ch. 4 for more on the stricter rules that apply to homestead exemptions.)
- The claimed item isn't exempt under the law. For example, a plumber who lives in New Jersey and selects his state exemptions might protect his plumbing tools under the "goods and chattels" exemption. The trustee and creditors are likely to object on the

ground that these are work tools rather than goods and chattels, and that New Jersey has no "tools of the trade" exemption.

- Within ten years before you filed for bankruptcy, you sold nonexempt property and purchased exempt property to hinder, delay, or cheat your creditors. (Ways to avoid this accusation are discussed in Ch. 3.)
- Property you claimed as exempt is worth more than you say it is. If the property's actual replacement value is higher than the exemption limit for that item, the item can be sold and the excess over the exemption limit distributed to your creditors (assuming you don't buy the property back from the trustee at a negotiated price).

EXAMPLE: In Courtney's state, clothing is exempt to a total of $2,000. Courtney values her vintage mink coat at $1,000 and her other clothes at $1,000, bringing her within the $2,000 exemption. A creditor objects to the $1,000 valuation of the coat, claiming that such mink coats routinely sell for $3,000 and up. If the creditor prevails, Courtney would have to surrender the coat to the trustee. She'd get the first $1,000 (the exempt amount of the coat's sale price). Or, Courtney could keep the coat if she gave the trustee a negotiated amount of cash ($2,000 or less) or other property of equivalent value.

- You and your spouse have doubled an exemption where doubling isn't permitted.

EXAMPLE: Peyton and Lauren, a married couple, file for bankruptcy using California's 704 exemptions. Each claims a $3,325 exemption in their family car, for a total of $6,650. California doesn't allow a married couple to double the 704 automobile exemption. They can only claim $3,325.

Responding to Objections

When objection papers are filed, the court schedules a hearing. The creditor or trustee must prove to the bankruptcy court that the exemption is improper. You don't have to prove anything. In fact, you don't have to respond to the objection or show up at the hearing unless the bankruptcy court orders, or local rules require, that you do so. Of course, you can—and probably should—either file a response or show up at the hearing to defend your claim of a legitimate exemption. If you don't show up, the bankruptcy judge will decide based on the paperwork filed by the objecting party and the applicable laws, which most often means you'll lose—especially if the trustee or a bankruptcy attorney is objecting.

A Creditor Objects to the Discharge of a Debt

There are a variety of reasons a creditor can object to the discharge of a debt. In consumer bankruptcies, the most common is that the creditor believes you made fraudulent statements to borrow the money in the first place (for example, on a credit card application). (See Ch. 9 for more on this and other potential grounds for objecting to the discharge of a debt.)

You Want to Get Back Exempt Property Taken by a Creditor

You might have filed for bankruptcy after a creditor:

- repossessed collateral (such as a car) under a security agreement, or
- seized some of your property as part of a judgment collection action.

If so, you should have described the event in your Statement of Financial Affairs, which you filed along with your bankruptcy petition and schedules. Repossessions are difficult to undo, because they occur under a contract that you voluntarily entered into. However, property seized to satisfy a judgment can be pulled back into your bankruptcy estate if the seizure occurred within the three months before you filed. If the property is not exempt (or at least some of it is not exempt), the trustee might go after it so that it can be sold for the benefit of your unsecured creditors. If the property is exempt (meaning you are entitled to keep it), you can go after it yourself. However, you'll have to file a formal complaint in the bankruptcy court against the creditor.

The process for getting the bankruptcy judge to order the property returned to you is complex; you'll probably need the assistance of an attorney. Given the cost of attorneys, it's seldom worth your while to go after this type of property unless it's valuable or an irreplaceable family heirloom. Keep in mind that most property is only exempt up to a specific value—for example, a car might be exempt up to $5,000, furnishings up to $2,500. So even if you get the property back, you'll receive only the exempt amount from the proceeds if the trustee decides to sell it.

You Want to Dismiss Your Case

If you change your mind after you file for bankruptcy, you can ask the court to dismiss your case.

Common reasons for wanting to dismiss a case include the following:

- You discover that a significant debt you thought was dischargeable isn't. You don't have enough other debts to justify your bankruptcy case.
- You realize that an item of property you thought was exempt isn't. You don't want to lose it in bankruptcy.
- You come into a sum of money and can afford to pay your debts.
- You realize that you have more property in your estate than you thought and decide that you don't have to file for bankruptcy after all.
- Your bankruptcy case turns out to be more complex than you initially thought. You need a lawyer, but you don't have the money to hire one.
- The emotional stress of bankruptcy is too much for you.

It is within the court's discretion to dismiss your case. That means the court can grant or refuse the dismissal. How the courts make this decision varies from district to district. In some districts, dismissing a case is next to impossible if your bankruptcy estate has assets that can be sold. However, if yours is a no-asset case and no creditor objects to the dismissal, you might have better luck dismissing it.

If you want to dismiss your case, you must file a request with the court. Instructions on how to do this follow. Depending on how receptive your local bankruptcy court is to dismissal, you may need the help of a lawyer.

Step 1: Check your court's local rules for time limits, format of papers, and other requirements for voluntary dismissals. (See Ch. 10 for information on finding local rules online.) If you can't find the information you need from reading your local rules, ask the court clerk, the trustee assigned to your case, a local bankruptcy petition preparer, or a bankruptcy lawyer for help.

Step 2: Refer to the sample Petition for Voluntary Dismissal and a sample Order Granting Voluntary Dismissal on the companion page (www.nolo.com/back-of-book/HFB.html). Follow along with the sample as you type your caption, inserting your own information in the blanks.

Step 3: If you're using a typewriter, make a few photocopies of what you have typed so far, so you can make two different documents with that one caption.

Step 4: On one copy of your caption, center and type "PETITION FOR VOLUNTARY DISMISSAL." The text of the petition will be similar to the sample but tailored to the facts of your case. In particular, you will put your filing date in Paragraph 1; in Paragraph 3, you will explain your own reason for wanting to dismiss the case.

Step 5: Sign and date the petition. If you filed together with your spouse, both of you must sign. Otherwise, leave the spouse's signature line blank.

Step 6: On another photocopy of the caption you made, center and type: "[PROPOSED] ORDER GRANTING VOLUNTARY DISMISSAL." Then type the text of the order from the sample at the end of this chapter. Include the blanks; the judge will fill them in.

Step 7: Make at least three copies of your signed petition and your blank order.

Step 8: Take your originals and copies to the bankruptcy court clerk. When you get to the court clerk, explain that you are filing a petition to dismiss your case. The clerk will take your originals and one or more of your copies. Ask the clerk the following:

- What notice to your creditors is required?
- If there is a problem, will you be contacted? If not, how will you learn of the problem?
- If the judge signs the order, when can you expect to get it?
- Once you have a signed order, who sends copies to your creditors—you or the court? If you send the copies, do you also have to file a Proof of Service?

Step 9: Once you receive the signed order, put it away for safekeeping if you don't have to notify your creditors. If you do, make copies and send one to each.

Step 10: If you have to file a Proof of Service, follow the instructions in Ch. 5.

You Want to Reopen Your Case

At several places in this book, we've suggested that you might have to reopen your case (for example, to file a motion to avoid a lien or to file Form 423 proving that you completed budget counseling). You'll start by filing what's called an "ex parte motion." This simply means that you don't have to provide formal notice to the other parties in your case. Instead, you just prepare and file your request and an accompanying order, and demonstrate that you have given written notice of your motion to the trustee and the U.S. Trustee. You don't have to schedule a hearing; the judge will consider your request and either grant or deny it based solely on your paperwork.

You'll find copies of the forms necessary to reopen your case to allow you to file Form 423 asking the court for a discharge on the companion page.

There are four forms in all:

- a request to reopen the case
- an order reopening the case
- a request for a discharge, and
- an order that a discharge be entered.

If you want the court to reopen your case for a different reason, you'll have to change the forms. Describe why you need the case reopened and tailor the forms to request the ultimate relief you want the court to grant (for example, to avoid a lien). If you have trouble completing these forms or figuring out what to say, talk to a bankruptcy lawyer.

Life After Bankruptcy

Congratulations! After receiving your discharge, you can get on with your life and enjoy the fresh start bankruptcy offers. There could still be a few things left to do, however. For example, you might want to rebuild your credit. You might also need to take action if any of the following occurs:

- You receive or discover new nonexempt property.
- A creditor tries to collect a nondischargeable debt.
- A creditor attempts to collect a debt that has been discharged in your bankruptcy.
- A creditor or the trustee asks the court to revoke your bankruptcy discharge.
- A government agency or private employer discriminates against you because of your bankruptcy.

This chapter explains how these events typically unfold and how you can respond to them. But don't worry: Very few people face these circumstances. If you were complete and honest in your paperwork, it's unlikely that you'll run into any postbankruptcy problems. We provide the information in this chapter just in case you're one of the rare exceptions.

Newly Acquired or Discovered Property

If you omit property from your bankruptcy papers or acquire certain types of property soon after receiving a discharge, the trustee might reopen your case. The trustee probably won't take action unless the property is nonexempt and is valuable enough to justify reopening the case, seizing and selling the property, and distributing the proceeds to creditors. Even so, if the property you acquire or discover is of little value, you should still tell the trustee about it. Reopening the case is the trustee's decision, not yours.

Notifying the Trustee

It's your legal responsibility to notify the bankruptcy trustee if either of the following occurs:

- Within 180 days of filing for bankruptcy, you receive or become entitled to receive the type of property discussed below.
- You discover you failed to list some of your nonexempt property in your bankruptcy papers.

Newly Acquired Property

If you receive or become entitled to receive the following types of new property within 180 days after your bankruptcy filing date, you must report it to the trustee, even if you think the property is exempt or your case is already closed:

- an inheritance (property you receive or become entitled to because of someone's death)
- property from a divorce settlement, or
- proceeds of a life insurance policy or death benefit plan. (11 U.S.C. § 541(a)(5).)

(These categories are discussed in more detail in Ch. 3.)

If you don't report it and the trustee learns of your acquisition, the trustee could ask the court to revoke your discharge. (See "Attempts to Revoke Your Discharge," below.)

To report this property to the trustee, use the Supplemental Schedule for Property Acquired After Bankruptcy Discharge form. A blank copy is on the companion page. The other option is to add the property to the Schedule A/B form and check the "amended" box. You might want to call the trustee's office and ask the trustee's preference. When you've filled out one of the forms, follow these steps:

Step 1: Photocopy a Proof of Service by Mail (a blank copy is on the companion page) and fill it out, but don't sign it.

Step 2: Make three photocopies of the Supplemental Schedule and the Proof of Service forms.

Step 3: Have a friend or relative mail the original Supplemental Schedule and a copy of the Proof of Service to the trustee and the U.S. Trustee. Then, sign the Proof of Service.

Step 4: File a copy of the Supplemental Schedule and the original Proof of Service with the bankruptcy court. No additional filing fee is required.

Step 5: Keep a copy of the Supplemental Schedule and the Proof of Service for your records.

In some areas, the court might require you to file amended bankruptcy papers. If that happens, follow the instructions in Ch. 7 in "Amending Your Bankruptcy Papers."

Property Not Listed in Your Papers

If you discover that you forgot to list property in your bankruptcy papers after your bankruptcy case is closed, you don't need to file any documents with the court. You must, however, notify the trustee. A sample letter is shown below.

Letter to Trustee

1900 Wishbone Place
Wilkes-Barre, PA 18704
October 22, 20xx

Francine J. Chen
Trustee of the Bankruptcy Court
217 Federal Building
197 S. Main St.
Wilkes-Barre, PA 18701

Dear Ms. Chen:

I've just discovered that I own some property I didn't know about when my bankruptcy case was open. Apparently, when I was a child, I inherited a bank account from my uncle, the proceeds of which were supposed to be turned over to me when I turned 21. Although I turned 21 eight years ago, for some unknown reason, I never received the money.

The account is in the Bank of New England, 1700 Minuteman Plaza, Boston, MA 02442, and has a balance of $4,975.19. As you know, I opted for the federal exemptions in my case and do not own a home, so I believe this property would be exempt under 11 U.S.C. § 522(d)(5). Please let me know how you intend to proceed.

Sincerely,

Ondine Wallace

Ondine Wallace

CAUTION

Omitting property could put your discharge at risk. If the trustee believes you were playing fast and loose with the bankruptcy court by intentionally omitting the property from your petition, the trustee can reopen your case and attempt to cancel your discharge. If it would appear to a neutral person that your omission could have been deliberate, consult a bankruptcy lawyer before talking to the trustee.

Trustee's Motion to Reopen Your Bankruptcy Case

If the newly discovered property is valuable and nonexempt, the trustee might reopen your case, take the property, and have it sold to pay creditors. As noted above, the trustee will probably do this if it looks like the profit from selling the property will be greater than the cost of reopening your case and administering the sale.

To get to these new assets, the trustee files a motion to reopen the case. Judges usually grant these motions unless they think the property isn't valuable enough to justify reopening or too much time has passed. How much time constitutes "too much" varies with the facts of the case. Once reopened, the trustee will ask for authorization to sell the new assets and distribute the proceeds.

CAUTION

Get help if you're fighting the trustee's attempt to reopen your case. If you can bear to lose the property, consider consenting to what the trustee wants. But if your discharge or valuable property is at stake, consult a bankruptcy lawyer. You could oppose the motion to reopen on your own, but you will need to do a lot of legal research. (See Ch. 10 for tips on lawyers and research.)

Newly Discovered Creditors

Perhaps you inadvertently failed to list a particular creditor on your schedule. As we pointed out in Ch. 7, you can always amend if you discover the omission while your bankruptcy case is still open. But suppose you don't become aware of your omission until your bankruptcy is closed. Does that mean that the debt survives your bankruptcy? Not at all. If the creditor had actual knowledge of your bankruptcy, then it's the same as if the creditor were actually listed in your papers.

Suppose, however, that the omitted creditor didn't have actual knowledge, or you lost track of one or more of your creditors and had no way to identify them in your bankruptcy schedules. Even then, the chances are great that the debt will be considered discharged.

If yours was a no-asset case (all your property was exempt), the debt is considered discharged. The exception would be if leaving out the debt caused your creditor to lose the opportunity to contest the discharge on the grounds of fraudulent or embezzling behavior or a willful and malicious act (such as assault or libel). It is often possible to reopen the bankruptcy and let the bankruptcy judge rule on whether the debt is, in fact, dischargeable. If the creditor sues you in state court for a judgment, you could argue the issue in that forum or have the case removed to bankruptcy court.

Suppose yours was an asset case and your unsecured creditors received funds from your bankruptcy estate. In that case, your situation will be more complicated. Because your nonexempt assets were already distributed to your other unsecured creditors, the omitted creditor would be unfairly discriminated against if the debt were discharged. So you can expect to remain responsible for such a debt. If the debt is large, you might want to hire a lawyer to reopen the case and argue that the debt should be discharged in your particular circumstances. (See Ch. 10 for advice on finding and working with a lawyer.)

Postbankruptcy Attempts to Collect Debts

After bankruptcy, creditors whose debts haven't been discharged are entitled to be paid. Creditors whose debts have been discharged cannot pursue the obligation further. But it isn't always clear into which category a creditor falls. The bankruptcy court doesn't give you an itemized list of your discharged debts. Instead, your final discharge paper merely explains the types of debts that are erased in general terms. Because of this lack of specificity, it can be tough to figure out whether a particular debt has been wiped out.

How do you know which debts have been discharged and which debts must still be paid? Here's the general rule: All debts listed in your bankruptcy papers are discharged unless a creditor successfully objected to the debt's discharge or it falls into one of these categories:

- most student loans (unless you obtained a court ruling that it would be an undue hardship for you to repay them)
- most taxes
- debts you took on to pay nondischargeable taxes
- domestic support, such as child support or alimony
- fines, forfeitures, penalties, and criminal restitution obligations
- debts the court decided are not discharged
- some debts not properly listed
- debts covered by a reaffirmation agreement
- debts related to personal injury or death caused by your intoxicated driving
- debts not discharged in a previous bankruptcy because of fraud or misfeasance
- condominium and cooperative fees incurred after your filing date, or
- loans owed to a pension, profit sharing, stock bonus, or retirement plan.

A creditor can collect a discharged debt from anyone else responsible for paying the debt, such as a cosigner or insurance company. Ch. 9 discusses all of these categories in more detail.

Finally, as noted above, even if a debt is not listed in your bankruptcy papers, it will be considered discharged if yours was a no-asset case—unless the creditor could have successfully challenged the discharge in bankruptcy court if the creditor were properly notified of your case.

Even if you think some of your debts weren't discharged in bankruptcy, the creditors might never try to collect. Many creditors believe that bankruptcy cuts off their rights, period; even attorneys often don't understand that some debts survive bankruptcy.

If a creditor tries to collect a debt after your bankruptcy, inform the creditor that your debts were discharged. Unless you're absolutely sure that the debt wasn't discharged—for example, a student loan the court didn't discharge after an adversary proceeding—this is a defensible position to take.

Letter to Creditor

388 Elm Street
Oakdale, WY 95439
March 18, 20xx

Bank of Wyoming
18th and "J" Streets
Cheyenne, WY 98989

To Whom It May Concern:

I've received numerous letters from your bank claiming that I owe $6,000 for charges between September 20xx and September 20xx. I received a bankruptcy discharge of my debts from the United States Bankruptcy Court, District of Wyoming, on February 1, 20xx, in Case No.: 20xx-01234. A copy of the discharge is enclosed for your reference.

Sincerely,

Brenda Woodruff

Brenda Woodruff

If the creditor ignores your letter and continues collection efforts, there are other ways to respond:

- **Amend your bankruptcy papers.** Remember that an unlisted debt is discharged in a no-asset case unless the creditor was deprived of a chance to oppose the debt's discharge. You can reopen the bankruptcy, amend your papers to list the debt, and then see what the creditor does.
- **Do nothing.** The creditor knows you've just been through bankruptcy, have little or no nonexempt property, and probably have no way to pay the debt, especially all at once. Thus, if you don't respond to collection efforts, the creditor may decide to leave you alone, at least for a while.
- **Try to get judgments wiped out.** If a creditor sued you and won before you filed for bankruptcy, the creditor might try to collect on that judgment unless you can convince a state court that the judgment was discharged in bankruptcy. Creditors with a lien can try to

enforce judgments years after they won them, so it's a good idea for you to reopen the bankruptcy case and file a motion asking the judge to rule that the judgment is discharged and that the lien extinguished. (See Ch. 7 for information on reopening your case.)

- **Negotiate.** If the debt is arguably nondischargeable, you can try to negotiate for a lower balance or a payment schedule that works for you. Again, the creditor knows you've just been through bankruptcy and might be willing to compromise.

- **Defend in court.** If the creditor sues you for a nondischargeable debt, you can raise any defenses you have to the debt itself.

EXAMPLE: The Department of Education sued Emma for failing to pay back a student loan she received. Emma refused to make the payments because the trade school she enrolled in went out of business before classes even began. Because this is a valid defense to collecting a student loan, Emma should talk to a lawyer who will likely ask the court to delay her case while she applies for a discharge.

- **Protest a garnishment or another judgment collection effort.** A creditor who has sued you and won a court judgment for a nondischargeable debt is likely to try to take (garnish) your wages or other property to satisfy the judgment. But the creditor can't take it all. What was exempt during bankruptcy under your state's general exemptions is still exempt. (You'll find lists of exempt property on the companion page.) Nonetheless, the creditor can still request that 25% of your wages be taken out of each paycheck. If the debt was for child support or alimony, the creditor could take even more: up to 60% if you don't currently support anyone and up to 50% if you do. Those amounts could increase by 5% if you haven't paid child support in more than 12 weeks.

Soon after the garnishment—or, in some states, before—the state court must notify you of the garnishment, what's exempt under your state's laws, and how you can protest. You can protest a garnishment if it isn't justified or causes you hardship. To protest, you'll have to file a document in the state court. That document goes by different names in different states. In New York, for example, it's called a Discharge of Attachment; in California, it's a Claim of Exemption. If you protest, the state court must hold a hearing within a reasonable time, where you can present evidence as to why the court should not enforce the garnishment. The court may not agree, but it's certainly worth a try.

Protesting a wage garnishment is usually a relatively straightforward procedure. Because states are required to tell you how to proceed, you'll probably be able to handle it without the assistance of a lawyer.

Most states also have procedures for objecting to other types of property garnishments, such as a levy of a bank account. You'll have to a bit of research at a law library to learn the exact protest procedure, which is generally similar to the one for protesting a wage garnishment. (See Ch. 10 for tips on doing your own research.)

Dealing With Difficult Debts After Bankruptcy

For some debts, such as taxes, child support, or alimony, exempt property may be taken, so a garnishment protest will do little good. Don't be surprised if the U.S. Treasury Department initially garnishes a significant portion of your back federal income taxes. The best strategy is to attempt to negotiate the amount, not to fight the creditor's right to garnish in the first place.

Attempts to Collect Clearly Discharged Debts

A creditor trying to collect a discharged debt will usually stop if you provide three things: the bankruptcy court, case number, and filing date. Why? Because creditors know that continuing could result in penalties. If that doesn't work, try a letter like the one shown above or below (both will work). Again, you can assume a debt was discharged if you listed it in your bankruptcy papers, the creditor didn't successfully object to its discharge, and it doesn't fall into one of the nondischargeable categories listed under "Postbankruptcy Attempts to Collect Debts," above. Also, if yours was a no-asset case, you can assume the debt was discharged even if the debt wasn't listed.

If a debt was discharged, the law prohibits creditors from filing a lawsuit, sending you collection letters, calling you, withholding credit, and threatening to file or actually filing a criminal complaint against you.

Letter to Creditor

1905 Fifth Road
N. Miami Beach, FL 35466

March 18, 20xx

Bank of Miami
2700 Finances Hwy
Miami, FL 36678

To Whom It May Concern:

I've been contacted once by letter and once by phone by Rodney Moore of your bank. Mr. Moore claims that I owe $4,812 on Visa account number 1234 567 890 123.

I've already informed Mr. Moore that this debt was discharged by the United States Bankruptcy Court, Southern District of Florida, on February 1, 20xx. Your collection efforts are in violation of the bankruptcy court's discharge order under federal law, 11 U.S.C. § 524. If the collection attempts continue, I will be forced to pursue my legal rights.

Sincerely,

Dawn Schaffer

Dawn Schaffer

Suppose the collection efforts don't immediately stop. In that case, you'll likely need a lawyer to write the creditor again. If that doesn't work, the next step will be suing the creditor in bankruptcy court (after reopening your case). If the creditor sues you over the debt, consider raising the discharge as a defense and sue the creditor yourself to stop the illegal collection efforts. The bankruptcy court has the power to hold the creditor in contempt.

The court might fine the creditor for the humiliation, inconvenience, and anguish you suffered and order the creditor to pay your attorneys' fees. (See, for example, *In re Barbour*, 77 B.R. 530 (Bankr. E.D. N.C. 1987), where a creditor paid $900 for attempting to collect a discharged debt.)

You can bring a lawsuit to stop collection efforts in state court or federal bankruptcy court. Bankruptcy courts are often more familiar with collection prohibitions and might be more sympathetic. If the creditor sues you in state court, consider requesting a transfer to the bankruptcy court (a local bankruptcy lawyer can help you develop a sound strategy).

A debt collector's attempt to collect a debt discharged in bankruptcy may also violate the federal Fair Debt Collection Practices Act (FDCPA). The FDCPA prohibits debt collectors from engaging in deceptive practices, including misrepresenting a debt's legal status. Several courts have ruled that by stating that payment was due on discharged debts, debt collectors misrepresented the legal status of the debts, and therefore violated the FDCPA. Although the FDCPA applies to debt collectors and not creditors (with a few exceptions), some states have fair debt laws that apply to creditors. If a creditor in one of those states attempts to collect a debt discharged in bankruptcy, you might have a state fair debt claim against it.

Attempts to Revoke Your Discharge

In rare instances, a trustee or creditor might ask the bankruptcy court to revoke the discharge of *all* your debts. If the trustee or a creditor attempts to revoke your discharge, consult a bankruptcy attorney. (See Ch. 10 for tips on finding a lawyer.)

Your discharge can be revoked if the creditor or trustee proves any of the following:

- You obtained the discharge through fraud discovered after you received your discharge.
- You intentionally withheld information about property acquired from an inheritance, a divorce settlement, or a life insurance policy or death benefit plan within 180 days after filing for bankruptcy.
- Before your case was closed, you refused to obey a bankruptcy court order or, for a reason other than the privilege against self-incrimination, refused to answer an important question asked by the court.

For the court to revoke your discharge based on fraud, the trustee or creditor must file a complaint within one year of your discharge. For the court to revoke your discharge based on fraudulent failure to report property or refusal to obey an order or answer a question, the complaint must be filed either within one year of your discharge or before your case is closed, whichever is later. You're entitled to receive a copy of the complaint and to respond. Also, the court must hold a hearing before deciding whether to revoke your discharge.

If your discharge is revoked, you'll owe your debts as if you'd never filed for bankruptcy. However, any payment your creditors received from the trustee will be credited against what you owe.

Postbankruptcy Discrimination

Be aware that current bankruptcy debtors can be denied eligibility for some government programs. For instance, bankruptcy debtors do not qualify for the CARES Act Paycheck Protection Program (PPP).

Although declaring bankruptcy has adverse consequences, discrimination shouldn't be a problem. Laws exist to protect you from most types of postbankruptcy discrimination by the government and private employers.

Government Discrimination

All federal, state, and local governmental units are prohibited from denying, revoking, suspending, or refusing to renew a license, permit, charter, franchise, or other similar grant solely because you filed for bankruptcy. (11 U.S.C. § 525(a).) This law provides important protections, but it does not insulate debtors from all negative impacts of filing for bankruptcy. Lenders, for example, can consider your bankruptcy filing when reviewing an application for a government loan or extension of credit. (See, for example, *Watts v. Pennsylvania Housing Finance Co.*, 876 F.2d 1090 (3rd Cir. 1989) and *Toth v. Michigan State Housing Development Authority*,

136 F.3d 477 (6th Cir. 1998).) Still, under this provision, the government cannot use your bankruptcy as a reason to:

- deny employment or fire you
- deny or terminate your public benefits
- evict you from public housing (although if you have a Section 8 voucher, you might not be protected)
- reject or refuse to renew your state liquor license
- withhold your college transcript
- refuse to issue a driver's license, or
- fail to consider you for a contract, such as a contract for a construction project.

In addition, lenders cannot exclude you from government-guaranteed student loan programs. (11 U.S.C. § 525(c).)

Once a government-related debt has been discharged, all acts against you arising from the debt also must end. For instance, suppose you lost your driver's license after an accident because you didn't pay a court judgment. In that case, you must be granted a license once the debt is discharged. If your license was suspended for lack of insurance, you might need to first meet your state's financial responsibility requirements.

If, however, the judgment wasn't discharged, you can still be denied your license until you pay up. (If you and the government disagree about whether or not the debt was discharged, see "Postbankruptcy Attempts to Collect Debts," above.)

Keep in mind that only government denials based on your bankruptcy are prohibited. You might be denied a loan, job, or apartment, not for reasons related to the bankruptcy but rather your future creditworthiness. For example, the government could doubt whether you'd repay a Small Business Administration loan.

Nongovernment Discrimination

Private employers cannot fire you or otherwise discriminate against you solely because you filed for bankruptcy. (11 U.S.C. § 525(b).) While the law expressly prohibits employers from firing you, employers may refuse to hire you because you went through bankruptcy.

Unfortunately, other forms of discrimination in the private sector aren't illegal. Suppose you want to rent an apartment. The landlord does a credit check, discovers your bankruptcy, and refuses to rent to you. In that case, there's not much you can do other than try to show that you'll be a responsible tenant. Being able to prepay your rent can be helpful, or, if it is permitted under your state's laws, provide a more sizeable security deposit. (However, if you file for bankruptcy during your lease, your landlord cannot use this as a reason to evict you before the lease term is up.)

If a private employer refuses to hire you because of poor credit history—not because you filed for bankruptcy—you might have little recourse. If you suffer illegal bankruptcy discrimination, you can sue in state court or in bankruptcy court. And you'll probably need the assistance of an attorney.

Rebuilding Credit

Although a bankruptcy filing can remain on your credit record for up to ten years, you can rebuild your credit quickly. If you're diligent, you likely won't be turned down for a major loan after three years. Most creditors look for steady employment and a history of making and paying for credit purchases after bankruptcy. And many creditors disregard a bankruptcy after about five years.

RESOURCE

Rebuilding your credit. For more information on rebuilding your credit, see *Credit Repair*, by Amy Loftsgordon and Cara O'Neill (Nolo).

Create a Budget

The first step to rebuilding your credit is to create a budget. Making a budget will help you control impulses to overspend and help you start saving money—an essential part of rebuilding your credit. The budget counseling you received during your bankruptcy case should give you a good start.

Should You Rebuild Your Credit?

Habitual overspending can be just as hard to overcome as excessive gambling or drinking. If you think you might be a compulsive spender, rebuilding your credit might not be a good idea. Consider focusing on curbing spending rather than creating more opportunities to indulge your compulsion.

Debtors Anonymous is a 12-step support program similar to Alcoholics Anonymous. It has programs nationwide. If a Debtors Anonymous group or a therapist recommends staying out of the credit system, follow that advice. Even if you don't feel you're a compulsive spender, paying as you go may still be the best strategy.

Debtors Anonymous meets all over the country. Take a look at its website, which is extremely informative, at www.debtorsanonymous.org. To find a meeting near you, consult the website or send a self-addressed stamped envelope to Debtors Anonymous, General Services Office, P.O. Box 920888, Needham, MA 02492-0009. Or call and speak to a volunteer or leave a message at 800-421-2383.

Before limiting your spending, take time to find out exactly how much you spend now. For the next 30 days, document all your expenses: $5 for your morning coffee, $10 for lunch, $6 for the toll, and so on. Be compliant. Omitting anything will skew the overall picture and render your budget inaccurate.

At the end of the 30 days, review your ledger. Are you surprised? Are you impulsively buying things, or do you tend to make the same purchases consistently? If it's the latter, you'll have an easier time planning a budget than if your spending varies tremendously.

Think about the changes you need to make to put away a few dollars at the end of every week. Even if you think there's nothing to spare, try to set a small goal—even $5 a week. It will help. Spending $5 per day on coffee adds up to $35 per week and at least $140 per month. Making coffee at home might save you most of that amount. If you subscribe to multiple television services, consider canceling those used less frequently.

Avoiding Financial Problems

These nine rules, suggested by people who have been through bankruptcy, will help you stay out of financial trouble.

1. **Create a realistic budget and stick to it.**
2. **Don't buy on impulse.** When you see something you hadn't planned to purchase, go home and think it over. It's unlikely you'll decide to return to the store and buy it.
3. **Avoid sales.** Buying a $500 item on sale for $400 isn't a $100 savings if you didn't need the item in the first place.
4. **Get medical insurance.** Because you can't avoid medical emergencies, living without medical insurance is an invitation to financial ruin.
5. **Charge items only if you can pay for them now.** Don't charge based on future income; sometimes future income doesn't materialize.
6. **Avoid large house payments.** Obligate yourself only for what you can afford now and increase your mortgage payments only as your income increases. Again, don't obligate yourself based on future income that you might not have.
7. **Think long and hard before agreeing to cosign or guarantee a loan for someone.** Your signature obligates you as if you were the primary borrower. You can't be sure that the other person will pay.
8. **Avoid joint obligations with people who have questionable spending habits**—even your spouse or significant other. If you incur a joint debt, you're probably liable for it all if the other person defaults.
9. **Avoid high-risk investments,** such as speculative real estate, penny stocks, and junk bonds. Invest conservatively in things such as certificates of deposit, money market funds, and government bonds. And never invest more than you can afford to lose.

Once you understand your spending habits and identify the changes you need to make, you're ready to make a budget. At the top of a sheet of paper, write down your monthly net income—that is, the amount you bring home after taxes and other mandatory deductions. At the left, list everything you spend money on in a month. Include any bank or other deposit accounts you use or plan to use for saving money and any nondischarged, reaffirmed, or other debts you make payments on. To the right of each item, write down the amount paid each month. Finally, if the total amount exceeds your monthly income, make some changes by eliminating or reducing unnecessary expenditures. Or start over. Once your budget is final, stick to it.

Check Your Credit Report for Accuracy

Some credit reporting agencies temporarily increased the number of free reports provided to help alleviate the effects of COVID-19. The same often occurs after significant security breaches. Check availability independently. Because many benefits expire before printing, we aren't including details here.

Rebuilding your credit requires you to keep incorrect information out of your credit file. Start by obtaining a copy of your file from one of the "big three" credit reporting agencies:

- Equifax
- Experian, and
- TransUnion.

To get your report, don't contact the credit reporting agency itself. Instead, request the report from the Annual Credit Report Request Service, P.O. Box 105283, Atlanta, GA 30348-5283, www.annualcreditreport.com/index.action.

You will need to provide your name and any previous names, addresses for the last two years, telephone number, year or date of birth, employer, and Social Security number.

You are entitled to a free copy of your credit report once a year from each of the three major credit reporting agencies, thanks to an amendment to the Fair Credit Reporting Act (FCRA). If you'd like to monitor your credit, consider requesting a report from one bureau every four months throughout the year. For more information, follow the links at www.ftc.gov.

You can also get a free copy of your report for the following reasons:
- you were denied credit
- your credit account was terminated
- you weren't granted the amount of credit requested
- a creditor made unfavorable changes to your account
- a creditor took adverse actions related to your application for credit
- you are on public assistance
- you're unemployed and planning to look for work in the next 60 days, or
- you believe your file contains errors due to identity theft (fraudulent use of your name, Social Security number, and so on) or someone's fraud.

If you are not entitled to a free copy of your report, expect to pay no more than $20 for a copy from one of the credit reporting agencies.

CAUTION
Don't pay for a credit score. The credit reporting agency might offer to tell you your credit *score* for a fee. You don't need that now. Your goal is to check your credit report to make sure the information in it is accurate.

In addition to your credit history, your credit report will tell you the sources of its information. You'll also see the people or institutions that received your file within one year and potential employers who requested your file within two years.

Credit reports can contain negative information for up to seven years, except for bankruptcy filings, which can remain for ten years. You will want to challenge outdated entries and incorrect or incomplete information. The credit reporting agency must investigate the accuracy of challenged items within 30 days and either correct it or, if it can't verify it, remove it.

Letter to Credit Reporting Agency

74 Ash Avenue
Hanover, NH 03222

March 18, 20xx

Credit Reporters of New England
4118 Main Blvd.
Manchester, NH 03101

To whom it may concern,

Your records incorrectly show that I am unemployed. In fact, I am a self-employed cabinetmaker whose work is known in the community. I receive customers by referral, and, like many, I work out of my home as a result of the COVID-19 pandemic.

Please make the appropriate adjustments to your records.

Sincerely,
Dennis Porter
Dennis Porter

If the agency keeps incorrect information in your file, you're entitled to write your version in a statement of up to 100 words. An example of such a statement is shown above. Be sure it's tied to a particular item in your file so the statement will be removed along with the item. If you write a general "my life was a mess and I got into debt" statement, it will stay for a full seven years even if the negative items are removed sooner.

Your statement, or a summary of it, must be given to anyone who receives your credit report. Also, if you request it, the agency must give a copy to anyone who received your report within the past year, or two years if your report was requested for employment-related reasons.

You also want to keep new negative information out of your file. To do this, remain current on your bills. What you owe, as well as how long it takes you to pay, will show up in that file.

Avoid Credit Repair Agencies

You've probably seen ads for companies that claim they can fix your credit, qualify you for a loan, and get you a credit card. Stay clear of these companies. Their practices are almost always deceptive and sometimes illegal. Some steal the credit files or Social Security numbers of people who have died or live in Guam or the U.S. Virgin Islands and replace your file with these other files. Others create new identities for debtors by applying to the IRS for taxpayer ID numbers and telling debtors to use them in place of their Social Security numbers.

But even the legitimate companies can't do anything you can't do yourself. If items in your credit file are correct, these companies cannot get them removed. The only difference between using a legitimate credit repair agency and doing it yourself is the money you will save by going it alone.

In addition to information about credit accounts, credit reports also contain information from public records, including arrests and lawsuits.

After receiving your bankruptcy discharge, be sure to modify public records to reflect what occurred in the bankruptcy, so wrong information won't appear in your credit file. For example, if a state court case was pending when you filed for bankruptcy and, as part of the bankruptcy, the potential judgment against you was discharged, be sure the state court case is formally dismissed. You might need the help of an attorney. (See Ch. 10 for information on finding a lawyer.)

When Discharged Debts Appear on Your Credit Report

On occasion, a creditor will continue to report a debt that has been discharged in bankruptcy. Although some courts have ruled that listing a discharged debt on a credit report is an attempt to collect the debt in violation of the federal discharge injunction, other courts have allowed it. If a clearly discharged debt shows up on your credit report, make sure it says "discharged in bankruptcy." If it doesn't, see a bankruptcy lawyer and determine whether it makes sense to take action against the creditor or the credit reporting agency.

Negotiate With Some Creditors

If you owe a debt that shows up as past due on your credit file, try to make it current. Contact the creditor and ask that the item be removed in exchange for either full or partial payment. On a revolving account (such as a department store), consider asking the creditor to "re-age" the account—that is, make the current month the first repayment month and show no late payments on the account.

! CAUTION
Think carefully before asking a creditor to re-age your account. If you later fail to keep your payments current, the creditor can report your account to the credit reporting agencies as delinquent based on the later missed payment date rather than the original missed date. The delinquent account will remain on your credit report longer—seven years from the later missed payment date. If you're sure you can keep the account current, re-aging may be a good plan for you.

Stabilize Your Income and Employment

Your credit history is not the only thing lenders will consider in deciding whether to give you credit. They also look carefully at the stability of your income and employment. And, if you start getting new credit before you're back on your feet financially, you'll end up in the same mess that led you to file for bankruptcy in the first place.

Get a Credit Card

Once you have your budget and some money saved, you can begin to get some positive information in your credit file. One way to do this is by getting a secured credit card.

Some banks will give you a credit card and a line of credit if you deposit money into a savings account. These are called secured credit cards. In exchange, you cannot remove the money from your account. If you're worried that it will be difficult to guarantee a hotel reservation or rent a car without at least one major credit card, get such a card if you truly believe you'll control any impulses. Also, keep in mind that many hotels and car rental agencies will do business with you if all you have is a debit card—just be prepared to have a refundable deposit withdrawn from your account.

> **CAUTION**
> **Avoid credit card look-alikes.** Some cards allow you to make purchases only from the issuing company's own catalogs. The items in the catalog tend to be overpriced and of mediocre quality. And your use of the card isn't reported to credit reporting agencies, so you won't be rebuilding your credit.

Another reason to have a credit card is that, in a few years, banks and other large creditors will be more apt to grant you credit if you've made and paid for purchases on credit. However, a significant drawback is that they often have extremely high interest rates. So use the card to buy inexpensive items you can pay for when the bill arrives. Otherwise, you'll pay a bundle in interest and could end up back in financial trouble.

Be sure to shop around before signing up for a secured credit card. Even though you just filed for bankruptcy, you'll probably still get offers for unsecured cards in the mail. Often, these cards have better terms than do secured cards. If you do choose a secured credit card, be sure it isn't secured by your home. And make sure the card issuer reports to the credit reporting agencies. Some don't—which means the card will do little to rebuild your credit.

Work With a Local Merchant

Another step to consider in rebuilding your credit is approaching a local merchant (such as a jewelry or furniture store) about purchasing an item on credit. Many local stores will work with you, but be prepared to pay a deposit of up to 30% and a high interest rate or possibly find a cosigner for the loan.

Borrow From a Bank

Bank loans provide an excellent way to rebuild credit. A few banks offer something called a passbook savings loan. But, in most cases, you'll have to apply for a standard bank loan. You probably won't qualify for such a loan unless you bring in a cosigner, offer some property as collateral, or agree to a very high rate of interest.

The amount you can borrow will depend on how much the bank requires you to deposit (in the case of a passbook loan) or its general loan term limits.

Banks that offer passbook loans typically give you one to three years to repay the loan. But don't pay the loan back too soon—give it about six to nine months to appear on your credit file. Standard bank loans are paid back on a monthly schedule.

Before you take out any loan, be sure you understand the terms:

- **Interest rate.** The interest rate on your loan will probably be between two and six percentage points more than what the bank charges its customers with the best credit.
- **Prepayment penalties.** Usually, you can pay the loan back as soon as you want without incurring any prepayment penalties. Prepayment penalties are fees banks sometimes charge if you pay back a loan early and the bank doesn't collect as much interest from you as expected. The penalty is usually a small percentage of the loan amount.
- **Whether the bank reports the loan to a credit reporting agency.** This is key; the whole reason you want to take out the loan is to rebuild your credit, so you want the loan to appear in your file. You might have to make several calls to find a bank that reports loans.

Which Debts Are Discharged

Not all debts can be discharged in a Chapter 7 bankruptcy. Some debts survive the bankruptcy process—they remain valid and collectable, just as they were before you filed for bankruptcy. To understand what bankruptcy will do for you, you need to know which of your debts, if any, you will still owe after your bankruptcy case is over.

When granting your final discharge, the bankruptcy court won't specify which of your debts have been discharged. Instead, you'll receive a standard form from the court stating that you have received a discharge. (A copy appears on the companion page.) This chapter helps you figure out exactly which of your debts are discharged and which obligations might survive.

Here's the lay of the land:

- Certain kinds of debts are routinely discharged in bankruptcy, except in rare circumstances.
- Some types of debts are never discharged in bankruptcy.
- Student loan debts are not discharged unless you can prove that your situation is an exception to the rule.
- Income tax debts aren't discharged unless they're old—approximately three years or older—and you meet other state law requirements.
- Some types of debts are discharged unless the creditor comes to court and successfully objects to the discharge.

Debts Your Creditors Claim Are Nondischargeable

Some of your creditors may claim that the debts you owe them cannot be wiped out in bankruptcy. For example, computer leases—for software and hardware—often contain clauses stating that if you're unable to complete the lease period, you can't eliminate the balance of the debt in bankruptcy.

Don't fall for it. The only debts you can't discharge in bankruptcy are the ones specifically listed in the Bankruptcy Code as nondischargeable—and we'll describe them in this chapter. Don't let your creditors intimidate you into thinking otherwise.

Debts That Will Be Discharged in Bankruptcy

Certain types of debts will be erased when you receive your Chapter 7 discharge—that is, you will no longer be responsible for repaying them. If you have nonexempt assets, the bankruptcy trustee will divide the proceeds among your creditors, and at the end of your case, the court will discharge any balance that remains unpaid.

Credit Card Debts

Without a doubt, the vast majority of those who file for bankruptcy want to get rid of credit card debts. Happily, most bankruptcy filers succeed in this mission. Credit card debts are typically wiped out in bankruptcy, with the exception of a few rare cases involving fraud or luxury purchases made immediately before filing for bankruptcy. (See "Debts That Survive Chapter 7 Bankruptcy," below).

Medical Bills

Many people who file for bankruptcy got into financial trouble because of medical bills. Despite attempts to make health insurance more affordable, many Americans either have inadequate insurance from their employers or can't afford the deductibles in the available plans.

Luckily, bankruptcy provides an out: Your medical bills will be discharged at the end of your bankruptcy case. In fact, an enormous amount of medical bills are discharged in bankruptcy every year.

Lawsuit Judgments

Most civil court cases are about money. If someone wins one of these lawsuits against you, the court issues a judgment ordering you to pay. If you don't come up with the money voluntarily, the judgment holder can collect it by, for example, grabbing your bank account, levying your wages, or placing a lien on your home.

Money judgments are usually dischargeable in bankruptcy, regardless of the facts that led to the lawsuit in the first place. There are a couple of exceptions (discussed in "Debts That Survive Chapter 7 Bankruptcy," below), but in the vast majority of cases, money judgments are discharged. You can even cancel liens on your home arising from a court money judgment if they interfere with your homestead exemption. (See Ch. 5 for more on how bankruptcy affects a judicial lien on your home.)

Debts Arising From Car Accidents

Car accidents usually result in property damage and sometimes in personal injuries. Often, the driver responsible for the accident is insured and doesn't have to pay personally for the damage or injury. But sometimes the driver at fault has insufficient insurance and remains financially responsible for the harm.

If the accident resulted from the debtor's negligence—careless driving or failing to drive in a prudent manner—the debtor can discharge the debt arising from the accident. This is true even if the accident was the result of reckless driving. If, however, the accident was due to the driver's willful and malicious act or impaired driving, it will survive bankruptcy. (See "Debts Not Dischargeable in Bankruptcy If the Creditor Successfully Objects," below).

Obligations Under Leases and Contracts

It's becoming more common for people to lease things rather than own them. However, financial problems can arise when severe penalty clauses kick in because you can't make the monthly payment or fail to do something required by the lease.

Some debtors also have contractual obligations to do things like sell real estate, buy a business, deliver merchandise, or perform in some other way. If you can't uphold your end of the deal, the other party might want to force you to by suing you for breach of contract damages.

Typically, you can discharge your liability for both types of obligations in bankruptcy. A bankruptcy filing will convert your lease or contractual obligation into a dischargeable debt unless the trustee believes the lease or contract will produce money to pay your unsecured creditors or the court finds that you've filed for bankruptcy to get out of a personal services contract (such as a recording contract).

Personal Loans and Promissory Notes

The money you borrow in exchange for a promissory note—or even a handshake and an oral promise to pay the money back—is almost always dischargeable in bankruptcy. As with any debt, the court could refuse to discharge a loan debt if the creditor can prove that you acted fraudulently; however, that rarely happens. (See "Debts That Survive Chapter 7 Bankruptcy," below.)

Other Obligations

Not all debts are dischargeable in bankruptcy. So how do you know whether you can wipe out all of your debts? The rule is simple. You can eliminate an obligation or debt unless it fits within one of the exceptions discussed in "Debts That Survive Chapter 7 Bankruptcy," below.

Debts That Survive Chapter 7 Bankruptcy

In Chapter 7, several categories of debt are "not dischargeable." That is, you'll still owe them after your bankruptcy is final. For instance, some debts:
- can't be discharged under any circumstances
- will not be discharged unless you convince the court that they fit within a narrow exception to the rule, and
- will be discharged unless the creditor convinces the court that they shouldn't be.

> ### Are Secured Debts Dischargeable?
>
> Secured debts are contractually linked to specific items of property, called collateral. If you don't pay the debt, the creditor can take the collateral. The most common secured debts include loans for cars and homes. If you have a debt secured by collateral, bankruptcy eliminates your personal liability for the underlying debt—that is, the creditor can't sue you to collect the debt itself. But bankruptcy doesn't eliminate the creditor's hold, or "lien," on the property that served as collateral under the contract. Other types of secured debts arise involuntarily, often due to a lawsuit judgment or an enforcement action by the IRS on taxes that are old enough to be discharged (covered below). In these cases, bankruptcy eliminates the underlying debt but might not extinguish a lien placed on your property by the IRS or a judgment creditor.
>
> Chapter 7 offers several options for dealing with secured debts, such as buying the property from the creditor for its replacement value, reaffirming the contract, or surrendering it. You'll find options for dealing with secured debts in Ch. 5.

Debts Not Dischargeable Under Any Circumstances

Bankruptcy doesn't affect certain debts at all. You will continue to owe these debts after your case closes.

Domestic Support Obligations

Debts defined as "domestic support obligations" are not dischargeable. Domestic support obligations include child support, alimony, maintenance, and spousal support. For example, suppose a spouse agreed to pay some of the other spouse's or the children's future living expenses (shelter, clothing, health insurance, and transportation) in exchange for a lower support obligation. The bankruptcy court could treat the obligation to pay future living expenses as nondischargeable support owed to the other spouse even though a family law court didn't order it.

But the rule doesn't apply to all debts owed between ex-spouses. To be nondischargeable under this section, a domestic support obligation must have been established or be capable of being established in:

- a separation agreement, divorce decree, or property settlement agreement
- an order of a court authorized by law to impose support obligations, or
- a determination by a child support enforcement agency or another government unit legally authorized to impose support obligations.

A support obligation assigned to a private entity for reasons other than collection (for example, as collateral for a loan) is dischargeable, but this exception rarely applies. Almost all assignments of support to government or private entities are for support collection.

Other Debts Owed to a Spouse, Former Spouse, or Child

Under the old bankruptcy law, debts owed to a spouse or child, with the exception of support arising from a divorce or separation, were discharged unless the spouse or child appeared in court to contest the debt. Under the 2005 bankruptcy law, this category of debt is now automatically nondischargeable. The most common of these types of debts is when one spouse agrees to assume responsibility for marital debt or promises to pay the other spouse in exchange for his or her share of the family home. These types of obligations will now be nondischargeable if they are owed to a spouse, former spouse, or child, and arose out of "a divorce or separation or in connection with a separation agreement, divorce decree, or other order of a court of record, or a determination made in accordance with State or territorial law by a governmental unit." (11 U.S.C. § 523 (15).)

It is important to realize that Chapter 13 treats these types of debts differently. If a court finds that an obligation arising out of a divorce is not in the nature of support, then it is treated like other general unsecured debts in the Chapter 13 plan. An example would be a property division agreement wherein one spouse pays to keep more property than they're entitled to. An outstanding balance could be eliminated in Chapter 13, but not Chapter 7. (*In re Nelson*, 451 B.R. 918 (Bankr. D. Or. 2011).)

However, debts that are not nondischargeable against an exspouse might still be dischargeable against the actual creditor. For instance, suppose that the debtor erases a joint credit card debt the debtor was obligated to pay pursuant to a settlement agreement. In that case, the creditor would sue the exspouse for payment of the debt, and the exspouse would seek reimbursement from the debtor (check with your family law attorney to determine whether this applies in your jurisdiction).

Fines, Penalties, and Restitution

You can't discharge fines, penalties, or restitution that a federal, state, or local government has imposed to punish you for violating a law. Examples include:

- fines or penalties imposed under federal election law
- charges imposed for time spent in a court jail (*In re Donohue*, No. 05-01651 (Bankr. N.D. Iowa 2006))
- fines for infractions, misdemeanors, or felonies
- fines imposed by a judge for contempt of court
- fines imposed by a government agency for violating agency regulations
- surcharges imposed by a court or an agency for enforcement of a law restitution you are ordered to pay to victims in federal criminal cases, and
- debts owed to a bail bond company as a result of bond forfeiture.

However, one court has held that a restitution obligation imposed on a minor in a juvenile court proceeding can be discharged, because it isn't punitive in nature. (*In re Sweeney*, 492 F.3d 1189 (10th Cir. 2007).)

Overpayments by a government entity are not by themselves nondischargeable. Often the overpayment is due to a clerical error by the agency and not attributable to the recipient's wrongdoing. In such cases, the debt is dischargeable unless one of the following applies:

- The agency makes a finding after a hearing was held or offered, that the overpayment was fraudulent.
- The overpayment is a fine or penalty.

Otherwise, the debt will be discharged unless the agency comes into bankruptcy court and proves fraud.

Certain Tax Debts

While regular income tax debts are dischargeable if they're sufficiently old and meet other jurisdictional requirements, other taxes are frequently not dischargeable. The specific rules depend on the type of tax and the rules where you live. (See "Debts Not Dischargeable Unless You Can Prove That an Exception Applies," below.)

Fraudulent income taxes. You cannot discharge debts for income taxes if you didn't file a return or you were intentionally avoiding your tax obligations. Returns filed on your behalf by the IRS are not considered filed by you, and therefore don't make you eligible for a discharge of income tax debt. Also, your state might have other rules. For instance, in California, you can't discharge income taxes if you filed a late return.

Property taxes. Property taxes aren't dischargeable unless they became due more than a year before filing for bankruptcy. And even if your personal liability to pay the property tax is discharged, any tax lien on your property will remain. So from a practical standpoint, this discharge won't help if you'll have to pay off the lien to transfer the property with clear title. And you might face a tax foreclosure action if you take too long to come up with the money.

Other taxes. Business-related payroll taxes, excise taxes, and customs duties aren't dischargeable. Sales, use, and poll taxes are likely not dischargeable.

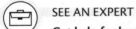 SEE AN EXPERT

Get help for business tax debts. If you owe any of these nondischargeable tax debts, see a bankruptcy attorney before you file.

Court Fees

Prisoners can't discharge a fee imposed by a court for filing a complaint, motion, or appeal, or for other costs and expenses assessed for that court filing, even if you claim an inability to afford the fees. (You can discharge these fees in Chapter 13, however.)

Intoxicated Driving Debts

If you kill or injure someone while driving under the influence of alcohol or drugs, any debts resulting from the incident won't be dischargeable. The debt might even be nondischargeable if a judge or jury finds you liable for the accident but remains silent on intoxication if the bankruptcy court (or a state court in a judgment collection action) determines that you were, in fact, intoxicated.

This rule applies only to personal injuries. Debts for property damage resulting from your intoxicated driving are dischargeable.

> **EXAMPLE:** A state court convicted Christopher of driving under the influence after he injured Destiny and damaged her car in a motor vehicle accident. Several months later, Christopher listed Destiny as a creditor when he filed for bankruptcy. After the bankruptcy case was over, Destiny sued Christopher, claiming that the debt wasn't discharged because Christopher was driving while intoxicated. (She didn't have to file anything in the bankruptcy proceeding.) If Destiny shows that Christopher was illegally intoxicated under his state's laws, she will be able to pursue her personal injury claim against him. She is barred, however, from trying to collect the damage to her car.

Condominium, Cooperative, and Homeowners' Association Fees

You can discharge these fees if you incurred them before filing for bankruptcy. However, you cannot discharge fees for a condominium or housing cooperative assessed by the membership association *after* your bankruptcy filing date. As a practical matter, the rule that applies to any qualified debt incurred after your bankruptcy filing applies here, as well: Fees that come due after filing for Chapter 7 will survive the bankruptcy, but you can discharge fees you owed before filing.

You might be wondering why we bring this up if the rule is essentially the same. Here's why.

It's not uncommon for condominium ownership to continue after a bankruptcy filing even though the debtor has already moved out. For instance, suppose a condo owner facing foreclosure files for bankruptcy and vacates the property. Even though the condo fees assessed before the bankruptcy will be discharged, condo fees (and property taxes) will continue to accrue in the owner's name until the unit is sold and ownership is transferred to a third party. Filing for bankruptcy affects debt, but it doesn't change property title.

Debts for Loans From a Retirement Plan

If you've borrowed from your 401(k) or another retirement plan that qualifies for tax deferred status under IRS rules, you'll be stuck with that debt. Bankruptcy doesn't discharge 401(k) loans because you can only discharge debts owed to another person or entity. You loan funds borrowed from a 401(k) to yourself. (However, you can discharge a retirement loan plan in Chapter 13.)

Debts You Couldn't Discharge in a Previous Bankruptcy

If a bankruptcy court dismissed a previous bankruptcy case because of your fraud or other bad acts (for instance, misfeasance or failure to cooperate with the trustee), you cannot discharge any debts listed in the earlier bankruptcy. This rule doesn't affect debts you incurred after filing the earlier bankruptcy case.

Debts Not Dischargeable Unless You Can Prove That an Exception Applies

Some debts can't be discharged in Chapter 7 without proving to the bankruptcy court that it falls within an exception. You can take one of two approaches:

- While your case is open, ask the bankruptcy court to rule that the debt should be eliminated. To do this, you have to file and serve a Complaint to Determine Dischargeability of a Debt and then show, in court, that your debt isn't covered by the general rule. (The grounds and procedures for getting such debts discharged are discussed in "Disputes Over Dischargeability," below.) If you succeed, the court will rule that the debt is discharged, and the creditor won't be allowed to collect it after bankruptcy.

- In the alternative, you might decide not to take any action during your bankruptcy. If the creditor attempts to collect after your case is closed, you can try to reopen your bankruptcy and raise the issue then (by bringing a contempt motion or by filing a Complaint to Determine Dischargeability). Or, you can wait until the creditor sues you over the debt or tries to collect on the judgment, then argue in state court that the debt has been discharged.

By not raising the issue while your bankruptcy case is open you can avoid the hassle of litigating the issue. And the problem might never come up again if the creditor doesn't pursue the debt. However, questions about whether the debt has been discharged will be left hanging over your head after the bankruptcy case is over.

Generally, you are better off litigating dischargeability issues in the bankruptcy court—either during or after your bankruptcy—because bankruptcy courts tend to tilt in the interest of giving the debtor a fresh start, and might be more willing to give you the benefit of the doubt. This is especially true when your creditor is a federal or state taxing agency or a student loan creditor, as well. However, you might be better off not doing so if you're up against an individual creditor whose claim isn't big enough to justify hiring a lawyer. These creditors are probably less likely to pursue you—or even know that they can—after your bankruptcy is over.

Student Loans

Whether made by the government, a nonprofit, or a private lender, virtually all student loans are not dischargeable unless the debtor shows undue hardship.

To discharge your student loan based on undue hardship, you must file a separate action in the bankruptcy court (a Complaint to Determine Dischargeability of Student Loan) and obtain a court ruling in your favor. Succeeding in an action to discharge a student loan debt typically requires the services of an attorney. However, it's possible to do it yourself if you're willing to put in the time and deal with skeptical judges. (See "Disputes Over Dischargeability," below.)

When determining whether undue hardship exists, courts use several tests (depending on where the court is located). In two of the more commonly used tests, courts look at either:

- the three factors listed below (these come from a case called *Brunner v. New York State Higher Education Services, Inc.*, 46 B.R. 752 (S.D.N.Y. 1985), aff'd, 831 F.2d 395 (2nd Cir. 1987)), or
- the totality of the circumstances, which essentially means the court will consider all of the facts it deems relevant in deciding whether undue hardship exists.

The majority of courts use the *Brunner* three-factor test. You must show that all three factors tilt in your favor to demonstrate undue hardship. The factors are:

- **Poverty.** Based on your current income and expenses, you cannot maintain a minimal standard of living and repay the loan. The court must consider your current and future employment and income (or your employment and income potential), education, and skills; how marketable your skills are; your health; and your family support obligations.
- **Persistence.** It's not enough that you can't repay your loan right now. You must also show that your current financial condition is likely to continue for a significant part of the repayment period. For example, a debtor with bipolar disorder lost her job after stopping her medication. Because her history demonstrated that she could remain employed as long as she took her medication, however, the court found that her economic condition would not necessarily persist—and it rejected her undue hardship claim. (*In re Kelly*, 351 B.R. 45 (Bankr. E.D.N.Y. 2006).)
- **Good faith.** You must prove that you've made a good-faith effort to repay the debt. Someone who files for bankruptcy immediately after getting out of school or after the period for paying back the loan begins will not fare well in court. Nor will someone who hasn't tried hard to find work. And if you haven't made payments, it helps to show that you've applied for a deferment or forbearance. (See *In re Kitterman*, 349 B.R. 775 (Bankr. W.D. Ky. 2006), in which the court found that the debtor lacked a good faith effort to repay his

student loans because he didn't reapply for a deferment after his first request for a deferment was denied.) In the past, many courts also found that the debtor's failure to apply for one of the federal flexible repayment programs was grounds to deny a request to discharge student loans. But that is changing somewhat. Some courts have discharged student loans even when the debtor did not apply for a reduced payment plan under one of the federal student loan repayment programs, a forbearance, or deferment. (See *In re Roth*, 490 B.R. 908, 919 (BAP 9th Cir. 2013).) Those courts insist that it's important to look at each debtor's particular situation.

In the past it was challenging to discharge student loans under most circumstances and that is still the case in some jurisdictions. This doesn't mean that the factors cannot be met, however—they can. (See *In re Lamento*, 520 B.R. 667 (Bankr. N.D. Ohio 2014).) Fortunately, other courts are beginning to discharge loans that they might not have ten years ago. For example, a Nebraska court discharged the student loans of a 28-year-old woman who could not secure higher paying employment after diligently trying for several years. (*In Matter of DeLaet*, 2015 WL 850629 (Bankr. D. Neb. 2015).) In Illinois, the court did not require proof that the debtor made actual student loan payments in the past when the overall circumstances evidenced a lack of ability to pay. (*Krieger v. Educ. Credit Mgmt. Corp.*, 713 F.3d 882 (7th Cir. 2013).)

The bottom line is that while it is still difficult to meet the standard necessary to discharge student loans, courts will do it in the right circumstances, and, as the new student loan crisis unfolds, it appears some courts may even soften the traditionally harsh application of *Brunner*.

Getting Your Transcript

If you don't pay back loans obtained directly from your college, the school can withhold your transcript. But if you file for bankruptcy and receive a discharge of the loan, the school can no longer withhold your records. In addition, while your bankruptcy case is pending, the school cannot withhold your transcript, even if the court eventually rules your school loan nondischargeable. (*In re Aleckna*, 543 B.R. 717 (M.D. Pa. 2016).)

SEE AN EXPERT

Consult with a lawyer about discharging your loan. There are dozens of court cases that interpret the three factors from the *Brunner* case or explain what the "totality of the circumstances" include. If you are filing for bankruptcy and you have substantial student loan debt, you should talk to an attorney who is knowledgeable on these issues.

If the cost of an attorney seems impossibly high, do a quick cost–benefit analysis. If you have an excellent chance of getting your loan discharged, paying an attorney $5,000 to help you discharge a $30,000 loan would not be a bad deal. On the other hand, if your loan is $10,000, the deal won't look as good.

Because no lawyer can guarantee a successful outcome no matter how good your case is, to some extent, you are gambling $5,000 to win $30,000 (win in the sense that you wouldn't have to pay back the loan). To minimize the risk, you might consider paying one or two attorneys a few hundred dollars each for opinions on your likelihood of success. If they agree that you would probably get the loan discharged, you might feel better paying $5,000 (or more) for help in getting the student loan discharged.

Regular Income Taxes

People who are considering bankruptcy because of tax problems are almost always concerned about income taxes they owe to the IRS or the state equivalent. It's a myth that income tax debts can never be discharged in bankruptcy. However, this is not true if the debt is relatively old and you can meet several other conditions. Tax debts that qualify under these rules are technically discharged; however, you might have to file a complaint in the bankruptcy court to determine dischargeability of the debt and have the judge order the IRS to honor the discharge.

Income tax debts are dischargeable if you meet all of these conditions:

- You filed a legitimate (nonfraudulent) tax return for the tax year or years in question. If the IRS completes a Substitute for Return on your behalf that you neither sign nor consent to, your return is not considered filed. (See *In re Bergstrom*, 949 F.2d 341 (10th Cir. 1991).)
- You want to discharge the liability for a tax return (not a Substitute for Return) that you actually filed at least two years before you filed for bankruptcy.

- The tax return for the liability you wish to discharge was first due at least three years before you filed for bankruptcy. (If you filed for an extension, the three-year period begins on the extended due date, not the original due date.)

- The IRS has not assessed your liability for the taxes within the 240 days before you filed for bankruptcy. You're probably safe if you do not receive a formal notice of assessment of federal taxes from the IRS within that 240-day period. If you're unsure of the assessment date, consider seeing a tax lawyer—but don't rely on the IRS for the date. If the IRS gives you the wrong date—telling you that the 240 days have elapsed—the IRS won't be held to it if it turns out to be incorrect. (See, for example, *In re Howell*, 120 B.R. 137 (BAP 9th Cir. 1990).) Under the 2005 bankruptcy law, the 240-day period is extended by the time collections were suspended because you were negotiating with the IRS for an offer in compromise or because of a previous bankruptcy.

  EXAMPLE: Andrew filed a tax return in August 2014 for the 2013 tax year. In March 2016, the IRS audited Andrew's 2018 return and assessed a tax due of $8,000. In May 2022, Andrew files for bankruptcy. The taxes that Andrew wishes to discharge were for tax year 2018. The return for those taxes was due on April 15, 2019, more than three years before Andrew's filing date. The tax return was filed in August 2019, more than two years before Andrew's bankruptcy filing date, and the assessment date of March 2021 was more than 240 days before the filing date. Andrew can discharge those taxes.

- You didn't willfully evade payment of a tax. What constitutes willful tax evasion is a subjective matter, depending on the view of the IRS personnel making the judgment. (See "Willful Evasion of Tax," below, for a list of factors that might cause the IRS to suspect willful tax evasion.) The Sixth Circuit Court of Appeals ruled that the mere fact that a debtor did not pay income tax is not enough for the IRS to prove that the nonpayment was willful or intentional without other evidence. (*U.S. v. Storey*, 640 F.3d 739 (6th Cir. 2011).)

TIP

Get an account transcript to make sure you've got the dates right. If you want to make sure you have met all the requirements to get a tax debt discharged, you can obtain an account transcript from the IRS. To find out how, visit www.irs.gov and type "account transcript" in the search box.

If you meet each of these five requirements, your personal liability for the taxes should be discharged. However, any lien placed on your property by the taxing authority will remain after your bankruptcy. The result is that the taxing authority can't go after your bank account or wages, but you'll have to pay off the lien before you can sell your real estate (or other property to which the lien is attached) with a clear title.

Penalties and interest on dischargeable taxes are also dischargeable. If the underlying tax debt is nondischargeable, courts are split as to whether you can discharge the penalties or not.

> **EXAMPLE:** Jenna failed to file a tax return for 2015. In 2019, the IRS discovered Jenna's failure and, in January 2021, assesses taxes of $5,000 and penalties and interest of $12,000. Jenna files for bankruptcy in January 2022. Because Jenna didn't file a return for 2015, she can't discharge the tax, even though it became due more than three years past (and more than 240 days have elapsed since the taxes were assessed). Jenna might be able to discharge the IRS penalties for failure to file a tax return and failure to pay the tax. Or course, the IRS is likely to argue that she cannot discharge the penalties, and some courts will agree.

CAUTION

Debts incurred to pay nondischargeable taxes will also be nondischargeable. If you borrowed money or used your credit card to pay taxes that would otherwise not be discharged, you can't eliminate that loan or credit card debt in a Chapter 7 bankruptcy. In other words, you can't turn a nondischargeable tax debt into a dischargeable tax debt by paying it on your credit card. This is true for any type of nondischargeable tax owed to a governmental agency. You might consider using Chapter 13 instead, which allows you to discharge this type of debt.

Different Rules Apply Out West

If you try to discharge your student loans in one of the federal courts that make up the 9th Circuit Court of Appeals (which includes Alaska, Arizona, California, Hawaii, Idaho, Montana, Nevada, Oregon, Utah, and Washington), a much wider variety of factors might be considered. Circumstances that could potentially allow a discharge include:

• The debtor or debtor's dependent has a severe mental or physical disability preventing employment or advancement.
• The debtor must care for dependents.
• The debtor has a lack of, severely limited, or poor quality education.
• The debtor has a lack of usable or marketable job skills.
• The debtor is underemployed.
• The debtor's income potential has maxed out and the debtor doesn't have other lucrative job skills.
• The debtor has limited work years remaining in which to pay back the loan.
• The debtor's age or other factors prevent retraining or relocation as a means of earning more to repay the loan.
• The debtor lacks assets that could be used to repay the loan.
• The debtor's potentially increasing expenses outweigh any potential appreciation in the debtor's assets or increases in the debtor's income.
The debtor lacks better financial options elsewhere.
(See *Educational Credit Management Corp. v. Nys*, 446 F.3d 938 (9th Cir. 2006).)

Some western courts have used the *Nys* factors in discharging student loans of relatively young, able-bodied, working debtors. For example, in *Scott v. U.S. Dept. of Ed.*, 417 B.R. 623 (Bankr. W.D. Wash. 2009), the court discharged the student loans of a young couple with children who had no realistic prospects of earning more income in the future and could not maintain a minimum standard of living while making loan payments. And in *Hedlund v. Educational Resources Institute*, 718 F.3d 848 (9th Cir. 2013), the 9th Circuit discharged a portion of a thirty-something man's law school loans because he never passed the bar exam, did not have a realistic possibility of earning more than his $40,000 per year salary as a probation officer, repeatedly tried to work out a payment plan, and could not maintain a minimum standard of living for himself and his family while paying back $85,000 in student loans. Despite these rulings, however, the bar is still high for discharging student loans, so be sure to consult with an experienced bankruptcy lawyer (or two) to get an opinion in your case.

Willful Evasion of Tax

The IRS views certain facts as red flags of possible willful tax evasion. They include:

- membership in a tax protest organization
- a pattern of unfiled returns
- filing a fraudulent, frivolous, blank, or incomplete return
- repeatedly understating income or overstating deductions on returns
- serial failure to pay taxes
- concealing, giving away, or trading away valuable assets or transferring title
- selling assets way below fair value (especially to insiders)
- setting up an abusive trust or sham tax shelter and transferring assets to it
- creating a corporation and transferring assets to it
- changing banks or bank accounts frequently
- closing bank accounts and conducting business in cash only
- adding another person's name to a bank account
- depositing income in another's bank account
- using a foreign bank account
- changing your name or the spelling of your name
- changing your Social Security number
- an altercation with a revenue officer
- engaging in money laundering
- withdrawing cash from a bank and hiding it
- claiming an incorrect number of exemptions on your tax return
- purchasing property in someone else's name
- refusing to cooperate with a revenue officer or deliberately obstructing an audit or investigation
- losing, concealing, or destroying financial documents
- maintaining inadequate records
- hiding your actual residence address or business address
- trading valuable assets for less valuable assets
- devising clever schemes such as divorcing your spouse, directing all income to him or her, and renting a room in his or her house, and
- living a lavish lifestyle knowing that delinquent taxes have not been paid.

Debts Not Dischargeable in Bankruptcy If the Creditor Successfully Objects

Four types of debts survive Chapter 7 bankruptcy if, and only if, the creditor both:

- files a formal objection—called a Complaint to Determine Dischargeability—during the bankruptcy proceedings, and
- proves that the debt fits into one of the categories discussed below.

> **TIP**
>
> **Creditors might not bother to object.** Even though bankruptcy rules give creditors the right to object to the discharge of certain debts, many creditors—and their attorneys—don't fully understand this right. Even a creditor who knows the score might sensibly decide to write off the debt rather than contest it. It can cost a lot to bring a dischargeability action (as this type of case is known). If the debt isn't huge, a cost–benefit analysis might show that it will be cheaper to forgo collecting the debt than to fight about it in court.

Debts Arising From Fraud

For a creditor to prove that one of your debts should survive bankruptcy because you incurred it through fraud, the debt must fit one of the categories below.

Debts from intentionally fraudulent behavior. If a creditor can show that a debt arose because of your dishonest act, and that the transaction wouldn't have occurred had you been honest, the court probably will not let you discharge the debt. Here are some common examples:

- You wrote a check for something and stopped payment on it, even though you kept the item.
- You wrote a check against insufficient funds but assured the merchant that the check was good.
- You rented or borrowed an expensive item and claimed it was yours, to use it as collateral to get a loan.
- You got a loan by telling the lender you'd pay it back, when you had no intention of doing so.

For this type of debt to be nondischargeable, your deceit must be intentional, and the creditor must have relied on it when extending credit. Again, these are facts that the creditor has to prove before the debt will be ruled nondischargeable by the court.

Debts from a false written statement about your financial condition. If a creditor proves that you incurred a debt by making a false written statement, the debt isn't dischargeable. Here are the rules:

- The false statement must be written—for instance, made in a credit application, rental application, or résumé.
- The false statement must have been "material"—that is, it was a potentially significant factor in the creditor's decision to extend you credit. The two most common materially false statements are omitting debts and overstating income.
- The false statement must relate to your financial condition or the financial condition of an "insider"—a person close to you or a business entity with which you're associated.
- The creditor must have relied on the false statement, and the reliance must have been reasonable.
- You must have intended to deceive the creditor. The creditor would likely try to show deceptive behavior on your part, such as by inflating your income on a credit application.

Recent debts for luxuries. If you run up more than $725 in debt to any one creditor for luxury goods or services within the 90 days before you file for bankruptcy, the law presumes that your intent was fraudulent. If the creditor presents these facts to the bankruptcy court, all the charges will survive your bankruptcy unless you prove that your intent wasn't fraudulent. "Luxury goods and services" do not include things that are reasonably necessary for the support and maintenance of you and your dependents. What that means is decided on a case-by-case basis, but generally, items such as food, inexpensive clothing, utilities, and gas to get to work would likely be considered necessary for support.

Recent cash advances. If you get cash advances from any one creditor totaling more than $1,000 under an open-ended consumer credit plan within the 70 days before you file for bankruptcy, the debt is non-dischargeable if the creditor presents these facts to the court. "Open-ended" means there's no date when the debt must be repaid, but rather, as with most credit cards, you may take forever to repay the debt as long as you pay a minimum amount each month.

Debts Arising From Debtor's Willful and Malicious Acts

If the act that caused the debt was willful *and* malicious (that is, you intended to inflict a specific injury to person or property), the debt isn't dischargeable if the creditor successfully objects. However, for reasons probably related to ignorance of their rights, creditors don't often object in this situation.

Generally, crimes involving intentional injury to people or damage to property are considered willful and malicious acts. Examples are assaults, rape, intentionally setting fire to a house (arson), or vandalism.

Your liability for personal injury or property damage the victim sustained in these types of cases will almost always be ruled nondischargeable—but (once again) only if the victim-creditor objects during your bankruptcy case. Other acts that would typically be considered to be willful and malicious include:

- kidnapping
- deliberately causing extreme anxiety, fear, or shock
- libel or slander, and
- illegal actions by a landlord to evict a tenant, such as removing a door or changing the locks.

Debts From Embezzlement, Larceny, or Breach of Fiduciary Duty

A debt incurred due to embezzlement, larceny, or breach of fiduciary duty is not dischargeable if the creditor successfully objects to its discharge.

"Embezzlement" means taking property entrusted to you for another and using it for yourself. "Larceny" is another word for theft. "Breach of fiduciary duty" is the failure to live up to a duty of trust you owe someone, based on a relationship where you're required to manage property or money for another, or where your relationship is a close and confidential one. Common fiduciary relationships include those between:

- spouses
- business partners
- attorney and client
- estate executor and beneficiary
- in-home caregiver and recipient of services, and
- guardian and ward.

Debts or Creditors You Don't List

Bankruptcy requires you to list all of your creditors on your bankruptcy papers and provide their most current addresses. This gives the court some assurance that everyone who needs to know about your bankruptcy will receive notice. As long as you do your part, the debt will be discharged as long as it's otherwise dischargeable under the rules, even if the official notice fails to reach the creditor for some reason beyond your control—for example, because the post office errs or the creditor moves without leaving a forwarding address.

Suppose, however, that you forget to list a creditor on your bankruptcy papers or carelessly misstate a creditor's identity or address. In that situation, the court's notice may not reach the creditor and the debt may not be discharged. Here are the rules:

- If the creditor knew or should have known of your bankruptcy through other means, such as a letter or phone call from you, the debt will be discharged even though the creditor wasn't listed. In this situation, the creditor should have taken steps to protect its interests, even though it didn't receive formal notice from the court.
- If all of your assets are exempt—that is, you have a no-asset case— the debt will be discharged unless the debt is nondischargeable in any circumstances. In this situation, the creditor wouldn't have benefited from receiving notice because there is no property to distribute. However, if the lack of notice deprives a creditor of the opportunity to successfully object to the discharge by filing a complaint in the bankruptcy court (such as for a fraudulent debt), the obligation may survive your bankruptcy.

If an Unknown Creditor Pops Up After Bankruptcy
If a creditor comes out of the woodwork after your bankruptcy is closed, you can always reopen it, name the creditor, and then seek an amended discharge. (See Ch. 7 for more on reopening a case.) If it's the kind of debt that will be discharged anyway, many courts won't let you reopen because there is no need to. The debt is discharged by law and most creditors know this. However, if the creditor continues to try to collect the debt, you can haul the creditor into bankruptcy court on a contempt charge.

Disputes Over Dischargeability

If your debt is not one that's automatically discharged, there could be a dispute over whether the debt should survive your bankruptcy. For example, if the debt is one you must prove should be discharged, you might have to file a Complaint to Determine Dischargeability. Or, if the creditor must prove that the debt should not be discharged, you might have to defend yourself in court against the creditor's claims.

Complaints to Determine Dischargeability

If you want to have a student loan or tax debt wiped out, you will have to prove to the court that you meet all of the requirements for discharge. To do this, you must file a formal complaint with the bankruptcy court along with a summons that the court generates when you file the complaint. Generally, you can file your complaint any time after you file for bankruptcy. Some courts may impose their own deadlines, however, so check your court's local rules.

Can You Litigate the Dischargeability of a Debt Without a Lawyer?

It's not uncommon for a bankruptcy filer to qualify for a student loan discharge or a discharge of a tax debt, but not be able to afford a lawyer to handle the case. In such a situation, it might make sense for you to handle your own case without a lawyer. But, you must be prepared to receive a fair amount of problems from the judge and from the opposing lawyers. They, after all, are familiar with the proper forms and procedures whereas you are a first-timer.

Remember, though, that neither the judge nor the lawyers can do you harm if you make honest mistakes. If you file the wrong paperwork or make the wrong arguments, you will almost always be allowed to correct your errors.

If you plan to go it alone, get a copy of *Represent Yourself in Court*, by Paul Bergman and Sara Berman (Nolo), and do some online research (for example, search for "discharging student loans in Chapter 7 bankruptcy" and "bankruptcy adversary actions"). Ch. 10 has more about legal research.

If you are shot down at some point in the process, simply ask the court what's needed to correct the problem. After all, you have a right to represent yourself, and it is wrong of the judge to rule against you simply because you are unfamiliar with the process.

If the judge tells you to "get a lawyer," and that helping you would impinge on his or her impartiality, you can try another approach. Explain that you really can't afford a lawyer, that you'd like a clear explanation of what you did wrong and what's needed to get on the right track. But keep in mind that there's no guarantee this will work, and a judge can only do so much. Although most judges will do what they can, most aren't going to provide legal advice.

You also might want to consider hiring a lawyer to handle the adversary proceeding but not to represent you in your entire bankruptcy case. For instance, you'll likely need to present expert testimony, which requires paying for, disclosing, and examining the expert—none of which is simple.

Suppose, for example, that you want to have a student loan discharged. As discussed above, you will have to prove that it would be an undue hardship to repay the loan. You will file at least two forms: a Complaint to Determine Dischargeability (see sample form on the companion page), stating the facts that make repayment an undue hardship, and a Proof of Service (see example on the companion page), showing that you served the complaint on the affected creditor and the trustee. These forms are intended only to give you an idea of what a complaint to determine the dischargeability of a student loan looks like. Your court may require more or different forms. If you plan to file a complaint yourself, you must familiarize yourself with the rules of bankruptcy procedure regarding pleadings and service of process. For example, Bankruptcy Rule 7004 provides the basic rules for serving different defendants in an adversary process such as this one.

> **CAUTION**
>
> **Get help from a lawyer if you need it.** Before you charge off into court, here is a heartfelt warning: Embarking upon federal litigation in bankruptcy court can be quite a challenge if you don't have substantial coaching from someone who has experience in the field.

Creditor Objections to Discharges

To object formally to the discharge of a debt, the creditor must file a document called a Complaint to Determine Dischargeability of a Debt. The creditor must give you and the trustee a copy of the complaint. To defend against the objection, you must file a written response within a specified time limit and be prepared to argue your case in court.

If the debt is one of the types that will be discharged unless the creditor objects, the creditor has the burden of proving that the debt fits within the specified category. For instance, if the creditor claims that the debt arose from a "willful and malicious injury" you caused, the creditor will have to prove that your actions were willful and malicious. Similarly, suppose the creditor is arguing that a particular debt arose from your fraudulent acts. In that case, the creditor will have to prove that all the required elements of fraud were present. Absent this proof, the bankruptcy court will reject the creditor's lawsuit and maybe even award you attorneys' fees (if you use an attorney).

However, keep in mind that if you plead guilty to a criminal charge involving fraud, a document from the court showing your conviction could be all that's necessary to convince the judge to rule the debt nondischargeable. A no-contest plea, on the other hand, would not have the same effect because that type of plea can't be used as evidence in a later civil case (such as a bankruptcy case).

The fact that the creditor has the burden of proof doesn't mean that you should sit back and do nothing. You should be prepared to prove that the creditor's allegations in the complaint are not true (unless, of course, you already admitted your guilt in a prior case by pleading guilty or being convicted after trial).

CAUTION

If sued, seek legal advice. If a creditor in a civil case obtains a judgment based on fraud, willful or malicious conduct, or some other "nondischargeable" basis, the bankruptcy court could give it great weight and declare the debt nondischargeable without a new full-blown evidentiary trial. Ultimately, it will depend on how well the state court identified the wrongdoing in the court's findings. If all the legal elements exist (each fact that must be proven), the state court judgment will have a preclusive effect that the bankruptcy court must follow. On summary judgment motion in the adversary hearing, the bankruptcy court will have to find the debt nondischargeable without proceeding to trial. (*In re Dekhtyar,* 2019 WL 1282753 (Bankr. E.D. Cal. Mar. 19, 2019).) If this could be a possibility and you're facing a significant judgment, you'll likely want to file your bankruptcy case immediately.

Objections Based on Credit Card Fraud

Increasingly, the creditors most likely to object to the discharge of a debt are credit card issuers. Except for charges made shortly before filing for bankruptcy, few rules explain what constitutes credit card fraud in bankruptcy. But courts are looking to the following factors to determine fraud:

- **Timing.** A short time between incurring the charges and filing for bankruptcy may suggest fraudulent intent.
- **Manipulation of the system.** Incurring more debt after consulting an attorney may lead a judge to conclude that you ran up your debts in anticipation of your bankruptcy filing.
- **Amount.** As mentioned earlier, recent charges of over $725 for luxuries will be presumed to be fraudulent.
- **Crafty use of the card.** Multiple charges under $50 (to avoid preclearance of the transaction by the credit card issuer) will start to look like fraud when you've reached your credit limit.
- **Deliberate misuse.** Charges after the card issuer has ordered you to return the card or sent several "past due" notices don't look good.
- **Last-minute sprees.** Changes in your pattern of use of the card (for instance, much travel after a sedentary life), charges for luxuries, and multiple charges on the same day could lead to problems.
- **Bad-faith use.** Charges made when you were clearly insolvent and unable to make the required minimum payment (for instance, you had lost your job and had no other income or savings) are a no-no. Banks claim that insolvency is evidenced by any of the following:
  - A notation in the customer's file that the customer has met with an attorney (perhaps because the customer told the creditor he or she was considering bankruptcy and had talked to an attorney about it).
  - A rapid increase in spending, followed by 60–90 days without activity.
  - The date noted on any attorney's fee statement if the customer consults a lawyer for help with a bankruptcy.

Questions for Credit Card Companies

If you find yourself facing a dischargeability action over a credit card debt, you'll have an opportunity to send questions (called interrogatories) to the company, to be answered under oath. Here are some you might consider asking:

- You (the card issuer) have alleged that I obtained funds from you by false pretenses and false representations. Please state with particularity the nature of the false pretenses and false representations.
- State all steps taken to determine my creditworthiness.
- Identify all means that you, the card issuer, used to verify my income, expenses, assets, or liabilities. Identify any documents obtained in the verification process.
- Identify your general policies concerning the decision to grant credit and how those policies were applied to me.
- You have alleged that at the time I obtained credit from you, I did not intend to repay it. State all facts in your possession to support this allegation.
- Identify all credit policies you allege were violated by me. State how such policies were communicated to me, and identify all documents that contained those policies.
- Identify the dates on which you claim any of the following events occurred:
  - I consulted a bankruptcy attorney.
  - I had a reduction in income.
  - I formed the intent not to repay this debt.
  - I violated the terms of the credit agreement.
- State whether you believe that every credit card user who does not later repay the debt has committed fraud.
- If the answer to the preceding question is no, state all facts that give rise to allegations of fraud in this debtor's use of the card.

After receiving a list of questions like these, the credit card issuer is likely to conclude that you are serious about defending yourself. It might even withdraw its complaint.

Of course, the mere fact that a creditor challenges your discharge of a credit card debt doesn't mean the creditor will win in court. In most cases, the creditor files a standard 15- to 20-paragraph form complaint, which states conclusions without supporting facts. The creditor rarely attaches your account statements, but only a printout of the charges to which it is objecting.

Research Tips

If you want to read cases supporting the debtor's position when a credit card issuer claims fraud, visit a law library or search online for some of these cases:

- *In re Hearn*, 211 B.R. 774 (N.D. Ga. 1997)
- *In re Etto*, 210 B.R. 734 (N.D. Ohio 1997)
- *In re Hunter*, 210 B.R. 212 (M.D. Fla. 1997)
- *In re Davis*, 176 B.R. 118 (W.D.N.Y. 1994)
- *In re Kitzmiller*, 206 B.R. 424 (N.D. W.Va. 1997)
- *In re Christensen*, 193 B.R. 863 (N.D. Ill. 1996)
- *In re Chinchilla*, 202 B.R. 1010 (S.D. Fla. 1996)
- *In re Grayson*, 199 B.R. 397 (W.D. Mo. 1996), and
- *In re Vianese*, 195 B.R. 572 (N.D. N.Y. 1995).

For tips on doing your own legal research, see "Legal Research" in Ch. 10.

Some very sophisticated debtors might be able to represent themselves in this type of case. If you decide to do this, you'll need lots of time to familiarize yourself with general litigation procedures and strategies, as well as the bankruptcy cases in your district that deal with this issue. Start by getting a copy of *Represent Yourself in Court*, by Paul Bergman and Sara Berman (Nolo).

CAUTION

Consider getting help from a lawyer. Allegations of fraud should make you seriously consider consulting an attorney. If a creditor challenges discharge of a debt by claiming you engaged in fraud, but the judge finds in your favor, the judge may order the creditor to reimburse you for the money you spent on attorneys' fees.

Help Beyond the Book

Although this book covers routine bankruptcy procedures in some detail, it doesn't come close to covering everything. That would require thousands of pages, most of them irrelevant for nearly all readers. That said, here are some suggestions if you need more information or advice than this book provides.

The major places to go for follow-up help are:

- **bankruptcy petition preparers,** when you're ready to file for bankruptcy but need assistance in typing the forms and organizing them for filing in your district

- **lawyers,** when you want information, advice, or legal representation, and

- **law libraries and the Internet,** when you want to do your own research on issues raised in the course of your bankruptcy.

Before we discuss each of these resources in more detail, here's a general piece of advice: Maintain control of your case whenever possible. By getting this book, you've taken responsibility for your own legal affairs. If you decide to get help from others, shop around until you find someone who respects your efforts as a self-helper and recognizes your right to participate in the case as a valuable partner.

Debt Relief Agencies

Under bankruptcy law, any person, business, or organization that you pay or otherwise compensate for help with your bankruptcy is considered a debt relief agency—and must identify itself as such. The two main types of debt relief agencies are lawyers and bankruptcy petition preparers (BPPs). Credit counseling agencies and budget counseling agencies are not debt relief agencies. Nor are any of the following:

- employers or employees of debt relief agencies (for instance, legal secretaries)
- nonprofit organizations that have federal 501(c)(3) tax-exempt status
- any creditor who works with you to restructure your debt
- banks, credit unions, and other deposit institutions, or
- an author, publisher, distributor, or seller of works subject to copyright protection when acting in that capacity (in other words, Nolo and the stores that sell its books aren't debt relief agencies).

This section explains what the bankruptcy law requires of debt relief agencies generally, so you'll know what you can expect for your money.

Mandatory Contract

Within five days after a debt relief agency assists you, it (or he or she) must enter into a contract with you that explains, clearly and conspicuously:

- what services the agency will provide
- what the agency will charge for the services, and
- the terms of payment.

The agency must give you a copy of the completed, signed contract.

Mandatory Disclosures and Notices

Debt relief agencies must inform you, in writing, that:

- All information you are required to provide in your bankruptcy papers must be complete, accurate, and truthful.
- You must completely and accurately disclose your assets and liabilities in the documents you file to begin your case.
- You must undertake a reasonable inquiry to establish the replacement value of any item you plan to keep before providing the value on your forms.
- Your current monthly income, the amounts you provide in the means test, and your computation of projected disposable income (in a Chapter 13 case), as stated in your bankruptcy papers, must be based on a reasonable inquiry into their accuracy.
- Your case could be audited, and your failure to cooperate in the audit could result in the dismissal of your case or some other sanction, including a possible criminal penalty.

In addition to these stark warnings—which most debt relief agencies would rather not have to give—a debt relief agency must also give you a general notice regarding some basic bankruptcy requirements and your options for help in filing and pursuing your case. Failure to provide you with this notice—in a timely manner—can land the agency in big trouble.

Finally, every debt relief agency has to give you some plain-English written information about the basic tasks associated with most bankruptcies, such as how to deal with secured debts and choose exemptions. Ideally, debt relief agencies would freely distribute this book, which has all of the information required (and much more, of course).

Restrictions on Debt Relief Agencies

A debt relief agency may not:

- fail to perform any service that the agency told you it would perform in connection with your bankruptcy case
- counsel you to make any statement in a document that is untrue and misleading or that the agency should have known was inaccurate or deceptive, or
- advise you to incur more debt in order to pay for the agency's services (for instance, accepting a credit card or steering you to a cash advance business).

Any contract that doesn't comply with the requirements of debt relief agencies can't be enforced against you. A debt relief agency is liable to you for costs and fees, including legal fees, if the agency negligently or intentionally:

- fails to comply with the law's restrictions on debt relief agencies, or
- fails to file a document that results in dismissal of your case or conversion to another bankruptcy chapter.

In sum, debt relief agencies are on the hook if they are negligent in performing the services required by the bankruptcy law or other services they have agreed to provide.

Bankruptcy Petition Preparers

Even though you feel you're capable of handling routine bankruptcy procedures yourself, you might want someone familiar with the bankruptcy forms and courts in your area to enter your data on the official forms and print them out for filing with the court. For this level of assistance—standard form preparation and organization—consider using a bankruptcy petition preparer (BPP).

What a Bankruptcy Petition Preparer Can't Do for You

BPPs are very different from lawyers. BPPs are prohibited from giving you legal advice, which includes information such as:

- whether to file a bankruptcy petition or which chapter (7, 11, 12, or 13) is appropriate
- whether your debts will be discharged under a particular chapter
- whether you will be able to hang on to your home or other property if you file under a particular chapter (that is, which exemptions you should choose)
- information about the tax consequences of a case brought under a specific chapter or whether tax claims in your case can be discharged
- whether you should offer to repay or agree to reaffirm a debt
- how to characterize the nature of your interest in property or obligations, and
- information about bankruptcy procedures and rights.

Fees

All fees charged by debt relief agencies are reviewed by the U.S. Trustee for reasonableness. However, unlike lawyers' fees, which can vary widely according to the circumstances, a BPP's fees are subject to a cap imposed by the particular district. Caps differ widely in the 91 court districts and can range from $75 to $200. The rationale offered by the U.S. Trustee for this cap—and by the courts that have upheld it—is that BPP fees can be set according to community standards. Because BPPs aren't lawyers and can't give legal advice, they're limited to filling out the forms. Therefore the services they're allowed to provide don't warrant charging the rates for professional assistance.

BPPs are an excellent choice for people who want some help transferring their information to the proper forms.

How Bankruptcy Petition Preparers Are Regulated

Anyone can be a BPP. Yes, anyone. There is nothing in the bankruptcy code that requires BPPs to have any particular level of education, training, or experience. How, then, are BPPs regulated? Regulation is provided by the U.S. Trustee's office, which reviews all bankruptcy petitions prepared by a BPP. BPPs must provide their name, address, telephone number, and Social Security number on the bankruptcy petition, as well as on every other bankruptcy document they prepare. The U.S. Trustee uses this information to keep tabs on BPPs.

BPPs are also regulated at the 341 hearing, where the bankruptcy trustee can ask you how the BPP conducts business. For instance, if you represent yourself, the trustee might ask how you got the information necessary to choose your exemptions (see Ch. 3) or decided which bankruptcy chapter to use.

Can BPPs Give You Written Information?

Under the Bankruptcy Code, BPPs are supposed to prepare your bankruptcy forms under your direction. A BPP isn't a cheap alternative to hiring a bankruptcy lawyer. You must do your homework before attempting to file for bankruptcy on your own. For instance, you decide the exemptions to choose, chapter to file, approach to take with secured debts (car note, mortgage, and so on), and values to place on property.

If the BPP provided you with this information, the trustee might refer the case to the U.S. Trustee's office. The BPP will be required to explain the rule violation against giving legal advice. The consequences could include being forced to return your payment or, if it's not the first offense, being banned from practicing as a BPP. Other than the inconvenience of being dragged into court, none of this will affect your case.

BPPs can be fined for actions and inactions spelled out in the bankruptcy code (11 U.S.C. § 110). These are:

- failing to put their name, address, and Social Security number on your bankruptcy petition
- failing to give you a copy of your bankruptcy documents when you sign them
- using the word "legal" or any similar term in advertisements, and
- accepting court filing fees from you. You must pay the court filing fee yourself or, in some districts, give the BPP a cashier's check made out to the court.

Finally, a BPP must submit a statement under oath that includes the amount paid over the previous 12 months and any outstanding unpaid amounts. If the charges are more than are permitted, the BPP will be ordered to return the excess payment.

A BPP who engages in any fraudulent act or fails to comply with the rules governing behavior could be required to return your fee and pay a $500 fine for each violation. Serious fraud can result in a fine up to $2,000 and three times your fee, and an order to cease providing BPP services. Simply put, BPPs who take your money without providing services or counsel you to play fast and loose with the bankruptcy system are likely to be weeded out in a hurry.

How to Find Bankruptcy Petition Preparers

You're more likely to find a BPP if you live on the West Coast. The best way to find a reputable BPP a is to get a recommendation from someone satisfied with a BPP's work. You can try checking online, but it might be difficult because they go by different names in different states. In California, your best bet is to find a legal document assistant (the official name given to independent paralegals in California) who also provides BPP services. Check the website maintained by the California Association of Legal Document Assistants (www.calda.org). In Arizona, hunt for a legal document preparer. In other states, especially Florida, search for paralegals who directly serve the public (often termed independent paralegals or legal technicians).

> **CAUTION**
> **A bankruptcy petition preparer cannot represent you.** If you decide to use a BPP, remember that you are representing yourself and are responsible for the outcome of your case. You must not only learn about your rights under the bankruptcy law and understand the proper procedures but accept responsibility for correctly completing the bankruptcy petition and schedules. For instance, if you lose your home because the homestead exemption available to you didn't cover your equity, you can't blame the BPP. Nor can you blame the BPP if other property is taken from you because you didn't get the necessary information to properly claim your exemptions. The point is that unless you hire a lawyer to represent you, you are solely responsible for acquiring the information necessary to competently pursue your case.

When You Might Need a Lawyer

Most Chapter 7 bankruptcies move through the process without a problem. However, there are some situations in which you might need some help from a bankruptcy lawyer:

- Your average gross income during the six months before you file won't allow you to pass the means test. (See Ch. 1 and Ch. 6 for more information on these calculations.)
- You want to hold onto a house or motor vehicle and you still have questions.
- You want to get rid of a student loan or income tax debt that won't be wiped out in bankruptcy unless you convince a court that it should be discharged.
- A creditor files a lawsuit in the bankruptcy court claiming that one of your debts should survive your bankruptcy because you incurred it through fraud or other misconduct.
- The bankruptcy trustee requests the dismissal of your bankruptcy case because you didn't give honest and complete answers to questions about your assets, liabilities, and economic transactions.
- The U.S. Trustee asks that your case be dismissed or converted to Chapter 13 because your Chapter 7 filing is an abuse of process.

- You have given away or sold valuable property for less than it is worth within the last two years.
- You went on a recent buying spree with your credit card (especially if you charged more than $725 on luxury goods within the past 90 days or took out more than $1,000 in cash advances within the past 70 days).
- You want help negotiating with a creditor and the amount involved justifies hiring a bankruptcy lawyer to assist you.
- You have a large lien on your property because of a court judgment against you, and you want to remove the lien in your bankruptcy case.
- A creditor asks the court for permission to proceed with a collection action (such as foreclose because you're behind on your mortgage payments) and you oppose the request.
- You are being evicted by your landlord because you have fallen behind on your rent.

Even if you aren't facing one of these complications, you might still want a lawyer's help. A lawyer can take charge of your case and relieve you of the responsibility to get everything done. For instance, the lawyer can complete and file your paperwork on time, accompany you to the 341 hearing, and handle other details to ensure a successful bankruptcy case.

Although representation comes at a price, you will have the peace of mind of knowing that someone is watching your back. Because while many people can handle their own Chapter 7 bankruptcies, it isn't suitable for everyone. People with other sources of stress or who don't feel up to the task will benefit from getting help.

Full-Service Lawyer Representation

In a general sense, you are represented by a lawyer if you contract with the lawyer to handle some or all of your bankruptcy case for you. More specifically, there are two types of representation—the type where you hire a lawyer to assume complete responsibility for your bankruptcy, and the type where you represent yourself but hire a lawyer to handle one particular aspect of your bankruptcy case.

When providing full-service representation, a bankruptcy lawyer is responsible for ensuring that all of your paperwork is filed on time and that the information in your paperwork is accurate. These duties require the lawyer to review various documents—for instance, your credit report, tax returns, and home value—to ensure accuracy and confirm you're filing under the appropriate chapter. Most full-service bankruptcy lawyers typically are also responsible for appearing with you at the 341 hearing (see Ch. 7). A lawyer who fails to fulfill required duties could be required to return your fees.

The attorneys' fees are unlikely to include unusual events, such as representing you if a creditor opposes the discharge (see Ch. 9) or eliminating liens that can be stripped from your property (see Ch. 5).

Sometimes, a case appears simple but becomes complicated later on. In that event, you might start out representing yourself but later decide to hire an attorney to handle a tricky issue that arises. However, keep in mind that it takes a lot of effort to fix an issue that could have been avoided. Many bankruptcy lawyers won't take cases that have become problematic.

Also, bankruptcy lawyers often won't assist with a single issue because a bankruptcy court might hold an attorney who has appeared on one matter responsible for the entire case. Once an attorney has "appeared," the attorney must get permission from the court to end the representation. Since courts tend to prefer that the debtor has legal counsel, getting off of a case isn't guaranteed, and not being able to do so could prove costly.

Litigation Services

Even though lawyers will be hesitant to take on a problematic case midstream, you'll likely be able to find a bankruptcy attorney to help you with motion or litigation work. For instance, a litigation attorney can help you remove a lien from your property during your case (or even after it closes) or represent you in a dischargeability action brought by you or a creditor. These types of services are sufficiently separate from the underlying bankruptcy case and tend to require different expertise than that possessed by many bankruptcy lawyers.

Also, nothing prevents a lawyer from appearing for you in a limited capacity and putting his or her own name on associated documents.

Lawyers providing such services usually charge an hourly fee. As a general rule, you should bring an hourly attorney into the case only if a dispute involves something valuable enough to justify the attorney's fees. If a creditor objects to the discharge of a $500 debt, and it will cost you $400 to hire an attorney, you might be better off trying to handle the matter yourself, even though this increases the risk that the creditor will win.

How to Find a Bankruptcy Lawyer

For many people, a book won't replace talking to a human being. If you decide to retain legal counsel, you should use an experienced bankruptcy lawyer, not a general practitioner.

There are several ways to find the right bankruptcy lawyer for you:

- **Personal referrals.** This is your best approach. If you know someone was pleased with the services of a bankruptcy lawyer, call that lawyer first.
- **Legal Aid.** Legal Aid offices offer legal assistance in many areas, but most don't provide bankruptcy service. To qualify for Legal Aid, you must have a very low income.
- **Legal clinic.** Many law schools sponsor legal clinics and provide free legal advice to consumers. Some legal clinics have the same income requirements as Legal Aid; others offer free services to low- and moderate-income people.
- **Group legal plans.** If you're a member of a plan that provides free or low-cost legal assistance and the plan covers bankruptcy, make that your first stop in looking for a lawyer. Keep in mind that these services pay bankruptcy lawyers less than average for the area, so research the attorney before retention.
- **Lawyer referral panels.** Most county bar associations will give you the names of bankruptcy attorneys who practice in your area. But bar associations might not provide much screening. Take the time to check out the credentials and experience of the person to whom you're referred.

- **Online lawyer directories.** If you need a bankruptcy lawyer, Nolo's lawyer directory can help you find one who's right for you. Another excellent source is the National Association of Consumer Bankruptcy Attorneys (NACBA at www.nacba.org/find-an-attorney). NACBA provides members with excellent education and training on all aspects of bankruptcy and foreclosure.
- **ABI pro bono resources.** The American Bankruptcy Institute maintains a list, by state, of Legal Aid or other organizations that provide free bankruptcy services. Often these services consist of bankruptcy clinics where you can get help completing forms or ask questions about bankruptcy in general or your case in particular. A few organizations will prepare forms or represent you in bankruptcy. Go to the ABI's website at www.bankruptcyresources.org, choose "Find Help," choose your state, and then click on "Pro Bono Resources."

Fees

For a routine Chapter 7 bankruptcy, a full-service lawyer will likely charge you somewhere between $1,000 and $2,000 (plus the $338 filing fee). You'll also have to pay additional fees for credit counseling. Also, you will have to pay the attorney in full before the attorney will file your case. Once filed, any money owed the attorney would be discharged with your other dischargeable unsecured debts.

For some people needing bankruptcy, coming up with a few thousand dollars to pay an attorney and cover the filing fee can be a struggle. One option is to stop making payments on credit cards and sock that money away for your bankruptcy lawyer fees. Don't do this until you first consult with a lawyer, though. If bankruptcy ends up not working for you, it'll be tough to get back on track with your credit card payments. Another option is to ask for help from a relative. Unlike you, a relative can use a credit card to pay your attorney.

On your bankruptcy papers, you must state the amount you are paying your bankruptcy lawyer. Because every penny paid to a bankruptcy lawyer is a penny not available to your creditors, the court has the authority to make the attorney justify the fee. However, this rarely happens because attorneys, knowing the range of fees allowed, set their prices accordingly.

The scope and range of services that the attorney promises you in return for your initial fee will be listed in Form 2030 Disclosure of Compensation of Attorney for Debtor. This form is filed as part of your bankruptcy papers. In the typical Chapter 7 case, attorneys' fees will include routine tasks associated with a bankruptcy filing: counseling, preparing bankruptcy and reaffirmation forms, and attendance at the 341 hearing. Any task not included in the disclosure is subject to a separate fee.

If your case requires attorney time for services not included in the original fee, you might be charged according to the attorney's hourly fee or other criteria. A typical bankruptcy attorney charges between $200 and $300 an hour, so you could expect to pay roughly $400 to $600 for a court appearance.

However the attorney charges you, you are protected against fee gouging. An attorney must file a supplemental form to obtain the court's permission for any postfiling fees.

What to Look for in a Lawyer

No matter how you find a lawyer, these three suggestions will help you make sure you have the best possible working relationship.

First, hire someone with whom you feel comfortable working. Keep looking if the price or personality isn't right.

Second, ask to talk directly to the lawyer for the simple reason that a paralegal can't give you legal advice. If you can't, this might give you a hint as to how accessible he or she will be. Of course, if you're told that a paralegal will be handling the routine aspects of your case under the supervision of the lawyer, you might be satisfied with that arrangement.

During your meeting, ask specific questions. Do you get clear, concise answers? If not, try someone else. Also, pay attention to how the lawyer responds to your knowledge. If you've read this book, you're already better informed than most clients. You'll be in a good position to determine whether the lawyer has sufficient bankruptcy experience versus an attorney who takes the occasional case.

Finally, once you find a lawyer you like, make an appointment to discuss your situation. The lawyer or a paralegal in the lawyer's office will tell you what to bring to the meeting. Some lawyers will want to see a recent credit report and tax return. In contrast, others will send you a questionnaire to complete before your visit.

Depending on the circumstances, you might also be asked to bring bills and documents regarding your home and other real estate you own. Some lawyers prefer not to deal with details during the first visit and won't require you to bring anything.

Your main goal at the initial conference is to find out what the lawyer recommends in your particular case and how much it will cost. If your lawyer's suggestions don't make sense or you have other reservations, call someone else.

Legal Research

Legal research can vary from very simple to complex. In this section, we are staying on the simple side. If you would like to learn more about legal research or if you find that our suggestions come up a bit short in your particular case, we recommend that you obtain a copy of *Legal Research*, by the Editors of Nolo (Nolo), which provides a plain-English tutorial on legal research in the law library and online.

Sources of Bankruptcy Law

Bankruptcy law comes from a variety of sources:
- federal bankruptcy statutes passed by Congress
- federal rules about bankruptcy procedure issued by a federal judicial agency
- local rules issued by individual bankruptcy courts
- federal and bankruptcy court cases applying bankruptcy laws to specific disputes
- laws (statutes) passed by state legislatures that define the property you can keep in bankruptcy, and
- state court cases interpreting state exemption statutes.

Not so long ago, you would have had to visit a law library to find these resources. Now you can find most of them online. However, if you can visit a decent-sized law library, your research will be better for it. Using actual books allows you to more easily find and read relevant court interpretations of the underlying statutes and rules—which are crucial to getting a clear picture of what the laws and rules really mean. There is another important reason to visit the law library, if possible.

While you can find superficial discussions and overviews of various aspects of bankruptcy online, you'll find in-depth encyclopedias and treatises in the law library that delve into every part of bankruptcy. In other words, you can find not only the law itself but also what the experts have to say about issues that have arisen over the years. Also, books in a law library are almost always subjected to a rigorous quality control process, whereas you never know what you're getting online. Follow our suggestions below for researching bankruptcy law online and avoid the temptation to settle for the first hit in a Google search.

Below, we show you how to get to the resources you'll most likely be using, whether you are doing your research on the Internet or in the law library.

Bankruptcy Background Materials: Overviews, Encyclopedias, and Treatises

Before digging into the primary law sources (statutes, rules, cases, and so on that we discuss below), you might want to do some background reading to get a firm grasp of your issue or question.

Online Research

Some online sites have large collections of articles written by experts about various aspects of bankruptcy. A good starting place is Nolo's website at Nolo.com. You'll find lots of information and resources.

Another approach to searching for bankruptcy-related materials is using a basic Google search or Google Scholar (https://scholar.google.com). For example, if you want to know more about discharging student loans, you would use Google Scholar, click the "Articles" radio button and enter "discharging student loans in bankruptcy" in the search box to pull up links to related articles. Similarly, if you want to read court opinions about discharging debts in bankruptcy you would do the same search but use the "Case law" button.

The Law Library

Providing you with a good treatise or encyclopedia discussion of bankruptcy is where the law library shines. This type of resource is not typically available online unless you find a way to access the expensive legal databases—Westlaw and LexisNexis—marketed almost exclusively to lawyers.

How to Use Law Libraries

Law libraries that are open to the public are most often found in and around courthouses. Law schools also frequently admit the public (typically, not during exam time, over the summer, or during other breaks in the academic year).

Almost without exception, law libraries come with law librarians who are very helpful when you ask them the right questions. For example, the law librarians will direct you to specific library resources, such as the federal bankruptcy statutes or rules. Still, they usually won't teach you the ins and outs of legal research. Nor will they give an opinion about what a law means, how you should deal with the court, or how your particular question should be answered. For instance, if you want to find a state case interpreting a specific exemption, the law librarian will show you where your state code is located and might even point out the volumes that contain the exemptions. The librarian won't, however, help you interpret the exemption, apply the exemption to your specific facts, tell you how to raise the exemption in your bankruptcy case, or explain additional research steps you can take. When it comes to legal research in the law library, self-help is the order of the day.

Collier on Bankruptcy

It's a good idea to get an overview of your subject before trying to find a precise answer to a particular question. The best way to do this is to find a general commentary on your subject by a bankruptcy expert. For example, if you want to determine whether a particular debt is nondischargeable, you should start by reading a general discussion about the type of debt you're dealing with. Or, if you don't know whether you're entitled to claim certain property as exempt, a good overview of your state's exemptions would get you started on the right track.

The most complete source of this type of background information is a set of books known as *Collier on Bankruptcy*, by Alan N. Resnick, et al. (Matthew Bender). It's available in virtually all law libraries. *Collier* is both incredibly thorough and meticulously up to date; semiannual supplements, with all the latest developments, are in the front of each volume. In addition to comments on every aspect of bankruptcy law, *Collier* contains the bankruptcy statutes, rules, and exemption lists for every state.

Collier is organized according to the bankruptcy statutes. This means that the quickest way to find information in it is to know what statute you're looking for. (See the Bankruptcy Code sections set out below.) If you still can't figure out the governing statute, start with the *Collier* subject-matter index. Be warned, however, that the index can be difficult to use because it contains a lot of bankruptcy jargon you may be unfamiliar with. A legal dictionary will be available in the library.

Bankruptcy (National Edition) published by The Rutter Group

This four-volume set authored by Judge Judith K. Fitzgerald, et al. provides crisp treatments of all the pesky little issues that can arise in a bankruptcy case. Because of its relatively low cost, you are more likely to be able to find it in small county and court law libraries.

Foreclosure Resources

If you are facing foreclosure, try *The Foreclosure Survival Guide,* by Amy Loftsgordon (Nolo). This book explains the options available to you and walks you through the steps to handle your particular situation.

Other Background Resources

For general discussions of bankruptcy issues, there are several other good places to start. An excellent all-around resource is called *Consumer Bankruptcy Law and Practice*. This volume, published by the National Consumer Law Center, is updated every year. It contains a complete discussion of Chapter 7 bankruptcy procedures, the official bankruptcy forms, and a helpful bibliography.

Bankruptcy Code Sections (11 U.S.C.)

§ 101 Definitions

§ 109 Who May File for Which Type of Bankruptcy; Credit Counseling Requirements

§ 110 Rules for Bankruptcy Petition Preparers

§ 111 Budget and Credit Counseling Agencies

§ 302 Who Can File Joint Cases

§ 326 How Trustees Are Compensated

§ 332 Consumer Privacy Ombudsmen

§ 341 Meeting of Creditors

§ 342 Notice of Creditors' Meeting; Informational Notice to Debtors; Requirements for Notice by Debtors

§ 343 Examination of Debtor at Creditors' Meeting

§ 348 Converting From One Type of Bankruptcy to Another

§ 349 Dismissing a Case

§ 350 Closing and Reopening a Case

§ 362 The Automatic Stay

§ 365 How Leases and Executory Contracts Are Treated in Bankruptcy

§ 366 Continuing or Reconnecting Utility Service

§ 501 Filing of Creditors' Claims

§ 506 Allowed Secured Claims and Lien Avoidance

§ 507 Priority Claims

§ 521 Paperwork Requirements and Deadlines

§ 522 Exemptions; Residency Requirements for Homestead Exemption; Stripping Liens From Property

§ 523 Nondischargeable Debts

§ 524 Effect of Discharge and Reaffirmation of Debts

§ 525 Prohibited Postbankruptcy Discrimination

§ 526 Restrictions on Debt Relief Agencies

§ 527 Required Disclosures by Debt Relief Agencies

§ 528 Requirements for Debt Relief Agencies

§ 541 What Property Is Part of the Bankruptcy Estate

§ 547 Preferences

§ 548 Fraudulent Transfers

§ 554 Trustee's Abandonment of Property in the Bankruptcy Estate

§ 707 The Means Test; Dismissal for Abuse; Conversion From Chapter 7 to Chapter 13

§ 722 Redemption of Liens on Personal Property

§ 727 Chapter 7 Discharge; Financial Management Counseling Requirements

Another good treatise is a legal encyclopedia called *American Jurisprudence, 2nd Series*. Almost all law libraries carry it. The article on bankruptcy has an extensive table of contents, and the entire encyclopedia has an index. Between these two tools, you should be able to zero in on helpful material. Finally, some large and well-stocked law libraries carry a looseleaf publication known as the *Commerce Clearing House (CCH) Bankruptcy Law Reporter (BLR)*. In this publication, you can find all three primary source materials relating to bankruptcy: statutes, rules, and cases.

If you are looking for information on adversary proceedings (such as how to defend against a creditor's challenge to the dischargeability of a debt), turn to *Represent Yourself in Court*, by Paul Bergman and Sara J. Berman (Nolo). It has an entire chapter on representing yourself in adversary proceedings in bankruptcy court. If you need information on court procedures or the local rules of a specific court, consult the *Collier Bankruptcy Practice Guide*.

Finding Federal Bankruptcy Statutes

Title 11 of the United States Code contains all the statutes that govern your bankruptcy.

Online

If you use the Internet, go to the Legal Information Institute of Cornell University Law School, www.law.cornell.edu. Cornell lets you browse laws by subject matter and also offers a keyword search. Below you'll find a helpful table setting out the various subject matter sections of the U.S. Code that apply to bankruptcy.

The Law Library

Virtually every law library has at least one complete set of the annotated United States Code ("annotated" means that each statute is followed by citations and summaries of cases interpreting that provision). If you already have a citation to the statute you seek, you can use the citation to find the statute. However, if you have no citation—which is frequently the case— you can use either the index to Title 11 (the part of the Code that applies to bankruptcy) or the table we set out just below, which matches various issues that are likely to interest you with specific sections of Title 11.

Once you have found and read the statute, you can browse the summaries of written opinions issued by courts interpreting that particular statute. You will be looking to see whether a court has addressed your specific issue. If so, you can find and read the entire case in the law library. Reading what a judge has had to say about the statute regarding facts similar to yours is an invaluable guide to understanding how a judge is likely to handle the issue in your case, although when and where the case was decided might be important.

Finding the Federal Rules of Bankruptcy Procedure (FRBP)

The Federal Rules of Bankruptcy Procedure govern what happens if an issue is contested in the bankruptcy court. They also apply to routine bankruptcy procedures, such as deadlines for filing paperwork. Because most cases sail through the court without any need for the bankruptcy judge's intervention, you may not need to be familiar with these rules. However, certain types of creditor actions in the bankruptcy court must proceed by way of a regular lawsuit conducted under both these rules and the Federal Rules of Civil Procedure—for example, complaints to determine dischargeability of a debt. If you represent yourself in such a lawsuit, you'll want to know these rules and look at the cases interpreting them. Any law library will have these rules. Your bankruptcy court's website will also have a link to the rules, as does www.law.cornell.edu.

Finding Local Court Rules

Every bankruptcy court operates under a set of local rules that govern how it does business and what is expected of the parties who use it. Throughout this book, we have cautioned you to read the rules for your particular court so that your dealings with the court will go smoothly—and so you won't end up getting tossed out of court if you become involved in litigation, such as an action to determine the dischargeability of a debt or a creditor's motion to lift the automatic stay.

Your bankruptcy court clerk's office will have the local rules available for you. Most courts also post their local rules on their own websites. To find the website for your court, take these steps:

Step 1: Go to www.uscourts.gov.

Step 2: Use the Court Locator to find the bankruptcy court near you.

Step 3: Browse the list until you find your bankruptcy court.

Step 4: Click on the link to your court's website.

Court websites usually contain other helpful information, including case information, official and local bankruptcy forms, court guidelines (in addition to the local rules), information for lawyers and BPPs, information about the court and its judges, and the court calendar.

Collier Bankruptcy Practice Manual also has the local rules for most (if not all) of the nation's bankruptcy courts.

Finding Federal Court Bankruptcy Cases

Court opinions are vital to understanding how a particular law might apply to your individual case. The following levels of federal courts issue bankruptcy-related opinions:

- the U.S. Supreme Court
- the U.S. Courts of Appeals
- the Bankruptcy Appellate Panels
- the U.S. District Courts, and
- the bankruptcy courts.

Most bankruptcy-related opinions are, not surprisingly, issued by the bankruptcy courts. By comparison, very few bankruptcy opinions come out of the U.S. Supreme Court. The other courts are somewhere in the middle.

Online

Depending on the date the case was decided, U.S. Supreme Court decisions and U.S. Court of Appeals decisions are available for free on the Internet. You can also subscribe to VersusLaw for a low monthly fee (at www.versuslaw.com). It provides U.S. Court of Appeals cases for an earlier period than you can get for free—often back to 1950. VersusLaw doesn't require you to sign a long-term contract and provides a free trial period. VersusLaw also publishes many U.S. District Court cases on its website. Opinions by the bankruptcy courts are generally not yet available over the Internet unless you subscribe to LexisNexis or Westlaw, both of which are pricey.

U.S. Supreme Court. To find a Supreme Court case, go to www.supreme court.gov. Use one of the search options to locate a particular case.

Other U.S. Courts. If you know the case name, you can find a U.S. Court of Appeals case back to 1924. Follow these steps:

Step 1:   Go to www.justia.com.

Step 2:   Click on the "US Courts" link.

You can also find many cases through a Google search. If you don't know the case name and instead want to search by keyword, you'll have to use VersusLaw or sign up for one of the pricier services that lawyers use, like Westlaw, LexisNexis, or FastCase (www.fastcase.com).

The Law Library

U.S. Supreme Court cases are published in three different book series:
- *Supreme Court Reports*
- *Supreme Court Reporter,* and
- *Supreme Court Lawyer's Edition.*

Some law libraries carry all three of these publications; others have only one. The cases are the same, but each series has different editorial enhancements.

U.S. Court of Appeals cases are published in the *Federal Reporter* (abbreviated simply as "F."). Most law libraries, large and small, carry this series.

Many U.S. District Court cases are published in the *Federal Supplement* (F.Supp.), a series available in most law libraries.

Written opinions of bankruptcy judges, and related appeals, are published in the *Bankruptcy Reporter* (B.R.), which is available in most mid- to large-sized libraries. To accurately understand how your bankruptcy court is likely to interpret the laws in your particular case, you'll need access to the *Bankruptcy Reporter.*

State Statutes

The secret to understanding what property you can keep frequently lies in the exemptions that your state allows you to claim. These exemptions are found in your state's statutes.

Online

Every state has its statutes online, including its exemption statutes. This means that you can read your state's exemption statutes for yourself. Follow these steps:

Step 1: Go to the exemptions on the companion page. At the top of your state's exemption table, you'll see a general reference to the collection of laws for your state that contain the exemption statutes.

Step 2: Google the name of your state and "statutes" or "code." You'll likely find yourself on your state's legislative website—most states maintain the entire code there.

The Law Library

Your law library will have your state's statutes in book form, usually referred to as your state's code, annotated statutes, or compiled laws. Go to the exemption chart on the companion page (www.nolo.com/back-of-book/HFB.html) to find a reference to the exemption statute you want to read, then use that reference to locate the exemption statute in the code. Once you find and read the statute, you can browse the summaries of court opinions interpreting the statute and, if you wish, read the cases in their entirety.

Alternatively, if your library has a copy of *Collier on Bankruptcy* (see above) or *Bankruptcy* by the Rutter Group, you can find the exemptions for your state, accompanied by annotations summarizing state court interpretations.

State Court Cases

State courts are sometimes called on to interpret exemption statutes. If a court has interpreted the statute in which you are interested, you'll definitely want to chase down the relevant case and read it for yourself.

Online

All states make their more recent cases available free on the Internet—usually back to about 1996. To find these cases for your state:

Step 1: Go to www.law.cornell.edu/opinions.html#state.

Step 2: Click on your state.

Step 3: Locate the link to the court opinions for your state. This might be one link, or there could be separate links for your state's supreme court and your state's courts of appeal (the lower trial courts seldom publish their opinions, so you probably won't be able to find them).

If you want to go back to an earlier case, consider subscribing to VersusLaw at www.versuslaw.com. As mentioned earlier, you don't have to sign a long-term contract.

The Law Library

Your law library will have a collection of books that contain opinions issued by your state's courts. If you have a citation, you can go right to the case. If you don't have a citation, you'll need to use a digest to find relevant bankruptcy cases. Finding cases by subject matter is a little too advanced for this brief summary. (See *Legal Research,* by the Editors of Nolo (Nolo), for more help.)

Other Helpful Resources

The most helpful bankruptcy website is probably maintained by the Office of the United States Trustee at www.usdoj.gov/ust. This site provides lists of approved credit and financial management counseling agencies, median income figures for every state, and the IRS national, regional, and local expenses you will need to complete the means test. You can download official bankruptcy forms from www.uscourts.gov/forms/bankruptcy-forms. However, this site doesn't include required local forms; for those, you'll have to visit your court or its website. You can find either one using the court locator tool at www.uscourts.gov/court-locator.

As part of the bankruptcy process, you are required to give the fair market value for all of the property you list in Schedule A/B. These figures are also the key to figuring out which of your property is exempt. Here are some tips on finding these values:

- Cars: Use the *Kelley Blue Book* at www.kbb.com or the National Auto Dealers Association website at www.nada.com.
- Other personal property: Check prices on eBay, www.ebay.com.
- Homes: Check comparable homes and sales history, bedrooms and baths, and square footage at Zillow.com, Trulia.com, and Realtor.com.

Glossary

341 hearing. A hearing that the debtor is required to attend in a bankruptcy case, at which the trustee and creditors might ask the debtor questions about his or her property, information in the documents and forms he or she filed, and his or her debts.

341 notice. A notice sent to the debtor and the debtor's creditors announcing the date, time, and place for the first meeting of creditors. The 341 notice is sent along with the notice of bankruptcy filing and information about important deadlines by which creditors have to take certain actions, such as filing objections.

342 notice. A notice that the court clerk is required to give to debtors pursuant to Section 342 of the bankruptcy code to inform them of their obligations as bankruptcy debtors and the consequences of not being completely honest in their bankruptcy cases.

707(b) action. An action taken by the U.S. Trustee, the regular trustee, or any creditor, under the authority of Section 707(b) of the bankruptcy code, to dismiss a debtor's Chapter 7 filing on the ground of abuse.

Abuse. Misuse of the Chapter 7 bankruptcy remedy. This term is typically applied to a Chapter 7 bankruptcy filing that should have been filed under Chapter 13 because the debtor appears to have enough disposable income to fund a Chapter 13 repayment plan.

Accounts receivable. Money or other property that one person or business owes to another for goods or services. Accounts receivable most often refer to the debts owed to a business by its customers.

Administrative expenses. The trustee's fee, the debtor's attorneys' fee, and other costs of bringing a bankruptcy case that a debtor must pay in full in a Chapter 13 repayment plan. Administrative costs are typically 10% of the debtor's total payments under the plan.

Administrative Office of the United States Courts. The federal government agency that issues court rules and forms to be used by the federal courts, including bankruptcy courts.

Adversary action. Any lawsuit that begins with the filing of a formal complaint and formal service of process on the parties being sued. For instance, an adversary action can be brought to determine the dischargeability of a debt or recover property transferred shortly before filing for bankruptcy.

Affidavit. A written statement of facts, signed under oath in front of a notary public.

Allowed secured claim. A debt secured by collateral or a lien against the debtor's property, for which the creditor has filed a proof of claim with the bankruptcy court. The claim is secured only to the extent of the value of the property—for example, if a debtor owes $5,000 on a note for a car that is worth only $3,000, the remaining $2,000 is an unsecured claim.

Amendment. A document filed by the debtor changing one or more documents previously filed with the court. A debtor often files an amendment because the trustee requires changes to the debtor's paperwork based on the testimony at the meeting of creditors.

Animals. An exemption category in many states. If your state simply allows you to exempt "animals," you can include livestock, poultry, or pets. Some states exempt only domestic animals, which usually covers all animals except pets.

Annuity. A type of insurance policy that pays out during the insured's life unlike life insurance, which pays out at the insured's death. Once the insured reaches the age specified in the policy, he or she receives monthly payments until death.

Appliance. A household apparatus or machine, usually operated by electricity, gas, or propane. Examples include refrigerators, stoves, washing machines, dishwashers, vacuum cleaners, air conditioners, and toasters.

Arms and accoutrements. Arms are weapons (such as pistols, rifles, and swords); accoutrements are the furnishings of a soldier's outfit, such as a belt or pack, but not clothes or weapons.

Arms-length creditor. A creditor with whom the debtor deals in the normal course of business, as opposed to an insider (a friend, relative, or business partner).

Articles of adornment. See "jewelry."

Assessment benefits. See "stipulated insurance."

Assisted person. Any person contemplating or filing for bankruptcy who receives bankruptcy assistance, whose debts are primarily consumer debts, and whose nonexempt property is valued at less than $192,450. A person or an entity that offers help to an assisted person is called a "debt relief agency."

Automatic stay. An injunction issued by the bankruptcy court when a debtor files for bankruptcy. The automatic stay prohibits most creditor collection activities, such as filing or continuing lawsuits, making written requests for payment, or notifying credit reporting bureaus of an unpaid debt.

Avails. Any amount available to the owner of an insurance policy other than the actual proceeds of the policy. Avails include dividend payments, interest, cash or surrender value (the money you'd get if you sold your policy back to the insurance company), and loan value (the amount of cash you can borrow against the policy).

Bankruptcy Abuse Prevention and Consumer Protection Act of 2005. The formal name of the new bankruptcy law that took effect on October 17, 2005.

Bankruptcy administrator. The official responsible for supervising the administration of bankruptcy cases, estates, and trustees in Alabama and North Carolina, where there is no U.S. Trustee.

Bankruptcy Appellate Panel. A specialized court that hears appeals of bankruptcy court decisions (available only in some regions).

Bankruptcy assistance. Goods or services provided to an "assisted person" for the purpose of providing information, advice, counsel, document preparation or filing, or attendance at a creditors' meeting; appearing in a case or proceeding on behalf of another person; or providing legal representation.

Bankruptcy Code. The federal law that governs the creation and operation of the bankruptcy courts and establishes bankruptcy procedures. (You can find the bankruptcy code in Title 11 of the United States Code.)

Bankruptcy estate. All of the property you own when you file for bankruptcy, except for most pensions and educational trusts. The trustee technically takes control of your bankruptcy estate for the duration of your case.

Bankruptcy lawyer. A lawyer who specializes in bankruptcy and is licensed to practice law in the federal courts.

Bankruptcy petition preparer. Any nonlawyer who helps someone with bankruptcy. Bankruptcy petition preparers (BPPs) are a special type of debt relief agency, regulated by the U.S. Trustee. Because they are not lawyers, BPPs can't represent anyone in bankruptcy court or provide legal advice.

Benefit or benevolent society benefits. See "fraternal benefit society benefits."

Building materials. Items, such as lumber, brick, stone, iron, paint, and varnish, used to build or improve a structure.

Burial plot. A cemetery plot.

Business bankruptcy. A bankruptcy in which the debts arise primarily from the operation of a business, including bankruptcies filed by corporations, limited liability companies, and partnerships.

Certification. The act of signing a document under penalty of perjury. (The document signed is also called a certification.)

Chapter 7 bankruptcy. A liquidation bankruptcy in which the trustee sells the debtor's nonexempt property and distributes the proceeds to the debtor's creditors. At the end of the case, the debtor receives a discharge of all remaining debts, except those that cannot legally be discharged.

Chapter 9 bankruptcy. A type of bankruptcy restricted to governmental units.

Chapter 11 bankruptcy. A type of bankruptcy intended to help a business reorganize its debt load and remain in business. A Chapter 11 bankruptcy is typically much more expensive than a Chapter 7 or 13 bankruptcy because it is more complicated and lawyers must be paid out of the bankruptcy estate.

Chapter 12 bankruptcy. A type of bankruptcy designed to help small farmers reorganize their debts.

Chapter 13 bankruptcy. A type of consumer bankruptcy designed to help individuals reorganize their debts and pay all or a portion of them over three to five years.

Chapter 13 plan. A document filed in a Chapter 13 bankruptcy in which the debtor shows how all of his or her projected disposable income will be used over a three- to five-year period to pay all mandatory debts—for example, back child support, taxes, and mortgage arrearages—as well as some or all unsecured, nonpriority debts, such as medical and credit card bills.

Claim. A creditor's assertion that the bankruptcy filer owes a debt or an obligation.

Clothing. Most states exempt the everyday clothes you and your family need for work, school, household use, and protection from the elements. In many states, luxury items and furs are not included in the clothing exemption category.

Codebtor. A person who assumes an equal responsibility, along with the debtor, to repay a debt or loan.

Collateral. Property pledged by a borrower as security for a loan.

Common law property states. States that don't use a community property system to classify marital property.

Community property. Certain property owned by married couples in Arizona, California, Idaho, Louisiana, New Mexico, Nevada, Texas, Washington, Wisconsin, and, if both spouses agree, Alaska. Very generally, all property acquired during the marriage is considered community property, belonging equally to both spouses, except for gifts and inheritances by one spouse. Similarly, all debts incurred during the marriage are considered community debts, owed equally by both spouses, with limited exceptions.

Complaint. A formal document initiating a lawsuit.

Complaint to determine dischargeability. A complaint in an adversary action asking the court to decide whether a particular debt should be discharged at the end of the debtor's bankruptcy case.

Condominium. A building or complex in which separate units, such as townhouses or apartments, are owned by individuals and common areas (lobby, hallways, stairways, and so on) are jointly owned by the unit owners.

Confirmation. The bankruptcy judge's ruling approving a Chapter 13 plan.

Confirmation hearing. A court hearing conducted by a bankruptcy judge in which the judge decides whether a debtor's proposed Chapter 13 plan appears to be feasible and meets all applicable legal requirements.

Consumer bankruptcy. A bankruptcy in which a preponderance of the debt was incurred for personal, family, or household purposes.

Consumer debt. A debt incurred by an individual for personal, family, or household purposes.

Contingent debts. Debts owed if certain events happen or conditions are satisfied.

Contingent interests in the estate of a decedent. The right to inherit property if one or more conditions to the inheritance are satisfied (for example, a debtor who will inherit property only if he survives his brother has a contingent interest).

Conversion. When a debtor who has filed one type of bankruptcy switches to another type—as when a Chapter 7 debtor converts to a Chapter 13 bankruptcy, or vice versa.

Cooperative housing. A building or another residential structure that is owned by a corporation formed by the residents. In exchange for purchasing stock in the corporation, the residents have the right to live in particular units.

Cooperative insurance. Compulsory employment benefits provided by a state or federal government, such as old age, survivors, disability, and health insurance, to assure a minimum standard of living for lower- and middle-income people. Also called social insurance.

Court clerk. The court employee responsible for accepting filings and other documents and generally maintaining an accurate and efficient flow of paper and information in the court.

Cramdown. In a Chapter 13 bankruptcy, the act of reducing a secured debt to the replacement value of the collateral securing the debt.

Credit and debt counseling. Counseling that explores the possibility of repaying debts outside of bankruptcy and educates the debtor about credit, budgeting, and financial management. Under the new bankruptcy law, a debtor must undergo credit counseling with an approved provider before filing for bankruptcy.

Credit insurance. An insurance policy that covers a borrower for an outstanding loan. If the borrower dies or becomes disabled before paying off the loan, the policy will pay off the balance due.

Creditor. A person or an institution to which money is owed.

Creditor committee. In a Chapter 11 bankruptcy, a committee representing the unsecured debtors in reorganization proceedings.

Creditor matrix. A specially formatted list of creditors that a debtor must file with the bankruptcy petition. The matrix helps the court notify creditors of the bankruptcy filing and the date and time set for the first meeting of creditors.

Creditors' meeting. See "341 hearing."

Crops. Products of the soil or earth grown and raised annually and gathered in a single season. Thus, oranges (on the tree or harvested) are crops; an orange tree isn't.

Current market value. What property could be sold for. This is how a debtor's property was previously valued for purposes of determining whether the property is protected by an applicable exemption. Under the new bankruptcy law, property must be valued at its "replacement cost."

Current monthly income. A bankruptcy filer's total gross income (whether taxable or not), averaged over the six-month period immediately preceding the month in which the bankruptcy is filed. The current monthly income determines whether the debtor can file for Chapter 7 bankruptcy, among other things.

Debt. An obligation of any type, including a loan, credit, or promise to perform a contract or lease.

Debt relief agency. An umbrella term for any person or agency—including lawyers and bankruptcy petition preparers, but excluding banks, non-profit and government agencies, and employees of debt relief agencies—that provides bankruptcy assistance to a debtor. See "bankruptcy assistance" and "assisted person."

Debtor. Someone who owes money to another person or business. Also, the generic term used to refer to anyone who files for bankruptcy.

Declaration. A written statement that is made under oath but not witnessed by a notary public.

Declaration of homestead. A form filed with the county recorder's office to put on record your right to a homestead exemption. In most states, the homestead exemption is automatic—you are not required to record a homestead declaration in order to claim the homestead exemption. A few states do require such a recording, however.

Disability benefits. Payments made under a disability insurance or retirement plan when the insured is unable to work (or retires early) because of disability, accident, or sickness.

Discharge. A court order, issued at the conclusion of a Chapter 7 or Chapter 13 bankruptcy case, which legally relieves the debtor of personal liability for debts that can be discharged in that type of bankruptcy.

Discharge exceptions. Debts that are not discharged in a bankruptcy case. The debtor continues to owe these debts even after the bankruptcy ends.

Discharge hearing. A hearing conducted by a bankruptcy court to explain the discharge, urge the debtor to stay out of debt, and review reaffirmation agreements to make sure they are feasible and fair.

Dischargeability action. An adversary action brought by a party who asks the court to determine whether a particular debt qualifies for discharge.

Dischargeable debt. A debt that is wiped out at the conclusion of a bankruptcy case unless the judge decides that it should not be.

Dismissal. When the court orders a case closed without providing the relief available under the bankruptcy laws. For example, a Chapter 13 case might be dismissed because the debtor fails to propose a feasible plan; a Chapter 7 case might be dismissed for abuse.

Disposable income. The difference between a debtor's "current monthly income" and allowable expenses. This is the amount that the bankruptcy law deems available to pay into a Chapter 13 plan.

Domestic animals. See "animals."

Domestic support obligation. An obligation to pay alimony or child support to a spouse, child, or government entity pursuant to an order by a court or other governmental unit.

Doubling. The ability of married couples to double property exemption amounts when filing for bankruptcy together. The federal bankruptcy exemptions allow doubling. State laws vary—some permit doubling and some do not.

Education Individual Retirement Account. A type of account to which a person can contribute a certain amount of tax-deferred funds every year for the educational benefit of the debtor or certain relatives. Such an account is not part of the debtor's bankruptcy estate.

Emergency bankruptcy filing. An initial bankruptcy filing that includes only the petition and the creditor matrix, filed right away because the debtor needs the protection of the automatic stay to prevent a creditor from taking a certain action, such as a foreclosure. The court will dismiss an emergency filing case if the debtor doesn't file other required documents and forms in a timely manner.

Endowment insurance. An insurance policy that gives an insured who lives for a specified time (the endowment period) the right to receive the face value of the policy (the amount paid at death). If the insured dies sooner, the beneficiary named in the policy receives the proceeds.

Equity. The amount you get to keep if you sell property—typically the property's market value, less the costs of sale and the value of any liens on the property.

ERISA-qualified benefits. Pensions that meet the requirements of the Employee Retirement Income Security Act (ERISA), a federal law that sets minimum standards for such plans and requires beneficiaries to receive certain notices.

Executory contract. A contract in which one or both parties still have a duty to carry out one or more of the contract's terms.

Exempt property. Property described by state and federal laws (exemptions) that a debtor is entitled to keep in a Chapter 7 bankruptcy. Exempt property cannot be taken and sold by the trustee for the benefit of the debtor's unsecured creditors.

Exemptions. State and federal laws specifying the types of property creditors are not entitled to take to satisfy a debt, and the bankruptcy trustee is not entitled to take and sell for the benefit of the debtor's unsecured creditors.

Farm tools. Tools used by a person whose primary occupation is farming. Some states limit farm tools of the trade to handheld items such as hoes, axes, pitchforks, shovels, scythes, and the like. In other states, farm tools also include plows, harnesses, mowers, reapers, and so on.

Federal exemptions. A list of exemptions contained in the federal bankruptcy code. Some states give debtors the option of using the federal exemptions rather than the state exemptions.

Federal Rules of Bankruptcy Procedure. A set of rules issued by the Administrative Office of the United States Courts, which govern bankruptcy court procedures.

Filing date. The date a bankruptcy petition is filed. With few exceptions, property owned before the filing date is part of the bankruptcy estate, while property acquired after the filing date is not. Similarly, debts incurred after the filing date are not discharged.

Fines, penalties, and restitution. Debts owed to a court or a victim as a result of a sentence in a criminal matter. These debts are generally not dischargeable in bankruptcy.

Foreclosure. The process by which a creditor with a lien on real estate forces a sale of the property in order to collect on the lien. Foreclosure typically occurs when a homeowner defaults on a mortgage.

Fraternal benefit society benefits. Benefits, often group life insurance, paid for by fraternal societies, such as the Elks, Masons, Knights of Columbus, or the Knights of Maccabees, for their members. Also called benefit society, benevolent society, or mutual aid association benefits.

Fraud. Generally, an act intended to mislead another for the purpose of financial gain. In a bankruptcy case, fraud is any writing or representation intended to mislead creditors to obtain a loan or credit, or any act intended to mislead the bankruptcy court or the trustee.

Fraudulent transfer. In a bankruptcy case, a transfer of property to another for less than the property's value for the purpose of hiding the property from the bankruptcy trustee—for instance, when a debtor signs a car over to a relative to keep it out of the bankruptcy estate. The trustee can recover and sell fraudulently transferred property for the benefit of the creditors.

Fraudulently concealed assets. Property that a bankruptcy debtor deliberately fails to disclose as required by the bankruptcy rules.

Furnishings. An exemption category recognized in many states, which includes furniture, fixtures in your home (such as a heating unit, furnace, or built-in lighting), and other items with which a home is furnished, such as carpets and drapes.

Good faith. In a Chapter 13 case, when a debtor files for bankruptcy with the sincere purpose of paying off debts over the period of time required by law rather than for manipulative purposes—such as to prevent a foreclosure that by all rights should be allowed to proceed.

Goods and chattels. See "personal property."

Group life or group health insurance. A single insurance policy covering individuals in a group (for example, employees) and their dependents.

Head of household. A person who supports and maintains, in one household, one or more people who are closely related to the person by blood, marriage, or adoption. Also referred to as "head of family."

Health aids. Items needed to maintain their owner's health, such as a wheelchair, crutches, a prosthesis, or a hearing aid. Many states require that health aids be prescribed by a physician.

Health benefits. Benefits paid under health insurance plans, such as Blue Cross/Blue Shield, to cover the costs of health care.

Heirloom. An item with special monetary or sentimental value, which is passed down from generation to generation.

Home equity loan. A loan made to a homeowner based on the equity in the home and secured by the home in the same manner as a mortgage.

Homestead declaration. See "declaration of homestead."

Homestead exemption. A state or federal exemption applicable to property where the debtor lives when filing for bankruptcy. Some states allow debtors to use the homestead exemption to protect boats and mobile homes used as a residence.

Household good. As an exemption category, an item of permanent nature (as opposed to items consumed, like food or cosmetics) used in or about the house. This includes linens, dinnerware, utensils, pots and pans, and small electronic equipment like radios. Many state laws specifically list the types of household goods that fall within this exemption, as do the federal bankruptcy laws.

Householder. A person who supports and maintains a household, with or without other people. Also called a "housekeeper."

Impairs an exemption. When liens prevent a debtor from collecting the exemption amount the debtor would be entitled to receive had the property been free of liens. For example, suppose the debtor is entitled to a $5,000 exemption on property worth $15,000. In that case, a lien exceeding $10,000 would impair the debtor's exemption. Certain types of exemption-impairing liens can be removed (avoided) by the debtor if the court so orders.

Implement. As an exemption category, an instrument, tool, or utensil used by a person to accomplish his or her job.

In lieu of homestead (or burial) exemption. Designates an exemption available only if the debtor doesn't claim the homestead (or burial) exemption.

Individual Debtor's Statement of Intention. An official bankruptcy form that debtors with secured debts must file to indicate what they want to do with the property that secures the debt. For instance, a debtor with a car note must indicate whether he or she wants to keep the car and continue the debt (reaffirmation), pay off the car note at a reduced price (redemption), or give the car back to the creditor and cancel the debt.

Injunction. A court order prohibiting a person or an entity from taking specified actions—for example, the automatic stay that prevents most creditors from trying to collect their debts is a type of injunction.

Insider creditor. A creditor with whom the debtor has a personal relationship, such as a relative, friend, or business partner.

Intangible property. Property that cannot be physically touched, such as an ownership share in a corporation or copyright. Documents—such as a stock certificate—can serve as evidence of intangible property.

Involuntary dismissal. When a bankruptcy judge dismisses a case because the debtor fails to carry out his or her duties—such as filing papers in a timely manner and cooperating with the trustee—or because the debtor files the bankruptcy in bad faith or engages in abuse by wrongfully filing for Chapter 7 when he or she should have filed for Chapter 13.

Involuntary lien. A lien placed on the debtor's property without the debtor's consent—for instance, when the IRS places a lien on property for back taxes.

IRS expenses. A table of national and regional expense estimates published by the IRS. Debtors whose "current monthly income" is more than their state's "median family income" must use the IRS expenses to calculate their average net income in a Chapter 7 case, or their disposable income in a Chapter 13 case.

Jewelry. Items created for personal adornment, such as rings, necklaces, bracelets, and watches.

Joint debtors. Married people who file a bankruptcy petition together and pay a single filing fee.

Judgment proof. A description of a person whose income and property are such that a creditor can't (or won't) seize them to enforce a money judgment—for example, a dwelling protected by a homestead exemption or a bank account containing only a few dollars.

Judicial lien. A lien created by the recording of a court money judgment against the debtor's property—usually real estate.

Lease. A contract that governs the relationship between an owner of property and a person who wishes to use the property for a specific period of time. Examples include car and real estate leases.

Lien. A legal claim against property that must be paid before title to the property can be transferred. Liens are often collected through repossession (personal property) or foreclosure (real estate), depending on the type of lien.

Lien avoidance. A bankruptcy procedure in which certain types of liens can be removed from certain types of property. Liens that can't be avoided survive the bankruptcy even if the underlying debt is canceled—for instance, a lien remains on a car even if the debt evidenced by the car note is discharged in the bankruptcy.

Life estate. The right to live in, but not own, a specific home until your death.

Life insurance. A policy that provides for the payment of money to an individual (called the beneficiary) in the event of the death of another (called the insured). The policy matures (becomes payable) only when the insured dies.

Lifting the stay. When a bankruptcy court allows a creditor to continue with debt collection or other activities that are otherwise banned by the automatic stay. For instance, the court might allow a landlord to proceed with an eviction or a lender to repossess a car because the debtor has defaulted on the note.

Liquid assets. Cash or items that are easily convertible into cash, such as a money market account, stock, U.S. Treasury bill, or bank deposit.

Liquidated debt. An existing debt for a specified amount arising out of a contract or court judgment. In contrast, an unliquidated debt is a claim for an as-yet uncertain amount, such as for injuries suffered in a car accident before the case goes to court.

Lost future earnings. The portion of a lawsuit judgment intended to compensate an injured person for the money he or she won't be able to earn in the future because of the injury. Also called lost earnings payments or recoveries.

Luxuries. In bankruptcy, goods or services that a court decides don't qualify as food, utilities, or other necessary items needed to live. This might include vacations, jewelry, costly cars, or frequent meals at expensive restaurants.

Mailing matrix. See "creditor matrix."

Marital debts. Debts owed jointly by a married couple.

Marital property. Property owned jointly by a married couple.

Marital settlement agreement. An agreement between a divorcing couple that sets out who gets what percentage (or what specific items) of the marital property, who pays what marital debts, and who gets custody and pays child support if there are children of the marriage.

Materialmen's and mechanics' liens. Liens imposed by statute on real estate when suppliers of materials, labor, and contracting services used to improve the real estate are not properly compensated.

Matured life insurance benefits. Insurance benefits currently payable because the insured person has died.

Means test. A formula that uses predefined income and expense categories to determine whether a debtor whose income is more than the state's median family income qualifies to file a Chapter 7 bankruptcy.

Median family income. An annual income figure for which there are as many families with incomes below that level as there are above that level. The U.S. Census Bureau publishes median family income figures for each state and for different family sizes. In bankruptcy, the median family income is used as a basis for determining whether a debtor must pass the means test to file Chapter 7 bankruptcy, and whether a debtor filing a Chapter 13 bankruptcy must commit all his or her projected disposable income to a five-year repayment plan.

Meeting of creditors. See "341 hearing."

Mortgage. A contract in which a loan to purchase real estate is secured by the real estate as collateral. If the borrower defaults on loan payments, the lender can foreclose on the property.

Motion. A formal legal procedure in which the bankruptcy judge rules on a dispute in the bankruptcy case. To bring a motion, a party must file a document explaining the requested relief, the facts of the dispute, and the legal reasons why the court should grant the relief. The party bringing the motion must mail these documents to all affected parties and let them know when the court will hear argument on the motion.

Motion to avoid judicial lien on real estate. A motion brought by a bankruptcy debtor that asks the bankruptcy court to remove a judicial lien on real estate because the lien impairs the debtor's homestead exemption.

Motion to lift stay. A motion in which a creditor asks for court permission to continue a court action or collection activities in spite of the automatic stay.

Motor vehicle. A self-propelled vehicle suitable for use on a street or road. This includes a car, truck, motorcycle, van, and moped. See also "tools of the trade."

Musical instrument. An instrument having the capacity, when properly operated, to produce a musical sound. Pianos, guitars, drums, drum machines, synthesizers, and harmonicas are all musical instruments.

Mutual aid association benefits. See "fraternal benefit society benefits."

Mutual assessment or mutual life. See "stipulated insurance."

Necessities. Articles needed to sustain life, such as food, clothing, medical care, and shelter.

Newly discovered creditors. Creditors whom the debtor discovers after the bankruptcy is filed. If the case is still open, the debtor can amend the list to include the creditors; if the case is closed, it usually can be reopened to accommodate the amendment.

Nonbankruptcy federal exemptions. Federal laws that allow a debtor who has not filed for bankruptcy to keep creditors away from certain property. The debtor can also use these exemptions in bankruptcy if the debtor is using a state exemption system.

Nondischargeable debt. Debt that survives bankruptcy, such as back child support and most student loans.

Nonexempt property. Property in the bankruptcy estate that is unprotected by the exemption system available to the debtor (this is typically—but not always—the exemption system in the state where the debtor files bankruptcy). In a Chapter 7 bankruptcy, the trustee will sell it for the benefit of the debtor's unsecured creditors. In a Chapter 13 bankruptcy, debtors must propose a plan that pays their unsecured creditors at least the value of their unsecured property.

Nonpossessory non-purchase-money lien. A lien placed on property already owned by the debtor and used as collateral for the loan without being possessed by the lender. In contrast, a non-purchase-money, possessory lien exists on collateral held by a pawnshop.

Nonpriority debt. A type of debt that is not entitled to be paid until priority debts are paid in full. Nonpriority debts are almost always discharged in Chapter 7 and do not have to be paid in full in Chapter 13.

Nonpriority, unsecured claim. A claim that is not for a priority debt (such as child support) and is not secured by collateral or other property. Typical examples include credit card debt, medical bills, and student loans. In a Chapter 13 repayment plan, nonpriority, unsecured claims are paid after all other debts are paid.

Notice of appeal. A form filed with a court when a party wishes to appeal a judgment or an order issued by the court. Often, the notice of appeal must be filed within ten days of the date the order or judgment is entered in the court's records.

Objection. A document one party files opposing a proposed action by another party—for instance, when a creditor or trustee files an objection to a bankruptcy debtor's claim of exemption.

Order for relief. The court's automatic injunction against certain collection and other activities that might negatively affect the bankruptcy estate. Another name for the "automatic stay."

Oversecured debt. A debt secured by collateral and worth more than the outstanding debt amount.

PACER. An online, fee-based database containing bankruptcy court dockets (records of proceedings in bankruptcy cases) and federal court documents, such as court rules and recent appellate court decisions.

Pain and suffering damages. The portion of a court judgment intended to compensate for past, present, and future mental and physical pain, suffering, impairment of ability to work, and mental distress caused by an injury.

Partially secured debt. A debt secured by collateral worth less than the debt itself—for instance, when a person owes $15,000 on a car worth only $10,000.

Party in interest. Any person or entity that has a financial interest in the outcome of a bankruptcy case, including the trustee, the debtor, and all creditors.

Pension. A fund into which payments are made to provide an employee with income after retirement. Typically, the beneficiary can't access the account before retirement without incurring a significant penalty, usually a tax. There are many types of pensions, including defined benefit pensions provided by many large corporations and individual pensions (such as 401(k) and IRA accounts). In bankruptcy, most pensions are not considered part of the bankruptcy estate and are therefore not affected by a bankruptcy filing.

Personal financial responsibility counseling. A two-hour class intended to teach budget management. Every consumer bankruptcy filer must attend such a class in order to obtain a discharge in Chapter 7, Chapter 12, or Chapter 13 bankruptcy.

Personal injury cause of action. The right to seek compensation for physical and mental suffering, including injury to body, reputation, or both. For example, someone hit and injured by a car might have a personal injury cause of action against the driver.

Personal injury recovery. The portion of a lawsuit judgment or insurance settlement intended to compensate someone for physical and mental suffering, including physical injury, injury to reputation, or both. Bankruptcy exemptions usually do not apply to compensation for pain or suffering or punitive damages—in other words, that part of the recovery can be taken by the trustee in a Chapter 7 case.

Personal property. All property not classified as real property, including tangible items, such as cars and jewelry, and intangible property like stocks and pensions.

Petition. The document a debtor files to officially begin a bankruptcy case and ask for relief. Other documents and schedules must be filed to support the petition at the time it is filed or shortly afterward.

Pets. See "animals."

Preference. A payment made by a debtor to a creditor within a defined period prior to filing for bankruptcy—within three months for arms-length creditors (regular commercial creditors) and one year for insider creditors (friends, family, or business associates). Because a preference gives that debtor an edge over other debtors in the bankruptcy case, the trustee can recover the preference and distribute it among all of the creditors.

Prepetition. Any time prior to the moment the bankruptcy petition is filed.

Prepetition counseling. Debt or credit counseling that occurs before the bankruptcy petition is filed—as opposed to personal financial management counseling, which occurs after the petition is filed.

Presumed abuse. In a Chapter 7 bankruptcy, when the debtor has a current monthly income in excess of the family median income for the state where the debtor lives, and has sufficient income to propose a Chapter 13 plan under the "means test." If abuse is presumed, the debtor has to prove that his or her Chapter 7 filing is not abusive in order to proceed further.

Primarily business debts. When the majority of debt owed by a bankruptcy debtor—in dollar terms—arises from debts incurred to operate a business.

Primarily consumer debts. When the majority of debt owed by a bankruptcy debtor—in dollar terms—arises from debts incurred for personal or family purposes.

Priority claim. See "priority debt."

Priority creditor. A creditor who has filed a Proof of Claim showing that the debtor owes it a priority debt.

Priority debt. A type of debt that is paid first if there are distributions to be made from the bankruptcy estate. Priority debts include alimony and child support, fees owed to the trustee and attorneys in the case, and wages owed to employees. With one exception (back child support obligations assigned to government entities), priority claims must be paid in full in a Chapter 13 bankruptcy.

Proceeds for damaged exempt property. Money received through insurance coverage, arbitration, mediation, settlement, or a lawsuit to pay for damaged or destroyed exempt property. For example, a debtor with a $30,000 homestead exemption can exempt $30,000 in insurance proceeds if the home was destroyed by fire.

Projected disposable income. The monthly amount of income remaining after deducting allowable expenses, payments on mandatory debts, and administrative expenses. A debtor must pay the disposable income amount toward unsecured nonpriority debts in a Chapter 13 plan.

Proof of Claim. A formal document bankruptcy creditors file to assert a right to payment from the bankruptcy estate when money is available to pay creditors.

Proof of Service. A document signed under penalty of perjury by the person serving a document that states how, when, and who effectuated service.

Property of the estate. See "bankruptcy estate."

Purchase-money loans. Loans including an agreement allowing the purchased property to serve as collateral. Examples include car loans and mortgages that give the lender the right to seize the car or home if the purchaser fails to pay per the agreement.

Purchase-money security interest. A claim on property owned by the holder of a loan that was used to purchase the property and that is secured by the property (as collateral).

Reaffirmation. An agreement entered into after a bankruptcy filing (postpetition) between the debtor and a creditor in which the debtor agrees to repay all or part of a prepetition debt after the bankruptcy is over. For instance, a debtor makes an agreement with the holder of a car note that the debtor can keep the car and will continue to pay the debt after bankruptcy.

Real property. Real estate (land and buildings on the land, usually including mobile homes attached to a foundation).

Reasonable investigation. A bankruptcy attorney's obligation, under the new bankruptcy law, to look into the information provided to them by their clients.

Redemption. In a Chapter 7 bankruptcy, when the debtor obtains legal title to collateral for a secured debt by paying the secured creditor the replacement value of the collateral in a lump sum. For example, in some situations, a debtor can redeem a car note by paying the lender the replacement value of the car (what a retail vendor would charge for the car, considering its age and condition).

Reopen a case. To open a closed bankruptcy case—usually for the purpose of adding an overlooked creditor or filing a motion to avoid an overlooked lien. A debtor must request that the court reopen the case.

Repayment plan. An informal plan to repay debts outside of bankruptcy. Also refers to the plan proposed by a debtor in a Chapter 13 case.

Replacement cost. What it would cost to replace a particular item by buying it from a retail vendor, considering its age and condition—for instance, when buying a car from a used car dealer, furniture from a used furniture shop, or electronic equipment on eBay.

Repossession. When a secured creditor takes property used as collateral after the debtor defaults on the loan secured by the collateral.

Request to lift the stay. A written request filed in bankruptcy court by a creditor seeking permission to engage in debt collection activity otherwise prohibited by the automatic stay.

Schedule A/B. The official bankruptcy form describing a debtor's property.

Schedule C. The official bankruptcy form listing the debtor's exempt property and the legal basis for the claims of exemption.

Schedule D. The official bankruptcy form a debtor must file to describe all secured debts owed by the debtor, such as car notes and mortgages.

Schedule E/F. The official bankruptcy form describing all priority debts owed by the debtor, such as back child support and taxes and all nonpriority, unsecured debts owed by the debtor, such as most credit card and medical bills.

Schedule G. The official bankruptcy form describing a debtor's leases and executory contracts (contracts under which one or both parties still have obligations) to which the debtor is a party.

Schedule H. The official bankruptcy form listing all codebtors that might be affected by the bankruptcy.

Schedule I. The official bankruptcy form describing the debtor's income.

Schedule J. The official bankruptcy form describing the debtor's actual monthly expenses.

Schedules. Official bankruptcy forms detailing the debtor's property, debts, income, and expenses.

Second deed of trust. A loan against real estate made after the original mortgage (or first deed of trust). Most home equity loans are second deeds of trust.

Secured claim. A debt secured by collateral under a written agreement (for instance, a mortgage or car note) or by operation of law—such as a tax lien.

Secured creditor. The owner of a secured claim.

Secured debt. A debt secured by collateral.

Secured property. Property that is collateral for a secured debt.

Security interest. A claim to property used as collateral. For instance, a lender on a car note retains legal title to the car until the loan is paid off.

Serial bankruptcy filing. A practice used by some debtors to file and dismiss one bankruptcy after another to obtain the protection of the automatic stay, even though the bankruptcies themselves offer no debt relief—for instance, when a debtor files successive Chapter 13 cases to prevent foreclosure of his or her home even though there are no debts to repay.

Sickness benefits. See "disability benefits."

State exemptions. State laws specifying the types of property creditors are not entitled to take to satisfy a debt, and the bankruptcy trustee is not entitled to take and sell for the benefit of the debtor's unsecured creditors.

Statement of Affairs. The official bankruptcy form a debtor must file to describe the debtor's legal, economic, and business transactions for the several years prior to filing, including gifts, preferences, income, closing of deposit accounts, lawsuits, and other information that the trustee needs to assess the legitimacy of the bankruptcy and the true extent of the bankruptcy estate.

Statement of Current Monthly Income and Disposable Income Calculation. The official bankruptcy form a debtor must file in a Chapter 13 case, setting out the debtor's current monthly income and calculating the debtor's projected disposable income that will determine how much will be paid to the debtor's unsecured creditors.

Statement of Intention. The official bankruptcy form a debtor must file in a Chapter 7 case to tell the court and secured creditors how the debtor plans to treat his or her secured debts—that is, reaffirm the debt, redeem the debt, or surrender the property and discharge the debt.

Statement of Social Security number. The official bankruptcy form a debtor must file to disclose the debtor's complete Social Security number.

Statutory lien. A lien imposed on property by law, such as tax liens and mechanics' liens, as opposed to voluntary liens (such as mortgages) and liens arising from court judgments (judicial liens).

Stay. See "automatic stay."

Stipulated insurance. An insurance policy that allows the insurance company to assess an amount on the insured, above the standard premium payments, if the company experiences losses worse than had been calculated into the standard premium. Also called assessment, mutual assessment, or mutual life insurance.

Stock options. A contract between a corporation and an employee that gives the employee the right to purchase corporate stock at a specific price mentioned in the contract (the strike price).

Strip down of lien. In a Chapter 13 bankruptcy, when the amount of a lien on collateral is reduced to the collateral's replacement value. See "cramdown."

Student loan. A type of loan made for educational purposes by nonprofit or commercial lenders with repayment and interest terms dictated by federal law. Student loans are not dischargeable in bankruptcy unless the debtor can show that repaying the loan would impose an "undue hardship."

Substantial abuse. Under the old bankruptcy law, filing a Chapter 7 bankruptcy when a Chapter 13 bankruptcy was feasible.

Suits, executions, garnishments, and attachments. Activities engaged in by creditors to enforce money judgments, typically involving the seizure of wages and bank accounts.

Summary of Schedules. The official bankruptcy form a debtor must file to summarize the property and debt information contained in a debtor's schedules.

Surrender value. See "avails."

Surrendering collateral. In Chapter 7 bankruptcy, the act of returning collateral to a secured lender in order to discharge the underlying debt—for example, returning a car to discharge the car note.

Tangible personal property. See "tangible property" and "personal property."

Tangible property. Property that can be physically touched. Examples include money, furniture, cars, jewelry, artwork, and houses. Compare "intangible property."

Tax lien. A statutory lien imposed on property to secure payment of back taxes—typically income and property taxes.

Tenancy by the entirety. A way that married couples can hold title to property in about half of the states. When one spouse dies, the surviving spouse automatically owns 100% of the property. In most cases, this type of property is not part of the bankruptcy estate if only one spouse files.

To ___ acres. A limitation on the size of a homestead that can be exempted.

Tools of the trade. Items needed to perform a line of work that a debtor is currently doing and relying on for support. For a mechanic, plumber, or carpenter, for example, tools of trade are the implements used to repair, build, and install. Traditionally, tools of the trade were limited to handheld tools. Most states, however, now embrace a broader definition, and a debtor can often fit many items under a tool of the trade exemption.

Transcript of tax return. A summary of a debtor's tax return provided by the IRS upon the debtor's request, usually acceptable as a substitute for the return in the instances when a return must be filed under the new bankruptcy law.

Trustee. An official appointed by the bankruptcy court to carry out the administrative tasks associated with bankruptcy and to seize and sell nonexempt property in the bankruptcy estate for the benefit of the debtor's unsecured creditors.

U.S. Trustee. An official employed by the Office of the U.S. Trustee (a division of the U.S. Department of Justice) who is responsible for overseeing the bankruptcy trustees, regulating credit and personal financial management counselors, regulating bankruptcy petition preparers, auditing bankruptcy cases, ferreting out fraud, and generally making sure that the bankruptcy laws are obeyed.

Undersecured debt. A debt secured by collateral that is worth less than the debt.

Undue hardship. The conditions under which a debtor can discharge a student loan—for example, when the debtor has no income and little chance of earning enough to repay the loan in the future.

Unexpired lease. A lease still in effect.

Unmatured life insurance. A policy that is not yet payable because the insured is still alive.

Unscheduled debt. A debt that is not included in the schedules accompanying a bankruptcy filing, perhaps because the debtor overlooked or intentionally left it out.

Unsecured priority claims. Priority claims that aren't secured by collateral, such as back child support or taxes for which no lien has been placed on the debtor's property.

Valuation of property. The act of determining the replacement value of property for the purpose of describing it in the bankruptcy schedules, determining whether it is protected by an applicable exemption, redeeming secured property, or cramming down a lien in Chapter 13 bankruptcy.

Voluntary dismissal. When a bankruptcy debtor dismisses a a Chapter 13 case without coercion by the court.

Voluntary lien. A lien agreed to by the debtor. Examples include a lien given pursuant to a mortgage, car note, or second deed of trust signed by the debtor.

Weekly net earnings. The earnings a debtor has left after mandatory deductions, such as income tax, mandatory union dues, and Social Security contributions, have been subtracted from the debtor's gross income.

Wildcard exemption. A dollar value that the debtor can apply to any type of property to make it—or more of it—exempt. In some states, filers can use the unused portion of a homestead exemption as a wildcard exemption.

Willful and malicious act. An act committed with the intent to cause harm. In a Chapter 7 bankruptcy, a debt arising from the debtor's willful and malicious act is not discharged if the victim proves to the bankruptcy court's satisfaction that the act occurred.

Willful or malicious act resulting in a civil judgment. A bad act that was careless or reckless but necessarily intended to cause harm. In a Chapter 13 case, a debt arising from the debtor's act that was either willful or malicious is not discharged if it is part of a civil judgment.

Wrongful death cause of action. The right to seek compensation for having to live without a deceased person. Usually, only the spouse and children of the deceased have a wrongful death cause of action.

Wrongful death recoveries. The portion of a lawsuit judgment intended to compensate a plaintiff for having to live without a deceased person. The compensation is intended to cover the earnings and the emotional comfort and support the deceased would have provided.

How to Use the Downloadable Forms on the Nolo Website

This book comes with downloadable files that you can access online at: **www.nolo.com/back-of-book/HFB.html**

To use the files, your computer must have specific software programs installed. The files provided by this book are in PDF form. You can view these files with *Adobe Reader*, free software from www.adobe.com. Government PDFs are sometimes fillable using your computer, but most PDFs are designed to be printed out and completed by hand.

> **CAUTION**
> In accordance with U.S. copyright laws, the forms provided by this book are for your personal use only.

List of Forms Available on the Nolo Website

To download any of the files listed on the following pages go to: **www.nolo.com/back-of-book/HFB.html**

Form Title	File Name
State and Federal Exemption Charts	StateFederalExemptions.pdf
Bankruptcy Forms Checklist	FormsChecklist.pdf
Bankruptcy Documents Checklist	DocumentsChecklist.pdf
Median Family Income Chart	MedianFamilyIncome.pdf
Amendment Cover Sheet	AmendmentCoverSheet.pdf
Notice of Change of Address	ChangeofAddress.pdf
Supplemental Schedule for Property Acquired After Bankruptcy Discharge	SupplementalScheduleProperty.pdf
Proof of Service by Mail	ProofofServicebyMail.pdf
Pleading Paper	PleadingPaper.pdf

Form Title	File Name
Chapter 1	
Current Monthly and Yearly Income Worksheet	IncomeWorksheet.pdf
Chapter 3	
Personal Property Checklist	PersonalProperty.pdf
Property Exemption Worksheet	PropertyExemption.pdf
Chapter 4	
Homeowners' Worksheet	HomeownersWorksheet.pdf
Chapter 5	
Judicial Lien Worksheet	JudicialLien.pdf
Sample Motion to Avoid Nonpossessory, Non-Purchase-Money Security Interest	MotionAvoidNonpossessory.pdf
Sample Notice to Avoid Nonpossessory, Non-Purchase-Money Security Interest	NoticeAvoidNonpossessory.pdf
Sample Order to Avoid Nonpossessory, Non-Purchase-Money Security Interest	OrderAvoidNonpossessory.pdf
Sample Notice of Motion and Motion to Avoid Judicial Lien on Real Estate	NoticeMotionAvoidJudicialLien RealEstate.pdf
Sample Request for Entry of Order by Default	RequestEntryOrderDefault.pdf
Sample Order to Avoid Judicial Lien on Real Estate	OrderAvoidJudicialLienRealEstate.pdf
Sample Agreement for Installment Redemption of Property	AgreementInstallmentRedemption.pdf
Sample Agreement for Lump Sum Redemption of Property	AgreementLumpSumRedemption.pdf
Chapter 6	
Sample Voluntary Petition	b_101.pdf
Sample Schedule A/B	form_b106ab.pdf
Sample Schedule C	form_b106c.pdf
Sample Schedule D	form_b106d.pdf
Sample Schedule E/F	form_b106ef.pdf
Sample Schedule G	form_b106g.pdf

Form Title	File Name
Sample Schedule H	form_b106h.pdf
Sample Schedule I	form_b106i.pdf
Sample Schedule J	form_b106j.pdf
Sample Summary of Your Assets and Liabilities and Certain Statistical Information	form_b106sum.pdf
Sample Declaration About an Individual Debtor's Schedules	form_b106dec.pdf
Sample Statement of Financial Affairs for Individuals Filing for Bankruptcy	form_b107.pdf
Sample Statement of Intention for Individuals Filing Under Chapter 7	form_b108.pdf
Sample Chapter 7 Statement of Your Current Monthly Income	form_b122a-1.pdf
Chapter 7 Means Test Calculation	form_b122a-2.pdf
Statement of Exemption from Presumption of Abuse	form_b122a-1supp.pdf
Notice Required by 11 U.S.C. § 342(b) for Individuals Filing for Bankruptcy	form_b2010.pdf
Chapter 7	
Order of Discharge	form_b318_0.pdf
Notice of Motion or Objection	b_420a_1216_0.pdf
Petition for Voluntary Dismissal	PetitionVoluntaryDismissal.pdf
Order Granting Voluntary Dismissal	OrderGrantingVoluntaryDismissal.pdf
Request to Reopen Case	RequestReopenCase.pdf
Order Granting Request to Reopen Case	OrderGrantingRequestReopenCase.pdf
Request for Discharge	RequestDischarge.pdf
Order Granting Request for Discharge	OrderGrantingRequestDischarge.pdf
Chapter 9	
Complaint to Determine Dischargeability of Student Loan	DischargeabilityStudentLoan.pdf
Chapter 10	
Sample Notice From Debt Relief Agency	NoticeDebtReliefAgency.pdf

Index

M